EMPIRE E PACIFIC

EMPIRES
ON THE
PACIFIC

World War II and the Struggle
for the Mastery of Asia

ROBERT SMITH THOMPSON

BASIC
BOOKS

A Member of the Perseus Books Group

Published by Basic Books,
A Member of the Perseus Books Group

Designed by Reggie Thompson

Library of Congress Cataloging-in-Publication Data
Thompson, Robert Smith
    Empires on the Pacific: World War II and the struggle for the mastery of
Asia/Robert Smith Thompson.—1st ed.
        p.   cm.
    Includes bibliographical references and index.
    ISBN 0-465-08576-8
    1. World War, 1939–1945—Asia. 2. World War, 1939–1945—Pacific Area. 3.
World politics—1900–1945. I. Title.
    D767.T49   2001
    909—dc21   2001036561

First Paperback Edition

03 / 10 9 8 7 6 5 4 3 2 1

To the memory of
Milton Needham Thompson
and
Marian Smith Thompson

CONTENTS

ACKNOWLEDGMENTS

To the staffs of numerous libraries and archives, listed under Sources, I owe a considerable debt: such persons have been invariably courteous, helpful, and professional. John Taylor at the National Archives was of the greatest assistance.

To three persons, who brought various kinds of expertise to reading the manuscript, I offer again my gratitude: Paul Hooper, Paul Aron, and Robert Angel. Many thanks.

To one person in the past I owe much of what underlies this work: the late Ellsworth C. Carlson.

For maps: Eric Stevens. For photos: James Zobel, Jack Green, Marilyn Rader, Allen Ruben, Laurie Lion, and Joanne Hartog.

I much appreciate the help of Dan Mandel, my agent, and the guidance of Don Fehr, the chief editor at Basic Books. I owe special thanks to Joan Benham, as hard-working, skilled, and helpful a developmental editor as one could imagine.

But words cannot express my acknowledgment of the love and support of those special two, Judy and Polly. I hope I return the love and support in kind.

PROLOGUE: WASHINGTON, DECEMBER 8, 1941

The crowds had been converging on the White House all morning long. Shivering, their collars turned up and their hands stuck in their pockets, men and women were packed together in rows, straining to peer past the posts of the tall iron fence. Just after noon, the throng stirred. The glass front doors under the north portico of the executive mansion slid open and President Franklin D. Roosevelt appeared, wearing a cape over his shoulders and gripping the arm of his son, James.

As he hobbled across the pavement, the president looked grim. Mrs. Roosevelt walked just behind him, wearing a stole and a hat with a veil. Flanked by two Secret Service agents, the Roosevelts clambered into the back of the waiting limousine. The agents closed the door and mounted the running boards, their overcoats and felt hats obscuring the view into the vehicle. Then, with one police car ahead and followed by seven more, all with their lights flashing and sirens blaring, the presidential limousine slid forward past the onlookers by the White House fence. The motorcade swung around the corner of the Treasury Building and raced through the intersections along Pennsylvania Avenue, heading east toward the Capitol. There, on the day after Japan's bombing of Pearl Harbor, President Roosevelt would ask Congress for a declaration of war.

The familiar story of America's official entry into World War II is that Japan's unprovoked attack on Pearl Harbor led the United States into the global conflict. Morally outraged, the United States struck back, crushing Japan and returning Asia and the Pacific to peace and stability. The good guys beat the bad guys.

But the story of World War II in Asia and the Pacific is more complicated, indeed more interesting, than that scenario suggests. To begin with, Japan's attack on Pearl Harbor was *not* unprovoked. Japan struck at Oahu preemptively: Its leaders saw the United States as threatening the very existence of their nation. In the Japanese view, that existence depended on imperial expansion in China. But to bring that war of conquest in China to an end, America was already preparing for war with Japan.

Many in the United States saw China as America's ward, a poor, backward, corrupt country that deserved our sympathy and help in becoming Christianized, democratized, and capitalized. Thus it was America's mission to save China, first from the old British and other European imperialists and then from the Japanese empire. But in China, Japan was impinging on America's own imperial interests, which dated well back into the nineteenth century. In the wake of the Boxer upheaval of 1900, the United States had forced the weak Chinese government to grant American gunboats treaty rights to ply Chinese rivers; the task of the gunboats had been to protect American factories, churches, and homes. In 1937 the Japanese sank one of those gunboats; and in the four years before Pearl Harbor, they had systematically destroyed American missionary compounds. At the war's end, Americans, who from the late nineteenth century onward had outcompeted the British commercially, rushed to replace what had been Great Britain's dominant position in the Chinese economy. In the course of the war, many Chinese came to see the Americans as just the newest imperialists, the latest barrier to China's dream of wealth and power.

The war's most enduring myth was that of undiluted American idealism, the cops-and-robbers version of the story. But in Asia and the Pacific, America was fighting two wars. One was the military struggle against Japan: There idealism, along with heroics and courage, existed aplenty; so did barbarism, and the sheer fact that in the end it was America's technology that defeated Japan. But the other was a political quest, America's hope to subjugate the force of Chinese nationalism and to render that ancient land America's postwar ally. In this, the United States failed.

America started to engage in a struggle for dominance in China even before the Japanese surrender. Enamored of their technology, Americans succumbed to a pride born of their very victory over Japan. Surely, Americans believed, the military triumph over Japan would be followed by political influence in China. The belief was the grand illusion of the end of the war in Asia and the Pacific.

PART I

THE ROAD TO WAR

I

THE FALL OF
IMPERIAL CHINA

1

Early September, 1793, a meeting took place that would prove to be the first great collision of East and West. King George III had commissioned George, Lord Macartney, a British diplomat, and his entourage, to create an embassy in China, expand British trade in the country, and introduce Christianity into the Middle Kingdom. The Chinese characters for China represent literally "middle" and "kingdom," signifying China's conception of itself as being halfway between heaven and earth, superior to all other lands. And indeed at the height of its power, the Chinese (more accurately Manchu, for the Manchus in 1644 had overrun China) empire dominated Korea, Taiwan, and Mongolia.

A few Europeans had established a presence in the empire: the Portuguese (and the Dutch temporarily) in Macao, an enclave in southern

China, and Italian Jesuits at the imperial court. No Europeans, however, had been able to establish diplomatic relations with China. Lord Macartney's task was to succeed where others had failed.

In command of three warships that had left from Portsmouth, Macartney had put in briefly at Macao; then he had gone ashore near Tianjin on the northern coast. After a sojourn of several weeks as the Chinese government's guests at the Summer Palace, just northwest of Beijing, Macartney and his staff left for Jehol, the imperial retreat high in the hills of northeastern China.

The terrain remained flat and dusty on the first day of the trip. On the second day, the road (such as it was) rose steadily, skirting a series of cliffs. When the procession neared an extension of the Great Wall, Macartney dispatched his engineers and artists to measure and sketch the ramparts, parapets, and towers. In his journal he rhapsodized over the stupendous size of the structure, as his men swarmed over the stones, notebooks in hand. Their Chinese escorts viewed such activity with apprehension: They suspected the "foreign devils" of dark designs. The hosts were not far from the mark. Lord Macartney's mission was in part one of gathering all information possible about China.

On the sixth day, the Britons saw before them on a hillside at Jehol an enormous monastery next to a lake. Taken on a boat trip, Macartney wrote in his journal: "Here was a large, magnificent yacht ready to receive us and a number of smaller ones for the attendants, elegantly fitted up and adorned with numberless vanes, pennants, and streamers. The shores of the lake have all the varieties of shape which the fancy of a painter can delineate, and are so indented with bays or projections, that almost every stroke of the oar brought a new and unexpected object to our view. . . . [W]e stopped at forty or fifty different palaces or pavilions. These are all furnished in the richest manner. . . ."

Ushering him into a huge tent, high-ranking mandarins presented Lord Macartney to the emperor, seated on an ornate throne. Defying custom, Macartney refused to kowtow. As he would to his own monarch, he merely knelt upon one knee. To the Manchu court, this insolence was outrageous. Macartney's action implied an unthinkable equality between the Chinese emperor and the British king.

Ignoring the Chinese sense of affront, Lord Macartney then proffered a gold box, embossed with diamonds and containing a letter from George III written in Latin (which Jesuits at the court could translate). "Many of Our subjects have . . . frequented for a long time a remote part of Your Majesty's dominions [the Pearl River delta] for the purpose of trade." For nearly half a century, British merchants had been trading in Canton (Guangzhou), but the Chinese authorities had ringed them with restrictions. The merchants could live in Canton only half the year and while there they had to stay on an island outside the city itself. They could do business only through *compradors,* or Chinese go-betweens, who exacted their cut. King George's subjects chafed under these restrictions and sometimes had resorted to violence. So he had declared: "We are . . . desirous to restrain Our subjects from doing evil or even of showing ill will in any foreign country, as We are [desirous that they] should receive no injury in it." His solution to the problem was to have a British embassy in China: "By such means every misunderstanding may be prevented [and] a firm and lasting friendship cemented . . . between our respective empires." The British monarch was proposing a breakdown of what he and his countrymen viewed as China's unreasonable hindering of free trade. The letter was signed, "Your Good Brother and Friend Georgius R."

After a week in Jehol and being ignored by the court, Lord Macartney set forth for the south. Back at Beijing, the answer to the king's epistle arrived, delivered by a Manchu officer. The response epitomized China's view of itself, indifferent and impregnable: "AN IMPERIAL EDICT TO THE KING OF ENGLAND: You, O King, are so inclined toward our civilization that you have sent a special envoy across the seas. . . . [But] The Celestial Court has pacified and possessed the territory between the four seas. . . . As a matter of fact, the virtue and prestige of the Celestial Dynasty having spread far and wide, the kings of the myriad nations come by land and sea with all sorts of precious things. Consequently there is nothing we lack, as your principal envoy and others have themselves observed [Lord Macartney had brought manufactured items as gifts]."

The message from Jehol ended on a note that was majestic, thunderous, and final. There would be no exchange of embassies, expansion of trade, or tolerance of any attempts to introduce the English religion into China. Any disregard of the restrictions would result in the expulsion of the British from the Canton harbor.

"Do not say that you have not been warned," the epistle concluded. "Tremblingly obey and show no negligence."

On his return to Macao and before sailing back to England, Lord Macartney in a long journal entry reflected on what he had seen. The empire of China, he penned insightfully and prophetically, "is an old, crazy, first rate man-of-war, which a fortunate succession of able and vigilant officers has contrived to keep afloat for these one and fifty years past, and to overawe their neighbors, but whenever an insufficient man [an emperor and his court, including the notoriously corrupt eunuchs] happens to have command upon deck, adieu to the discipline and safety of the ship. She may perhaps not sink outright; she may drift for some time as a wreck, and will then be dashed to pieces on the shore, but she can never be rebuilt on the old bottom."

2

China in the late eighteenth century was at the height of its wealth and prestige. This was the great age of China's decorative art: heavy, intricate cloisonné and multilayered lacquerware; enormous bronze temple bells and polychrome marbles; gilded jade tablets and variegated porcelain. The splendor dazzled foreign visitors.

By the time Macartney reached China, however, corruption had spread the length of the land. Tax revenues were falling. The population, the largest in the world, was eating more food than it could grow. And with millions of troops on army rolls to guard against the threat of rebellion, military costs were mounting fast.

The dynasty soon did face a major rural uprising, that of the White Lotus Society. Such peasant associations, often underground, were inimical to Confucian hierarchy and centralized authority. They were originally founded as mutual aid societies, the members bound together by oaths, religious rituals, and superstitious beliefs. Many worshipped purely local gods. But Buddhism, a peasant religion in China since the third century B.C., involved worship of an alien god, and so was inherently subversive. When times were tough, subversion could turn to revolution.

On the flat northern Chinese plain, a region often afflicted by droughts and floods, conditions at the end of the eighteenth century were particularly grim. With famine widespread, the White Lotus Rebellion erupted with fury, and it took the Manchus a decade to suppress the uprising. To do so, moreover, they had to rely on help from regional and local militias, a sure sign of dynastic decline.

The nineteenth century would also add a new element to the decline: outright imperialism. The British merchants in the Canton harbor had made a discovery worth emeralds and rubies.

China's demand for British manufactured goods had been slight. But in the second and third decades of the nineteenth century, sharp-eyed businessmen, mainly from Scotland, realized that the Chinese craving for opium was bottomless. Opium from China's own poppy fields, located in the hard-to-reach interior, was costly; opium smoking thus had been the preserve of the wealthy. But the British had easy access to the poppies of India and they had ships that could speed the opium processed from them up into the Pearl River delta. So British opium was plentiful and cheap.

As such it was a danger to public health, and so the Manchus in the 1830s sought to put a stop to the trafficking. In 1839 the emperor commissioned Lin Zexu, a high-ranking official, to proceed to Guangzhou, where Lin was to eradicate the opium trade, once and for all.

Lin first tried moral suasion. In an open letter to Queen Victoria, he stated: "We find that your country is sixty or seventy thousand *li* [three *li* made approximately one mile] from China. Yet there are barbarian ships that come here for trade for the purpose of making a good profit. . . . Even though the barbarians may not necessarily intend to do us harm, they have no regard for injuring others. Let us ask, 'Where is your conscience?' I have heard that the smoking of opium is very strictly forbidden in your country: that is because the harm caused by opium is clearly understood. Since it is not permitted to do harm in your own country, then even less should you let it be passed on to the harm of other countries—how much less to China!"

Lin's letter went unanswered. To the sealords of Britannia, what mattered was not the harm caused by opium but rather the cherished principle of free trade. The Manchu view was equally uncompromising. The great fear of the dynastic officials was that British opium trafficking would both harm the Chinese people and give the barbarians, as officialdom considered foreigners, such influence as to endanger the ruler's legitimacy. China therefore had to take active steps to impede the trade.

Following imperial instructions, Commissioner Lin ordered the British merchants in Guangzhou to hand over their opium crates. Lacking naval protection, they complied, and Lin dumped the opium in the harbor.

The British retaliation was swift and sure. In the middle of May, 1840, a fleet of British iron-clad, steam-powered gunboats reached the China coast. In a series of strikes over the next two years, which would become known as the First Opium War, the ships blasted away at Guangzhou, seized a fishing village called Shanghai, and in 1842 compelled the dynasty to sign the Treaty of Nanjing. According to the treaty, the Manchus ceded to Great Britain commercial access to five coastal cities (the first of the so-called "treaty-ports") and control "in perpetuity" of the Hong Kong island. China signed under duress.

From the British point of view, even so, the agreement proved unsatisfactory: Chinese authorities were still trying to block opium imports. So in 1859 and 1860, this time joined by the French, who were acquiring treaty-ports in Vietnam, the British again went to war. Under the command of the Eighth Lord of Elgin (son of the Lord Elgin who had snitched the marbles from the Parthenon), a punitive expedition captured Beijing. The foreigners soon withdrew. But in an expression of utter contempt for the dynasty, Elgin ordered the burning of the Old Summer Palace, where Lord Macartney once had sojourned.

Many of the stones from the Old Summer Palace still lie about what were the grounds. Carvings look European, baroque, which appears strange until one remembers that the Jesuits held a degree of influence in the Manchu court; their architects had designed the place. And the Chinese government allows one and all to walk and bicycle through the site: The ruins remind visitors of what was China's humiliation in the face of the West.

With the end of the Second Opium War, China fell decisively under the yoke of Western imperialism. A second treaty, the Convention of Beijing, forced China to accept foreign embassies and applied the treaty-port principle—the idea of extraterritoriality—to a dozen more cities. Using the spelling from the nineteenth century, these included Swatow, Amoy, and Ningpo below Shanghai on the coast, and Wusung, Nanking, and Hankow on the Yangzi River. In those British ports, Victoria's subjects were subject not to Chinese laws but rather to their own. Then the French, later the Germans and others, acquired similar rights. The treaty-port system amounted to colonization.

Each of the British enclaves fronted on a body of water, a bay, a river, or even a creek. Along the harbor ran the *bund,* a Hindi word meaning "water-front": The British in China imported lingo from elsewhere in their empire. They also built huge warehouses where local coolies (another Hindi term, standing for "dirt-cheap labor") labored and mansions like those along the Battery in Charleston, South Carolina, with verandas and tall windows designed to catch the sea breezes. In those stately homes dwelt the *taipans* (Chinese for "great managers") and the consuls general, legal authorities within the treaty-port. Aside from the climate, the Chinese in the streets, and the ever-pervasive stench of human feces, the British treaty-port was a little bit of home, albeit guarded by gunboats: The club, the church, and the race-course, and for Britons relegated to jobs as clerks, the pub, all seemed lifted directly from the suburbs of Birmingham, Glasgow, or London. And no British resident had to be tried in a Chinese court. All judicial proceedings took place before the bewigged judges and barristers of British tradition.

Compounding such legal colonization was the religious variety—the presence of missionaries, largely Methodists and Presbyterians from England, Wales, and Scotland. The missionaries of course did not see themselves as troublemakers. They were responding to the Call, Jesus's commission to his disciples to spread his message throughout the world. In large part, at that time the commission had come to mean the conversion of the "heathen Chinee." Confucian officials found Christianity profoundly subversive because it placed an alien God over the native rulers. And as peasant-based antimissionary riots made clear, to many Chinese, thrown out of work by foreign enterprises, the missionaries were part and parcel of the imperialist menace.

3

The menace to Manchu authority also came from within China. It took the form of an enormous uprising called the *Taiping* ("Great Peace") Rebellion.

Like the White Lotus affair, the *Taiping* movement was a response to hard times, especially in the southern reaches of China. By the 1850s, the Manchu government had grown increasingly degenerate and corrupt officials infested the country, afflicting the peasantry with onerous tax burdens. Added to the official rapaciousness, both droughts and floods were plaguing China south of the Yangzi, and the people there lacked food and clothing. Many became homeless, drifting migrants; others created a steady stream of emigration of Cantonese-speakers throughout the Pacific basin.

Near Guangzhou (Canton) a young man named Hong Xiuquan, who claimed to be a mystic, attracted countless adherents. Influenced by missionaries, he espoused a garbled Christianity; his real appeal was the promise of better times. He called his movement *Taiping*, or "Heavenly Peace," but organized his followers into a military force that came to dominate much of southern China. His force then pushed northward for a decade and by 1859 had captured Nanjing (the "Southern Capital") on the lower bank of the Yangzi River. Setting himself up as the new emperor, he launched a direct challenge to Manchu legitimacy.

In May, 1860, Hong and his legions headed down the river toward Shanghai, where he hoped to discredit the Manchus. As they marched to the ocean (Shanghai means "on the sea") the *Taiping* troops demonstrated the most rigid discipline. Soldiers who retreated in battle or threatened to desert had their heads cut off. The men and women who had joined the campaign (the movement had rejected the crippling custom of foot-binding and so young women were able to march) were forbidden to make contact; tobacco, alcohol, and opium were outlawed. The Chinese Communists later would emulate the *Taiping* puritanism.

In the mid-1860s, however, the *Taiping* movement collapsed. Prey to feuds and jealousies, the leaders fought each other rather than push ahead. Hong Xiuquan surrounded himself with an imperial luxury that detracted from military efficiency. Moving down the Yangzi valley, he overextended his lines of supply.

And the Manchus received help from the foreigners. A British officer named Charles George Gordon put together and trained a Chinese force, which the British dubbed the "Ever-Victorious Army." Using British rifles, British cannon, and British tactics, "China" Gordon helped to bring the *Taiping* Rebellion to an end.

Various Chinese provincial commanders also helped: Their regional armies contributed greatly to the *Taiping* defeat. As they did so, however, the local satraps exacted a price from the dynasty: freedom from taxation and other forms of interference from above.

Although the Manchu dynasty survived, China was starting a long slide into anarchy.

4

Seeking to restore the dynasty's power and prestige, a cluster of highly placed officials around the emperor in Beijing in the two decades after the *Taiping* uprising launched a program of national rejuvenation, the "self-strengthening movement." They mandated the construction of arsenals, set up a foreign language school, opened coal mines, organized a China Merchant's Steam Navigation Company, and sought to build a Chinese navy.

They also created the *Zongli Yamen,* a special board that in effect was a foreign ministry. Recognizing the futility of the earlier refusal to have normal diplomatic relations with the West, the "self-strengtheners" believed that the dynasty might be able to control the barbarians.

Expressing this hope, Feng Guifen, a high-ranking scholar, in 1889 brushed an essay entitled "On the Better Control of the Barbarians": "Today our country considers barbarian affairs to be the most important matter of government, and the suppression of the bandits [various rebels] to be the second. Why? Because the bandits can be exterminated but it is impossible to do so with the barbarians. . . . If a plan of controlling the barbarians is not devised, . . . the barbarian problem will become worse."

At last, Chinese officials were acknowledging their country's weakness. But no one had a plan for how China was actually to control the foreigners.

The self-strengthening movement was a fiasco. For financing, China had to turn to foreign banks, and the country fell into debt. Because of inept engineering, the coal mines went bankrupt. Plundered by its managers, the steamship company was obliged to sell out to the British. Foreign language learning proved slow going. The arsenals were inefficient. And as for a navy. . . . Northwest of Beijing stands the Park of Nurtured Harmony, identified in modern guidebooks as the

(New) Summer Palace. Rising to power after the 1860s, the Dowager Empress ordered up a new secondary imperial compound. In the midst of its palaces and temples was a lake, and in the lake was a boat. The boat still exists. It boasts two decks, stained glass windows, and elaborately carved facings, all financed for the Dowager's pleasure from the nearly empty Manchu treasury. Yet the boat could not float. It was made of marble.

Such was the extent of the Chinese navy. The marble boat symbolized much of what was going wrong in China. The vanity of the Dowager Empress, the emphasis upon imperial show rather than imperial might, the lack of realism that pervaded the court, and the wanton corruption all were driving the government into bankruptcy.

But even Chinese officials of good will knew no way to match the technical superiority of the industrialized world. And that world now was taking full advantage of its power.

5

The foreign powers were carving China apart like a melon. In 1858, the Russian army marched across huge tracts of territory north of the Amur River. In 1862, Indian units from the British Raj took over Lower Burma, once a Manchu client state. In 1871, Russia seized Ili, a vast area in Chinese Turkestan. In 1879, the Japanese navy grabbed the Ryukyu Islands (which included Okinawa), a chain that ran northeastward from Taiwan. In 1887, France completed its colonization of Indochina, another former Chinese tributary. In the late 1880s, German marines spread across the Shandong peninsula, in northeastern China. Russia acquired Port Arthur, at the southern tip of the Manchurian peninsula. The British acquired a lease to Weihaiwei, a small port on the northern side of Shandong, from which they could keep their telescopes trained on the Russians. And in 1898, British diplomats in Beijing obtained a ninety-nine-year lease (leasing being cheaper than fighting) to the New Territories, completing their creation of the Hong Kong territory.

Yet for China, the most traumatic of all such events took place in 1894–1895. Joining the ranks of the Western imperialists, a fully militarized Japan astonished the world with a resounding defeat of the Manchu armies. The conflict, fought in northern China, revealed China's extreme military weakness. After defeating a fleet of Chinese junks, the Japanese rapidly seized control of the seas, took over Korea, and pushed on into Manchuria. When they could see no way of stopping the Japanese army from moving on Beijing, the Chinese agreed to terms of surrender. China had to give up Taiwan, the Pescadore Islands, the Manchurian peninsula, any claim to Korea, and a huge indemnity; Japan also gained extraterritorial rights for her subjects in China, thus acquiring equal status with the Western treaty powers.

Japan's overwhelming success and ruthless exploitation of the victory alarmed competitors in the imperialist struggle. The foreign fears, however, were of little consequence in Japan. The Japanese were finding their very identity in imperialist expansion.

In the face of such humiliation, a group of Chinese intellectuals and officials once again sought to strengthen their country. In 1898, the eminent scholar Kang Yuwei, having startled officialdom with a study of Confucius as a reformer, obtained an audience with the young emperor. He convinced the monarch that the dynasty must embrace changes.

So in a period of 1898 called the "Hundred Days," the Manchu emperor ordered reforms in medicine, agriculture, education, and police and postal services, as well as in industry and military affairs. The upshot of the ruler's commitment to reform, however, was disastrous. Supported by the top Chinese general, Yuan Shikai, the Dowager Empress imprisoned the emperor (who was her nephew), made herself regent, and repealed the edicts. She had six of the reformers executed. Kang Yuwei fled to Japan; Japan was willing to succor any enemy of the Dowager Empress, who was now fully in control of the Manchu court.

One of the would-be reformers, a wealthy and powerful (and hence untouchable) official named Liang Qichao, wrote scathingly of the resistance to change. One group of officials, he contended, barely knew of the existence of the five continents. A second group was aware of the foreign aggression but, being advanced in years, wished simply to live out their days in peace. And a third group was unconcerned because even if the empire fell, their personal wealth would be unaffected. No reconstruction of the country, Liang concluded, could come from the Manchus or any of the officials in the Forbidden City.

Liang's pessimism was soon borne out, for the Manchu dynasty was on the brink of its last debacle, the Boxer upheaval.

6

On May 28, 1900, members of a Chinese association called the "Righteous and Harmonious Fists," or simply "Boxers," set fire to a train station on the outskirts of Beijing. The movement known to resident westerners as the Boxer Rebellion quickly reached the city; soon it would attain the edge of the Legation Quarter.

To the members of the foreign diplomatic corps, mainly British, American, French, German, Russian, and Japanese, the Legation Quarter had long been a haven. Wedged against the southern wall of the Forbidden City and flanked by another wall to the south, the area was open only to the east, where it faced a Methodist mission headquarters and a broad, busy thoroughfare that ran northward from one of the gates in the wall. Of Chinese doings beyond that thoroughfare the diplomatic community knew virtually nothing. Life in the Beijing compound, like life in the treaty-ports, meant manicured lawns, champagne at dinner, cards in the evening, and security from China's decades-old turmoil. All that was about to change.

After burning the train station, the Boxers, thousands of youths who had marched in from the parched plain of northern China, also cut the telegraph lines from Beijing to Tianjin. Being close to the coast, Tianjin served as the port for northern China and had a large foreign community. Then, on June 13, 1900, Boxers exploded into the streets just east of the Legation Quarter, smashing windows and setting fire to shops. As darkness fell, flames licked around to the north of the Quarter and, in the middle of the night, the cathedral went up with a roar.

Over the next two weeks, the violence escalated. A German official shot a Boxer to death and, aided by imperial troops, the Boxers retaliated by raining bullets down on the Legation Quarter from the surrounding walls. At the open end, Chinese erected a huge scaffold, which they proceeded to move ever closer into the foreign sector.

On June 29, runners carried to the British consul in Tianjin a note written by Sir Robert Hart, for decades in charge of China's tariffs. The message read: "Foreign community besieged. . . . Situation desperate. MAKE HASTE!"

In the world outside, telegraphed messages flew from capital to capital. Do we intervene? Yes. Shall we compose a multilateral force? Yes. Who shall command it? A German Count von Waldersee. Soon Tianjin received a host of foreign soldiers, Sikhs in turbans from British India, Italians with plumes, French Zouaves uniformed in red and blue, Russians, Germans, Japanese (the largest contingent), and, up from their post–Spanish-American War suppression of rebels in the Philippines, Americans. At the end of the first week of August, 1900, the international force set off for Beijing.

As dusk fell on August 13, shells from behind the scaffolding the Boxers had erected were poured into the Legation Quarter. Trumpets blared out of the darkness and from inside the Quarter foreigners could hear cries of "*Sha! Sha!*" ("Kill! Kill!"). Virtually everyone inside, even missionaries who had fled from the countryside, took up guns and secured themselves behind overturned desks or unemptied vats of nightsoil. Casualties had been few so far, but the Boxers were now entering the Legation Quarter.

Then, over the din and from outside the city walls, the foreigners began to hear the boom of cannon. The international relief force had reached Beijing.

The siege was over. Those Boxers not captured or executed fled to the countryside and the thousand foreign troops looted Beijing, forcing the dynasty to pay a huge indemnity. The Dowager Empress, who during the disturbance had fled Beijing disguised as a peasant, returned to the Forbidden City; but she soon died. All that was left of the Manchu dynasty was the emperor she had chosen to succeed her nephew, Henry Aisin Gyoro Pu Yi, only a small boy. The Manchus had run out of time.

Inspired by Sun Yatsen, a southern Chinese physician turned revolutionary and exiled in Japan (for Tokyo was happy to see China plunged into turmoil), peasant rebellions flared up in many parts of China. Attempted putsches against the dynasty did fail. But as George Morrison, a reporter, observed in 1911 in a cable to the London *Times*, "The Manchu dynasty is in danger. The sympathies of the immense mass of educated Chinese are all with the revolutionaries. Little sympathy is expressed for the corrupt and effete Manchu dynasty with its eunuchs and other barbaric surroundings. The court is in great anxiety and the outlook for the throne ominous."

The peasantry had rarely affected Chinese politics. But when onerous taxes combined with droughts and floods made life unbearable, the farmers did revolt.

Thus, on October 10, 1911, peasant rebels took over Guangdong (Canton) Province in the south, from which the *Taiping* movement had spread. Similar uprisings succeeded in most of the other provinces. One after another, military governors and leaders in provincial assemblies declared their independence. The anti-Manchu movement was sweeping the country.

In December the Manchu regent resigned and Yuan Shikai, who in 1898 had crushed the reform movement, staged a coup. On February 13, 1912, he forced the boy emperor to abdicate.

On that date, the Manchu dynasty ceased to exist and the Republic of China came into being. But the revolutionary spirit that had toppled the dynasty had been more anti-Manchu than pro-Yuan. Yuan Shikai, who had seized power, was a leader without a mandate, and the chaos of the preceding century now turned into the anarchy of warlordism.

7

In the first three decades of the twentieth century, China had no real government; in Beijing one warlord after another took power and then was defeated. The warlords—generals, bandit chieftains, and crime bosses—had reduced the country to anarchy. Here a warlord controlled a province, there a city, and over there a secret society ruled a forest.

One figure, however, did emerge as a national leader, Sun Yatsen's major disciple, Chiang Kaishek. Chiang's vehicle was the *Guomindang*, or Nationalist Party, a paramilitary organization with fascist leanings. Chiang was a professional soldier trained in Japan and based in Guangzhou, and in the mid-1920s he launched the Northern Expedition, eventually unifying southern and central China by force and forging an alliance with the bankers of Shanghai. Symbolizing that alliance was his marriage in 1927 to Soong Meiling, an American-educated daughter of China's wealthiest family. That year also saw Chiang's effort to crush the Chinese Communist Party, concentrated in Shanghai, China's one industrialized city.

The Party had its origins in the May Fourth Movement of 1919. Soon after the outbreak of World War I, Japan had declared war on Germany, then seized the German-held islands in the Pacific and China's Shandong peninsula, the German colony. Japan also had pressured China to accept the Twenty-One Demands, which without the diplomatic intervention of President Woodrow Wilson would have given Japan control over most of China's Yangzi valley basin. At the Paris peace talks of 1919, however, Wilson had acceded to Japan's continued occupation of Shandong and the warlord government-of-the-moment in Beijing had accepted the arrangement. Chinese students had erupted in fury, burning the Beijing home of the minister in question. Even after the fury had abated, Chinese intellectuals as never before turned to Western ideas as possible keys to national defense.

Out of the ideological ferment came an intense interest in Marxism-Leninism and the formation of the Chinese Communist Party.

Early in the 1920s the Communists had been part of the *Guomindang*, receiving training and advice from agents out of Moscow. Fearing Communist influence, however, Chiang Kaishek had instituted his purge.

Their ranks decimated, the Communists in the early 1930s gradually reassembled in the mountains of southeastern China. Their weapons were few, mostly picked up in raids on local warlords, and since most of the troops were peasants they had few financial resources. In time, encircled by Chiang's forces, they retreated again. Thus, on October 18, 1934, the Long March began.

"Around five o'clock in the morning," went one account, "Mao [Zedong] and about twenty others left Yutu [a town where they had been hiding] by the North Gate, and then turned to the left towards the river, which was all yellow, roaring and foaming. . . . Soon the sun set, and the gusts of bitter cold wind chilled us. The Chairman [Mao] wore a gray cloth uniform and an eight-cornered military cap, with no overcoat. He walked with enormous strides along the river-bank."

Forced out of the mountain redoubt, Mao Zedong led his columns westward below Hunan, his native province, then up toward the Yangzi River near Chongqing. Encountering Nationalist troops, the Reds skirted southward and to the west again, just above Kunming, then neared Tibet. Trails along the cliffs were rarely more than five feet wide, and were often icy. Many marchers plunged to their deaths. Then came the grasslands with swamps and quicksands. Rains made sleep difficult and mosquitoes brought fevers. Mao became ill and had to be carried much of the way. Of the 100,000 persons who had started with him, only 20,000 survived.

But a year after their departure, the Communists reached Yanan, in northwestern China. Far from Chiang Kaishek's centers of power, in 1936 they at last were safe from attack.

The next year, 1937, Edgar Snow, an American journalist who visited the Communist encampment and who later was Mao's trusted American confidant, described the setting: "[T]hough you see fields and cultivated land everywhere, you seldom see houses. The peasants are tucked away in . . . loess hills [porous topsoil blown down over the centuries from central Asia]. . . . Throughout the northwest, . . . men live in homes dug out of the hard fudge-colored cliffs—'*yao fang*,' or 'cave houses,' as the Chinese call them."

Holed up in the caves of Yanan, raising crops and ingratiating themselves with the local peasants, the Communists hoped to launch their own reconstruction of China. But then came the most devastating calamity in their country's experience: In 1937 Japan invaded China.

2

JAPAN'S RESPONSE
TO THE WEST

1

If superimposed on the East Coast of the United States, the map of the four main Japanese islands, Hokkaido, Honshu, Shikoku, and Kyushu, would stretch from southern Maine to southwestern Georgia; Tokyo Bay would lie along the Outer Banks of North Carolina. The Sea of Japan, corresponding in area to western New York and Pennsylvania, West Virginia, and Ohio, would separate Japan from the Asian continent, the one point of proximity to the mainland being the Tsushima Strait between Japan and Korea. The first waves of settlement, in the early part of the Christian era, of the people we call the Japanese came from Korea. The Japanese language, highly inflected, bears a resemblance to Korean and the other tongues of northeastern Asia, unlike the tonal and tenseless Chinese and Vietnamese. Geographical distance and linguistic difference over the centuries helped Japan preserve its cultural distinctiveness from China.

In the period of the Western Middle Ages, Japan did borrow Chinese ideographs, culinary implements, and architectural styles, as well as a reverence for the emperor. The Mongols, China's rulers in the thirteenth century, tried to invade Japan but were driven off by a *kamikaze*, a "divine wind." But China never was able to conquer Japan. The Japanese saw themselves as a people apart, with a warrior class, the *samurai*. In contrast to the luxury-loving upper classes of China, the *samurai* were often poor and bandit-threatened farmers for whom frugality was a virtue and mastery of the martial arts a necessity.

The armed warriors who accumulated wealth became the ruling nobility. Their ethic of self-discipline, along with their sense of uniqueness, helps explain why Japan eventually reacted so differently from China to the coming of the West.

By the mid-1800s, Japan had dwelt for two centuries in almost complete isolation from the rest of the world. After they had purged their islands of Catholic missionaries who had arrived in the sixteenth century and been regarded by the authorities as subversive of the existing order, the Japanese had all but vanished from the sight of Europeans. The only foreigners allowed were Protestant and decidedly nonproselytizing Dutch traders at Nagasaki. Through them, the Japanese had learned of the European imperial menace, right across the sea in China. As the British, the French, and others colonized the Chinese coast, Japan once again attracted European attention. Early in the nineteenth century, Russian diplomats explored ties with Japan; the Japanese authorities courteously but firmly rebuffed their requests for an embassy. British ships also explored Tokyo Bay and the Inland Sea; in 1824, British and Japanese sailors clashed by a small island off the southern tip of Japan.

Americans also had been making their presence known. From early in the nineteenth century, New England whaling ships had been sailing via Cape Horn into the North Pacific; the great circle route from California along the Aleutians had brought them close to Japan.

Crews had wanted supplies from Japanese ports and protection from capture and torture in case of shipwrecks; on some occasions men cast ashore by storms had been imprisoned. Then, with the advent of the age of steam, American captains wanted to erect coaling stations on the Pacific side of the Japanese coast. Responding to the New England lobbyists, President Millard Fillmore had sent Commodore Matthew Calbraith Perry to Tokyo Bay.

Matthew Perry, the younger brother of Oliver Hazard Perry (who after the Battle of Lake Erie in 1813 had proclaimed, "We have met the enemy and they are ours"), had been a hero of the Mexican War. As commander of the U.S. Navy's first steam frigate, he had been responsible for the taking of Veracruz. Perry was a taciturn disciplinarian who got things done. A portly man, he dressed immaculately. His neck and chin bulged over his stiff collars and his uniforms shone with gold braid. He was also so puffed up with religion that his journey to Japan was destined to carry "the gospel of God to the heathen"; the boast was similar to the British "white man's burden" and the French "civilizing mission."

Perry's flotilla, built in Brooklyn and Baltimore, consisted of two warships under sail and two side-wheelers under steam. No Japanese junk, the Navy Department was certain, could match the power of these vessels. Setting out from New York in the spring of 1853, they sailed around Africa and through the Indian Ocean. Perry put in first at Hong Kong, where the British gave him safe anchor, as they did routinely for sea captains. When he reached Okinawa, a Japanese dependency, his armed Marines marched along the crushed coral streets of Naha, the island's capital, and into the local palace. After thoroughly frightening the populace and the local satrap, Perry and his ships proceeded to Honshu, the main Japanese island.

On July 8, 1853, lookouts aboard Perry's black-hulled vessels spotted the snow-covered crest of Mount Fuji, rising above the horizon. As the warships entered Tokyo Bay and dropped anchor, fishing boats nearby put out oars and fled like wild birds for the shore. Temple bells in Uraga, a town at the water's edge, rang out in alarm, and women gathered along the beach prayed for a divine storm to drive the ships away.

Anchored off Uraga, Perry hoisted a signal flag on the mast of his flagship, the *Susquehanna*, telling his other ships: "Have no communication with shore; allow none from shore." When numbers of Japanese junks clustered about his ships and their sailors, armed with swords, tried to climb on board, Perry's men fended them off with pikes and bayonets.

But guard boats soon surrounded the American ships and then a larger boat came alongside. A black-and-white striped flag flew from its stern; its crew wore what seemed to be official uniforms. From its deck a voice called out, in English: "I can speak Dutch." One of the two interpreters whom Perry had brought along, H. A. L. Portman, was fluent in Dutch. After some haggling, Perry let the Dutch-speaking Japanese, and a man who claimed to be the vice governor at Uraga, on board. The Japanese were received in the captain's cabin. Perry remained in his own adjoining cabin, speaking to the Japanese only through his flag lieutenant. Perry, the lieutenant explained, bore a letter from the president of the United States to the emperor of Japan, which he would present only to an official equal in rank to himself. (Perry had passed himself off as the highest-ranking officer in the American Navy.) The Japanese vice governor replied that his country would do business with foreigners only at Nagasaki, at the far western tip of Japan. But Perry was adamant: He would go to Tokyo. And if the guard boats did not disappear, he would open fire. They dispersed. Perry had won his first important concession.

That night Perry's crews were uneasy. During the afternoon Japanese forts, fully manned, had been plainly visible. Now the Americans could see beacon fires upon the heights, a bell from somewhere on land sounded at regular intervals. Perry ordered sentinels for and aft and at the gangway of every ship. But the night passed without incident.

The next morning, two large boats approached the *Susquehanna* bringing a Japanese who announced himself as the local governor and his entourage. The Japanese again insisted that Perry go to Nagasaki and Perry again refused. As the conference continued, four fully armed surveying boats, one from each American ship, rowed farther to the north. Perry wanted accurate soundings of the bay, of course, but by inching closer to Tokyo itself he also was putting pressure on the Japanese.

Several days later, a Japanese delegation informed him that on July 14, a dignitary bearing proper credentials from the emperor would meet with him on land.

Wells Williams, Perry's other translator, on the morning of the fourteenth wrote that the "squadron was full of bustle, getting arms burnished, boats ready, steam up, men dressed and making all the preparations necessary to go ashore and be prepared for any alternative." Perry moved the two steamers into broadside formation so that their guns could command the landing area.

Then, shortly before ten o'clock, a Japanese launch arrived, bringing two officials dressed in elaborate brocade trimmed with velvet and gold lace; they were to guide the Americans to the reception point. Fifteen American launches and cutters followed them out from the flagship, carrying about one hundred Marines, a similar number of sailors, forty officers, and a brass band. Commodore Perry, bringing up the rear, now showed himself to the Japanese for the first time. Under a salute of thirteen guns from the *Susquehanna,* he stepped into his launch. His jacket was buttoned to the neck and his sword and epaulets gleamed in the sun; despite the July heat, he was in full dress uniform.

Upon reaching the shore, the boats let out their men on a pier of sandbags and straw, then pulled back about fifty feet and dropped anchor. Their crews were ready, if necessary, to dash to their comrades' defense. Behind them in the bay, the decks of the four ships were cleared for action.

On shore, the Americans stood in a line. At the head of the procession, all spit and polish, were the Marines. Then came a powerfully built sailor carrying Perry's colors, followed by two cabin boys bearing

President Fillmore's letter. Behind them waited Perry, flanked by two sailors holding American flags atop tall pikes. Next came the officers of the fleet, the rest of the sailors, and finally the musicians in blue caps with red, white, and blue bands. The players struck up "Hail, Columbia," an officer barked a marching command, and the grand parade stepped off toward the hastily erected meetinghouse.

Once inside the chamber, a tent carpeted in red and hung with violet-colored draperies, Perry and his aides were ushered to stiff-backed chairs. Opposite them, in silence, sat two Japanese officials, appointed to receive the American document.

Perry's aides brought the president's letter forward and the Japanese officials accepted it, placing it in a red lacquered box standing on gilt legs in the center of the room. A Japanese handed over an official receipt that read: "The letter of the president of the United States of North America is hereby received, and will be delivered to the emperor."

After the ceremony, Wells Williams wrote in his diary: "[T]hus closed this eventful day, one which will be a day to be noted in the history of Japan, one on which the key was put into the lock and a beginning made to do away with the long seclusion of this nation, for I am inclined to think that the reception of such a letter in such a public manner involves its consideration if not its acceptance. . . ."

But Williams's optimism was premature. The reply from the imperial court, delivered at a meeting on July 28, 1853, was evasive. Perry handed it back as unsatisfactory. He stated that he was going to leave Japan for Hong Kong for supplies, but would be back the next year. At that time, he threatened, Japan would accept an American presence on its soil, or face war.

In mid-February, 1854, when Perry returned to Japan, a change of attitude had taken place. Many influential Japanese had concluded that their swords and spears would be no match for the American guns. Through the Dutch at Nagasaki, they had learned of China's subjugation to the British and they had no wish to suffer a similar fate.

They would accept Perry's terms and then in time strive to make Japan invulnerable.

No Japanese war junks appeared when Perry's squadron once more reached the bay. The Japanese were friendly and agreed to a treaty-signing at Kanagawa, a larger port than Uraga. This time, furthermore, the Japanese would construct a real reception hall.

March 8, the day set for the opening of the new negotiations, dawned chilly but clear. Half an hour before noon, twenty-seven boats loaded with nearly five hundred armed Americans put off from the ships and rowed for shore. A cabin boy described the landing: "It was an imposing sight to see the bluff, burly commodore marching up between the bristling ranks, bareheaded and surrounded by his staff . . . sailors and soldiers presenting arms—the officers saluting—the bands from the various ships playing national airs . . . and last tho' not least the strange dresses, arms, and looks of the natives who came from all parts of the [Japanese] empire to view [this] strange, and to them, wonderful sight."

Having come ashore, Perry and his staff marched to the treaty house, a long, low, windowless building of unpainted pine. Ascending a flight of three steps, the American delegation went inside. Three-inch-thick straw mats, springy underfoot, carpeted the floor. A large blue flag with the imperial coat of arms almost completely covered the far wall. Along the side walls, hung with woodcuts, were low benches and tables draped with red cotton cloth. Copper bowls of glowing charcoal heated the room.

Perry, his aides, and his interpreters sat down on the left side of the room. Five Japanese commissioners entered, bowed, and, along with their own interpreters, sat on the right. After an exchange of polite greetings, Perry got down to business.

> We have in our country always regarded human life as of the first importance, and, therefore, whenever any of our countrymen—of course—or persons belonging to another country . . . reach our shores after having been shipwrecked,

we exert every effort to rescue them, and we treat them with kindness. I perceive no sign, however, that human life is counted in your country to be of great importance; for whenever a vessel of any foreign country approaches your shores, you repel it; and when shipwrecked persons reach the shore, you treat them like slaves, and keep them in harsh imprisonment.

If this sort of treatment continued, Perry warned, the United States might come to look upon Japan as an enemy; in that case, war might result. He pointed out that America had just concluded a war with a neighboring country, Mexico. "Circumstances may lead your country into a similar plight," Perry threatened. "It would be well for you to reconsider."

In the end it was the Japanese who again made the concessions; high officials believed that they had no choice. On March 13, 1854, they signed a treaty of "friendship and commerce." The term was a euphemism for Japan's agreeing to the coaling stations as well as the principle of extraterritoriality in selected port cities.

Losing no time introducing American goods to the Japanese, Perry presented his hosts a range of gifts: John James Audubon's drawings of American birds, farm tools, Colt pistols, a miniature electric train, and a telegraph. The telegraph especially intrigued the Japanese. Sailors rigged up transmitters and receivers a mile apart, strung a wire between them, and sent messages back and forth. Some of the Japanese tried to outrun the messages, but when they arrived huffing and puffing at the other end of the wire, the words were always there before them.

Everywhere the Americans noticed the Japanese with little brushes and sheets of rice paper, drawing pictures of all they saw. Unlike the Chinese, the Japanese were zealously learning all they could about the secrets of western technology.

On January 12, 1855, Commodore Perry finally returned to Washington. Receptions in his honor took place in New York, Boston, and

Newport, Rhode Island, his birthplace. The press likened him to Columbus, Vasco da Gama, and Captain Cook.

Privately, however, Perry was not jubilant. Although the British in Hong Kong had treated him well, their victory over China left him worried; he knew well the story of the opium war. The peoples of the region, he counseled the president and the secretary of state, needed the "national friendship and protection" of the United States. He had encouraged the Japanese to adopt the methods of Western industrialization and technology, in hopes that they would provide a balance to British power in the Far Pacific.

2

Japan was a land without substantial natural resources and with a coastline easily attacked by foreign navies. Such shortcomings led to what we might call the "Japanese problem": the possibility of suffering China's fate. One solution to the problem had been isolation; before Perry arrived, Japan had sought safety by withdrawing from the rest of the world. Perry's visit, however, had shown that isolation was impossible to maintain. Therefore, Japanese leaders turned to what Perry had counseled: a new answer to the problem—rapid economic modernization.

Beginning in the 1860s with the "Meiji Restoration," named after the new emperor whose reign was called *"Meiji,"* meaning "enlightened rule," businessmen and governmental officials ended the policy of isolation by emphasizing foreign trade. Starting with the export of silks, which Japanese artisans were already skilled at making, then other textiles and trinkets that were cheap to manufacture, Japan found niches in the markets of Europe and America; the emphasis on exports worked as long as these markets were open. Keeping domestic wages low and competition from other countries out (as Great Britain had done a century earlier at the time of its own industrial revolution), Japan's new capitalists, helped by tax breaks from the government, plowed the profits back into the further growth of exports. Additional expansion meant still more revenues with which resource-poor Japan could purchase raw materials abroad. Economic growth thus overcame some of Japan's deficiencies.

Until late in the nineteenth century, however, the problem of extraterritoriality remained. The country needed armed strength to induce the foreigners to leave. Japan therefore began to translate its economic advances into military prowess. Sending delegations overseas, Japan studied closely the tactics of the German Army, believed to be the most advanced in the world, and the naval architecture of the British fleet. Back home, the government drafted peasant boys and turned them into skilled soldiers and sailors. Blast furnaces for the production of armaments began to light up the night skies around Tokyo, Yokohama, and Osaka. The economic and military modernization secured its first objective: Impressed with Japan's progress, the foreign powers late in the nineteenth century gave up their extraterritorial rights on Japanese soil. Japan became the first non-Western nation to be accorded equality by the West.

Japan's very mode of development, however, led to a paradox. The progress reinforced the sense of uniqueness implicit in the old isolationism, and led the Japanese to see themselves as racially superior to other Asians. Yet Japan remained dependent on other countries for markets and raw materials. So it looked to Taiwan as a grain basket, Manchuria as a source of raw materials, and Korea as a barrier against Russian expansion into Manchuria. Taiwan, however, was part of the Chinese empire, and Korea was a Chinese client state. The prospect of war with China loomed large. To prepare the people at large for conquest abroad, the Japanese government promulgated the ideology of nationalism. Revering the emperor as a god, the Japanese people were taught in schools, newspapers, and mass meetings that they were not individuals but rather cogs in a mighty military machine. Their sacred task, an obligation buttressed by a Shintoism that had become a state religion, was the subjugation of China.

In 1875, a party of Japanese, landing from warships to map the Korean coast, came under gunfire from soldiers on the peninsula. A

Japanese fleet then anchored off Inchon, on the middle of the Korean west coast. In February, 1876, Japan imposed an unequal treaty modeled on the opium war treaties in China. The agreement opened three ports for Japanese trade, and it declared Korea an "independent state."

Over the next two decades, the Japanese in Korea erected schools, clinics, shops, restaurants, railroads, telegraph lines, and military encampments: collectively the infrastructure for invasion. Japan's refusal to acknowledge China's claim to sovereignty over Korea alarmed Beijing, which saw what remained of its own empire crumbling before its very eyes. China's fear was well founded. When a peasant revolt against the government broke out in southern Korea in 1894, China, at the Korean king's request, sent over a small contingent of troops; in response Japan sent more troops, seized Seoul, and on August 1 declared war on China.

Western diplomats thought that, with its masses of soldiers, China easily would overwhelm the Japanese. It did not work out that way. With their superior training, tactics, and weaponry the Japanese overran Korea and then invaded Manchuria, driving the Chinese out with ease. Next, on September 17, 1894, the Japanese navy off the mouth of the Yalu River destroyed a Chinese fleet in hours. The Japanese then besieged Weihaiwei, on the northern coast of the Shandong peninsula, bottling up what remained of the Chinese ships there. For good measure, Japan finally captured the naval base of Port Arthur, at the tip of the Manchurian peninsula. In the Treaty of Shimonoseki (a port in southwestern Japan), signed on April 17, 1895, China acknowledged its defeat.

In the eyes of the Europeans and the Americans, though, this was going too far. The Japanese were threatening to overturn the East Asian balance of power. On April 23, 1895, in a joint diplomatic intervention, Russia, Germany, and France (but not Great Britain, which was considering an alliance with Japan) "advised" Japan to give up Port Arthur, captured from the Chinese. Bowing to superior force, but holding onto Korea and Taiwan as colonies, and receiving a huge indemnity from China, the Japanese government complied.

Japan also complied with the Open Door Notes, promulgated by the United States in 1899 and 1900. These messages called for free trade and nonaggression in China. Japan's adherence to these principles, however, proved short-lived.

In 1898, threatening war, Russia forced China to cede Port Arthur. Lying at the tip of Manchuria's Liaodong peninsula, Port Arthur (the Chinese Lushun) was strategically well located. The only point along the Manchurian coast that was ice-free in winter, it gave any occupying fleet access to the Gulf of Zhili, the route to Beijing. The Japanese laid plans to capture Port Arthur again and to push on into mineral-rich Manchuria.

A visitor approaching Port Arthur by ship would have passed through a narrow harbor entrance into a landlocked bay where bare, rugged hills rose sharply on all sides. Off to the right, beneath a hill on which the Russian flag flew over a fort, were the naval basin, dockyard, and telegraph. On the left, a long peninsula sheltered calm-water moorings for torpedo boats. Straight ahead, beyond a row of white-painted houses along the waterfront, stood another fort, equipped with long-range artillery. Occupied by Russian troops that after the Boxer upheaval had not left the Far East, Port Arthur seemed inviolable.

On the moonless night of February 8, 1904, however, a Japanese torpedo boat flotilla out of Korea slipped through the narrows and (in an action that presaged Pearl Harbor) without warning sank the Russian fleet.

For Japan, the war went well. By the spring of 1905, it had driven the Russians back in Manchuria and captured Mukden, the provincial capital. In desperation, Russia sent its Baltic fleet to the rescue: forty-five obsolete and poorly equipped Russian ships, which British ports had refused to resupply en route, reached the Far East. In single file the ships had tried to make a dash through the Strait of Tsushima, between Japan and Korea. The Japanese sank all but a handful.

Japan, an Asian nation, had soundly defeated a European one. Fearing that the conflagration would spread, the European leaders looked about for an honest broker to negotiate an end to the war. Because Britain (in recognition of Japan's power) had allied with Japan, the German Kaiser was a first cousin to the Russian tsar, and France was allied to Russia, the role of an intermediary fell upon the president of the United States, Theodore Roosevelt.

TR had been eager to play the part. America in the era of Theodore Roosevelt was starting to displace Great Britain as the world's greatest power: America had enjoyed a spectacular (if easy) victory over Spain in 1898, and although Great Britain finally had won the Boer War in South Africa (1899–1902), it barely had been able to defeat a handful of Dutch-descended farmers. America certainly had the wealth to be the leader of nations, but its military and naval forces were slight. TR hoped that through diplomacy he could win recognition of America's stature.

On the afternoon of August 5, 1905, two American warships entered Oyster Bay on Long Island Sound just below the Roosevelt summer White House. One displayed the flag of the Rising Sun; the other the red and white emblem of imperial Russia. Launches from both ships transported frock-coated men to the presidential yacht, the *Mayflower,* at anchor by the pier. Out from the dock, a third launch also steered for the *Mayflower,* bearing President Roosevelt.

An accidental president by dint of the assassination of President William McKinley in September, 1901, Roosevelt had won election in his own right in the landslide victory of 1904. Then he had set out to make the American nation the guardian of peace abroad.

Roosevelt had wanted a Russo-Japanese meeting to take place in the United States. But where? Washington in the summertime was an oven and New York held too many distractions. TR wanted the sessions to take place on military property so that sentries could ensure privacy and near Oyster Bay so that, if necessary, he could intervene quickly. So he had chosen to stage the opening ceremonies on the *Mayflower* in view of his home. The delegates then would sail to the naval yard at Portsmouth, New Hampshire. While tending to duties

in the summer White House, Roosevelt would be in contact by telegraph and telephone.

On board the *Mayflower,* Roosevelt, speaking in French, invited
the Russians and the Japanese to lunch. With the two delegations'
leaders, Russia's Count Sergius Witte and Japan's Baron Komura Ju-
taro, on either arm, TR steered toward the door of the yacht's dining
room. He made certain that neither diplomat crossed the threshold
ahead of the other.

A buffet luncheon awaited the guests. Since Roosevelt wanted to
avoid the issue of who should sit at his right, the room contained no
tables. To avoid any appearance of partiality, TR ate sitting in a chair
with his back to the others. After the luncheon, he proposed a toast:
"I drink to the welfare and prosperity of the sovereigns and peoples
of the two great nations whose representatives have met one another
on this ship. It is my most earnest hope and desire that a just and lasting peace may speedily be concluded between them."

The inevitable news photographs followed: frock-coated, stripe-
trousered, and white-vested, President Roosevelt stood in the middle,
dwarfing Baron Komura and Minister Takahira Kogora on his left;
on his right stood the slender, elegant, white-bearded Baron Rosen
and the gigantic Count Witte. With the pictures taken, Roosevelt returned by launch to shore and the *Mayflower* set sail on the 300-mile
trip to Portsmouth.

At Portsmouth, the Russians and the Japanese squabbled. The
Japanese demanded reparations and the Russians, their treasury
bankrupted by the war, refused to pay. Alerted by State Department
personnel in attendance, TR intervened. Earlier in the year, a group
of Korean nationalists had asked Roosevelt to insist that Japan grant
the independence of their country. Roosevelt secretly had promised to
do so. Now, faced with a breakdown in the Portsmouth talks, he telephoned up an offer: If Japan would forego its demand for reparations, he would leave Korea to Japan. Breaking his word to the
Koreans, he closed the deal. Japan also got southern Manchuria.

At Portsmouth on September 5, 1905, the Russian and Japanese conferees signed a treaty of peace, drank champagne, and departed. For his efforts, Theodore Roosevelt won the Nobel Prize for Peace.

Two years later, Roosevelt sent sixteen battleships, the Great White Fleet (white signifying peaceful intentions) around the world: He wanted to put the world in general and Japan in particular on notice about America's own rising naval power. All along the route, from Virginia's Hampton Roads to Brazil, Cape Horn, California, Hawaii, New Zealand, Australia, the Philippines, Japan, Singapore, Suez, and back to the Chesapeake Bay, the voyage was a public relations hit.

Roosevelt learned from the American legation in Tokyo, however, that the Japanese were not impressed. The peace he had wrought was not to last.

In the five years after Roosevelt's departure from the White House in 1909, the Japanese turned Korea and Taiwan into economic appendages, forced suppliers of food for the Japanese population and of coal, metals, and other raw materials for the Japanese industrial machine. But an event that would change the East Asian imperial order further took place half a world away. On June 28, 1914, in Sarajevo, a young Bosnian Serb named Gavrilo Princip shot to death the archduke and archduchess of the Austro-Hungarian Empire. Six weeks later, because of its network of alliances, Europe was at war.

3

No sooner had the First World War broken out than Japan declared war on Germany. Tokyo had no real quarrel with Berlin. But China's Shandong peninsula was a German colony and Japan used the outbreak of European hostilities as a pretext for seizing the territory.

For a generation, Shandong had been subjected to proselytizing by foreign missionaries and had been the source of anti-Christian uprisings such as the Boxer movement. To young Chinese intellectuals, who had hoped that with Germany pinned down in Europe, Shandong again could become Chinese, the Japanese occupation was most galling.

Then, in January, 1915, Japan went further, secretly pressing China, now torn apart by the anarchy of warlordism, to accept a document that became known as the Twenty-One Demands. President Woodrow Wilson found out about most of the demands. Initially he thought they applied only to Shandong. But Secretary of State William Jennings Bryan heard from Chinese emissaries that additional demands would give Japan control of the Yangzi River valley, the heartland of central China. The Japanese ambassador in Washington went to the White House, denying the accusation. When Paul Reinsch, Wilson's ambassador in China, forwarded proof that the Japanese ambassador had lied, however, Wilson was furious. Like TR, he was committed to international stability; unlike Roosevelt, Wilson confronted a Japan decidedly on the march. In two tough notes of March and May, 1915, the president told the Japanese to back down. In his second missive, the president asserted that the United States would not tolerate any Japanese infringement of the "political or territorial integrity of China."

Although for many years an academic, Wilson had proven himself politically adept, moving from the presidency of Princeton University to the governorship of New Jersey, then to the White House in just two years. His greatest gift was his ability to articulate American principles. The freedom from aggression he called for in his notes to Japan was the most cherished of those ideals.

It was an ideal he would enunciate again when, in April, 1917, the United States entered into World War I. In justifying American participation, President Wilson announced the Fourteen Points, calling for free trade, the end of colonialism, and the self-determination of peoples. The next administration, that of President Warren G. Harding, applied the meaning of the Fourteen Points directly to Japan.

For the First World War had changed dramatically the antebellum imperial world order. The Russian and Austro-Hungarian empires were gone. Germany had lost its colonies in Asia and Africa. The British and the French were nearly bankrupt and faced uprisings in their own colonies, Ireland, India, and Indochina. The one empire that confronted no restraints, unless the United States provided them, was Japan.

4

On the chilly morning of November 12, 1921, limousines whisked down 17th Street in Washington and halted in front of Constitution Hall, letting out statesmen from Asia, Europe, and the United States. President Harding had convened them for an international gathering called the Washington Conference. The purpose of the meeting, the first multilateral session held in the United States, was to reach an arms control accord—and to build a diplomatic wall against Japanese aggression on the Asian mainland.

The conference produced the famous 5–5–3 agreement, whereby for every five British battleships, the United States could have five and Japan three. But it did more. Dominated by Secretary of State Charles Evans Hughes, the delegates agreed on two additional pledges. First, Japan got to keep its Pacific islands. Primarily these were the Carolines and the Marshalls, which along with Shandong the Japanese had taken from Germany; the Japanese pledged to keep the islands free of fortifications. Second, Japan would withdraw from Shandong and abide by the Nine Power Treaty, which guaranteed China's freedom from invasion. Signed on February 6, 1922, by the United States, the British Empire, France, the Netherlands, Portugal, Italy, Belgium, China, and Japan, the document began: "The Contracting Powers, other than China, agree . . . to respect the sovereignty, the independence, and the territorial and administrative integrity of China."

The United States in the Nine Power Treaty committed itself to deterring further Japanese incursions in China. And to make certain that Japan adhered to the agreement, the Harding administration arranged a flow of low-interest loans from Wall Street to Tokyo. The strategy worked as long as the loans kept coming.

But with the advent of the Great Depression in 1929, the loans stopped. Affronted by what it saw as a discriminatory American trade policy, the Smoot-Hawley Act of 1930, Japan embarked on a quest of what it considered a legitimate sphere of "autonomy," *jichiryo*. Autonomy was a euphemism for a self-contained empire on the Asian mainland.

5

On the night of September 18, 1931, a Japanese soldier wired some sticks of dynamite alongside a track of the Japanese-owned South Manchurian Railway. He was careful, burying the sticks so they would throw up dirt but leave the rails themselves unharmed. The job done, the soldier and his companions, sent out from a nearby garrison, lingered in the gloom, waiting for a Chinese patrol to come by. When the patrol appeared, one of the Japanese pushed the plunger, the powder exploded, and the Japanese unit opened fire on the Chinese.

The "Manchurian Incident," the Japanese euphemism for seizing the region, was under way. Claiming that the Chinese had triggered the explosion, Japanese forces quickly seized Mukden, the capital of Manchuria. Soon they took the entire province, which the Chinese had called *Manzhou* (continent or area of the Manchu people), renaming it *Manchuguo*, in Chinese meaning "Manchu Country," pretending that the province was an independent state. To maintain the pretense, they installed a ruler, Henry (to use his Western name) Aisin Gyoro Puyi, the last Chinese emperor, who had been living in Tianjin as a Japanese-supported playboy. They actually got a few countries, such as El Salvador, to recognize Manchuguo as a sovereign state.

But Manchuguo was no more than a puppet state, and Japan had seized the region in violation of the Nine Power Treaty. Americans were appalled. On January 7, 1932, President Herbert Hoover's secretary of state, Henry L. Stimson, announced that the United States refused to "admit the legality of any situation de facto [or] to recognize any treaty or agreement . . . which may impair the treaty rights of the United States or its citizens in China, including those which relate to the sovereignty, the independence, or the territorial and administrative integrity of the Republic of China, commonly known as the open-door policy."

"The Stimson Doctrine" was foreign policy by nonrecognition. Given America's lack of military preparedness then, it may not have seemed particularly potent. Stimson remarked soon after making his statement that he felt armed with "spears of straw and swords of ice." Yet by asserting the right to guarantee China's survival in the face of Japanese aggression, America acknowledged itself as a major player in the East Asian power game.

3

THE OPEN DOOR

1

Just past the middle of Japan's long period of isolation, Britain's American colonies won their independence. The fledgling United States, however, was anything but isolated. Pioneers were venturing beyond the Appalachians and merchants were looking for profits abroad. The British Parliament in 1789 did decree that Americans could not trade with the British West Indies and that American exports, largely furs and tobacco, had to be carried in British ships. Enterprising Americans, however, soon discovered a market that the British could not close: China. Thus emerged the first contact between the United States and the Far East.

Just after the end of the Revolutionary War, a group of American financiers converted a privateer to business use, hired John Green, an experienced sea captain, and a crew; then they loaded the ship with furs, quantities of lead, barrels of Spanish silver dollars, and large stores of ginseng, prized as an aphrodisiac. All of these items, they had learned from the British experience, were in great demand in China. They named their vessel the *Empress of China*. It got under way on the morning of February 22, 1784, George Washington's birthday.

Late in August the same year, the *Empress of China* dropped anchor in Guangzhou harbor, fifty miles up the Pearl River in southern China. Most of the Western ships around it carried the Union Jack, as the British enjoyed a near-monopoly of Western trade in the port. Captain Green nonetheless was able to sell his goods and return to New York with a shipment of tea, porcelains, and silk: His profit was thirty percent.

Up and down the Atlantic Coast newspapers published accounts of the voyage, further igniting mercantile imaginations. In Portsmouth, Salem, and Newport, and elsewhere, other ships, too, made fortunes from trade with China. Many who acquired fortunes dealt in opium, which, starting in the 1820s, they acquired from the Ottoman Empire. But they chafed at China's anti-opium restrictions. If they were to do business, they were convinced, they would need some measure of protection. So the American merchants lobbied Washington; protected by the First Amendment, lobbying dated back to the first Congress. Now, in the late 1830s and early 1840, the merchants inquired why they should not enjoy the privileges accorded to the British after the Opium War of 1839–1842 in the Treaty of Nanjing.

President John Tyler responded by sending a special envoy to China, Caleb Cushing. Cushing's mission was to win from the Manchu dynasty the concessions already granted to Great Britain in the Nanjing agreement.

2

Caleb Cushing had grown up in Newburyport, one of those Massachusetts villages that lived by and off the sea. He had graduated from Harvard, become a lawyer, and won election to the U.S. House of Representatives. There he had served as a member of the Committee on Foreign Affairs; so he had gained some knowledge of the world.

Late in the 1830s, he also had lent several thousand dollars to the eloquent but always cash-needy Senator Daniel Webster.

In 1841, under President Tyler, Webster became secretary of state and was willing to repay Cushing's favor with an appointment. Ambitious to be a diplomat, Caleb Cushing became America's first envoy to China.

Upon reaching Macao, a tiny peninsula on the mouth of the Pearl River occupied by the Portuguese since the sixteenth century, Cushing agreed to meet a Chinese official in a temple on the narrow strip of land called Wangxia that joined the peninsula to China itself. Cushing's biographer described the ceremonial call on June 18, 1844: "[Kiyeng, the official, made an entrance] preceded by axe bearers, like the ancient Roman lectors. Behind and on either side of him were troops of infantry; while he himself, richly attired, was born aloft in a sedan chair upon the shoulders of bearers." Trying to overawe the American, Kiyeng demanded that Cushing proceed to Beijing. It was a delaying tactic.

Cushing stood his ground. In a return visit to the temple, this time for the actual negotiations, he staged his own entry "with as much pomp and state as could be mustered for the occasion. The . . . temple was massive and spacious, formed of connected buildings with courts between, and approached by a flight of broad and high stone steps. As the Americans approached, [their] band struck up and they fired a salute of three guns. [Then] they were led through the courts to an inner building, where Cushing was received by Kiyeng."

The Chinese commissioner was about sixty years of age, with an expression both stern and inscrutable; he appeared to be a tough negotiator. So Cushing was surprised at his willingness to make concessions. By the end of the day, Kiyeng had signed the Treaty of Wangxia, extending to the United States the same rights imposed by Great Britain two years before in the Treaty of Nanjing: most-favored-nation treatment, extraterritoriality, and the establishment of businesses, churches, and hospitals in the five ports of the earlier accord.

How had Caleb Cushing, one man with a handful of aides, been able to extract such terms from the Manchu dynasty? He had indicated that America and Great Britain were close allies. The Chinese may have been dubious: They regarded the Americans as "second chop" or second-rate Britons. Nonetheless, they feared a return of the British gunboats, this time on behalf of the Americans.

Only two years after Cushing opened China to merchant interests on America's East Coast, the United States won the war with Mexico and acquired most of America's West Coast. The United States now possessed the basis for its own empire on the Pacific.

3

On the evening of Saturday, February 19, 1846, an American diplomat named James Freaner reached Washington. Two weeks earlier, having completed negotiations with the Mexican government, he had left Mexico City on horseback and headed through mountain passes to the port of Vera Cruz. From there he had arrived by ship at Mobile and taken a stagecoach north. Once in the American capital, he immediately sought out the residence of the secretary of state, James Buchanan. In Buchanan's study, Freaner delivered the Treaty of Guadalupe Hidalgo, the prized document of the Mexican surrender: Mexico had ceded territories including Texas, New Mexico, Arizona, Nevada, and California.

Until the end of the Mexican War, Americans had continued to expend vast energies in the conquest of their continent. New Englanders had migrated out along the Great Lakes, Southerners across the Appalachian Mountains into the Tennessee Valley and out to the Mississippi. Following the Louisiana Purchase, pioneers had pushed their way along the Missouri into the Great Plains and up along the Canadian border. With the bays at San Diego and San Francisco acquired in the Treaty of Guadalupe Hidalgo, Americans gained jumping off points for expansion even farther west.

Next, in 1867, America bought Alaska from Russia. Referring to Canada, Secretary of State William H. Seward claimed that the purchase would "cage the British Lion on the Pacific coast" and provide a bridge between America and Asia. The same year, American naval officers, authorized by President Andrew Johnson, placed the flag on the Midway atoll, so named because it lay halfway between California and Japan. In 1871, Commander R. W. Meade, authorized by the Grant administration, got a lease for the harbor of Pago Pago in Samoa. In 1875, President U. S. Grant and his secretary of state, Hamilton Fish, negotiated a reciprocity treaty with Hawaii, then an independent monarchy. American planters, farming the islands since before the Civil War, could now ship their sugar and pineapples to the United States. The agreement integrated the islands with the mainland American economy.

And in 1882, Commodore Robert Shufeldt, authorized by President Chester Arthur, in Perry-like fashion forced Korea to sign a treaty opening itself to American trade. An ardent expansionist, Shufeldt expressed his view of America's Pacific destiny thus: "The Pacific is the ocean bride of America—China and Japan and Korea— with their innumerable islands hanging like necklaces about them, are the bridesmaids, California is the nuptial couch, the bridal chamber, where all the wealth of the Orient will be brought to celebrate the wedding. Let us as Americans—let us determine while yet in our power, that no commercial rival or hostile flag can float with impunity over the long swell of the Pacific sea."

Then came the Spanish-American War. We know of Commodore George Dewey steaming into Manila Bay, Teddy Roosevelt charging up San Juan Hill, and perhaps General Nelson Miles taking over Puerto Rico. The war now seems a trivial military episode. Yet, climaxing America's nineteenth-century outward thrust, it gave the United States command of Puerto Rico, Cuba (temporarily), Guam, and the Philippines. To ardent expansionists such as Theodore Roosevelt and Massachusetts senator Henry Cabot Lodge, the new island empire signaled America's entrance onto the stage of world power politics. It also saddled the nation with the responsibility of governance and of defense, particularly of the Philippines, the jumping off point for the China market.

The establishment of America's oceanic empire, furthermore, coincided with a rush on the part of the European continental and Japanese imperial powers for the complete colonization of the coast of China. So to preserve the prerogatives of America's merchants and missionaries in the Middle Kingdom, the McKinley administration took steps to establish and preserve the "Open Door."

But Great Britain also wanted to protect its own rights and privileges in China. To do so, it sought help from the United States of America.

4

In 1899 an English diplomat named Alfred E. Hippisley went to Washington. His wife, an American, hailed from nearby Baltimore and wished to visit her family; such was the pretext for the trip. In reality, Hippisley was on a mission. He had served in China in the 1890s and had observed that Great Britain increasingly faced French, German, Russian, and Japanese encroachments upon its domains. Britain had championed free trade (largely for itself), but now the other imperialist countries were erecting tariff barriers against British goods. Britain's preeminent position in China stood threatened.

Underscoring the threat was the fact that with declining economic productivity and an obsolete industrial base, Britain's armed might was slipping. Abandoning the "splendid isolationism" of the Victorian era, London in 1902 would bring about an alliance with Japan. But the greater prize was the United States. The British governors hoped to forge a special relationship with America.

The hope was based on history. Although the British government had sided tacitly with the Confederacy during the Civil War, allowing Southerners to purchase warships built in British yards, ever since then it had been cultivating American friendship. In the 1872 Washington Treaty, London had agreed to pay an indemnity for damages wrought to Union ships by the Liverpool-built, Confederate-owned, blockade-runner *Alabama*. And in 1896, during a border dispute between Venezuela and British Guiana, London submitted its case to an American arbitration board and accepted its negative ruling: Britain was recognizing the importance of the United States in the Western Hemisphere.

Three years later, the Foreign Office sought a return on the investment, sending Hippisley to his old friend and State Department official, W. W. Rockhill, to seek help in China.

Tall and blond, and independently wealthy, Rockhill was a diplomat who had spent several years reporting on China and Tibet. He had fallen in love with the region and feared for its future. China was disintegrating and the Russians and the Japanese both were perched like vultures, waiting for the death. As an American governmental official (what today would be known as the assistant secretary of state for East Asian affairs) Rockhill also felt responsibility to protect American business interests in China. So the ideals and interests he represented overlapped with those of Hippisley.

They overlapped but were not the same. Rockhill had considered Victoria's empire "as great an offender in China as Russia itself": to augment America's trade and investment abroad, U.S. officials hoped for the end of all colonialism.

Still, the "Open Door," a term long used by the missionaries to China, had its appeal. So in a letter to a State Department counsel, Rockhill stated: "I cannot, however, think that, at the present stage, it will be sufficient for this country to insist that no discrimination shall apply to any of our merchandise entering the various spheres of interest [in China]. We must go much farther than that. Our action . . . should be such that the very vague assurances given by Great Britain, Russia, and other powers as to their desire to maintain and insure the integrity of the Chinese Empire . . . should be expressed in much stronger terms and assume tangible shape." Using this justification, Rockhill sent a draft of the first Open Door Note to Secretary of State John Hay.

Hay had served as President Lincoln's private secretary, made a fortune as a Cleveland steel magnate, and then served under President McKinley, a fellow Ohioan, as ambassador to the Court of St. James before becoming secretary of state. Small, bearded, and elegantly dressed, he was the very embodiment of the American establishment. The establishment wanted safeguards for American commerce in China.

Using Rockhill's language, Hay's first initiative with regard to China was an 1899 note, sent through diplomatic channels, that asked the other powers (especially Russia, Germany, and Japan) to respect China's territorial integrity. Knowing that with its growing industrial power the United States could undersell any competitor in the China market, Hay also urged an international acceptance of "fair field and no favor."

The competitors at first scoffed, and so in a second note, endorsed by President McKinley and sent around in 1900 during the Boxer upheaval, Hay now insisted that all the powers pledge to preserve "Chinese territorial and administrative integrity." Hay, who was a sophisticated diplomat, knew full well that words alone could not save China and thus America's market. As he wrote to McKinley from his sickbed in New Hampshire, where he had retreated in the hope of recovering from cancer, "The inherent weakness of our position is this: we do not want to rob China ourselves, and our public opinion will not permit us to interfere, with an army, to prevent others from robbing her. Besides, we have no army. The talk of the papers about 'our pre-eminent moral position giving the authority to dictate to the world' is mere flap-doodle." Yet Hay had articulated fundamental American interests. In the first note he had expressed the American principle of free trade and in the second nonaggression. America was committing itself to China's defense and thus to the containment of Japan.

Between 1900 and the First World War, no other nation could or would hold Japan back. Russia was weak, Germany was concentrating on the buildup of its fleet, and France's interests lay far to the south in Vietnam. And in 1905, pursuant to its alliance with Japan,

Britain removed its major warships from the China coast. So the commitment to the containment of Japan fell to the United States.

That commitment became evident in Woodrow Wilson's denunciation of the Twenty-One Demands in 1915, and in the antiaggression strictures of the 1921–1922 Washington Conference and its Nine Power Treaty. And Japan accepted those limitations. After World War I, the spirit of democracy and internationalism that swept the industrialized world touched Japan. Influenced by the West, liberal schools of thought blossomed. But the Great Depression hit Japan hard. Against a background of starving peasants eating the bark of pine trees or digging for the roots of wild plants, anger surged and the people turned to the military for salvation. For the military believed that it had the answer to the country's woes: conquering all Manchuria, extracting its deposits of iron, zinc, and gold for use in Japanese industry, and slamming the Open Door shut against the British and the Americans.

5

Even before the Great Depression, Japanese goods had replaced once-dominant American cotton textiles in Manchuria. But American investments in the late nineteenth century in ores, transportation, and communications had remained in place. With the invasion of Manchuria in 1931, the Japanese expropriated them.

In Manchuria, W. B. Courtney, an American China hand and journalist, wrote in *Collier's* in the mid-1930s that the Japanese were "transforming an entire country—nearly half a million square miles—one sixth the size of the whole United States . . . into a single unified fortress. A nation where every railway, every road, every town and village, is designed first of all for its military effectiveness; where a population of nearly 40 million lives [is] always under martial law. . . ; and where there is no free commerce, except under military passes."

Step by step, American mining and railroad enterprises in the region were being squeezed out. As Japanese forces took over from Americans the various public utilities, railways, and electric plants, each enterprise, Carl Crow, another reporter, explained, was supplied with a Japanese "adviser." The Japanese "advised" American engineers right out of their jobs. American salesmen were compelled to deal with Japanese purchasing agents who could not speak English. Later the Americans ran into an even more noxious obstacle: specifications asking for supplies were written in Japanese instead of English, as before. And when the Japanese also set up an oil monopoly, banishing Texaco, Socony-Vacuum, and the British-owned Asiatic Petroleum Company, British and American protests that this was a direct violation of the Open Door policy were fruitless.

One is "unprepared for the . . . Japanese success in claiming the cities [in Manchuria] as their own," Edgar Snow wrote in 1936 in the first of several pieces published in *The Saturday Evening Post*. "Where formerly you rarely saw a spangled kimono or heard the drag of the wooden *geta,* today in many places the streets . . . seem imported bodily from Japan, with the drably clad natives a mere background for the costumes and homes of Japanese." In Dairen, near Port Arthur, Snow reported, every "shop bursts with neatly packaged goods—Japanese predominating, of course—every street is the scene of brisk building activity. . . . [F]uturistic . . . office buildings, numerous playgrounds, public gardens [abound] in circles from which the wide streets radiate spokelike. . . . On its spacious macadam roads that spread for miles beyond the town, out beyond old Port Arthur, thousands of substantial new buildings and suburban homes are being erected, served by luxurious buses, by clean Japanese-made trams and trains, by the cheap taxies that have driven the rickshaws almost out of existence." Japan was remaking Manchuria in its own image.

But it was not stopping with Manchuria. Just below the Great Wall, the Japanese were duplicating the Manchurian model. Snow explained: "The South Manchurian Railway, . . . spearhead of the Japanese conquest above the Wall, . . . moves into China proper, with the cooperation of the Chinese bureaucracy. It opens branches in Tianjin, Beijing, Qingdao, . . . and Shanghai. . . . It is establishing numerous dependent companies to monopolize—by special agree-ment with ... northern puppets ... the exploitation of North China's ... coal, her remaining resources of iron and other valuable minerals, her annual cotton crop, and her airways and railways de-velopment. Meanwhile, the Japanese are ... detaching the northern salt, land, opium, railways, telegraphs, and surtax revenues, as well as the maritime customs from Nanjing's control, to convert the re-gion [North China] into an exclusive Japanese market. ..."

Snow went further: "We may be sure of one more thing. Japan's se-cret agents have contacts with leading rebels in every subject country [subject to the European and American colonialists]. Through them, when war comes, Japan will instigate rebellions against white imperi-alism in India, Burma, Malaya, the Dutch Indies, Borneo, Indo-China, the Philippines, and elsewhere."

Where was it all going to end? "The Japanese advance," Snow con-cluded, "is not going to end—until it meets determined opposition."

Actually, the Japanese already were meeting "determined opposi-tion" in the form of China's ancient secret societies. Even during World War I, as the Japanese began to infiltrate China, they found themselves confronted with economic boycotts organized by the Mafia-type organizations. In 1931 as they invaded Manchuria, they also launched their first attack on Shanghai. So fierce was the city's resistance (again conducted by clandestine associations) that the in-vaders had to withdraw. Finally, as they spread from Manchuria into the northern Chinese plain, they and their Chinese collaborators were subject to further boycotts and even murders.

Then, for the Japanese, a crisis arose. China's government, led by Chiang Kaishek, for nearly a decade had been waging war against the Communists. Led by Mao Zedong, the Reds had made their Long March into northwestern China. In December, 1936, however, the Nationalists and the Communists formed a united front against Japan: The Japanese saw the prospect of a united China as a direct threat to their position in Manchuria. Indeed, it was just that.

6

Early in December, 1936, a passenger plane circled the mountains of northern China and aligned itself with the runway near Xian, beginning its descent. Snow lay over the hillsides and only the landing strip was clear. The airplane landed and out stepped Chiang Kaishek.

Having aligned himself with China's nascent capitalist class, Chiang was obsessively anti-Communist. But he had been unable to dislodge the Reds from the village called Yanan. Now, in flying to Xian, a city in northwestern China, Chiang hoped through a prearranged meeting to persuade (perhaps by bribery) the local warlord, Zhang Xueliang, to flush out Mao and his Communist followers.

As Chiang trotted down the airplane's ramp, Zhang's officers in down-filled jackets and caps with earflaps came up to greet him. Chiang spoke briefly with the warlord. Then he repaired to a hotel at the foot of the mountains where he set up his headquarters for the completion of his campaign against the Chinese Communists.

Up before dawn on December 12, 1936, Chiang performed martial arts exercises, splashed water on his face, and then stood motionless. From somewhere outside the hotel, gunshots sounded. A messenger came to his room: Mutineers, soldiers of the warlord, were forcing their way into the hotel and Chiang should leave at once. Still in his nightshirt, barefoot, his false teeth resting on a ledge, the *generalissimo* fled into the darkness. Climbing the wall that surrounded the hotel, he fell and sprained an ankle. He whispered for help. Hearing him, a few nearby aides hauled him up and dragged him over the snow to a cave.

As the day dawned, Chiang Kaishek later told a biographer, "I could see from the cave that the Li Mountain was surrounded by a large number of troops. . . . The rebels were looking for me. Twice they passed the cave in which I took cover but failed to discover me. . . . Then [they] made a more thorough search. I heard one of the mutineers above the cave saying, 'Here is a man in civilian dress; probably he is the *generalissimo*.'. . . I then raised my voice and said,

'I am your *generalissimo*. Don't be disrespectful. If you regard me as your prisoner, kill me, but don't subject me to indignities.' The mutineers . . . fired three shots in the air and shouted, 'The *generalissimo* is here!'"

Limping out of the cave, Chiang stormed, "Shoot me and finish it all!"

The leader of the group, however, replied: "We will not shoot you. We only ask you to lead our country against Japan."

In his drive against the Communists, Chiang had largely ignored the Japanese menace; he had hoped to crush the Reds, fully unify China under his command, and only then, sure of national solidarity, expel the Japanese. Now he was going to have to change his strategy. Back at the hotel, but this time in captivity, Chiang received a stream of important visitors: his wife, Soong Meiling; her banker brother, T. V. Soong; and since the local warlord out of patriotism had arranged the kidnapping with the help of the Reds, Zhou Enlai, the Communists' main negotiator. The Communists had seen the political advantage of taking a patriotic stance against the Japanese.

Who said what and to whom in the Xian hotel we shall never know; no records seem to exist. In the end, however, Chiang Kaishek signed a pledge, soon made public, to "admit all parties to share the joint responsibility of national salvation," to "stop all civil war immediately," and to "adopt the policy of armed resistance against Japan."

Free again, Chiang flew back to Nanjing. As he did so, almost immediately Communists in the countryside and Nationalists working with their gangland friends in the cities launched a wave of terror against Japanese residing in China. And Tokyo began to look for a pretext for war.

7

Just southwest of Beijing stood the Luguoqiao, or Marco Polo Bridge. The bridge itself was of little import, but it happened to be the site of a critical incident. On the night of July 7, 1937, the commander of a

Japanese regiment discovered that one of his men was missing; Chiang Kaishek's power had not extended to Beijing and corrupt local warlords had allowed a Japanese military presence in the region. Approaching a Chinese fort located at one end of the bridge, he demanded entry; he may have wanted to search for the missing soldier or he may have wished to provoke a fight. When the Chinese commander refused the demand, the Japanese regiment on the bridge opened fire upon the fort and the Chinese soldiers inside fired back.

In the morning, the local Chinese and Japanese commanders met in Beijing and agreed to end the fighting then and there. In Nanjing and Tokyo, however, the governments of the two countries decided to go to war. The Chinese government did so because Chiang Kaishek's deal in Xian had engendered an anti-Japanese united front (one that during the war itself would disintegrate). The Japanese government did so because it wished to put a stop to what it saw as Chinese terrorism and because the Japanese military considered the conquest of China to be their nation's divine right. To most Chinese leaders, unity was the only way to national salvation; to most Japanese authorities, since the Chinese seemed to menace Manchuria, and Manchuria was the key to Japan's own national salvation, war was the only solution.

Thus began what the Japanese called the "China Incident," in fact no "incident" but the invasion of the Middle Kingdom. Japanese troops fanned out across northern China; Chinese troops moved up to meet them. Japan sent ships to Shanghai, for Shanghai was crucial to the dominance of the lower Yangzi valley. Nationalist and Communist Chinese troops commanded by Chiang Kaishek reinforced the city. And a warship called the *Izumo* dropped anchor in the harbor off the city's Japanese sector.

8

Just before the Huangpu River flows into the Yangzi, just in from the ocean, its north to east bend forms the Shanghai harbor. The Japanese sector lay just to the north of the bend and the international settlement,

administered by Britain and America, was on the west, stretching behind the Bund. The Chinese parts of the city lay all around.

High over the Bund on the afternoon of August 14, 1937, the
Palace Hotel was crowded with people. An awning, rust-brown like
the sail of a Chinese junk, shaded about half the terrace. Out in the
other half, potted ferns spread their leaves and umbrellas sheltered
the tables. The tiles of the floor gleamed, sprinkled by Chinese servants hourly to temper the heat. Waiters glided and bowed, carrying
silver trays. Some of the patrons were drinking tea, others whiskey,
wine, or vodka. Under the awning a Russian string quartet played Vi-
valdi, the *pizzicati* barely audible over the burble of talk. Conversations were taking place in many languages: German, Russian, French,
a little Chinese, a great deal of English. Then, suddenly, the chatter
ceased. There was a distant thudding.

A few of the foreigners walked to the terrace railing. The streets
were in turmoil. From the waterfront to the facades of the tall, West-
ern-style bank buildings, beggars, old women, children, and coolies
pulling rickshaws or running with poles on their shoulders and
squeezing past limousines all were racing away from the waterfront.
For beyond the piers, the guns of the *Izumo* were blazing away. The
Sino-Japanese War, prelude to World War II in Asia, had begun.

4

NEW ORDER IN
EAST ASIA

1

The "China Incident," as the Japanese euphemistically called their invasion of China, had its roots in their earlier conquest of Manchuria. For the Japanese, Manchuria had been an outlet for domestic overpopulation, a source of raw materials, and proof that Japan had joined the ranks of the imperial powers. Some Japanese factions, to be sure, were uneasy about expansion. How far could Japan go, they wondered, in the face of British and American disapproval? But China's Nationalist-Communist united front seemed to threaten Japan's self-proclaimed "right" to Manchuria. So most Japanese considered the attack on China justified.

As that attack began, the guns of the *Izumo* and other Japanese warships in the Shanghai harbor were trained on the city's Chinese sector. But four nights later, with shells falling around them, residents of the international zone crowded together on the piers, clutching their children and their luggage and preparing to board the American liner, *President McKinley,* anchored nearby. As they clambered into small boats that set off for the liner, Chinese gunners were shooting at the Japanese ships from both sides of the river. Flashes of fire arched through the darkness, and wherever the shells hit, smoke billowed upward, reddened by the glow of the flames below.

The foreign refugees reached the *McKinley* unharmed. Seamen aboard the USS *Augusta,* a cruiser that had steamed down from the northern China coast, were less fortunate. A shell landed on the deck and exploded, injuring eighteen sailors and killing one, a young Louisianan named Freddie John Faigout.

Elsewhere in China, other Americans also were having trouble. In Beijing, Otto Geissberger, a young marine from North Bergen, New Jersey, ventured outside the American consulate and photographed a column of marching Japanese. To his surprise, he found himself surrounded by their military police, who grabbed and smacked him, trying to haul him away. He escaped only by yanking the film out of his camera. U.S. troops in China thereafter were under standing orders to take no photographs recording the Japanese conquest of northern China.

To celebrate their conquest, the Japanese floated balloons over the Forbidden City in Beijing. Streamers hung from the balloons announced a new slogan: "The Japanese Army Preserves the Peace of East Asia." In Shanghai the Japanese were preserving the peace in vicious block-by-block street fighting. The Chinese resistance was fierce but the Japanese artillery and machine guns took their toll. Late in October, 1937, Shanghai fell and the Japanese began to push up the Yangzi River.

As you steamed into the river's mouth, you could have seen the northern shoreline, or the southern, but not both at once: At its aperture the Yangzi was less a river than an ocean. Fleets of vessels, junks, sampans, and steamers plied the Yangzi's lower reaches. More than

14,000 foreign ships each year chugged inland from the Shanghai piers. Nearly half the population of China lived along the Yangzi and its tributaries.

After gaining control of Shanghai, China's largest city and busiest port, Japan's next task therefore was obvious: It had to sever the Yangzi River valley from the rest of the world. Otherwise the river could be a conduit of supplies to the Nanjing government, 200 miles upstream.

On November 18, 1937, hoping to shut off the supplies, Japanese authorities seized the British-run customs service, situated in Shanghai's international settlement. On November 29, Japanese marines boarded an American-owned launch anchored off the French concession at Shanghai, ripped off the American flag, and threw it into the water. On December 3, Japanese troops marched into the international settlement. Stringing out barbed wire barricades, they closed down major avenues (at one intersection, Japanese machine guns were pointing in all four directions) and took command of several foreign clubs. On December 5, at Suhu, a Yangzi River city near Nanjing, Japanese airplanes bombed a British gunboat and two British merchant vessels that displayed the Union Jack.

In his Nanjing headquarters, guarded by a dragon-roofed gate and overlooking willows and a lake, Chiang Kaishek the same day sat with his leading generals to make an urgent decision. The Japanese were approaching the capital fast. Should the Nationalist government surrender? Or should it flee three hundred miles inland to Chongqing and establish a war-time capital there?

The decision, joined by the Communists present, was to retreat. But the retreat was an acknowledgment of failure. Since it was far from Beijing and the weak warlords who had ruled that city, Nanjing had symbolized China's hope for wealth and power; and midway along the lower Yangzi, Chiang's capital had been close to the bulk of China's population. But Chongqing was medieval and remote, a place from which Chiang and his ministers could only watch from afar as the Nanjing holocaust unfolded.

To understand what happened at Nanjing, Tillman Durdin reported to the *New York Times*, "it is necessary to note that the city lies in a bend of the Yangzi at a point where the river turns from a northward course and flows east. It can easily be seen that a defending force occupying only the area within the city walls and the immediate suburbs could be surrounded on three sides."

That was exactly what occurred. As the Japanese forces approached the city from those three sides, the terror began: Nanjing, Durdin wrote, took on "an appearance of awesome frightfulness." As the Japanese scaled the walls, the remaining Chinese troops panicked. The gates of the city were locked, but some of the soldiers thought they knew a way out. A tunnel some seventy feet long led under one of the gates and from there out to the riverbank. A few dozen soldiers, then hundreds more, then thousands, crammed into the mouth of the tunnel. Civilians behind them formed a human tide almost three miles long that pushed its way forward toward the far end of the tunnel. But the gate of the tunnel was locked. Then an ammunition truck in the procession caught fire and exploded. Rickshaws, automobiles, and carts went up in flames and the momentum of the mob pushed hundreds into the roaring blaze. At just that moment, according to a Western eyewitness, "Japanese planes, sweeping low, mowed down refugees and soldiers alike with wide open machine guns. For the weak and the aged there was no escape." The Reverend John Magee, an Episcopal medical missionary, climbed over what he described as "mountains" of the dead. On one avenue, he found "charred bodies . . . everywhere, in places six and eight deep."

Over the next several weeks the Japanese troops, taught to believe in their racial superiority over the Chinese, went on an orgy of burning, rape, and murder. At least 200,000 persons, civilians and military alike, lost their lives in what came to be called the "Rape of Nanjing." Tillman Durdin reported on *how* many died. Very old men, he cabled back to New York, "were to be seen face downward on the pavements . . . shot in the back at the whim of some Japanese soldier." Soldiers would tie up Chinese prisoners in bundles of forty or fifty, douse them with gasoline, and set them on fire. "Bloated bodies lay everywhere," a British missionary wrote. "Dogs wandered from carcass to carcass. The stench was terrific."

> "Practically every building in the city, including the American [and] British . . . embassies, has been robbed repeatedly by [Japanese] soldiers," an American professor reported. "Most of the shops, after free-for-all pilfering, were systematically stripped by gangs of Japanese soldiers working with trucks, often under the direction of officers, and then burned deliberately. Most of the refugees were robbed of . . . their scanty clothing, and bedding and food. . . . You can imagine the outlook for work and life in this city with shops and tools gone, everything else plundered, no banks or communications, the people facing starvation.

But the Japanese atrocities only aroused the patriotism of the masses of the Chinese people (as well as the outrage of readers of the major American newspapers that carried missionary accounts of the Nanjing horror). And the Japanese made another major miscalculation: Their pilots sank the American gunboat USS *Panay,* which under the terms of a 1903 treaty was allowed to be on Chinese waters.

The *Panay* resembled a Mississippi River paddlewheel steamer without the paddlewheel. Its lower deck was almost level with the waterline and its upper deck, which served as roof for most of the cabins, ran almost the length of the vessel. Awnings shaded the top deck fore and aft and across both awnings, lying flat and thus plainly visible from overhead, were painted two large American flags.

At noon on December 12, 1937, the *Panay* was anchored in the Yangzi, close to the Nanjing shoreline. The gunboat had taken that position to serve as a refuge for American diplomats and other westerners fleeing the horror in the city. Several indeed had come aboard, including Norman Alley, a newsreel cameraman for Universal Studios. Joining the officers, Alley went to the mess below for lunch, after which most of the men retired to their bunks for naps. Alley went onto the bottom deck for a stroll. He happened to be carrying his Bell & Howell newsreel camera. The time was 1:37 P.M.

At precisely that moment, the spotter in the bridge called out a warning—airplanes were approaching from the southeast. Down in his cabin, where he had just fallen asleep, Lt. Commander James J. Hughes scrambled up, put on his uniform cap, and headed for the bridge. As he bounded up the steps, he glanced around: All the American flags and emblems were in place. From the air, the Panay's nationality would be unmistakable. Reaching the bridge, Hughes grabbed a pair of binoculars. Adjusting the lenses, he made out six aircraft, strung out in a line, speeding toward the Panay. The first three were dropping into a power-dive!

Standing beside Hughes, Chief Quartermaster John L. Lang cried out: "They're letting go bombs! Get under cover!" As Hughes scrambled back down to the pilot house—the only cover on the bridge was a strip of canvas—the first of the Japanese bombs went off. It seemed to hit directly overhead; Hughes, wounded in the right leg, passed out. Then the airplanes were gone.

On the lower deck, Alley recorded the scene on film. "My first reaction," he said later to reporters in the United States, "was that the Japanese, mistaking the Panay for an enemy ship, had realized their error and were leaving." They were not leaving: Almost immediately a squadron of six small pursuit-type bombers flew over at a much lower altitude than the earlier planes, power-diving and releasing what seemed to be 100-pound bombs. A reporter later asked Alley if the Japanese had made a mistake. "Hell no," he retorted, "when they started dive bombing they would have had to see our flags. They came straight out of the sun. And they came over and over."

The Panay's return fire did little good, with the gunboat suffering about two dozen hits. When he recovered consciousness, Commander Hughes ordered everyone to abandon ship. As the crew and passengers climbed into lifeboats, the *Panay* behind them was beginning to sink. By the time the men reached the reeds by the shore, the gunboat was about half under water.

As they hid in the reeds, they heard a throbbing sound growing closer. Then they saw two launches, both Japanese. The *Panay* now was nearly submerged, with nothing showing but its upper deck. The Japanese vessels fired upon it anyway.

Then the launches went away. One of the crew of the *Panay,* wounded while still aboard, died in the attack. The others survived. As soon he could, Norman Alley flew back to the United States.

By 8:30 A.M., December 30, 1937, a crowd had started to gather in front of New York City's Rialto Theater even before the *Panay* newsreel reached the projectionist. When the doors finally opened, so many customers jammed their way inside that many had to stand. The theater went dark, the screen lights came on, and the first footage appeared before the audience: the Yangzi River; Commander Hughes, immaculate in his dress whites; the cloudless sky; the decks of the *Panay;* and the American flags painted across the awnings.

High above the mast, the black silhouette of an airplane suddenly zoomed across the screen. It went into a dive, followed by another plane, and another, and in a moment they were diving, swooping, bombing. Sometimes the airplanes zipped so close that viewers in the theater could see the pilots' helmets and goggles. The *Panay*'s crewmen were shown trying to defend the gunboat with machine guns so old they looked straight out of World War I, which they were. The audience then saw the riverside, the reeds, and a close-up of Commander Hughes forcing a smile despite the agony of his wound.

When the newsreel finished, a man in the audience rose from his seat and commanded: "Everybody stand up!" The entire audience rose to its feet.

In response to a note of protest from the American government, Japan proffered an apology for the incident, although it claimed the bombing had been a pilot's mistake. Unable to see how the pilots could have taken the *Panay* for anything but an American vessel, however, President Roosevelt at the end of 1937 notified Congress that he wished to expand American naval power.

2

The government-controlled Japanese press portrayed the "China Incident" in glowing terms. The papers mentioned neither the horrors at Nanjing nor the attack on the *Panay,* giving the populace no reason to oppose the war. The mood in Japan was one of national celebration.

The "munitions boom which helped to make the last New Year prosperous has become a full war boom and the [Japanese] nation, exalted by a succession of victories and happy with prosperity, is preparing for the holidays in a spirit of hectic exuberance." Thus went an account by Hugh Byas, a Scot, one of the few Japanese-speaking foreign journalists in Tokyo, and a stringer for both the *New York Times* and the *Times* of London. Byas filed the story early in February, 1938, at the beginning of the Lunar New Year.

Trying to understand Japan, Byas wrote, was like feeling organs through a membrane: He could tell that something was there but usually he failed to discern quite what. From the time of his arrival back in the 1920s, Japanese officialdom had kept Byas under tight control. He did have an office adjacent to his flat in the yellow stone Imperial Hotel, a place with "three tall windows that rattled like the devil." From those windows, Byas wrote, "you could see half Tokyo and, on the horizon, a long saw-toothed ridge of mountains." Tokyo itself was a "great noisy city with eight- and ten-story buildings that look[ed] as if they had been imported from Seattle."

Byas must have spent a lot of time looking out at those buildings: His sources were censored. Police agents followed him everywhere, he believed, even on excursions he and his wife took by train out to the suburbs and villages. Fearing harassment or even arrest if they talked with any openness with a foreign reporter, Japanese passengers in the cars, and the vendors and hotel keepers, showed masks of politeness and little else.

Byas did what he could. From his office he could translate posters on the street below, banners that proclaimed this or that victory of Japanese forces in China. He could walk the pavements and observe the tractors drawing artillery, the soldiers taking bayonet practice in the parks, and the delegations parading with flags and bugles as they escorted new draftees to their barracks. Back in the hotel, he walked through a lobby usually packed with Japanese businessmen in their Western suits; the Japanese would not converse with him, but at the bar Byas sat with his fellow journalists, comparing notes.

Just after the Lunar New Year, Byas and his foreign colleagues received invitations to a press conference, to be held in the Imperial Palace. Within the Outer Palace's massive, mortarless stone walls, ponds, gardens, and stands of miniature trees gave way to the Inner Palace. Passing the sentries, Byas and his fellow correspondents walked down a long hallway and entered the audience hall. There they sat, and waited. At last Emperor Hirohito entered the chamber, followed by Premier Prince Konoye Fumimaro and the rest of the top level of the Japanese government. Byas described the scene as "singularly characteristic of present-day Japan, with its mixture of ancient and modern. In the hall, decorated with gold screens and the famous wall painting called 'The Thousand Sparrows,' the emperor in khaki and his generals, admirals, and ministers in uniforms or frock coats sat stiffly before tables draped with priceless brocades. The few speeches were of extreme formality and the proceedings . . . a solemn repetition and ratification in irrevocable form of measures already agreed upon."

As they left the palace grounds, Byas and the other journalists compared translations of what they had heard. The Japanese speakers, they realized, had used a critical word, a use sanctioned by the presence of the emperor. The word was "annihilation"—of China. Byas did not know if the Japanese government really believed it could exterminate the Chinese people. Byas reported that propaganda organs, nonetheless, were employing "annihilation" to whip up the martial spirit of the people.

The propaganda was necessary. In northern China especially, Communist guerrillas, ragged, surviving on gruel and turnips, and trekking barefoot over the ice in remote mountain passes, were perfecting the art of the ambush. A Japanese column would ensconce itself in a village along the Yellow River and build fires for the evening rice, only to be beset by Chinese swarming down from the hillsides, wielding swords, knives, clubs, and bare knuckles, who then, before Japanese aircraft could arrive to help the troops, would fall back to friendly villages.

Falling back was China's strategy for survival. The farther back the Chinese fell, the longer the Japanese had to stretch their supply lines, incurring shortages of fuel and food. Though at home they claimed to be winners, the Japanese in the field were starting to look like losers, bogging down in the stubble of the Chinese countryside. And complicating the Japanese problems were the overseas Chinese, who for patriotic reasons were starting to smuggle money and materiel into China. These Chinese lived in communities from Singapore to Los Angeles and San Francisco, and thus were conducting their smuggling from British and American soil.

Despite its official neutrality, the American government by 1938 was starting to support the Chinese cause. By purchasing tung oil and other commodities, which China could ship from the interior in sampans down the Pearl River and out through Hong Kong, the Treasury Department was propping up the Chinese currency. The American policy left the Japanese enraged.

The American ambassador to China, Nelson T. Johnson, early in March cabled President Roosevelt that the Japanese were trying hard to eliminate "all [American] influence among the Chinese." Plump as a pillow, Johnson had golden hair and his face was perpetually pink. Tilted back in a rickshaw, some thought, he looked like a tire salesman.

His looks were deceiving. Fluent in Chinese, he was an old Asia hand, and he thoroughly distrusted the Japanese.

Mirroring Johnson's view, Admiral Harry E. Yarnell in command of the *Augusta* in the Shanghai harbor cabled William D. Leahy, the chief of naval operations: "The policy of Japan was announced unofficially to a US naval attache by a [Japanese] official to be (a) to drive all whites out of China; (b) to destroy all Chinese industrialism; and (c) to obtain control of the customs . . . and other financial organs of the Chinese government." Yarnell had a recommendation. With "our allies," he went on, referring to Britain, France, and Holland, "we could control roughly 90 percent of the world's resources of iron, coal, and oil, as well as a major portion of other raw materials." Japan, Yarnell concluded, "can be strangled to death" by a naval blockade.

In his headquarters in the Washington Navy Yard, Admiral Leahy the year before had prepared a plan for a joint blockade of Japan by American, British, and Soviet forces. The idea was to deploy British ships at Singapore, Soviet vessels at Vladivostok, and American warships at Panama and Pearl Harbor, thereby isolating Japan completely. "No war plan was ever simpler," Leahy had reported to President Roosevelt. "We place our fleet at Panama and Hawaii. The British place 24 ships at Singapore. The Russians have 50 submarines at Vladivostok. They send them down to harass Japanese lines of communication between Shanghai and Nagasaki. The Japanese cannot live without supplies. . . . Within three months . . . Japan will be broken economically. We tell the Japanese we are going to blockade you until you get out of China."

Nothing came directly of Leahy's proposal. For the Soviet Union the war had not yet started; Britain, with its Royal Navy concentrated in the Mediterranean, in the home waters, and guarding Singapore, was unable to spare the ships; and Roosevelt feared that a blockade would be anathema to isolationist opinion.

Leahy, however, was a classic Washington bureaucrat, and never gave up on a fight. He may have looked more like a "ship chaplain" than the commander of the U.S. fleet, as a colleague described him, but he knew how to move the bureaucracy.

Having steered contracts to shipbuilding firms in Savannah and Baltimore, Leahy had won the political friendship of Senator Joseph Tydings of Maryland, an advocate of a big navy, and of Representative Carl Vinson of Milledgeville, Georgia, the soft-spoken, tobacco-chewing chairman, or perhaps monarch, of the House Naval Affairs Committee. Working with the two politicians, Leahy forged the Vinson-Tydings bill, designed to increase naval spending by twenty percent.

The bill's passage produced a shock in Tokyo. "Our view," a Japanese navy spokesman told foreign reporters on March 28, 1938, "is that if Americans are not thinking of naval operations against Japan, they would not need a fleet of that size." In light of America's historical expansion across the Pacific, the Japanese admiralty viewed the U.S. ship buildup with alarm.

Had the Japanese admiralty known of changes in War Plan ORANGE, it might have been even more alarmed. Dating back to the administration of Theodore Roosevelt, when Japan's naval strength had become evident, ORANGE had provided the guidelines of the U.S. Navy's Pacific strategy; its emphasis had been on defensive war. Now, under Admiral Leahy the Navy was reviewing the plan, shifting the momentum to offensive war.

ORANGE, to be sure, was only a contingency plan, not necessarily to be put into effect. But the language of the new War Plan ORANGE was strong. The 1938 version of ORANGE went beyond efforts to expel Japan from China. It called for broad "military and economic pressure"—a blockade—to be imposed in the event of war and increased in severity until the United States, even without a declaration of war, had attained its "national objective," the defeat of Japan.

3

On June 10, 1938, inside the arched and colonnaded façade of the old State Department just east of the White House, Secretary of State

Cordell Hull met with Stanley Hornbeck and Maxwell Hamilton, top aides from the Far Eastern Division. Although the State Department by tradition was not so aggressive as the Navy, the recent course of events abroad worried the diplomats. Hitler had annexed Austria and he had set his sights upon the Sudetenland, the German-speaking part of Czechoslovakia.

Furthermore, by the time of the meeting, Japanese bombings of American properties in China, especially chapels and clinics, had become intolerable; under instructions from the State Department, the American embassy in Tokyo had protested repeatedly, but always to no avail. Japan would apologize, then resume the attacks. So the issue was how tough the United States should get with Japan. Hornbeck, formerly a professor of Far Eastern history but nonetheless possessed of a belligerent viewpoint, thought "very"; Hamilton, imbued with the career officer's caution, was more moderate. Hull listened to both men with his characteristic care.

White-haired and handsome, Cordell Hull, as his eventual successor Dean Acheson would remember, "looked like a gentleman in the classic American tradition—the tradition of the great Virginia dynasty, of Henry Clay, of Daniel Webster (but handsomer, more like Warren Harding). His well-structured face was sad and thoughtful, his speech slow and gentle, except when he was aroused. . . . Suspicious by nature, he brooded over what he thought were slights and grievances." And from the White House he perceived plenty of snubs. As a representative and then a senator from Tennessee, Hull certainly was no part of the Roosevelt clique. Starched, pressed, buttoned, and scowling, he resembled a grandfather in someone's Victorian photograph. His exactitude drove President Roosevelt wild. Over evening cocktails in the White House, the evening ritual to which the secretary was never invited, the president sometimes mimicked the secretary's lisp.

FDR nonetheless appreciated Hull's importance. "You must realize," Roosevelt once said when asked by a reporter why he kept Hull on at State, that "Cordell Hull is the only member of the cabinet who brings me any political strength that I don't have in my own right."

As a politician, Hull was just as attuned as Roosevelt to the isolation-ist mood of the country. Both men nonetheless thought Japan danger-ous; both were coming to the conclusion that the United States could restrain Japan only by force.

For Stanley Hornbeck, at the June 10 meeting, the time to go to war was then, and he won the argument by reinforcing Hull's own view. The public, he pointed out, was restive: Americans might still be isolationist with regard to Germany, but not with regard to Japan. Newsreels were showing horrific pictures from China and the major newspapers were carrying stories of unending Japanese brutalities. Prominent citizens such as Nebraska's Senator George W. Norris, Professor John Dewey, Alma Gluck Zimbalist, wife of the violinist, Paul Robeson, and Dr. Reinhold Niebuhr, despite the neutrality acts of 1935, 1936, and 1937, had signed an appeal demanding a boycott of Japanese goods. Labor unions, too, were insisting upon boycotts, and longshoremen were refusing to handle Japanese products. All across America people were uniting in the wish to end cotton, oil, machine tool, and scrap iron sales to Japan. People called these sales the "blood trade."

At least, Hornbeck said to Hull, the government could block the sale of airplanes to Japan. Hull, at last, agreed with Hornbeck. The State Department, a spokesman announced the next day, would be reluctant to "issue any licenses authorizing exportation . . . of any aircraft . . . to countries the armed forces of which are making use of airplanes for attack upon civilian populations." The restriction clearly applied to Japan. And the State Department by the end of the year heard the Japanese reaction.

4

At breakfast time on November 3, 1938, the voice of Prime Minister Prince Konoye crackled out of Tokyo radio sets. In the U.S. embassy, translators listened closely, scribbled as fast as they could, and showed a transcription of the speech to Ambassador Grew. "It is my great pleasure," Prince Konoye had said, "on this occasion of the birthday anniversary of the late Emperor Meiji and once more remembering the high virtues of the emperor, to enunciate the views of the government in connection with the establishment of peace in the Far East." He proclaimed a "New Order in East Asia."

After the September, 1938, Munich Conference, Hitler had made the German-speaking part of Czechoslovakia, the Sudetenland, part of the *Reich*. In doing so, he had promulgated the slogan "New World Order." Undoubtedly encouraged by Hitler's successes, Prince Konoye applied the same term to East Asia.

What Japan "sincerely desires," Konoye was stating, "is the development and not the ruin of China. It is China's cooperation and not conquest that Japan desires. Japan desires to build up a stabilized Far East by cooperating with the Chinese people who have awakened to the need of self-determination." China's "true" self-determination, Konoye made clear, could emerge only through tutelage by, and union with, Japan. In that union, China and the rest of Asia would be purged of communism, colonialism, and Western influence. All of this Japan was willing to bring about, at great sacrifice, for China. But China would have to do its part. China, Konoye insisted, must recognize Manchuguo, allow Japan to station troops in the country indefinitely, let Japanese citizens set up special zones of business and residence in China wherever they wished, and grant Japan exclusive rights to the exploitation of China's mineral resources. Japan, of course, would cooperate with others, as long as those others acknowledged that Japan had first claim to China's assets.

Ambassador Grew was shocked. Here, on the typescript, he believed, was Japan's arrogance unmasked. Always judicious, however, and wishing to double-check his impressions, Grew went to talk with Arita Hachiro, Japan's foreign minister. Their conversation, conducted through an interpreter, left him even more shocked than before.

Arita, square-faced with a bristling crew cut, and a believer in the idea that John Hay's Open Door policy was history, snapped at Grew. "It is the firm conviction of the Japanese government, that now, at a time of continuing development of new conditions in East Asia, an attempt to apply to present and future conditions without any changes concepts and principles which were applicable to conditions prevailing before the present incident [the "China Incident"] does not ... contribute to the solution of immediate issues." Grew understood his meaning: As far as Japan was concerned, the Open Door policy, the Washington Conference system, Japanese cooperation with the West, all were dead. Japan at all costs would continue its effort to force China to surrender.

5

To stop the flow of supplies into China, Japan by now had occupied all the ports on the China coast except British Hong Kong. But China did have an outlet to the outside world, a road from Chongqing down to the Burmese border, then a jungle trail that led partway to Rangoon. The British and Americans called the trail the "Burma Road."

In December, 1938, Ambassador Nelson T. Johnson went down that road in the company of a Marine named James M. McHugh, who was the American assistant naval attaché to China. Like the ambassador, McHugh was fluent in Chinese and had lunched almost every day in Chongqing with Chiang Kaishek; Chiang had used these luncheons to present himself and his government as worthy recipients of American support. Although Chiang's armies (as later became apparent) were doing little to combat the Japanese, McHugh had written regularly to General Thomas Holcomb, the commandant of the Marine Corps. In these epistles, which Holcomb showed to Roosevelt, McHugh had insisted on increased American aid to Chiang Kaishek. Roosevelt, in turn, cabled the embassy with a request to consult with McHugh and Johnson.

The two men set off from Chongqing by car. "We started our ... trip," McHugh wrote in his diary on December 12, 1938, "from the south bank of the Yangzi River. ... Mr. Johnson and I left Chongqing at 7:30 A.M. Driving was very difficult. It had rained all night and soon started again. We crossed five passes—the last 3,500 feet above Chongqing." Then McHugh and Johnson reached the start of the Burma Road, if indeed it could be called a road. Some stretches, McHugh wrote, were "little more than bullock paths, without any metal surface; others were footpaths ages old, trodden by the foot of man and beast for generations, too narrow for any large vehicles."

McHugh and Johnson nonetheless inched their Chevrolet along as far as a British rail line in Burma. By Christmas, 1938, they were in Rangoon; a week later, flying the Pacific in a Pan American Clipper, they were in Washington.

On New Year's Day, Ambassador Johnson spoke with President Roosevelt. "Unless we begin to show our teeth and indicate to the world and specifically to Japan that we mean business, we may forever find ourselves stopped from taking action." So Johnson remembered his part of the conversation. "Time is with China in its conflict with Japan, but time is with the totalitarian states in their relations with the democracies. We should do what we can to assist and encourage the Chinese in their fight for an independent national existence."

Ambassadors often represent their own country in the courts of the host nation and plead that nation's cause back home; so it was with Nelson Johnson. But it was not China's cause alone that moved Roosevelt: Reports reaching the White House from Europe as well as from Asia had convinced the president that totalitarianism would lead to global war. And soon after Johnson's visit, an event took place on the China coast that let FDR see the rapid decline of Great Britain's role in the Far East.

In the nineteenth century, Britain had been the world's premier guarantor of peace. But in Roosevelt's eyes now, the Pax Britannica was a thing of the past. Roosevelt believed that the United States had the obligation to pick up Britannia's shield and sword and take over from Britain the role of master of the world.

5

THE ROAD TO
PEARL HARBOR

1

Late in the morning on Friday, June 8, 1939, a special train reached Washington's Union Station; a young woman in a summer dress and hat and her husband in a British admiral's full dress uniform stepped to the platform. At the invitation of President Roosevelt, King George VI and Queen Elizabeth (the mother of Elizabeth II), after a tour of Canada, had come for an official visit to the American capital, the first time a British monarch had set foot on American soil. After the president, standing with a hand on the arm of an aide, and Mrs. Roosevelt had greeted the royal couple, the Marine Band played "God Save the King" and the "Star-Spangled Banner." Leaving the station, an open limousine, with the king and the president in the rear seat, proceeded to First Street, just below the Capitol dome. Two huge American flags hung from in front of the Capitol. George VI snapped off a salute and a huge crowd of watching Americans went wild. Later, at Mount Vernon, the king placed a wreath on the tomb of George Washington.

Roosevelt had staged the visit to show Americans that, despite United States neutrality laws of the 1930s, the crowned head of the British Empire had come to the United States as a suppliant. The implication, despite the pomp and circumstance of the monarchy, was that the empire was declining and that the United States would have to fill the void—as an event by the northern coast of China made clear.

The previous April, four Chinese who had resided in the British zone in Tianjin had murdered a Chinese official suspected of Japanese sympathies, then fled for safety back into the sector. The Japanese had demanded that the assassins be handed over, but the British authorities had refused.

The Japanese responded with a litany of accusations. The British concession, they claimed, had become a sanctuary for Chinese assassins, not to mention Chinese-run propaganda presses and radio stations. These accusations were true but they were also pretexts. The British banks in Tianjin held reserves of Chinese silver and had maintained the value of the northern Chinese currency, refusing to give preference to Japan's own bank notes. The real issue in Tianjin was one of power and the Japanese meant to wield that power.

On June 13, 1939, with their launches suddenly massing along the Tianjin Bund, Japanese troops ringed the British zone with an electrified barbed-wire fence. Anyone who wished to go in or out of the zone would have to cross a Japanese-manned barricade.

Incidents in Tianjin mounted. Japanese soldiers shot two Chinese peddlers to death for the crime of passing a basket of vegetables over the barricade. Japanese policemen subjected various British subjects—a newspaperman, a couple employed by a country club, an officer from a coastal steamer, a New Zealander, and many others—to taunts, slaps, and on occasion strip searches. Any Briton in Tianjin faced what Vice Admiral Hibino Masahuso, chief of the Japanese naval forces in the northern China region, termed "chastisement"; he did not define the word.

In Tokyo, a mob in front of the British embassy charged the gates and retreated only after a series of skirmishes with the Royal Marines. As the rioters departed, they left behind a poster that read: "Britain is Dead!"

In the wake of Japan's invasion of Manchuria, London had severed its alliance with Tokyo. Now Britain was trying to hold on to its treaty-ports in China.

To settle the Tianjin issue, Foreign Minister Arita Hachiro, late in June, 1939, called in Sir Robert Craigie, the British ambassador to Japan. The late June weather in Tokyo was hot and Arita was making things hotter: A week later a cartoonist in a British newspaper portrayed Craigie hunched over a tiny table, shoeless, pantless, shirtless, except for his bowler and his heavy horn-rimmed glasses, stark naked.

The drawing got to the truth. Craigie had to capitulate. "His Majesty's Government," a communiqué issued in early July stated, "recognize the actual situation in China, where hostilities on a large scale are in progress. . . . The Japanese forces in China have special requirements for the purpose of safeguarding their own security and maintaining public order. . . . His Majesty's Government have no intention of countenancing any acts or measures prejudicial to the attainment of the above-mentioned objects." The British also stopped giving the Chinese currency preference over the Japanese.

In plain language, the British had caved in to the Japanese demands. A Tokyo newspaper trumpeted: "A SECOND MUNICH!"

Pledged to defend Poland and preparing for the coming war in Europe, the British government under Prime Minister Chamberlain regarded the Far East as a theater of declining importance. The days when Britannia had ruled the China coast were gone.

Like many Americans, President Roosevelt had hoped that the British Empire could serve as a bulwark against Japanese aggression in China. Now even his own ambassador to the Court of James, Joseph

P. Kennedy, was contending that the British Empire was a lost cause. The Tianjin affair reinforced Roosevelt's belief that the task of containing Japan was going to fall to the United States. But how to put that restraint into effect? In the summer of 1939, American military might was slight. The best Roosevelt could do then was to authorize a warning.

2

Before the warning was issued, Europe reached the point of crisis. Early in September, 1939, and just after the signing of the Nazi–Soviet Pact, Germany invaded Poland and Britain and France jointly declared war on the *Reich*. Although the adversaries settled into what the British press dubbed the "Phony War," the French *"la drole de guerre,"* and the Germans the *"Sitzkrieg,"* both sides (Germany and Italy were allies) were preparing for the explosion to come.

Against this dark background, Joseph C. Grew, the American ambassador to Japan, on the evening of October 19, 1939, spoke in Tokyo to a meeting of the America–Japan Society; present were American businessmen and their wives, and Japanese from the highest financial, diplomatic, and court circles. Grew began diplomatically, saying that he was glad to be back after a sojourn in America.

Then he changed his tack. What he was about to say, Grew stated, came "straight from the horse's mouth." To the puzzled Japanese, he explained that he was going to relay the thinking of the president of the United States.

On "returning from a long stay in America," Grew told his audience, "would it not insult your intelligence if I were to talk of trivialities?" He proposed instead to speak of important things, of how and why Americans so strongly resented Japan's atrocities in China. Anticipating what many in the audience might be thinking, Grew acknowledged: "There are two sides to every picture.... In America ... I did my best to show various angles of the Japanese point of view." He continued: "Let me therefore try to remove a few utterly fallacious conceptions of the American attitude as I think they exist in Japan today."

Any notion of America's hostility to Japan being based on misunderstanding, Grew held, was mistaken. "The facts as they exist today are accurately known by the American people. I do not suppose any country in the world today is better served by the press and radio with accurate foreign information than the United States."

Grew then became even franker. "Many of you are not aware of the increasing extent to which the people of the United States resent methods which Japanese armed forces are employing in China, and what appear to be their objectives. The American people regard with growing seriousness the violation and interference with American rights by Japanese armed forces in China in disregard of treaties and agreements." His compatriots, Grew went on, were not being merely "legalistic." They were angry and feared that Japan's New Order for East Asia would leave their own Open Door principle "truncated and emasculated." The injuries suffered by Chinese—and by Americans in China—appeared "wholly needless."

Grew paused before concluding with his warning to Japan. When "such opinion tends toward unanimity," he declared, referring to the American viewpoint, "it is a force which a government cannot possibly overlook and will not fail to reflect in its policies and actions."

Reaction in the United States to Grew's speech was ecstatic. The *New York Times* praised it as "the strongest ever made by a diplomat in Japan." Editorial writers in other papers described Grew's message variously as "a thunderbolt," "good if bitter medicine," "bare-knuckle diplomacy," and "straight from the horse's mouth."

In Tokyo, however, the day after Grew gave his speech, Nomura Kichisaburo, Japan's new foreign minister, was unmoved. He told reporters that the "determination of the entire Japanese nation to bring about a New Order in East Asia, is too strong to be changed or affected by the interference of a third power."

Even in the comparative safety of the United States the winter of 1939–1940 looked bleak. The Soviet Union, which in September, 1939, had taken over a slice of Poland, also overran the Baltic republics and invaded Finland. And in Asia nothing seemed able to quench the spirit of Japanese militarism. Hallett Abend, a stringer with the *New York Times,* asked in a report filed early in 1940:

> What could be drearier than a land long occupied by a hated and arrogant enemy, a land with half-ruined cities, with farms laid waste, with sullen men and thousands of shamefaced women? A conquered land, with trade throttled, with insecurity on all sides. From Harbin ... in the far north to Guangzhou in the far south the story is the same, except that the far north is a frozen land in winter.... The winter ... is the worst Beijing and Tianjin have known for decades.... Dust and sand from the Gobi Desert are whirled across the empty courtyards of the one-time Forbidden City.... In the great mat-shed structures thousands of beggars and homeless Chinese are given one bowl of millet gruel a day, but scores die of hunger and cold on the streets every night. The Legation Quarter, deserted by diplomats of higher rank than secretaries, waits, powerless and unimportant. About 500 American marines [posted in China under a treaty that allowed the presence of gunboats], divided half-and-half between Beijing and Tianjin, are the only remaining symbols of the power of the western world. In Tianjin, foreign business is dead. The Japanese Army monopolizes the trade in the exports of [the] hinterland, whether it be sausage casings, furs, or wool from Inner Mongolia.

The Japanese zone of control ranged from Inner Mongolia across northern China, up into Manchuria, then in a band that varied between about 100 and 200 miles down the coastline. The Communists occupied much of the interior and the Nationalist armies, centered on Chongqing, 500 miles up the Yangzi, kept receiving supplies smuggled in from abroad.

The Japanese could not, at least not without widening the war, quench the flow of goods into China. Down in the Hong Kong harbor, where the ferries plied the waters between the island and the Kowloon peninsula, Hallett Abend had a good look at the piers. Along the waterfront, he cabled to the *Times*, "block after block . . . was piled high with goods ordered by Chongqing," machinery, tires, huge coils of barbed wire, and, he estimated, over 2,000 motor trucks. These goods represented a crucial factor in the China war: Fueled with funds from abroad, especially from overseas Chinese business communities, China was purchasing materiel, storing it in Hong Kong, shipping it through Haiphong, the major port in northern Vietnam, and hauling it by rail in through China's southern Yunnan Province and up to Chongqing. China was staying alive.

3

And Washington continued putting pressure on Japan. With no more formality than the midnight ticking of the grandfather clock in the office of Secretary of State Cordell Hull, the 1911 United States–Japan most-favored-nation commercial treaty expired. The resumption of trade as before, the State Department in a terse note informed the Japanese ambassador, would depend on Japan's behavior.

Japan replied with a threat. A United States–imposed embargo on the export of oil to Japan would oblige Tokyo to obtain its petroleum from the Netherlands Indies, the Foreign Ministry warned. So that everyone would get the point, Tokyo placed a list of demands on the Dutch colonial government in Batavia (now renamed Djakarta): a "lowering of trade restrictions; greater facilities for Japanese enterprise in the Indies; easier entry for Japanese merchants, employees, and workers; mutual control of the press." Recognizing their vulnerability, Dutch officials in Batavia cabled Washington that "if we give in on the so-called less important points, if we give the Japanese even a finger's breadth of their demands, they will quickly ask the whole of our country [the East Indies]."

Privately, Hull and Roosevelt were worried. If Japan was looking toward the Indies today, where would it look tomorrow? Australia? New Zealand? Wake Island and Guam? Hawaii? Beyond?

In the middle of March, 1940, American newspapers ran an article about a previously undisclosed naval mission. According to a government report, six U.S. Navy bombers out of Hawaii had landed southwest of Hawaii at Canton Island, which was under joint British-American control. The bombers' next run would be to Johnston Island, where the Navy was building a seaplane base.

In an implicit threat to Japan, the report emphasized the matter of distance: Together the two legs of the flight equaled 3,750 miles. That was roughly the distance from Honolulu to Tokyo.

In the early months of 1940, Hitler made detailed plans to seize Narvik, the northern Norwegian port through which Germany imported Swedish iron ore. At the end of the first week of April, 1940, Hitler ordered the *Blitzkrieg* up through Denmark and Norway. With the Germans beating the Royal Navy to Narvik, Prime Minister Chamberlain's political reputation plummeted.

But at the same time, Japan was experiencing trouble. All around Southeast Asia, wherever one found sizable Chinese communities, from Indochina and the Philippines to Thailand, Malaya, Singapore, and the Indies, Chinese chambers of commerce, often fronts for Mafia-type gangs, were persuading their members to boycott Japanese goods. The methods of persuasion were not subtle: For uncooperative Chinese, their ears were sliced off or their doors smeared with dung. Such steps were effective. The boycotts reduced Japanese exports of manufactured products to Southeast Asia to about half of what they had been before 1937. And throughout the region, Chinese boycott leaders substituted American goods for Japanese, thus buying American sympathy for China.

The Japanese government searched for ways to break what it saw as an ever-tightening encirclement. The approach it decided upon at the time of Hitler's Scandinavian invasion was threefold.

First, Lieutenant General Yasuda Takeo, director of the Japanese Military Aeronautic Technical Laboratory, summoned a young staff officer, Suzuki Tatsusaburo. Yasuda was certain that America had an atomic bomb program. (In 1939, Albert Einstein had warned President Roosevelt that Germany was developing a super-bomb; FDR almost immediately had authorized the Manhattan Project, and all American atomic research had become classified.) Suzuki had studied physics at Tokyo University; his professor there, Sagane Ryokichi, had studied with Ernest O. Lawrence, inventor of the cyclotron, at Berkeley and at the Cavendish Laboratory at Cambridge University. Back in Japan, Sagane in 1936 had built the largest cyclotron outside the United States. At the request of his commanding officer, Suzuki went to see Sagane, who told him that in America, Lawrence and others most certainly were working on the super-bomb: American physics journals already had published the basic research. Japan could do so, too, especially if it exploited uranium deposits in its Korean colony. Suzuki went right to work.

Furthermore, in response to America's Tydings-Vinson measure of 1938, Japan had launched a renewed ship construction program, with the goal of eighty fresh vessels of war. Among these were the carriers that eventually would attack Pearl Harbor.

And finally, given its problems in Southeast Asia, the Japanese government began to prepare its people for what increasingly seemed certain to come, an expansion of the war into Southeast Asia. At a press conference on April 15, 1940, Foreign Minister Arita asserted that with "the South Seas regions, especially the Netherlands East Indies, Japan is economically bound by an intimate relationship of mutuality in ministering to one another's needs. Similarly, other countries of East Asia maintain close economic relations with those regions. That is to say, Japan, these countries and these regions together are contributing to the prosperity of East Asia through mutual aid and interdependence. Should hostilities in Europe be extended to the Netherlands and produce repercussions . . . in the Indies, it . . . would give rise to an undesirable situation from the standpoint of the peace and stability of East Asia. . . . The Japanese government cannot but be deeply concerned over any development accompanying the aggravation of the war in Europe that may affect the status quo of the

Netherlands East Indies." If the Netherlands fell, Arita was announcing, and if Roosevelt extended American military protection to the Indies, Japan would regard such a step as an act of aggression.

On May 10, 1940, Hitler ordered his forces westward. After the *Wehrmacht* overran the Low Countries, Queen Wilhelmina of the Netherlands and the top officials of her government fled to London; the colonial authorities in the Dutch East Indies remained free, protected for the moment by the Netherlands East Indian Navy. The *Wehrmacht* reached Paris almost without opposition. France capitulated: on June 18, 1940, a new government, seated at Vichy and prepared to collaborate with the Nazis, surrendered.

For Japan, the fall of the Netherlands and France opened opportunities. The fall of France left Indochina defenseless; the Indies were similarly vulnerable. Desperate to defend the home island against a German invasion, Winston S. Churchill, who had succeeded Chamberlain as prime minister, reduced British forces in Singapore, Burma, and India.

Japan now moved swiftly into the vacuum. The Japanese government demanded that the British close the Burma Road; with its forces in Burma diminished, Great Britain in June, 1940, complied, thereby impeding the flow of supplies to China. To press the British further, Tokyo sent agents into Rangoon and stirred the Burmese people to rebellion and riot. Japanese radio broadcasts pictured a vast new aggregation of satellite states in East Asia and the South Seas, all revolving harmoniously around Japan. The satellite region, the newspaper *Nichi Nichi*, an official mouthpiece, explained, would include French Indochina, the Dutch East Indies, British Hong Kong, Singapore, Malaya, and Burma, in addition to China.

On the day of France's formal surrender to Germany, a group of Japanese officials marched up the steps of Government House, the French colonial administrative center on the Avenue Puginier in Hanoi. Threatening to shut down rail traffic from Haiphong into China, the Japanese delegation demanded the right to station observers at the Chinese border. The French authorities, aligned with Vichy, obeyed.

News of the action in Vietnam set off alarms in Washington. Japan seemed on the verge of overturning the imperial status quo in the Far East—a point being emphasized by a Chinese lobbyist in Washington.

4

"A Chinaman comes flying into Washington. He takes a room in a hotel, he talks to a couple of people, he tells a story, and he sticks to it. And the first thing you know, that Chinaman walks off with $100 million in his pocket. $100 million! Just think of it!"

This was *Life,* in midsummer 1940, quoting an official with the Depression-era Reconstruction Finance Corporation (RFC). The "Chinaman" was T. V. Soong. A Harvard graduate, brother-in-law of Chiang Kaishek, scion of China's wealthiest family, and director of the Bank of China, Soong now was a Washington lobbyist. Upon his arrival in the capital in the summer of 1940, *Life* reported, Soong called on the treasury secretary "Henry Morgenthau and Jesse Jones [head of the RFC]. Soong explained that he wanted money in vast amounts [for China] but that he did not propose to beg for it. Told that it might be a good idea to contact a few congressmen..., T. V. Soong snorted. He had come to Washington with a business proposition and the president, the Congress, and Mr. Jones could take it or leave it." They took it.

For Soong, the connection with Morgenthau and Jones was critical. A huge man and a hard worker, Jones had started as a real estate developer in Dallas and Houston, then gone to Washington during the Hoover administration to head the RFC, through which he had lent money to thousands of enterprises. With the interest that had returned from those loans, he had expanded his fiefdom, adding the Federal Housing Administration, the Electric Home and Farm Authority, the Home Owner's Loan Corporation, and the federal Home Loan Bank system; he also controlled the Export-Import Bank. So powerful was Jesse Jones that when Roosevelt nominated him to be secretary of commerce, no one in the Senate had so much as peeped.

So when Mr. Soong went to Washington, he went straight to Morgenthau and Jones for the funding that China desperately needed.

Building on those ties, Soong expanded his Washington network to include Secretary of the Navy Frank Knox, Justice Felix Frankfurter who, as a Harvard law professor, had been a one-man employment agency for the New Deal, and Thomas "Tommy the Cork" Corcoran, a Frankfurter protégé and the Mr. Fix-It aide in the Roosevelt White House. In the large fieldstone house Soong and his wife had bought near the Washington Cathedral and decorated with rare Chinese paintings, they hosted lavish dinners for people such as Jones, the Morgenthaus, and Warren Lee Pierson of the Export-Import Bank.

Soong's Washington operation proved effective. Bespectacled and corpulent (some thought he resembled a whale in a frock coat), he won two $50 million loans for China. One was for currency stabilization; the other for food, gasoline, trucks, ammunition, machine guns, and pursuit planes, all to be procured in the United States.

Soong was hardly alone in such lobbying. Britons such as Leslie Howard, the actor in *Gone With the Wind*, were speaking for their own country's cause. Despite the neutrality laws, Churchill eventually obtained American destroyers and other forms of military aid. Such politicking from both sides of the world had rendered American neutrality null. And the Japanese knew it.

Tokyo was hot and sultry on the morning of July 27, 1940. But as Japan's highest admirals and generals convened in the palace for a "liaison conference" with the emperor, the mood was even more stultifying than the heat. The Japanese economy was in shambles. The China war was a terrible drain on resources, manpower, and morale. In China, the Japanese military was descending further into barbarity, practicing germ warfare on Chinese subjects. And on the home front, the government was using every device from enforced uniformity of dress to spy scares to mountains of words in the newspapers about Japan's "just cause," all to make sure that no dissent arose. The government could not back out of China: To do so would be to abandon the imperative that had led Japan into Manchuria in the first place. But as long as China kept getting aid from abroad, it could not go forward either.

At the Tokyo conference, General Tojo Hideki, the new hard-hitting Army chief of staff, seized the agenda by presenting the group with a plan entitled "Main Japanese Policy Principles for Coping with the Situation Which Has Developed in the World." The proposal called for new steps to cut off Western aid to Chiang Kaishek and for a Japanese economic and military thrust into Southeast Asia. The plan stated that positive "arrangements must be undertaken to include the English, French, Dutch, and Portuguese [a reference to Macao] islands of the Orient within the substance of the New Order."

The Navy chief of staff, Admiral Yamamoto Isoroku, who as a young man had lost two fingers in the Russo-Japanese War, protested. What about the United States, he asked? Expansion into the European colonies inevitably would lead to a war with the United States, he argued; and in a Pacific war the United States inevitably would win.

The conference flared with debate. The generals accused the admirals of cowardice; the Navy accused the Army of stupidity.

But the generals won the day, citing the need to carry on the war in China at all costs. On August 1, 1940, Tokyo announced its intention of creating a "Co-Prosperity Sphere in Greater East Asia"—meaning an extension of Japanese dominion over not only Korea, Manchuria, and China, but also all of Southeast Asia.

The pace of action and counteraction quickened. On July 26, President Roosevelt restricted export licenses for selling heavy scrap steel, tetraethyl lead, lubricating oil, and aviation gasoline to Japan. On July 27, Tokyo threatened restrictions of the sale of rubber and tin from Malaya and the Indies to the United States. On August 7, a former American steamship now flying the Panamanian flag reached Manila: It was carrying sixty-four American-made airplanes and 1,000 tons of munitions. Then came a series of news reports.

August 13: Harold Callender, a reporter for the *New York Times* traveling with other American correspondents on Pan America's inaugural flight from San Francisco to Australia, filed a story from

Pearl Harbor listing the vessels he had seen: "ten battleships; two aircraft carriers; fifteen cruisers; about 50 destroyers; and many submarines, some painted blue, some black." All in all, he wrote, "one gets the impression that [military] preparations are going forward rapidly."

August 18: The White House announced that the United States and Canada had agreed on the creation of a Joint Defense Board to coordinate bilateral efforts in both the Atlantic and the Pacific. Roosevelt wanted the American Navy to have access to the ports at Halifax and Vancouver.

August 22: Cabling the *New York Times* from Canberra, Callender reported an exchange with the Australian prime minister, Robert G. Menzies. The Australian leader asked the assembled American correspondents if the joint U.S.–Canadian defense board would have any bearing on American relations with Australia and New Zealand. Would America tighten ties with the countries down under as it had with Canada? A flotilla of American warships had just reached Sidney: Menzies, one of the reporters replied, had only to think about the significance of American warships in an Australian harbor.

August 23: The State Department publicly warned that if Japan pursued its course, pushing into Southeast Asia, the "time of reckoning" would come.

August 27: In Batavia, the capital of the Dutch East Indies, the touring American reporters inspected the naval yard, machine shops, repair facilities, seaport, and airport: The Indies had received U.S.-made Curtiss pursuit planes and Glenn Martin bombers. Cabled Callender: "An interesting feature of [the naval air patrols] is the fact that the Netherlands patrol area overlaps the area [north of Borneo] covered by the United States Navy seaplanes based on Manila." That overlap symbolized "what the Netherlands [the Dutch authorities in the Indies] would like to think are our common interests in the Pacific."

September 2: The "traveler cannot help observing," Callender reported, "that in the air journey from Honolulu to and thence via Australia and the Netherlands Indies to Singapore he passes a vast series of actual or potential air and naval bases, strung out along United States, British, and Netherlands territories." The *Times* headline over the article proclaimed: "NEW DEFENSES RISE AT SINGAPORE."

September 3: The Tokyo daily, *Asahi,* declared: "Japan must take measures to prevent French colonies [Fiji and Tahiti] in the South Seas from falling under British control."

September 5: Secretary of State Cordell Hull said that a full Japanese invasion of Indochina would have an "unfortunate effect" on American public opinion. Secretary of the Navy Knox announced that the United States was building three new naval bases in Alaska.

September 8: An especially rabid Japanese newspaper, *Kokumin,* described United States–British cooperation as a "menace" to Japan's plans for a "Greater East Asia."

September 11: Upon returning to the United States from his Pacific junket, Harold Callender summarized his impressions in a story for the *Times:* "Everywhere [from Honolulu to Hong Kong], the scenes were similar—barbed-wire barriers, machine gun posts, new airfields equipped with the latest bombers, expanding mobile armies, swift naval vessels patrolling the coasts. The Manila base maintains constant air patrols, just as Surabaja [the port on the eastern end of Java], Batavia, and Singapore do. At Manila, they are called 'neutrality patrols,' but that is the only difference."

5

In a Chongqing restaurant in mid-October, 1940, an exchange of toasts took place. Britain had reopened the Burma Road and now, news reports stated, coolies in Lashio, at the Chinese–Burmese border, were lifting cargoes—lathes, rolls of adhesive plaster, flashlights, tins of high-octane gasoline, rifle barrels, barrels of kerosene, bales of raw cotton, even airplane wings—onto about 2,000 waiting American-made trucks smuggled on transport ships into Rangoon. The trucks now were rumbling up the Burma Road. *Time* reported that as the trucks left, thousands of coolies cheered.

The cheering soon stopped. On September 27, 1940, Japan had joined with Italy and Germany in signing the Tripartite, or Axis, Pact, a mutual defense treaty. By late October, emboldened Japanese pilots were bombing the Burma Road, strafing trucks, attacking bridges, killing dozens of people, and causing delays. But the trucks, paid for out of America's loan to T. V. Soong, kept going. Bridges went back up. Living laborers replaced the dead. On the Burma Road, the goods trickled through. However minor, that success was critical to a plan that was currently under way in Washington.

On December 20, 1940, Secretary Morgenthau summoned T. V. Soong to the Treasury. "I have good news for you," the secretary said. "Yesterday morning I had the chance to deliver . . . your memorandum to the president." Along with a note of explanation, Soong had provided a map of Chinese airfields from which bombers could reach Japan. "He was simply delighted, particularly . . . about the bombers. Yesterday after cabinet . . . the president had Hull, Stimson, and Knox stay, and we all had your map out. . . . I said, 'Should we work it out and come back?' and he said that was not necessary. He said, '[Y]ou work out a program.'"

At his home in Washington, Morgenthau the next afternoon met with Soong and Claire Chennault, an American aviator working for the Chinese. Their task was to work out details of what Roosevelt had called "a program." The president, Morgenthau informed them, was "seriously considering trying to make some four-engine bombers available to the Chinese in order that they might bomb Japan."

Chennault stuck in a caveat. B-17s, he pointed out, would require American crews, mechanics, bombardiers, and pilots. The neutrality laws prohibited active duty personnel from fighting for other countries. (Chennault long since had resigned from the Army Air Corps.)

Not to worry, Morgenthau retorted. The U.S. Army already was willing to release the persons required from active duty. And the White House also had other ways of getting around the law.

But Morgenthau himself had a question. Could the B-17s carry incendiary bombs, clusters of inflammatory devices? Japanese cities, after all, were made of wood and paper; American aviators as far back as Billy Mitchell in the 1920s had pointed out Japan's vulnerability.

Chennault assured Morgenthau that the B-17s could do the job.

A follow-up session was held on the twenty-second in the library of the Washington mansion of Secretary of War Henry L. Stimson. Stimson, Navy Secretary Frank Knox, and General George C. Marshall, Army chief of staff, were present. Morgenthau reviewed the matter of bombing Japan.

Now it was Marshall who raised questions. Could America spare the bombers? Should they not be sent to Britain instead?

After considerable discussion, Stimson brought Marshall around, arguing that with appropriate funding more bombers could be built for Britain. Marshall was, Morgenthau wrote in his diary, "going to work out a plan" for air bases in China and around the Pacific.

Thomas Corcoran, the White House aide, worked out the legal aspects of the plan. A dummy corporation called China Defense Supplies (CDS), chartered in Delaware, would do fake work for the Treasury Department. With U.S. government funds thus received, CDS would let out contracts for B-17 bombers and hire retired airplane personnel. Chennault would organize the force, train it, and supervise its movements across the Pacific; the major stopover would be Hawaii. The force, made up of B-17s (Flying Fortresses), would locate at various bases, in the Aleutians, Guam, Cavite in the Philippines, Hong Kong, Singapore, and Kunming in China.

Then, no later than early 1942, Chennault's pilots would take off from these various sites, all within flying distance of the Japanese islands, and proceed to firebomb Hirohito's cities into oblivion.

There was only one problem. Somehow, possibly through spies and possibly through leaks from the American side, Japanese intelligence learned about the bombing scheme. And the government in Tokyo believed it had no choice but to go to war. Going to war meant bombing Pearl Harbor.

6

Early in January, 1941, America, Britain, and Canada signed a treaty (the ABC agreement) wherein the United States pledged to defend the Atlantic against German submarines and to bomb Axis plants and railroads. Although the document was secret (not revealed until four days before Pearl Harbor, when the anti-Roosevelt *Chicago Tribune* printed the text in full), the effects soon became obvious. Beginning in April, 1941, the United States gradually increased the scope of its convoy protection for British merchant ships. By October 31, when a German submarine sank the American destroyer *Reuben James,* American warships stretched from the East Coast as far out as Iceland. Without a congressional declaration, America was in effect in the war on the side of Great Britain.

After invading the Balkans, Hitler on June 22, 1941, broke the 1939 Nazi–Soviet Pact and attacked the Soviet Union. Tokyo also moved again. On July 21, Japan took over all of Vietnam, turning Saigon and Camranh Bay into Japanese naval bases. Japan was now in a position to move south.

In response, President Roosevelt extended aid to the Soviet Union, froze Japanese funds in the United States, and signed an executive order placing an embargo on high-grade aircraft oil to Japan. With FDR's tacit approval, the State, Treasury, and War Departments agreed to prevent Japan from obtaining necessary export licenses for any oil at all. When the Japanese applied for such licenses, the relevant departments simply would stall, making the embargo on the sale of American-produced oil to Japan de facto and complete.

Roosevelt knew full well where an oil embargo would lead. "[T]o cut off oil altogether at this time [to Japan]," the president, maintaining the public pretense of a partial embargo, said in a press conference on July 19, "would probably precipitate an outbreak of war in the Pacific and endanger British communications with Australia and New Zealand."

At the end of July, Ambassador Nomura Kichisaburo made FDR's meaning clear. He reported to Tokyo a conversation held in the Oval Office: "The president said that if Japan attempted to seize oil supplies by force in the Netherlands East Indies, the Dutch would, without a doubt, resist, the British would immediately come to their assistance, war would then result between Japan, the British, and the Dutch, and, in view of [the Americans'] policy of assisting Great Britain, an extremely serious situation would immediately result."

In Tokyo, Prince Konoye was worried. With American economic sanctions in place and with American bombers crossing the Pacific, Japan had only one choice, he believed: to strike and strike first. To secure the oil to continue the war in China so that it could protect its "right" to Manchuria, Japan had to take all of Southeast Asia and keep the United States at bay until Japan could fortify its Pacific islands, surrounding itself with an impregnable shield. But how could Japan possibly do so? The only hope lay in the Pearl Harbor plan conceived by Admiral Yamamoto.

Renowned as a master game player, the purse-lipped Yamamoto as commander in chief of the Japanese fleet after 1939 was responsible for his nation's naval strategy. He was convinced that Japan's only chance to survive what he was sure would be a war with America was to cripple the United States Pacific Fleet, based in Pearl Harbor.

Training exercises for the Pearl Harbor attack began in August, 1941. At the Saeki Air Base in Kyushu, the southernmost of Japan's four main islands, naval pilots were practicing carrier takeoffs and landings. At Kagoshima Bay, also in the south, other pilots were learning to zoom over rooftops and chimneys, cut back their speed, drop to low altitudes, and release torpedoes while their airplanes skimmed the surface of the water. And at Mitsukue Bay, tucked into Shikoku Island, pilots waded around a miniature mock-up of Pearl Harbor, learning the profiles of the ships.

Early in September, the navy's top brass gathered at the War College in Meguro, a Tokyo suburb, to work out fleet directions. Convening around a tabletop, three teams, representing the Japanese fleets that would go south and east, and the American fleet at Pearl Harbor, moved miniature ships around on a chart. The southbound force encountered few problems, striking successfully at Manila, Hong Kong, Singapore, and Batavia. The eastbound fleet, however, ran into trouble. One of the admirals at the table moved tiny mock U.S. naval patrol planes out of Pearl Harbor and up toward Midway. There they crossed the path of the oncoming carriers.

On the table, Yamamoto's fleet had been detected. It would have to cross the Pacific under radio silence.

The Americans, the British, and the Dutch were also making preparations, concentrating their efforts at last on the fortification of Singapore. Location alone made Singapore important, for it sat at the end of the Malay peninsula and was a major commercial emporium; and with a rearming America clamoring for rubber and tin, Singapore's safety was critical.

Now, in the third week of September, 1941, the lobby of the famed Raffles Hotel was taken over by white and khaki uniforms, naval and army, and bearing American, British, and Dutch insignia. The officers, convened at the request of the Dutch in the Indies, who wished to preserve their fleet, had come to plan offensive action against Japan.

Their agreement called on their forces to: "Create subversive organizations in the China coast ports and in French Indo-China. These must commence operation as soon as possible concentrating on propaganda, terrorism, and sabotage of Japanese communications and military installations. . . . Reinforce the American garrison in the Philippines, particularly in air forces and submarines. . . . Prepare to defeat Japan without suffering grievous loss ourselves. . . . We must base mobile forces as near to Japan as possible. . . ." The Singapore conference proposed to confine Japan "as nearly as possible to the defense of her main islands" and to "cut Japan off from all sea communications with China and the outside world by intensive action in the air and waters around Japan, and to destroy her war industries."

Somehow, Japanese intelligence learned of the Singapore conference, at least in general terms. Decoded Japanese messages mentioned a British offer to the United States of use of the Singapore base, the arrival of Australian troops in Singapore, and the American intent, part of the Chennault mission, to build fourteen air bases in China.

The Japanese embassy in Washington also would have seen the October 31 issue of *US News*. The magazine carried a two-page relief map, a view of the Pacific Rim with Japan at the center. Then it portrayed arrows, with flying times indicated, of bomber lanes to Tokyo: thirteen hours from Singapore; ten and three quarters hours from Dutch Harbor; eight hours from Kunming; seven and a half hours from Cavite; seven and a quarter hours from Hong Kong; six and a quarter hours from Guam. The arrows and bombers in tiny outlines were colored red, as was a circle drawn around Honshu, Japan's main island. Tokyo itself was marked with a bull's-eye.

7

Completing its run from Tokyo and Honolulu on November 8, a Pan American seaplane crossed through the Golden Gate and pulled up to its berth at San Francisco's Embarcadero. When the passenger door opened, among the dozen or so passengers emerged a small, compact Japanese man, wearing a homburg and a Chesterfield coat. Dr. Kurusu Saburo was a special envoy from the government in Tokyo; he was bringing a peace overture from the new premier, Tojo Hideki.

From San Francisco, Kurusu flew to Los Angeles. As his plane put down at the Hollywood-Burbank airport, he would have seen the huge Vega and Lockheed plants nearby, which covered nearly 400 acres of the yellow-brown terrain, visible proof of the burgeoning might of the United States. Standing in the fields just outside the factories were hundreds of military airplanes in various stages of completion: fighters and seaplanes, and bombers that could fly nonstop to Hawaii and even 100 miles beyond. From southern California, Dr. Kurusu flew via TWA to a huge new U.S. Army airfield at Albuquerque, and thence to New York and down over Baltimore. Factories, including the giant Martin airplane plant, stretched in a continuous line from Baltimore through the piney woods to Washington.

At Washington's new airport, situated on the south bank of the Potomac, a single State Department official, Joseph Ballantine, was on hand to meet Kurusu. "Finishing my long and strenuous trip," Kurusu said in English (he had served in the Japanese consulate in Chicago), "I still feel I have a . . . chance for the success of my mission."

Kurusu's mission had no chance. The document he carried offered to the secretary of state a vague relaxation of tensions but made no mention of Washington's sine qua non for peace: Japan's withdrawal from China.

But other things, too, made peace impossible, as Dr. Kurusu must have realized. He most certainly would have read press clippings kept at the yellow stone Japanese embassy on Massachusetts Avenue. In its edition of November 21, 1941, *US News* held that "plans for a short war have been made [in Washington]." *Time,* on November 17, carried a cover story about Reuben Harris, the San Diego–based builder of the new B-24s, the so-called Liberators. The biggest bombers yet, and with a range of at least 5,200 miles, these giants already, said *Time,* were being ferried "to the Dutch in the Netherlands Indies."

And Kurusu scarcely could have missed Arthur Krock's article in the November 19 *New York Times* and the headline: "NEW AIR POWER GIVES [PHILIPPINE] ISLANDS OFFENSIVE STRENGTH."

On the morning of Saturday, November 14, 1941, in the office of General Marshall, a crucial press conference took place. Pledging the reporters to secrecy, a surefire way of ensuring leaks, he said: "We are preparing an offensive war against Japan."

"For two months," Marshall explained, "we have been moving troops and planes into the Philippines, and the movements are continuing. MacArthur has been unloading at night, no one has been allowed to approach the docks or other key points. . . . We have also been sending our Flying Fortresses, via Hawaii, Midway, Wake, New Britain [a Pacific island just east of New Guinea], and Port Darwin, Australia. We now have thirty-five Flying Fortresses in the Philippines—the greatest concentration of bomber strength in the world. . . . We are sending more as rapidly as we can get them and train crews."

The "trip [from Hawaii] to the main Japanese centers and back is just a little bit too far for the B-17s," General Marshall went on. The reporters must have been scribbling away frantically. "But they could fly from the Philippines, drop their loads, and continue to Vladivostok. . . . Japanese cities are very vulnerable—and so are their naval bases. . . . Also, we might add, where bases are securely held, [we can] bomb from China. Indochina, of course, would be within easy reach. . . . Our aim is to blanket the whole area with air power."

Marshall closed the press conference by repeating that what he had said was off-the-record. The leak would come from the most authoritative source of all, the *New York Times*.

On November 19, 1941, Arthur Krock, columnist for the *Times,* wrote:

> The changed condition [in the Far East and the Philippines] . . . is the consequence of two developments. . . . One is the naval alliance [a reference to the convoy patrols] with Great Britain, joining for all practical purposes the fleets of the two nations in the Pacific. The other is the coming of age of aircraft in battle. . . . And there are two other lesser factors responsible for the change—prepared air positions in Alaska, making possible a pincer attack by air on Japan, and the extension of the Lend-Lease program

to the Soviets, which opens up terminal and service points in Siberia for American fighter planes that have flown from Manila. . . . If the American commanders [of the Philippines] decided to "defend" by attacking, there are enough bombing planes, and of sufficient strength, to drop bombs on Japan, land in Siberia and refuel, and rebomb . . . on a return trip to Manila.

The implication of the arms buildup, Krock went on, was that as far as the Roosevelt administration was concerned, Japan had to get out of China or else. The message undoubtedly had come again from the horse's mouth. But Japan's unwillingness to leave China gave it only one choice: preemptive attack.

PART II

JAPAN'S
FAR-FLUNG
BATTLE LINE

6

THE ONSLAUGHT

1

On October 22, 1941, the Japanese ocean liner *Taiyu Maru* left Yokohama and began steaming across the Pacific toward Honolulu. Three officers, out of uniform but from the Navy General Staff in Tokyo, were among the passengers: Commander Maejima Toshihide, an expert on submarines; Sublieutenant Matsuo Keiu, a specialist on midget submarines; and Lieutenant Commander Suzuki Suguru, a pilot. Their task was to study the route to Pearl Harbor and to ascertain the chances of Admiral Yamamoto's plan for a surprise attack.

On the morning of November 1, Honolulu rose ahead, its backdrop of green mountains wreathed in white fog and early morning mist. As the *Taiyu Maru* slid alongside its pier, the three officers conferred. The results of their survey had been encouraging. Except for one brief storm, the weather had been fine. Sea currents had been tricky but manageable. No American reconnaissance planes had been visible anywhere around Midway Island. And throughout the voyage, the officers had not seen another vessel.

Fearing that dockside authorities in Honolulu might search the ship, the Japanese team had kept no notes. But no one examined the vessel and, on the return trip to Japan, the officers wrote out full reports.

Upon arriving in Yokohama, Suzuki Suguru took the first available launch to the battleship *Hiei,* anchored in Tokyo Bay, and delivered his findings to the commanding admiral. That same night, November 11, the *Hiei* steamed off for Tankan Bay, far to the north in the cold of the Kurile Islands. Tankan was the secret rendezvous for the ships of the Pearl Harbor mission.

One by one, never together and never with any apparent connection, battleships, cruisers, destroyers, submarines, oil tankers, and aircraft carriers slipped out of Yokohama, Nagasaki, Kobe, and other Japanese ports and assembled in Tankan Bay. Thirty-two ships were packed together in a gray bay ringed by snow-covered mountains.

To deceive American decoders in Hawaii, radio operators communicated with reference to their home port call numbers. Sailors were forbidden shore leave—not that the few fishermen's huts and a single concrete pier were inviting—and prohibited from throwing garbage overboard. On the night of November 23, at a conference aboard the carrier *Akagi,* Suzuki told Lieutenant Commander Fuchida Mitsuo about his trip to Hawaii. Fuchida, the pilot designated to lead the air strike at Pearl Harbor, took notes and the meeting ended with a toast of *saki* and three *banzais* for the emperor. Two mornings later, fueled and followed by a contingent of submarines (which carried midget subs, intended to slip into Pearl Harbor and release torpedoes during the bombing), six carriers with 363 bombers moved out.

Cruising on the surface by night and under the water by day, the submarine flotilla crossed the Pacific without incident. Late in the afternoon of December 6, the commanders could see Oahu through their periscopes. At nightfall they surfaced and eased to a point about ten miles off Pearl Harbor; despite moonlight, they were undetected.

From his conning tower, one commander, Hachimoto Mochitsura, became transfixed by the red and green lights around the Honolulu port, the glow of the twin towers of the Royal Hawaiian Hotel, and far off to the right the Elks Club whose windows glittered at the foot of Diamond Head. Shortly before dawn, the submarines released their half dozen midgets: These worked their way around the buoys and, just before it closed, the end of the steel mesh antisubmarine net that guarded the entrance of Pearl Harbor.

At the same time, the main decks of the carrier fleet, which had crossed the ocean in radio silence and now were positioned about 250 miles north of Oahu, were all action. Crews of mechanics were hauling the bombers up from the storage decks and tuning up the engines. Below the decks, pilots were rising from their bunks and pulling on freshly pressed uniforms. As they sat for breakfast, they picked up enameled chopsticks and ate *sehikan,* rice boiled with red beans, a dish reserved for the most important occasions.

Then aboard every ship everyone gathered in the briefing room: Sketches chalked on blackboards showed the previous day's position of every major ship in Pearl Harbor (reported in coded radio broadcasts from agents in the Japanese consulate in Honolulu). Pilots received one last instruction. Except for Commander Fuchida, no one was even to touch his radio.

Just at dawn, the pilots clambered to the main decks and up into their cockpits. Aboard the *Akagi,* a red and yellow tail stripe on Fuchida's plane marked it as the aircraft to follow. A flag above the *Akagi's* tower was lowered to half-mast, the signal for all the other carriers to turn and face southward toward Oahu.

At precisely 6:00 A.M., the *Akagi's* flag rose again to the top of its pole. From the deck of every carrier the pilots took off, the cheers of the crews drowned out by the roar of their engines.

The servicemen on duty at the U.S. Army's Opana radar station, near Kahuku Point on the northern coast of Oahu, were ready for breakfast. Even for a Sunday morning, their watch had been desultory.

Weekend spotters during the 0400 to 0700 shift usually would have noticed a dozen or more airplanes on the screen and would have occupied themselves by identifying the aircraft and plotting the probable routes. On this morning, December 7, 1941, however, they had seen scarcely a thing. Just before seven, the screen had flickered—two small airplanes came in from the north—but it had shown nothing else. The clock in the radar room pointed to seven and most of the men left for the mess hall.

Two privates, George Elliott, Jr., and Joseph Lockard, stayed behind. Elliott was at the controls of the radar. Noting a sudden formation on the oscilloscope, he motioned for Lockard to have a look. So many blips were showing up that for a moment they thought the machine must be broken: They were looking at about fifty airplanes in formation. Rushing to the plotting board, Elliott calculated that the formation was 132 miles away.

The clock showed two minutes past seven. Elliott said that they ought to call Fort Shafter, down in the valley below Kahuku Point; he called the fort switchboard operator. After several minutes, Lieutenant Kermit A. Tyler came on the line. The airplanes were now ninety miles from Oahu.

While Elliott was speaking with Tyler, Lockard got on a phone extension and said the blips were the biggest radar sightings he had seen, he said. What were they? Tyler hazarded a guess: Perhaps the airplanes were B-17s from the West Coast, part of the Chennault mission.

As they talked, Commander Fuchida in the lead Japanese bomber was using the radio beam of a Hawaii music station to calibrate his position. Only thirty-five miles off Oahu, he adjusted his course, and the armada of bombers behind him did the same.

The clouds below him were thick. Would they be so all the way to Pearl Harbor? Could bombing be accurate in such weather?

Then Fuchida glanced down. The clouds were thinning, revealing a white line of surf splashing up against the shore. He could make out palm trees and pink tile roofs. Then far off to his left, he saw the shimmering blue-gray water of Pearl Harbor.

In Pearl Harbor, the usual morning ritual was about to begin. At 0755 a blue flag ascended the pole on the signal tower atop the Navy's huge water tower. A minute later bandsmen reached their appointed station on the decks of the ships. The blue flag came down and throughout the harbor American flags suddenly fluttered in the clear air of the morning. But before the music could start, sailors aboard the battleship *Arizona* noticed specks in the sky.

A quartermaster aboard the destroyer *Helm* gave the approaching aircraft a wave. A pharmacist's mate on the battleship *California* heard someone say that maybe the Russians had a carrier nearby; America was giving Lend-Lease aid to the Soviet Union and the oncoming airplanes had red markings. Charles Flood, a signalman on the *Helena,* watched the airplanes through his binoculars: The way they were gliding seemed familiar.

Four years before, on duty in Shanghai aboard the cruiser *Augusta,* Flood had witnessed Japanese aerial attacks on Chinese ships. He had noted the way the pilots dropped their bombs. As they approached their targets they would go into a long glide, then dive. These aircraft with the red markings approaching the ships in Pearl Harbor were also going into a glide. And now they were diving.

2

Although President Franklin D. Roosevelt and his top officials had anticipated a Japanese attack on the Philippines and other points south, the bombing of Pearl Harbor came to them as a complete shock. Over the years some authors have contended that FDR knew of the attack beforehand. Not a shred of evidence supports this allegation. All accounts we have show that on December 7, 1941, President Roosevelt was overwhelmed with a sense of loss and defeat.

When the word of Pearl Harbor reached Chongqing, however, people greeted it with exultation. "[Nationalist] officials," Han Suyin, the author of many books about China, wrote in 1942, "went about congratulating each other as if a great victory had been won." America now would do what China could not: defeat Japan.

Chongqing actually was an unlikely place from which to win anything. The city, wrote the journalist Theodore White,

> sat on a wedge of cliffs, squeezed together by the Jialing and Yangzi Rivers. . . . The city wall with its nine gates had been built in the Ming dynasty, over five hundred years earlier. . . . Chongqing was still attached umbilically, as it had been forever, to the countryside. Rice fields reached up to the city wall itself; down below on the fringes of the Yangzi banks, peasants hopefully planted vegetables, gambling they could harvest before the summer floods overran their plots. . . . Rice came from upriver in flat-bottomed scows. . . . The city repaid the countryside by returning all its bowel movements; collectors [of night soil] emptied the thunder boxes of every home every morning, and padded barefoot down the alley stairs to the riverside, two buckets of liquid muck jiggling from their bamboo staves until they reached what foreigners delicately styled the "honey barges.". . . . From the same river, the water-bearers carried up buckets of muddy water, jiggling in the same staves. . . . The sloshings on the stone steps, up and down the alleys, left them always slipping, and one could never be sure what kind of slime one must avoid.

Such was Chongqing, the war-time capital of China, primitive, ageless, and, above all, remote. The Yangzi downstream narrowed into the Three Gorges, which were barriers against attack on the ground. Although the bombing had been going on for four years, the Japanese could not take Chongqing. So at the time of Pearl Harbor, Chiang Kaishek enjoyed prestige throughout China for simply being able to hold on. But survival alone would not win the war.

In Carmel, California, General and Mrs. Joseph W. Stilwell were holding open house for new junior officers from nearby Fort Ord on the morning of December 7. The weather was warm, the doors to the garden were open, and from the grounds the guests could see the Pacific Ocean as it sparkled, rolled, and crashed on the beach below. Since they were off duty, the guests wore civilian clothes, short sleeves and loafers. Some of them were reading the Sunday comics.

The telephone rang. Mrs. Stilwell answered.

"Turn on your radio," a friend cried over the line. "Pearl Harbor is being attacked!"

General Stilwell, the lean, wiry, bespectacled soldier known as "Vinegar Joe" for his acidic wit, drove rapidly back to Fort Ord, where he soon received orders from Washington. His mission was to organize the defense of the California coast against a further attack. With no artillery and small arms enough for only a few hours, Stilwell fired back his reply: "Good God, what the hell am I supposed to do? Fight 'em off with oranges?"

No attack materialized. But as the Japanese juggernaut drove into Southeast Asia, Stilwell wired a message to the War Department. "I'll go where I'm sent."

When it became apparent that the Japanese were not going to attack the American West Coast, the War Department summoned Stilwell to Washington.

"George [Marshall] sent for me—with him for over an hour," read Stilwell's diary entry for New Year's Day, 1942. The meeting with Marshall, held in the War Department's ramshackle headquarters on the Mall, Stilwell wrote, was "all about troubles in the Orient." Stilwell would go where he had served before, from 1926 to 1929 and 1935 to 1939, as an intelligence officer: China.

In Detroit, James H. Doolittle, a short, compact, cleft-chinned lieutenant colonel in the Army Air Corps in his mid-forties, had been chafing with boredom. One of the early dare-devil pilots, as well as an auto racer, Doolittle since 1940 had been assigned to help car and truck manufacturers convert to the production of jeeps, tanks, and airplanes. The work was important but it required paperwork, a daily grind of filling out forms in triplicate. He referred to his job as "flying a desk." Surely, he thought, he should be doing something else. But what?

The attack on Pearl Harbor, announced by radio stations throughout America, brought the answer. On December 8, 1941, he fired off a letter to General Henry H. ("Hap") Arnold, head of the Air Corps, requesting a transfer to a fighting unit. In January, 1942, he received command of a bombing mission whose target was Tokyo.

On the afternoon of December 7, 1941, a crowd gathered at the Polo Grounds in upper Manhattan to watch an intracity exhibition baseball game between the Brooklyn Dodgers and the New York Giants; the Dodgers hammered the Giants to defeat, 21 to 7. Halfway through the game, the stadium loudspeaker carried an announcement: "Colonel William Donovan, come to the box office at once. There is an important phone message."

A World War I hero and a Republican attorney in New York specializing in international law, William J. Donovan in many trips to Europe had served President Roosevelt as an unofficial intelligence agent. The previous July, FDR had established the top-secret Office of the Coordinator of Information (COI), America's first spy agency, with Donovan as chief.

Calling from COI's New York office, Robert Sherwood, the playwright and FDR speechwriter who also worked in the spy agency, told Donovan that the president wanted to see him immediately. Donovan caught the first train to Washington.

Just before midnight, Donovan reached Union Station and took a taxi to the White House. There he learned that Roosevelt wanted him to organize propaganda and clandestine warfare against Germany and Japan. Under Donovan, COI was to become the Office of Strategic Services, the forerunner of the Central Intelligence Agency.

At 9:00 P.M. Greenwich time on December 7, Winston S. Churchill turned on a portable radio. Ensconced for the weekend at Chequers, the official Tudor-style country residence of the British prime minister, he had been dining with John Winant, the American ambassador, and Averell Harriman, President Roosevelt's special emissary to Great Britain. They had been discussing Lend-Lease matters but they all wanted to hear the latest news from the BBC.

In smoothly modulated tones, the announcer spoke of fighting on the Russian front and of tank warfare in Libya. Then, almost casually, he mentioned that the Japanese had bombed Pearl Harbor.

In almost the same moment, the butler entered the room. "We heard it outside [on a radio in the pantry]," he said. "The Japanese have attacked the Americans."

"We looked at one another incredulously," Winant later remembered. "Then Churchill jumped to his feet and started for the door with the announcement, 'We shall declare war on Japan.' ... Without ceremony I too left the table and followed him out of the room.

"'Good God,' I said. 'You can't declare war on a radio announcement.'

"He stopped and looked at me half-seriously, half-quizzically, and then said quietly, 'What shall I do?'

"I said, 'I will call up the president and ask him what the facts are.'

"And he added, 'And I shall talk to him too.'"

Winant got through to the White House. When Roosevelt came on the line, the ambassador said that he had a friend who wanted to speak with the president. "You will know who it is, as soon as you hear his voice."

According to Churchill's account, he asked: "Mr. President, what's this about Japan?" to which Roosevelt replied, "It's quite true. They have attacked us at Pearl Harbor. We are all in the same boat now."

Churchill immediately made plans to go to Washington. Only four months before, he had met Roosevelt on board ship at Placentia Bay in Newfoundland. In promulgating the Atlantic Charter, they had pledged their two countries to the "final destruction of the Nazi tyranny." Now Churchill hoped to extract from Roosevelt a pledge to give the war in the Atlantic and Europe higher priority than the war in Asia and the Pacific.

Lord Privy Seal Marquis Kido Koichi, the emperor's most intimate civilian adviser, in his diary recorded his visit to the Imperial Palace on the morning of December 8: "Turning up Miyake slope as I climbed the Akasaka approach [to the palace] I saw the brilliance of the sunrise, in a clap, over the buildings, and I worshipped. I was reminded that today is the day in which we have embarked upon a great war against the two powerful nations, America and England. Earlier this morning our naval air force launched a large-scale attack upon Hawaii. Knowing this and worrying about the success or failure of the attack, I bowed involuntarily to the sun and closed my eyes and prayed in silence. At 7:30 A.M. I met with the prime minister and with the two chiefs of staff [General Sugiyama Hajime and Admiral Nagano Osani] and heard the good news of our tremendous success. . . . I felt deep gratitude for the assistance of the gods.

"I was received in audience by His Majesty from 11:40 to 12. I was struck to observe, if I may say so, that at this time when the nation has staked its future upon war, His Majesty seems completely self-assured and shows no trace of inner turmoil."

The composure seemed justified. Japan's tide of conquest rolled over barrier after barrier, as if nothing could stand in its way.

3

The first of the barriers to fall was Guam. About 1,000 miles east of the Philippines, Guam was the southernmost island of the Marianas. The Spanish had taken over the island chain in the seventeenth century, but had lost Guam in battle with the American warship *Charleston* in the Spanish-American War. A year after the war, Spain had sold the rest of the Marianas to Germany; during the First World War Japan had taken possession of all the islands except Guam. Three hours after the Pearl Harbor attack, Japan completed its conquest of the Marianas.

Guam had no real fortifications. Its marine and naval guard was tiny, 4,430 men equipped with World War I weaponry. At 2:00 A.M. on December 10, the third day of the war, Japanese landing boats, escorted by four destroyers, splashed ashore, disgorging more than 5,000 troops. By daybreak the fighting was over. The Americans suffered only slight casualties but U.S. Navy Captain George McMillin, the island's governor, left the Spanish-built palace to surrender. He became a prisoner of war.

The visible top of an active underwater volcano, Wake Island is an atoll in the central Pacific that the United States in the nineteenth century had used as a cable station; then in 1941 the Navy had started to transform it into an air and submarine base. Wake stretched out across the sea in the shape of a V, each arm about five miles long, and with an airstrip lying along one of the branches. Construction work for the submarine facility had destroyed much of the vegetation and so the low-lying island was largely devoid of cover. A few wooden barracks and a cement block house that served as headquarters provided the only shelter and a smattering of antiaircraft guns gave only a modicum of defense.

The Japanese bombing of Wake began on December 7, and continued for four more days. On December 11, a Japanese flotilla appeared off the island and tried an amphibious landing. The American coastal artillery thwarted the attempt. On December 23, however, Japanese reinforcements established a beachhead and later in the day forced the defenders to capitulate. The 1,200 Americans on Wake spent the rest of the war in Japanese prison camps.

Residents of the Anglo-American sector of Shanghai awoke to the sound of explosions shortly after four in the morning on the day of the Pearl Harbor attack. Some went to their roofs to observe. Japanese ships had set the British gunboat *Petrel* on fire and Japanese troops, armed with bayonets and rifles, were massing on the Bund. Toppling the statue of Sir Robert Hart, the Briton who during the Boxer Rebellion had sent out the plea for help, the Japanese by noon had brought the old International Settlement under their control.

Hong Kong was also in danger. On the morning of December 13, a launch put out of Kowloon, the peninsula across the harbor from the island and already in Japanese control. When the boat docked at Victoria Pier, a Japanese officer stepped out. Marching to Government House, he handed over a letter from his commanding general that advised the British authorities to surrender. Governor Mark Young refused to do so.

The next day, he and the island's 10,000 British, Indian, and Canadian troops received a wire from Churchill: "WE ARE ALL WATCHING DAY BY DAY AND HOUR BY HOUR YOUR STUBBORN DEFENSE OF THE PORT AND FORTRESS OF HONG KONG. YOU GUARD A LINK BETWEEN THE FAR EAST AND EUROPE LONG FAMOUS IN WORLD CIVILIZATION. WE ARE SURE THAT THE DEFENSE OF HONG KONG AGAINST BARBAROUS AND UNPROVOKED ATTACK WILL ADD A GLORIOUS PAGE TO BRITISH ANNALS. . . ."

There was no such glorious page. At dusk on December 18, Japanese artillery opened a bombardment of Hong Kong Island's northeastern coast. Then hundreds of launches pushed off from Kowloon, a miniature armada hidden by rain and black smoke billowing up from oil tanks along the waterfront. By daybreak on December 19, Japanese forces were ashore; by noon they had taken half the island, reaching Repulse Bay on the southern side. The view from Victoria Peak was ominous: From every quarter of the island, flames from oil tanks shot up, sending plumes of smoke curling high against the blue of the sky.

Governor Young had hoped for reinforcements from China. At four in the afternoon, however, the British military attaché in Chongqing cabled that no Chinese forces would reach Hong Kong until January 1, if then: Chinese commanders were unwilling to leave redoubts in the hinterland to take action in defense of the British imperialists. Young understood. Hong Kong was doomed.

Christmas in Hong Kong was bleak. The Japanese controlled the suburbs and even the air-raid tunnels. When night fell, the Britons in Government House did what they could do: They got drunk. Champagne, gin, whiskey, it hardly mattered which, contributed to a last, glorious, desperate binge.

The next day, December 26, was Boxing Day, in the British tradition a time for bank closings, servants' time off, and general relaxation. But now it was the Japanese who celebrated. As airplanes with red circles on their sides roared over the harbor, Japanese troops in Central, the island's principal business district, staged a victory parade. Thousands of Chinese rickshaw pullers left their vehicles by the sides of the streets and in support of their Japanese "liberators" waved little flags that displayed the rising sun.

On Boxing Day, Governor Young formally surrendered. The Japanese stuffed him away in the depths of his own jail, where he spent the duration of the war.

4

Two and a half hours after the first bombs fell on Pearl Harbor, Major General Lewis Brereton, commander of the U.S. Far East Air Force in the Philippines, arrived by staff car at No. 1 Victoria Street in the Walled City section of Manila. At five in the morning, the city was still dark. Brereton mounted the stone steps of the House on the Hill, headquarters of Douglas MacArthur, commanding general of the U.S. Army Forces in the Far East. Once past the sentries and inside, he approached General Richard K. Sutherland, General MacArthur's chief of staff. Brereton wished to speak with MacArthur immediately. Sullivan stated that MacArthur was unavailable. What MacArthur was doing remains unclear. He may well have been frozen with fear.

Brereton replied that he wished permission to get the B-17s, some of which had reached the Philippines under the Chennault bombing plan, up in the air before dawn.

Sutherland later claimed that he asked Brereton, "What are you going to attack? What's up there?" In Sutherland's account, Brereton admitted that he did not know, that he needed to send out a reconnaissance mission. But Brereton's version was different. In his recollection, he stated that intelligence had placed Japanese troop transports off Taiwan and heading for the Philippines. But since MacArthur was otherwise occupied, Brereton had no choice but to wait; he did not see MacArthur until several hours later.

Whichever interpretation of the conversation was correct, two facts are clear. First, MacArthur did nothing of his own accord to get the American bombers off the runways, either to attack the Japanese transports or to fly out of harm's way. And second, the dawn and the Japanese reached the Philippines at the same time.

MacArthur had graduated at the head of his class at West Point in 1903, been many times cited for bravery in World War I; in 1918 MacArthur had become the youngest American brigadier general. He also acquired a reputation for flamboyance and self-dramatization. In 1937 he had resigned from the U.S. Army to take the rank of field marshal in the Philippines; by all accounts he had regarded himself as a viceroy of the American empire. Chief of Staff General George C. Marshall recalled him to regular service in July, 1941. MacArthur now commanded a joint Filipino-American force. Living in a hotel penthouse high over Manila, he seemed as aloof and arrogant as ever. His failure to do anything regarding the bombers, however, led his subordinates to question his bravery, or at least his judgment.

In his capacity as head of the Philippine army, MacArthur, to be fair, had spent months doing all he could to prepare the islands' defenses. To his relief, late on Pearl Harbor Day, he received a message from General Marshall, assuring him that he enjoyed "the complete confidence of the War Department" and could expect "every possible assistance within our power." That very afternoon, however, an American convoy carrying artillery and planes and heading for

Manila received orders to divert to Fiji. And four other troopships bound for Manila, the *President Johnson, Bliss, Etolin,* and *President Garfield,* received orders to return to San Francisco.

The orders may have been the result of confusion: In the aftermath of Pearl Harbor, conflicting messages out of Washington abounded. When MacArthur learned of them, though, he felt betrayed, intimating to reporters that the War Department was writing the Philippines off.

At dawn on Pearl Harbor Day, two Japanese convoys out of Taiwan lay off Luzon, the main island of the Philippines. As 43,000 soldiers waded ashore at Lingayan Gulf, about 150 miles north of Manila, bombers flew on to Manila, where they unloaded on merchant ships in the bay. They also turned the American naval base at Cavite into a shambles.

Admiral Thomas Hart, head of the Asiatic Fleet, ordered most of the remaining ships, two destroyers, three gunboats, two minesweepers, two submarine tenders, and several submarines to Australia, which the American command believed to be beyond Japan's reach. Of all the naval defenses, only a few PT boats stayed behind.

A week after the Pearl Harbor attack, the Japanese still had only probed at the Philippines. But a full-fledged invasion, MacArthur knew, was bound to come. But would Washington help?

Back in the American capital, General Marshall had given a new brigadier general, Dwight D. Eisenhower, the task of assessing the Philippine defenses. Eisenhower had served under MacArthur for four years in the islands and saw no way of keeping the Japanese out: landing sites abounded. Moreover, "it will be a long time before major reinforcements can go to the Philippines," Eisenhower warned Marshall on December 17, "longer than the garrison can hold out with any driblet assistance, if the enemy commits major forces to their reduction. . . . Our base must be in Australia." Marshall agreed.

By early 1942, Eisenhower, who had been MacArthur's aide in the Philippines and regarded the general as bombastic, was arguing forcefully that the United States could not spread limited resources thinly around the world but must assemble as much of its force as possible in Britain. Eisenhower's message received White House support. MacArthur was out of luck.

Well before dawn on December 8, the periscope of an American submarine out of Manila Bay revealed the approach of an eighty-ship Japanese troop convoy, only forty miles north of Luzon. Word flashed to MacArthur's headquarters; awakened, he fired off a command: Every available B-17 was to fly northward to stop the fleet.

Starting at noon, Japanese air strikes destroyed half of them before they could leave the ground. The surviving bombers fled southward the same day. The B-17s had not launched a single strike.

That same day an even larger Japanese fleet, out of Taiwan and under the command of Lieutenant General Homma Masaharu, was steaming down toward Luzon's western coastline. At the same time, yet another Japanese flotilla was reaching the archipelago's southernmost bay at Davao, on the island of Mindanao. Upon receiving reports of the Japanese approach, MacArthur relocated his headquarters to Corregidor.

An island in the mouth of Manila Bay, Corregidor was a natural point of refuge. Nicknamed "The Rock," its main body rose more than five hundred feet from the water and concealed the Malinta Tunnel, with a main passageway and a number of wings or laterals that could house 10,000 men. Corregidor was a mighty fortress—and easily besieged.

The possibility of a siege loomed large. The Japanese had landed on Luzon without great difficulty and were pushing down across the island almost at will. MacArthur had hoped for a stalwart defense. On Christmas, however, he ordered a retreat to the mountainous peninsula that formed the western side of Manila Bay: Bataan. But even a retreat was risky. The roadways that wound back from the various outposts were easy targets for Japanese bombers; so was

Manila Bay. The day after Christmas, as MacArthur looked out from the cottage he had requisitioned on the heights of Corregidor, the sparkling water below was dotted with barges, steamers, launches, and tugs, all ferrying troops, food, and munitions to Corregidor and Bataan. All were vulnerable to attack from the air.

At noon that same day, a formation of Japanese bombers appeared over Manila. They concentrated their attack on the Walled City, then returned to Taiwan. As MacArthur through his field glasses surveyed the columns of smoke rising across the bay, he realized that he was seeing only the beginning.

On New Year's Eve, hundreds of vehicles loaded with Filipino and American troops rolled into the Bataan peninsula. For the moment they were in no danger. On New Year's Day, 1942, however, light bombers of the Japanese Fifth Air Group crossed and recrossed the mountains of Bataan, dropping no bombs but demonstrating that they could attack at will.

That same morning, Japanese army units reached the gates of Manila. Great clouds of smoke covered the city; its streets were filthy with ashes and soot, and once graceful Spanish palaces were heaps of rubble.

Marching into the defenseless city, the Japanese proceeded to the vacated residence of the American high commissioner, where they approached the flagpole and lowered the Stars and Stripes. As the flag reached the ground, a Japanese officer unfastened it, stomped on it, and in its place hooked up the flag of Japan. As the Japanese emblem ascended the pole, a band played the national anthem.

Then the Japanese force began to move beyond Manila, heading for the Bataan peninsula. The invasion of the Philippines was reaching its climax.

During the first week of January, General Homma Masaharu threw a veteran army against the forward United States defensive position on the peninsula, the Abucay line. In an unremitting assault, he pushed the Filipino and American troops ten miles back to their second redoubt, the Bagai-Orin line. There, in a ferocious battle in which neither side took prisoners—a foretaste of things to come—the defenders held firm.

By this point, more than a third of Homma's troops had been killed. Many of the rest were laid low by wounds, disease, or exhaustion.

So the fighting entered into a temporary stalemate while General Homma waited for reinforcements and supplies from Japan. They were slow in coming. But the Americans did not have the aircraft or ships to stem the flow. So, after two weeks, General Homma pushed on and this time he was unstoppable.

5

In their sweep into Southeast Asia, the Japanese had closed down all entry points for materiel into China, save one—the Burma Road. The trail was so muddy that trucks at times slipped off and hurtled toward the river bed a thousand feet below. But as it snaked its way some 750 miles from Lashio in Burma to Kunming in southwestern China, the Burma Road was Chiang Kaishek's lifeline. So if the Japanese succeeded in occupying Burma and closing the road, China's ability to survive would be greatly reduced.

On December 23, 1941, the Japanese launched their first raid on Rangoon. They ran into unexpected resistance. At Chiang Kaishek's request, General Claire Chennault had hooked up some of his pilots with Royal Air Force units out of India. Their task was the defense of Burma. Initially they were successful in forcing the Japanese raiders to retreat. But they did so at a cost: For the defenders of Rangoon, the loss of nine airplanes out of a dozen and their pilots was a disaster.

Just as crippling was the effect of the first Japanese bombing raid. Fires raged throughout the city, thousands of persons were wounded or killed, and many shorefront warehouses were damaged or destroyed. British officials cleaned up the rubble and tended to the injured; but they were powerless to arrest the flight of Indian and

Burmese workers to the countryside. By Christmas, business in Rangoon had ground to a halt. Fuel, food, and medicine were in short supply. To prevent looting and rioting, British colonial authorities imposed martial law.

It had little effect. On Christmas Day a Japanese aerial attack reduced Chennault's air force to four planes. On December 29, Japanese bombers knocked out the main railway station and demolished wharves and warehouses filled with Lend-Lease goods for China. Japanese troops then occupied Rangoon and moved northward to close the Burma Road.

It was "Vinegar Joe" Stilwell's task to open it again. If he was unable to do so, he was to organize an air route from India over the Himalayas (the "Hump") into China. But at all cost, he was to keep China in the war—as the British were about to go almost wholly out of the war in the Pacific.

6

"We are ready," declared Air Chief Marshall Sir Robert Brooke-Popham, British commander in chief for the Far East, from his headquarters in Singapore, in a public statement issued two hours after the Pearl Harbor attack.

> We have had plenty of warning and our preparations are made and tested. . . . We are confident. Our defenses are strong and our weapons efficient. . . . What of the enemy? We see before us a Japan drained for years by the exhausting claims of her wanton onslaught on China. . . . Confidence, resolution, enterprise, and devotion to the cause must and will inspire every one of us in the fighting services, while from the civilian population, Malay, Chinese, Indian, or Burmese, we expect that patience, endurance, and serenity which is the great virtue of the East and which will go far to assist the fighting men to gain final and complete victory.

Its racism aside, this pronouncement revealed much of the Britannic mind-set. Life as a privileged elite in a lush tropical setting had lulled Singapore's resident Britons into complacency. Malays, Indians, Chinese, and a smattering of Japanese had lived under British rule for more than a century, peacefully so.

Established as a colony at the end of the Napoleonic wars by Sir Thomas Stamford Raffles, one of the heroes of British imperial history, Singapore had flourished as the emporium that linked Shanghai, Hong Kong, and all the other treaty-ports on the China coast with India and eventually the Suez-to-Gibraltar commercial lifeline. Resident Britons had profited hugely, many purchasing London townhouses and estates in the English countryside. But the various "native" groups (the British had imported Indians and Chinese as laborers and clerks) had been distinctly subordinate to their Britannic overseers. By the 1940s, they were good and ready for British rule to end.

The Britons, however, could not imagine being expelled. Situated at the tip of the Malay peninsula, the island of Singapore was a walled fortress that bristled with huge antiaircraft guns: In a time-worn word, Singapore was "impregnable." Its naval defenses, moreover, were unsurpassed. In a blaze of publicity only a few days before, two of the most powerful warships afloat, HMS *Repulse* and *Prince of Wales,* had reached Singapore. With these two vessels at anchor in the harbor, Singaporeans felt secure.

So in a city that kept late hours, lights blazed throughout the night—beacons that guided Japanese bombers at 4:30 A.M., December 8, to the warehouses, docks, and ships in the harbor. And the vaunted guns of Singapore shot down not one Japanese bomber. The artillery pointed out to the South China Sea—and the Japanese airplanes had swept in from over the channel that separated the island from the peninsula.

The same day, December 8, intelligence reported, a Japanese convoy landed troops halfway up the east side of the Malay peninsula. Brooke-Popham sent *Repulse* and *Prince of Wales* up to intercept. Lacking an aircraft carrier, the high command could provide no fighter planes. But a destroyer escort was available. As the battleships set forth on the morning of December 9, rain and clouds provided a shroud of secrecy. The shield of bad weather remained in place for most of the day.

But the terrible ifs accumulated. If the sky had stayed overcast until nightfall, the British flotilla at daybreak could have caught the Japanese by surprise. If, after the sun late in the afternoon did break through the clouds, shipboard guns had been able to reach three Japanese reconnaissance aircraft spotted on the horizon, the Japanese might not have known of the British presence. And if a Japanese submarine had not been following undetected, then the ships might have gotten back to Singapore in safety. If. . . .

Just off the Malay peninsula, a task force of Japanese bombers and reconnaissance planes on the morning of December 9 was searching for the *Repulse* and the *Prince of Wales*. Rain and fog had returned, making detection all but impossible. As the fleet commander was about to turn back to the Japanese base in Saigon, however, he received a message: A submarine had pinpointed the battleships' exact location. Soon ninety-six bombers were descending through the clouds.

The battleships were on alert, steaming back to Singapore in zigzag patterns. Just after eleven o'clock on the morning of December 10, a loudspeaker on the *Repulse* announced: "Enemy aircraft approaching! Action stations!"

The Japanese air fleet approached in unending waves. Bombs burst in air. Torpedoes slashed through the water. Huge waves crashed over both British ships. Smoke enveloped the decks. Antiaircraft guns blazed forth but they barely could score a hit against the zipping attackers. From nearby carriers, nearly 1,000 Japanese planes now for hour after hour were diving and swooping at will. The accompanying destroyers were no match for the attackers and no fighter protection from Singapore materialized. Staggering, the two great ships could barely move. The *Prince of Wales* foundered, her beams almost awash. Lifeboats went out. Then, at 1:19 P.M., on December 11,

1941, the battleship rolled over; a minute later, dragging a destroyer with it, it disappeared beneath the waves. The *Repulse* soon followed it down.

News of the disaster shocked Singapore and London, too. Still in bed, Churchill received the news in a telephone call from First Sea Lord Sir Dudley Pound. To Churchill, the sinking of the *Prince of Wales* and the *Repulse* was the most shocking event of the war. To him, besides conveying the loss of more than 2,000 lives, it signaled the end of Great Britain's Far Eastern empire.

7

THE SINGAPORE
DEBACLE

1

Three days before Christmas, 1941, Prime Minister Winston S. Churchill and a large staff of military advisers, having crossed the Atlantic by battleship and docked at Annapolis, arrived in Washington. In a meeting code-named the Arcadia Conference, Churchill and Roosevelt coordinated their overall strategic decisions. Among their decisions was the establishment of the American–British–Dutch–Australian (ABDA) Command on the island of Java, headed by Lieutenant General A. P. Wavell. A square-jawed, taciturn Briton who had distinguished himself against the Germans in North Africa, Wavell soon found himself presiding over disaster.

With *Repulse* and *Prince of Wales* under water, General Yamashita Tomoyuki, the stocky, hard-driving, ruthless officer charged with the capture of Singapore, estimated that he could capture the island in 100 days. It took him seventy.

For the Japanese attackers, who had trained in the rugged, jungle terrain of Vietnam, the Malay peninsula was a straightforward matter. Carrying only light packs, canteens, small bags of pickles and rice, wearing not helmets but cloth Khaki hats, tee-shirts, shorts, and shower slippers, they advanced quickly to the southeast. Inured to forced marches, Japanese troops would hack their way through the vegetation and paddle small boats across swamps. Maps drawn earlier by spies enabled the Japanese to locate trails used by native hunters. Far inferior numerically to the British (mostly troops from India with white commanders), the Japanese used trumpets to convince the enemy of the imminence of hordes of soldiers. Tanks blasted away at British forward positions and truck-borne infantry would fall upon fleeing defenders. The Japanese furthered their advance in captured jeeps and trucks.

The most effective Japanese weapon, though, was the bicycle. As tanks moved forward, bicyclists preceded them to survey the land ahead, spotting the British positions. Then, with the enemy routed, the riders would pedal furiously, outpacing the tanks and keeping the pressure on the retreating defenders; often they crossed unbridged streams, holding their bicycles overhead. Malaya had been a good customer for Japan's prewar bicycle industry: Each jungle village had a repair shop with spare parts. Seeing the Japanese as liberators, villagers were happy to carry out repairs. Thus the two-wheelers just rolled on.

To escape the onrushing Japanese, the British units often had to dive into the surrounding vegetation. For them, the sweltering heat, thorny vines, and blood-sucking leeches were nightmarish. The tangle of growth limited visibility to a few feet. Worse yet was the eerie, all-pervasive stillness. A British colonel who visited an Indian unit reported: "They were thoroughly depressed. . . . The deadly ground silence emphasized by the blanketing effect of the jungle was getting on the men's nerves."

By early January, 1942, General Yamashita controlled two-thirds of the Malay peninsula. Alarmed, General Wavell flew to Singapore. Studying intelligence reports, he ordered an immediate retreat to Malaya's southernmost state, Johore, separated from Singapore by a shallow channel averaging less than a mile wide.

Somehow, Wavell seemed to believe, that channel would prove to be a sure defense. British planners considered Singapore, after all, to be impregnable: Its shore defenses included the most powerful artillery in the world.

2

Sunday in British Singapore was a time for relaxation. The week's work in the heat gave way to church in the morning, then to cricket, golf, tennis, yachting, swimming, and bridge. Up on the slopes, His Majesty's subjects who had chosen to rest in their bungalows, surrounded by gardens of hibiscus, wisteria, and bougainvillea, could browse through the Sunday edition of the *Straits Times*—as they were fanned by Indian and Malay servants. After tea, they could make their way to their clubs or to a dinner dance at the Raffles Hotel.

From the broad porch of the Raffles Hotel at night, the Britons could look out upon thousands of nautical lights, on the ships of many nations, twinkling in the darkness. Returning home by automobile or rickshaw, for Singapore had a huge population of Chinese coolies, the Britishers could go to sleep secure. In the morning the huge guns on the island that faced up toward the South China Sea guaranteed Singapore's safety. Life in Singapore was hot, sweaty, and placid.

On Sunday, December 8, 1941, the city on its island, suspended like an emerald below the scimitar blade of the Malayan peninsula, was preparing for the holiday season. Shops displayed holly and mistletoe; the streets were thronged with people, Britons and Chinese, Malays and Indians, civilians and soldiers, especially soldiers. Servicemen and nurses had assembled from Britain, India, Australia,

New Zealand, and the Netherlands East Indies. In the cinemas three-fourths of those present were in uniform. They were a comfort to the residents.

On Sunday night the first of the bombs began to fall. Almost immediately civil defense organizations sprang into action. Two nights after the bombing, the *Malayan Postscript* reported, "there was hardly a light to be seen. Zealous volunteers threw themselves into the task of blacking out Singapore. . . . The slightest chink of light provoke[d] frenzied shouts from the street below. Drivers of cars [were] stopped if their lights [were] thought to be the smallest degree on the bright side. Anyone attempting a cigarette on the street [at night was] fiercely pounced upon."

Still, Singaporeans remained calm. Even after the sinking of *Repulse* and the *Prince of Wales,* the citizenry tried to carry on with "business as usual." Shops and bazaars stayed open, housewives shopped, played bridge, or went to the movies, and their husbands worked in their offices. Restaurants had plenty to eat and drink. When military authorities informed the secretary of the Golf Club that they needed his greens for artillery, he said that he could not consent without a special committee meeting. A major wanted to cut down a row of banana trees to improve his field of fire, but civilian officials denied him permission.

Just before Christmas, though, the Japanese bombers returned. And the mood in Singapore changed dramatically.

On Christmas morning Cecil Brown, a correspondent with CBS Radio, broadcast a report from Singapore to the United States:

> This morning I talked with a number of people and it was not in their hearts to say or even think, "Peace on Earth—Good Will Toward Men." The Japanese were too near for that, and most people know that this Christmas Singapore is reaping the terrifying fruits of wishful thinking and unpreparedness. . . . On this Christmas, Singapore has the problem of rectifying almost overnight fifty

years of a strange kind of administration of the natives and one year of military apathy. During that year it was the conviction, almost a certainty of the military, that Japan would not move, that there would be no war in the Far East. And that conviction carried down to three days before war actually came. That's why this is a grim Christmas in Singapore, because the British out here are getting ready for a war with the war going on and the Japanese holding northwestern Malaya and dominating the skies over it.

Starting on the first day of the New Year, the people of Singapore experienced a month and a half of bombing. Hardly a day passed without its quota of raids. Air raid sirens would wail and everything would close—banks, post offices, shops, companies—then reopen in a frenzy as if to make up for lost time. Oddly, the city center, flanked with white-washed government buildings, was fairly safe; the Japanese early on were aiming primarily at the airfields and the waterfront. So civilians in the downtown enjoyed a degree of normality.

Not so the military command. What General Wavell discovered in Singapore left him shocked. The island's great guns all faced the sea—they could not be turned around to face Johore, a fact that no one had bothered to tell the prime minister. Wavell soon informed Churchill that "impregnable" Singapore was about to be raped.

Back in London from the Arcadia Conference, Churchill was outraged. "I must admit to being staggered by Wavell's telegram of January 16," he lambasted his chief of staff. "It never occurred to me for a moment . . . that . . . the fortress of Singapore, with its splendid moat half a mile wide to a mile wide, was not entirely fortified against an attack from the northward. What is the use of having an island for a fortress if it is not to be made into a citadel? . . . How is it that not one of you pointed this out to me at any time when these matters have been under discussion? More especially this should have been done because . . . I have repeatedly shown that I relied upon this defence of Singapore against a formal siege.

"Not only must the defence of Singapore Island be maintained by every means, but the whole island must be fought for until every single unit and every single strong point has been separately destroyed.

"Finally, the city of Singapore must be converted into a citadel and defended to the death. No surrender can be contemplated."

3

The order seemed sensible. General Yamashita's supply lines were stretched almost to the breaking point and his troops were running short of everything. Many were footsore and sick. Ranged against them were fresh Australian units, held in reserve in Johore. Joined by Indians pulled back from the peninsula, the Aussies in their slouch hats took the offensive. Setting up ambushes across Johore's ninety-mile northern border, they slowed the Japanese advance to a halt. Singapore breathed more easily.

Those on the island, though, failed to reckon with the matter of morale. Ordinary Australian troops did not see Singapore as their fight, and the Japanese were famously fanatical. A training manual distributed to the Japanese soldiers had roused them to a fever pitch. It was called "Read This Along—And the War Can Be Won!" Some excerpts:

> Once you set foot on the enemy's territory you will see for yourselves just what oppression by the white man means. Imposing splendid buildings look down from summits of mountains or hills onto the tiny thatched huts of the natives. Money that is squeezed from the blood of Asians maintains these small white minorities in their luxurious mode of life. . . .
>
> After centuries of subjection to Europe, these natives have arrived at a point of almost complete emasculation. We may wish to make men of them again quickly, but we should not expect too much. . . .
>
> When you encounter the enemy after landing, think of yourself as an avenger come at last face to face with his

father's murderer. Here is the man whose death will lighten your heart of its burden of brooding anger. If you fail to destroy him utterly you can never rest at peace. . . .

In that spirit, on January 15, 1942, Japanese troops on the Johore periphery drew their swords, approached some two hundred Australian prisoners, and cut their heads off. Then they turned toward Johore itself with renewed ferocity.

4

That same day, the docks of Singapore were ablaze. With their own bombers flying at will overhead, the Japanese had breached one end of the Johore front and were pouring on toward Singapore itself. The defenders withdrew again, beginning their exodus to the island. The Australians staged a last ambush, firing from within the jungle and knocking off most of two Japanese companies.

It was not enough. On the morning of January 31, 1942, remnants of the last British battalion on the peninsula—ninety exhausted Argyll and Sutherland Highlanders—stumbled across the thousand-yard causeway that linked Johore and Singapore. Two musicians playing "Hielan' Laddie" piped them across. When the last man reached the island, British engineers exploded the dynamite they had planted and the waters of the Johore Strait poured through a sixty-foot gap in the causeway. Few realized that at low tide the water in the gap was only four feet deep.

At the same time, General Yamashita set up his new headquarters. He chose a building of red brick and green tile—the so-called Green Palace owned by the Sultan of Johore—with a five-story tower.

Fabulously wealthy from tax revenues, the sultan dressed and spoke like an Englishman and in the weeks just past he had been generous in helping the British erect field hospitals. What they did not know was that he was a close friend of a relative of Emperor Hirohito, and that in offering the tower to Yamashita he was playing both sides against each other.

The tower sat atop a hillock, so it was plainly visible from across the water and thus vulnerable to British bullets. But from his command post at the top of the tower in a room with large windows, Yamashita enjoyed a bird's-eye view of the island of Singapore. From his overhead perch, he could radio his bombers as they hit the three-mile-long Singapore harbor with high explosives and incendiary bombs. He also ordered hundreds of folding boats and landing craft to be brought nearby under the cover of darkness and hidden behind bushes just inland from the strait.

From a height of 20,000 feet, twin-engined Japanese bombers based on captured British airfields in Malaya attacked Singapore in V-shaped clusters. Around them Zero fighters circled and weaved in escort. Occasionally one looped, flashing a reflection of the bright tropical sunshine.

Nothing could stop them. On its own bomb-blasted airfields, Singapore's fighters—Hurricanes, slower than the Zeros—were down to twenty-six. Every time they rose to counterattack, one or more was shot down. Antiaircraft shellbursts puffed below each onslaught of the bombers but the Japanese seldom broke their tidy packs.

On the night of January 31–February 1, four troopships, the *Empress of Japan, West Point, Wakefield,* and *Duchess of Bedford,* nosed into berths on the seaward side of Singapore's Empire Dock, bringing the troops of the Australian Eighteenth Division. The reinforcements sweated throughout the night to unload military stores. A procession of trucks came up empty and went away full by Main Entrance Road, then along Anson Road, and up through the city to the various British outposts. The unloading was urgent. The ships were due to sail in just a few hours, this time as mercy ships carrying away some 5,000 women and children to safety.

There was little safety. The ships were hardly underway when the Japanese resumed their attacks on Singapore. As a full moon outlined their targets, they plastered the harbor with bombs. The lead bomber in each formation carried an aiming device by which it located targets, then signaled the others when to drop their explosives. The loads crashed with roars that shook the whole island. Between the bombing raids, single fighters gunned the waterfront haphazardly.

Dockside coolies fled in terror. Only Chinese fishermen found life easier. As they rowed out at dawn, they found harvests of fish, stunned by the bombs, lying on the surface of the harbor. Fresh fish had been scarce in Singapore since the departure of Japanese fishermen—along with the small population of Japanese photographers, barbers, hairdressers, brothel-keepers, prostitutes, and clerks, who had either fled to the Malay peninsula or, arrested, been sent to British Ceylon for internment.

The government had feared a Japanese Fifth Column. But, in pep talks over the radio, Japanese officials urged workers back to their jobs. Few went; most were riveted in place by a Japanese voice on the air waves from somewhere on the peninsula: "Good morning, Singapore! How do you like our bombing? You saw what happened yesterday? That is a trifle compared to what is in store for you. Singapore will soon be a heap of ruins with not a living thing in sight. Today we are coming again to bomb the docks!"

In a broadcast from Java to Singapore on February 1, General Wavell tried to restore morale:

> It is certain that our troops on Singapore Island greatly outnumber any Japanese that have crossed the strait. We must defeat them. Our whole fighting reputation is at stake as is the honour of the British Empire. The Americans have held out on the Bataan peninsula against greater odds, the Russians are turning back the [best of] the Germans, the Chinese with almost complete lack of modern equipment have held the Japanese for four and a half years. It will be disgraceful if we yield our boasted fortress of Singapore to inferior enemy forces.
>
> There must be no thought of sparing troops or the civil population and no mercy must be shown to weakness in

any shape or form. Commanders and senior officers must lead their troops and if necessary die with them.

There must be no question or thought of surrender. Every unit must fight it out to the end and in close contact with the enemy. . . . I look to you and your men to . . . prove that the fighting spirit that won our empire still exists. . . .

That night the moon was full. Despite the brightness, the first of the Japanese had paddled across the Johore Strait in little rubber boats, undetected.

5

The morning of February 1 was hot and humid. The sky was a pale, steamy blue, tufted with dazzling white clouds. As the sun rose it pressed down like an iron, flattening the sea to a vast glittering sheet of corrugated glass. The wharves baked underfoot and the air by the waterfront reeked of rope, machinery, and the stench of burning.

The effects of the previous night's bombing raid were everywhere. The docks were nearly empty. The wreckage of the warehouses still smoldered. Offshore, a fuel tanker poured out a heavy column of smoke. Up by the Blue Funnel piers a freighter was on fire and sinking.

Nosing out through the minefields was a small Chinese vessel, painted white and bearing a Red Cross. Designed for the shallows of the Yangzi River, the ship was barely seaworthy. But it was the best Singapore now could manage by way of a hospital ship. Having somehow escaped the bombs, the boat was ferrying wounded persons to the Dutch Indies. And in the hotels, the clubs, and the bungalows around the heights, word went around: Not many boats were left.

The commanding officers that day allowed themselves a moment of optimism. Lt. General A. E. Percival, the tall, slender, somewhat buck-toothed, quiet-spoken man in charge of the Singapore garrison, told aides that he had a breathing spell of about eight days. He did have shells and his men could shoot out of the water any Japanese boats that tried to cross the Johore Strait. The Japanese bombs could make life on the island unpleasant but Singapore could survive. So he used the week ahead to strengthen the outposts.

On paper the task was simple: move artillery up to the strait. In reality it was difficult. The shoreline that faced the strait was jagged and the Japanese could attack at any number of inlets. Even with the reinforcements of the Eighteenth Division, the lay of the land would stretch his troops thin.

"There must be no panic, no spreading of rumors, no slackers, but steadfastness, re-doubled energy, and iron determination to win." Thus declared General Percival in a noontime radio broadcast on February 1. In almost the same moment, the Japanese opened machine-gun fire from the mainland.

Two days later they brought the full weight of their artillery upon Singapore's three northern airfields, the naval base, and major highway intersections. British cannon replied but the supply of shells was running low.

Despite the explosions, Singapore clung to a semblance of normality. Shops continued to do business. The brickworks kept on making bricks. Robinson & Company, a department store, carried on. Its shop in the Raffles Hotel had been demolished, but a new outlet provided what customers wanted—shoes, clothing, blackout curtains. Borneo Motors offered repairs, gasoline, and outboard motors—for cash only, because people wanted them for escape to Sumatra. The Alhambra Theater showed *Ziegfeld Girl*. Moviegoers escaped reality in the lovely atmosphere of American girls dancing and singing; then they stepped outside into the blazing tropical sun. They were halfway around the world from America and the Japanese were only a few miles away.

Along the Johore Strait, British troops dug trenches and threw up barbed wire—mostly at night, because during the day the Japanese from just across the water easily could see what they were doing. All this took place under mortar fire that lit up the darkness with streaks of red and white.

From only half a mile away over the Johore Strait British troops could hear the Japanese sawing and hammering as they repaired the gap in the causeway. One British officer spotted a Japanese staff car driving along the waterfront. The British along the strait also could make out, half-submerged in the ocean, the *Empress of Asia,* just arrived with rifles, automatics, and ammunition. But the cargo was useless. The ship was on fire.

Yet in its new store Robinson and Company reported record over-the-counter sales. Around the corner on Battery Road, beauticians supervised Elizabeth Arden treatments. Frazer and Neave still bottled soda water. Noisy drinkers filled the Cricket Club and sailors frequented the dance halls. The dining room of the Raffles Hotel was packed. The civilians of Singapore were in denial.

"All ranks must be imbued with the spirit of attack. . . . The endeavor of every soldier must be to locate the enemy and . . . to close with him." This was an order to all unit commanders from General Percival on February 3, 1942.

The same day, to their regular aerial attacks the Japanese added dive-bombers that shrieked down to shower "grass-cutters"—small bombs that burst above ground and scattered arcs of sharp-edged shrapnel—and fighters that cruised along the roads machine-gunning anything that moved, trucks, rickshaws, even bicycles.

Over the next two days, with long-range artillery positioned on the high ground in Johore, the Japanese began artillery fire. The shelling was of pinpoint accuracy. It sounded like a thunderstorm that just went on and on.

With Singapore thus softened up, the Japanese in launches, rowboats, and more rubber dinghies on the night of February 8–9 struck en masse at the northwestern flank of the island. The British made a mistake. As they heard the Japanese splash ashore, they could have illuminated the attackers in the blaze of searchlights. But the lights stayed dark: Switchmen had fled. So the Australians, who occupied this jungle corner of the island, had to fight in a blackness broken only by gun flashes. Panic ensued. Using the tactics by which they had conquered the Malay peninsula, the Japanese in the nighttime jungle were here, there, everywhere. Unlike the defenders, their squad leaders wore illuminated compasses strapped to their wrists.

By early morning, February 10, the Australians were in headlong retreat. Groups of men became separated. Many were lost. Many died. A few managed to straggle into Singapore City. By dawn, Yamashita's forces held nearly half the island, and General Percival ordered all troops back to prepare the city for surrender.

6

Preparing for surrender meant denying everything possible to the Japanese. Teams drawn from the Public Works Department, the Royal Engineers, and the Observer Corps worked day and night smashing plants and machinery, pouring out liquor stocks in warehouses, blowing up remaining cars, trucks, and small aircraft.

The streets daily were becoming more dangerous. In the twelve-hour equatorial nights, Japanese snipers had plenty of time to slip into the city and set themselves up in abandoned window frames. With the collapse of the *Straits Times* headquarters and the paper's once reliable reporting, rumors were as numerous as bullets.

The ranks of the wounded, military and civilian, increased daily. Every available office building and church turned into a makeshift hospital. St. Andrew's Cathedral became a first-aid station. Chairs, pews, hymnals, and hassocks disappeared from the nave: Beds and stretchers filled the space. Blood-splattered doctors and nurses moved in with drugs, antiseptic, splints, and rolls of bandages, but they could not begin to help the hundreds of wounded persons. People lay about screaming their lives away.

On February 11, all remaining British newspeople fired their presses and fled by motorboats to Batavia. Their departure nearly completed the foreign civilian exodus from Singapore—in most cases, they prevented native civilians from going along, often shoving them off the boats.

On the night of February 12–13, Japanese units entered a British military hospital and ran amok. An account written after the war by a British doctor who was present remains:

> During the morning the water supply was cut off. Shelling and air activity was intense. Bursting shells, mortar bombs, with an occasional shot from our own artillery. . . .
>
> Japanese fighting troops were about to enter the hospital from the rear. Lt. Weston went from the reception room to the rear entrance with a white flag to signify the surrender of the hospital. The Japanese took no notice of the flag and Lt. Weston was bayoneted to death. . . . The following events started at about the same time:
>
> (a) One party [of Japanese] entered the theater block. At this time operations were being prepared in the corridors between the Sisters' bunks and the main theater, this area being the best lighted and most sheltered part of the block. The Japanese climbed in through the corridors and at the same time a shot from the windows was fired. . . . About ten Japanese came into the corridor and the Royal Army Medical Corps personnel put up their hands. . . . The Japanese then motioned them to move along the corridor, which they did, and then for no apparent reason, set upon them with bayonets. . . .
>
> (b) Another party of Japanese went into the wards and ordered the medical officer and those patients who could [to] walk outside the hospital. In one ward two patients were bayoneted. . . .

(c) A party of Japanese came into the reception room shouting and threatening the staff and patients who had congregated there.

Bayoneting patients and staff alike, the Japanese killed more than three hundred persons. A few witnesses escaped. Their stories added to the growing sense of panic.

By the morning of Friday, February 13, the British forces had withdrawn to the city itself, where all hell was breaking loose. In the streets, black under the pall of oil smoke, hundreds of corpses lay unburied.

Troops skirting the dead saw that shops were shuttered and deserted. The soldiers themselves were out of control: They skulked through the downtown, hiding in the basements of government buildings or looting Chinese stores. Some of them clambered aboard departing motorboats. All Singapore seemed to be at the waterfront, searching desperately for a means of escape.

On the night of February 13, however, came a Japanese broadcast in broken English: "There will be no Dunkirk at Singapore. The British are not going to be allowed to get away with it this time. All boats leaving will be destroyed!"

The Japanese were true to their word. Some boats ran into mines in the harbor and exploded. Others came under fire from Japanese fighter planes and light naval craft. Then, too, a Japanese flotilla positioned itself in the Strait of Malacca between Singapore and neighboring Sumatra: Its guns blew more boats out of the water.

A few were able to flee, but most were not so lucky. A boat called the *Mary Rose* in the night received a signal from what the skipper took to be a Dutch trawler. Following instructions, he followed it up a Sumatran river where a second trawler materialized. At dawn the trawlers turned out to be Japanese. They sank the *Mary Rose* and most aboard drowned. A British motor launch, seventy-five feet long and carrying a group of British soldiers and nurses, smashed up on the beach of a nearby island. A party of Japanese soldiers appeared, marched the men out of sight, and returned to the beach, wiping their bayonets. They ordered the nurses, who wore Red Cross emblems, to walk into the sea. When the women were waist deep in the water, the Japanese fired upon them with machine guns. One soldier and one nurse survived.

The Japanese were right. Singapore was no Dunkirk.

That same morning, February 14, a Japanese airplane dropped a note from General Yamashita on General Percival's headquarters in Fort Canning. The message was couched in elaborately courteous terms, with compliments on British bravery—and a demand for surrender. Percival cabled the contents to General Wavell, stating that he was not prepared to dignify Yamashita's missive with a reply.

Percival soon learned that Singapore was about to run out of water: Breaks in the mains caused by the bombing and shelling meant that the supply in the reservoir was down to one-half. The water might last forty-eight hours, perhaps only twenty-four. Percival still refused to concede defeat. The bombing and shelling began anew. The wreckage of smashed buildings, broken telephone poles, and tangled wires blocked the streets. With the hospitals crowded to capacity, orderlies hauled the wounded on stretchers to the ground floors of the surviving hotels; they also dumped the dead in pits dug in the once smooth green lawns and flowerbeds. Despite the use of disinfectant, the air remained putrid all through the night.

As the sun rose on Sunday, February 15, Singapore was burning. Even the ocean seemed to be on fire. A blazing soap factory threw grotesque patterns on the walls of nearby buildings. On the northern coast the flaming oil tanks of the naval base—by this point in Japanese hands—poured a vast mantle of black smoke overhead. Tongues of flame from timber sheds reached a height of six hundred feet. Stocks of rubber smoldered and stank. Orbs of fire shone from nearby islands, where the British had fired oil reserves to keep them from the Japanese: The impression was that of minor setting suns come to rest upon the horizon.

"Today," Percival's immediate subordinate, General Gordon Bennett, wrote in his diary, "opened with a hopeless dawn of despair. There is no hope or help on the horizon. The tropical sun is sending its steamy heat onto the dying city which is writhing in its agony." Then he added: "Silently and sadly we decided to surrender."

7

A freshly starched General Percival that morning attended Anglican communion in the chapel at Fort Canning. After the service he dispatched two emissaries to discuss surrender terms with the Japanese.

In the afternoon, Percival and three top British officers entered a staff car and drove to Bukit Timah, a village about five miles west of the city. There, escorted by two Japanese officers, they marched to the enemy headquarters, now set up in an automobile assembly plant in the city itself. A photograph shows the two Japanese, in trousers, long sleeves, and cloth caps, dwarfed and flanked by the four Britishers wearing knee socks, khaki short pants, khaki shirts with the sleeves rolled up above the elbows, and almost flat, World War I–vintage helmets. One of the Britons carried the Union Jack on a pole over his shoulder. General Percival carried a white flag.

They entered the plant. In halting English, a Japanese who had been a university professor managed to translate. One of the escorting Japanese, Lt. Colonel Sugita Ichiji, and one of the Britons, Captain Cyril H. D. Wild, each of whom had picked up a bit of the other's language, helped.

General Yamashita entered the room; Percival handed him the white flag. Then, seated at a wooden table, Percival asked for an overnight delay. Yamashita declared that the bombardment would go on unless Percival surrendered immediately.

Percival hesitated.

"Yes or no?" Yamashita asked.

Percival bowed his head and whispered his assent.

At 8:30 P.M., February 15, 1942, the guns at Singapore fell silent. Japanese soldiers sang *Kimigaya,* their slow, stately national anthem. Assembling his staff at his headquarters, General Yamashita laid a white cloth over the wooden table and held the traditional victory celebration of dried cuttlefish, chestnuts, and *sake,* gifts of the emperor. Silently the officers faced northeast toward Tokyo and lifted little cups of wine in a solemn toast.

In Tokyo the *Asahi Shimbun* proclaimed: "To seize Singapore Island in as little time as three days could only have been done by our imperial army. Japan is the sun that shines for world peace. Those who bathe in the sun will grow and those who resist it shall have no alternative but ruin. Both the United States and Britain should contemplate the [triumphal] Japanese history. We solemnly declare that with the fall of Singapore the general situation of war has been determined. The ultimate victory will be ours!"

Why had Singapore fallen? Some in Britain put the blame on General Percival, claiming that while he was charming and able, he lacked the forcefulness to inspire his forces. Perhaps so. But his critics should have apportioned some of the blame to prewar British thinking, which in its complacency had conceived an attack on Singapore only by sea. British planners also underestimated the resolve of General Yamashita, who on the drive to Singapore inflicted more than 130,000 casualties on the defenders to only 10,000 for the Japanese.

In losing Singapore, Great Britain suffered its most degrading defeat in the Second World War. The ABDA Command dissolved ten days after the fall of Singapore. London switched General Wavell's headquarters to India and General Percival spent the rest of the war as a prisoner of the Japanese. And the Japanese juggernaut just pressed on.

8

WARRIORS OF
THE RISING SUN

1

In mid-March, 1942, the British Admiralty and the U.S. Navy Department issued a joint communiqué: "After dark on 28 February, 1942, HMAS [Australia] *Perth* and USS *Houston* left Tandjong Priok, Java, with the intention of passing through Sunda Strait [between Java and Sumatra]. The next day a report from HMAS *Perth* was received, indicating that it and USS *Houston* had come in contact with a force of Japanese ships off St. Nicholas Point. . . . Nothing, however, has been heard from HMAS *Perth* or USS *Houston* since that time. The next of kin . . . are being notified accordingly."

When Singapore fell, the Japanese creation of its East Asian empire was well under way. The Dutch East Indies were about to fall under Tokyo's dominion.

During the seventeenth century, the Netherlands had established a vast seaborne empire that stretched from the Hudson River valley to Cape Town on the southern tip of Africa across the Indian Ocean to the spice isles that ranged from Sumatra to New Guinea. Profits from the far-flung realms had furnished the luxurious homes depicted in the paintings of de Hooch and Vermeer. But the Anglo-Dutch maritime wars of that era had eliminated Dutch power in North America, and during the Napoleonic wars the British had hung the Union Jack over Cape Town. The Dutch Empire had receded to tiny islands in the Caribbean and the East Indies. Although the Indies had maintained a small fleet after the fall of Holland, the colony had depended for protection upon the British in Singapore. But with Singapore fast approaching disaster, the Indies were open to attack.

For the capture of the great archipelago, the Japanese had developed a three-pronged attack. Out of Davao, the southern Filipino port that the Japanese had taken late in December, 1941, one force was striking at Timor: That easternmost island of the Indies was to serve as a shield against reinforcements from Australia. From Davao another unit was approaching Borneo and Celebes in the north of the Indies. Then, with the surrender of Singapore assured, a third contingent steamed down from Camranh Bay on the coast of Vietnam; its destination was Sumatra, the Dutch island that flanked the Malay peninsula on the west. From these three locales—Timor, Celebes and Borneo, and Sumatra—the Japanese would converge on Java. Like Sumatra, Java was rich in oil. It also was the ABDA Command headquarters for the southeastern Asia theater. So it had to be taken.

Borneo and Celebes, lightly defended outer islands, succumbed without resistance. Most of New Guinea soon fell.

On February 20, the Japanese landed on two beaches in Timor. After only three days of fighting against Dutch and native defenders, that steamy island was wholly in their grip.

At the same time, 700 Japanese paratroopers floated down from the sky over the city of Palembang in southern Sumatra. Huge clouds of smoke billowed up to greet them: The defenders were torching the refineries and oil tanks of Royal Dutch Shell, trying to deny the Japanese access to high-grade aviation fuel. The Dutch and their Indonesian workers had been ready for the attack. With rifles and machine guns, they shot at the parachutes and killed many of the invaders.

But the defense soon crumbled. Only fifty miles north of Palembang, six Japanese cruisers, eleven destroyers, eight troop transports, and an aircraft carrier soon anchored off the mouth of the Musi River. A procession of motorboats carrying a full infantry division set out upriver toward the city. As bombs plastered Palembang, the outnumbered and outgunned defenders pumped a torrent of oil upon the river, setting it on fire. Hundreds of Japanese soldiers were burned to death in the flaming cascade. But the sheer size of the invading force prevailed. Sumatra fell and, imprisoning the Dutch and Malay defenders, the Japanese turned their attention to Java.

In his ABDA headquarters at Bandung, eighty miles southeast of Batavia (now Djakarta) in the mountains of central Java, General Wavell was close to despair. His assignment as ABDA commander of defending the Indies seemed impossible. Java was surrounded. By late February the Japanese had swallowed up all of Sumatra; and just to the east, off Bali, a Japanese convoy had appeared and anchored, its prows pointed toward Java.

At the end of February, 1942, Wavell was transferred to India, leaving behind the in-fighting American and Dutch commanders. American admiral Thomas Hart, aged sixty-four, was a thin, wiry, reserved sailor who considered the situation hopeless; the short, rotund, energetic Dutch admiral Conrad Helfrich wanted to take his little fleet straight into the guns of the Japanese navy. After hearing of Hart's vacillation, FDR recalled him, ostensibly because of age. Helfrich ordered preparations for battle.

In immediate charge of the Allied fleet of only sixteen warships was the dark-haired, balding, somewhat paunchy Dutch Admiral Karel W. F. M. Doorman. On the afternoon of February 26, he assembled his captains for a briefing at his headquarters in the leafy old residential quarter of Surabaya, near the Allied naval base in eastern Java. The atmosphere was hopeful. Decked out in starched whites and gold braid and ignoring the bombing all around them, the captains drank toasts and watched the sun set behind the harbor palms. That evening Doorman's flotilla lifted anchor, skirted through the mines in the Surabaya harbor, and headed out into the Java Sea.

Doorman nonetheless was fearful. His ships had never worked together as an integrated force at sea and had had no chance to develop joint tactics.

Under the stars, the ABDA warships gathered in fighting formation. Three British destroyers positioned themselves side by side to form a frontal screen. Following in a line were five cruisers: two Dutch, one British, one Australian, and one American. The last was the USS *Houston,* which the Japanese propagandists so often had reported sunk that the crew had nicknamed it the "Galloping Ghost of the Java Coast." Two Dutch destroyers flanked the procession; four American destroyers brought up the rear.

The force was hardly formidable. The ships were battered and the men exhausted. The vessels had no English–Dutch codes, no air support, and, most important, no reconnaissance. They were sailing blind, only groping for the Japanese.

At about four in the afternoon of February 27, they did make contact in the Java Sea: A spotter aboard the *Houston* detected two Japanese cruisers and reported the sighting. One of the ship's officers, Commander Walter Winslow, wrote that "I strained my eyes and finally made out two small dots on the far horizon. They grew larger every second until their ominous, pagoda-shaped superstructures became clearly visible." They were heavy cruisers, part of a force that consisted of one more cruiser, fourteen destroyers, and two convoys under the command of Admiral Takagi Takeo. Takagi gave the order to fire. Winslow wrote in his diary that "my heart pounds wildly as I realize the first salvo is on the way."

Doorman's ships roared back. A fire erupted on the bridge of one of the Japanese cruisers.

Yet Takagi had more ships, bigger guns, and a longer range than did the Allied fleet. A Japanese shell screamed into the *Exeter*, the British cruiser, exploding in the engine room and knocking the boilers out of action; the ship withdrew. A torpedo slammed into the Dutch destroyer *Kortenser*; folding in two, the ship vanished. Three Japanese destroyers surrounded their British counterpart, the *Electra*; it sank in a hail of shells.

Night fell but the darkness afforded the Allied ships no comfort. Dropping flares that made red streaks in the darkness, Japanese search planes marked out locations and Japanese ships closed in. Superpowered torpedoes sliced through the sea. The Dutch cruiser *Java* plunged to the bottom. At midnight, an explosion rocked Doorman's flagship, *DeRuyter*, and a pillar of fire leapt up into the sky. Then his ship went down. Along with 366 of his crew, Doorman drowned. Just before his death, he had sent open-coded signals in English, ordering *Perth* and *Houston*, the only remaining Allied destroyers, to make a run for Australia.

The next morning the *Perth* and the *Houston* tried to slip through the Sunda Strait, the narrow passage between the islands of Sumatra and Java. Without aerial intelligence or adequate radar, their officers had no idea that the Japanese had sealed off the passageway. So they were helpless when, suddenly, under the glare of the sun, three Japanese cruisers and nine destroyers materialized, pressing in upon them. Four torpedoes sank the *Perth*. Three more tore open a gash in the *Houston*'s hull. As the vessel listed, Commander Winslow found himself flung into the sea. "It seemed as though a breeze picked up the Stars and Stripes," he would write after being picked up by an Australian launch, "and waved them in one last defiant gesture."

With a shudder, the "Galloping Ghost of the Java Coast" was gone. The next day, March 1, ABDA ceased to exist: The Japanese had seized control of Java.

As they did so, the Dutch seaborne empire came to an end. And Japan had access to that most precious commodity, oil.

By January 23, 1942, Japanese ships already had captured Rabaul. An Australian naval base on the eastern tip of New Britain (an island just east of New Guinea), Rabaul possessed two usable harbors. From those bays the Japanese could dominate Dutch- and Australian-controlled parts of New Guinea and the Solomons, cutting the American line of communications with Australia. Rabaul lay on the easternmost edge of the great Allied shield that extended across the East Indies, along the Malay peninsula, and, finally, to that mountainous British colony through which ran the road to China—Burma.

2

Originating in the mountains along the border of China and running the full length of Burma, the Irrawaddy River as it descends becomes immensely wide and its waters reflect the blue of the sky, the green of the wilderness, and the glittering sand of its shores. On the eve of World War II, as now, villages straggled along those shores, their ramshackle bamboo huts half-hidden among the plantains that lined the banks. As the river passed through the plain of central Burma, in its mirror pagodas seemed to float amid the swaying of palm fronds. Water buffaloes lumbered through rice paddies. Sampans and junks proliferated. Then the river spread out into a delta. The main channel passed by outlying shacks, then middle-class suburbs, and finally the wharves and white becolumned official buildings of Rangoon.

One of the busiest ports on the Indian Ocean, Rangoon since the nineteenth century had been the capital and military headquarters of British Burma. Once Burma had seemed destined to remain a British colony forever. Like their counterparts in Singapore, British officials and merchants in Burma had sat on their verandas, lazing through the long, stifling midday hours and repairing to their clubs at night.

But at ten in the morning, two days before Christmas, 1941, the sound of air raid sirens shrieked through Rangoon. Soon after the warnings, about sixty Japanese bombers appeared overhead and blasted the docks and the airfield. More than 2,000 people who had

Devastation and carnage in the Shanghai International Settlement, August 14, 1937 (U.S. NAVAL HISTORICAL CENTER)

U.S.S. *Augusta* in the Shanghai Harbor, 1937
(U.S. NAVAL HISTORICAL CENTER)

Japanese bomber over
the *Panay*, December
12, 1937 (U.S. NAVAL
HISTORICAL CENTER)

Closeup of the *Panay*,
with the main deck
awash (U.S. NAVAL
HISTORICAL CENTER)

View of the *Panay* sinking in the Yangzi River
(U.S. NAVAL HISTORICAL CENTER)

Japanese miniature mock-up of Pearl Harbor
(U.S. Naval Historical Center)

The initial moments of the attack on Pearl Harbor
(U.S. Naval Historical Center)

President Franklin D. Roosevelt asking congress
for the declaration of war against Japan
(Franklin D. Roosevelt Presidential Library)

Japanese troops invading the Bataan Peninsula
(COURTESY OF DR. DISDADO M. YAP)

The Japanese landing on Corregidor
(MACARTHUR MEMORIAL)

The Bataan death march
(MACARTHUR MEMORIAL)

Doolittle's bombers en route to
Japan (UNITED STATES AIR FORCE)

flocked onto the streets were killed. Some had come to cheer: Long-simmering anti-British sentiments, stoked by an underground Burmese independence movement, suddenly had erupted.

Then the invasion began. On January 20, 1942, General Iida Sho-jiro's Fifteenth Army of about 35,000 men entered Burma east of Moulmein, where the Burmese panhandle runs southward along the border of Thailand; the Thais, never colonized by the Europeans and cordial to Japan, had allowed them passage. Headlong they spread northwestward into the British colony, slipping through the jungle in small groups. Their mobility was astonishing. Lightly clad and equipped, often riding bicycles or even elephants and carrying small-caliber weapons, they could avoid the major roads.

The British by contrast moved in trucks with heavy weapons and burdened themselves with boots and helmets. And their Burmese troops were not loyal. General Iida, devoted to the Japanese emperor, samurai code, and nation, also empathized with the Burmese and tried to prevent abuses by his troops. Pro-independence Burmese guerrillas accordingly guided the Japanese through the jungle right up to the British units.

By the third week of January, 1942, two Japanese divisions had passed through the eastern jungle to the rice fields and rubber planta-tions around Moulmein. Only ninety miles southeast of Rangoon, they were almost within sight of their final victory over Great Britain.

In response to the Japanese advance, Major General John Smyth on February 14 moved his troops from the Sittang to the more ford-able Bilin River, some thirty miles east of the Sittang, which lay about halfway between Moulmein and Rangoon. Only a week later, as he had feared, the Japanese overran his positions. He ordered a retreat back to the Sittang. Then disaster struck.

The only bridge across the Sittang was a single-lane railroad trestle. After rigging it for demolition, British engineers laid planks across the tracks so that Smyth's trucks could drive over. Before dawn on February 22, with their headlights out, the vehicles began to roll, headed for the west bank of the Sittang. Smyth, his staff, and part of one thinned-out brigade managed to get across, but at about four o'clock in the morning a truck slipped off the planks and lodged between railway ties. It could not be budged. All traffic came to a halt. Trucks, mules, and thousands of British and Indian troops were backed up for six miles along a narrow jungle trail. They were trapped.

At daybreak from both sides of the trail the Japanese emerged, firing, ducking back into the vegetation, and firing again. Smyth's column panicked. Many units broke and ran; some got lost in the jungle. Then came the airplanes, strafing at will. By nightfall, the Japanese had cut the column off from the bridge.

Over on the west bank of the Sittang the bridgehead commander, Brigadier Noel Hugh-Jones, had to make an agonizing choice. If he let the bridge stand, the Japanese would slip across it and march on Rangoon; if he blew it up, the British troops on the east bank would be doomed. He decided to trigger the dynamite.

Of the 8,500 troops who had gone east of that river, only 3,500 survived. The Japanese crossed anyway after laying pontoons, which Hugh-Jones had known nothing about.

On March 5, General Sir Harold Alexander, third son of an earl, commander of the British forces at Dunkirk and Burma's new military commander, reached Rangoon by air from Calcutta, replacing General Smyth. Seeing that a defense was impossible, on March 6 he ordered the firing of the storage tanks of the Burmah Oil Company. As he, Burma Governor Sir Reginald Dorman-Smith, an aide, and two journalists that same day made their way to a boat waiting in the harbor, they looked back upon Rangoon. According to the official report:

> [A] heavy pall of smoke hung over the town, but a light southerly wind kept the smoke off the foreshore. . . . The electric power station was ablaze; the port warehouses were blackening skeletons; . . . on the jetties the cranes, damaged by dynamite, leaned over at drunken angles. . . .

All along the normally thronged foreshore not a sign of human life was to be seen. . . . [I]t was almost dark and the flames, topped by columns of dense black smoke, rising thousands of feet into the air from the oil refineries, presented an awe-inspiring sight; and as the night fell the whole sky was lurid with the glare of that inferno.

In his last action in Rangoon, General Alexander ordered British forces to withdraw from the city and to retreat to the north; following them was a horde of refugees, fleeing up the valley of the Irrawaddy. The Japanese moved into a nearly empty Rangoon.

To stop a Japanese advance into India, the United States at this point sent air units to assist the British in defending the Raj. And General Joseph Stilwell went to India to organize efforts to keep China in the war.

3

Two days before the fall of Rangoon, General Stilwell and a staff of two dozen Army officers trained in the Chinese language reached New Delhi, the spacious, tree-lined city built in the 1920s as an imposing setting for the British Raj. Stilwell, who was to take command of the Chinese Fifth and Sixth armies, in northern Burma at the request of Wavell, attended a conference at the general headquarters. He barely contained his contempt for the British. The room was full of British "lieutenant generals and major generals and brigadiers, etc"; their numbers seemed out of all proportion to the mere three brigades left in Burma. He wrote in his diary that he "started asking questions and nobody but the quartermaster knew anything at all." The staff had no campaign plans, no intention of cooperating with the Chinese, and no intelligence from Burma. To Stilwell's amazement, the "British haven't taken a single prisoner yet."

A general made excuses. Stilwell then mocked the man's upper-class accent: "Well, it *might* just turn the scale. Miracles do happen in wah, don't they?" In his diary, Stilwell also recounted a comment made at a luncheon: "One does enjoy a cawktail, doesn't one? It's so seldom one gets a chawnce. In my own case, I hardly have time for a glahss of bee-ah!"

Stilwell, now a lieutenant general, and his team flew next to Calcutta, the teeming and squalid former British capital. On March 1 he dined in a gloomy old hall with General Wavell, who recently had arrived from the Indies.

With Wavell was an American, Major General Lewis Brereton of the Army Air Corps, who had served in the Philippines and now expected to head the Tenth Air Force based in India. Stilwell disliked Brereton immediately. A "shock to Brereton to learn he had anyone over him. Expected to be the Big Boy here [U.S. commander in chief]." Noticing that Brereton carried a riding crop, Stilwell muttered to an aide, "Why the hell does an Air Corps officer need a riding crop? To beat off the birds?"

On March 3, Stilwell and his entourage left Calcutta to continue their trek to China. The airplane rose above the dun-colored delta of the Ganges, passed over the green hills of Assam, then lifted up along the dark mountain ranges of Burma to Lashio, just below the Chinese border; it was the northern terminus of the Burma Road. There, in Porter House, a missionary edifice that hosted gatherings of foreigners, Stilwell met Chiang Kaishek; the *generalissimo* had flown down to inspect the scene.

China's Fifth and Sixth armies had fought well at first. But their foreign-supplied weapons were unfamiliar and their communications poor. Chiang had come to lift their morale.

Looking thoroughly military in a high-buttoned khaki uniform, Chiang ascended the upper porch of Porter House and gave a pep talk to his officers, assembled in the courtyard below. "[S]harp, clipped staccato voice of Chiang Kaishek [above]," Stilwell observed; "hushed quiet below." Chiang that afternoon flew back to China, giving his troops no further encouragement.

After his airplane refueled, Stilwell also flew over the twists and turns of the Burma Road into China. Landing at Kunming, he stayed overnight with General Claire Chennault, the American air commander in China. Many of the pilots Chennault had recruited before Pearl Harbor had formed the American Volunteer Group (nicknamed the "Flying Tigers") and had flown brilliantly against Japanese positions in China. After a cordial visit, Stilwell flew on to China's wartime capital.

The flight was rough—"Chinese passengers all puking"—but it lasted only two hours. Approaching Chongqing, the airplane descended to a landing strip at the edge of the Yangzi River. The runway was a sandbar paved with stone, and on both sides of the sandbar the river rushed by, carrying the silt of Inner Asia through the gorges below and to the ocean beyond. A footbridge led across an eddy of the river to the foot of a gray cliff, and there, high above the cliff, ran the city wall of old Chongqing. Stilwell, who had been there before, took "the same old tough climb" up 365 slippery stone steps. "Chongqing," Stilwell penned, "isn't half bad when the sun shines." It rarely shined.

The attitude toward Chiang Kaishek on the part of Americans in Chongqing seemed to range from "an intense dislike, even hatred" to being merely "fed up" with Chiang's unwillingness to fight. Carrying a "heavy mental burden," Stilwell on March 6 reported to the *generalissimo*: The American general was nominally subordinate to the Chinese leader.

Wanting to be sure of American aid, however, Chiang made Stilwell commander in chief over the Chinese forces.

Now officially in charge, although the divisions he commanded were not American, Stilwell and his staff soon developed a plan for dealing with Burma. With a swift northward drive, the Japanese had almost encircled a Chinese division in the center of the country. In doing so, however, they had exposed their flank. Stilwell saw an opportunity for a counterattack. To carry it off, he wanted to concentrate Chinese forces at a point on the rail line sixty miles above the front. From there they would try to rescue their enveloped comrades. Then they might be able to recapture Rangoon.

The plan depended on two things: the ability of the British to move from India back into Burma and the willingness of the Chinese to move into battle. On March 11, Stilwell flew back to northern Burma to oversee the operation.

4

He set up his field headquarters at Maymyo, the old summer capital with lawns and gardens laid out in the English manner. Stilwell moved into a red-brick mission compound overhung with bougainvilleas and planted with roses and honeysuckle. Up on a nearby hillside, Governor Dorman-Smith (whom Stilwell soon dubbed "Doormat-Smith") already had moved into Flagstaff House, a Victorian pile where guests still could sip beer from silver mugs. General Alexander flew in from India on Friday the thirteenth. "Very cautious," Stilwell observed: "Long sharp nose. . . . Astonished to find ME—mere me, a goddamn American—in command of Chinese troops. 'Extrawdinery!' Looked me over as if I had just crawled out from under a rock."

But the British were genuinely puzzled. Up at Flagstaff House, General Du Ling presented himself as commander of the Chinese armies. Governor Dorman-Smith asked how two men could hold the same position.

"Your Excellency," Du replied, "the American general only thinks he is commanding. In fact he is doing no such thing. You see, we Chinese think that the only way to keep the Americans in the war is to give them a few commands on paper. [That way] they will not do much harm."

Learning what Du had said, Stilwell realized that his mission in China was going to be frustrating. Roosevelt and Marshall had sent him out to safeguard China as a base from which the United States eventually could bomb Japan; in trying to regain Burma, Stilwell was seeking to ensure supplies for such attacks. To Chiang Kaishek, however, Stilwell was an alien intruder (a "foreign devil," as the Chinese said) whose brusque, sarcastic presence threatened to make the *generalissimo* lose face. Chiang wanted to win the war but he also wished to preserve his power. Since his generals were interested primarily in enriching themselves from American aid and not in risking their lives against the Japanese, Chiang's was a policy of doing nothing.

On March 22, with his British allies also demoralized and his Chinese allies privately prepared to let the Americans do the fighting, Stilwell ordered the execution of his plan. And nothing happened.

Or rather something *did* happen. With astonishing speed, the Japanese in the first week of April moved the 200 miles from Rangoon to Toungoo, the railhead Stilwell had chosen for his offensive. They were heading northward toward Mandalay, only fifty miles southwest of Maymyo.

The edge of the war moved from Toungoo along the Sittang and Irrawaddy Rivers. The air raids came first. Villages went up in flames. Long columns of oxcarts, women, children, and spindle-legged old men filled the roads. Then the Japanese airplanes strafed those columns and the jungle provided little room for escape. Cholera also struck. Corpses as thin as skeletons lay by the roadsides. Survivors pushed on past, intent on their destination.

Jack Belden, an American journalist, described the scene in Mandalay just before the Japanese attacked. Throngs of men and women still

> glittered beneath the noon-day tropic sun. The silk and cotton shirts of . . . passersby swirled and flashed in brilliant hues of red, green, and yellow, intermingled with purple, white, and blue. Blobs of color moved up and down, pausing here and there before some Western-style shop window or in front of hawk-nosed Indians in the sidewalk bazaars. The rumble of trolley cars, the clack-clack of

ponies pulling carts, and the Donald Duck honk of old-fashioned rubber automobile horns sounded through the wide-paved streets. Oxen, bicycles, and foot-propelled one-seater carriages all passed back and forth, giving an air of busy motion to this metropolis on the Irrawaddy River. . . . In back of the town a small eminence covered with red temples [and] white pagodas . . . coruscated beneath the sun. In the heart of the city, people walked leisurely by a moat filled with lilies shining on a green and white circle about the red-washed stone walls of the palace. . . . Everywhere was beauty, charm, richness. . . . [B]rilliant color, gilded temples, bazaars heavy with commerce and the vocal sound of bargaining—shone forth from Mandalay the morning of April 4, 1942.

Then, in a surprise attack, the Japanese bombers came.

The carnage was horrific. An ox stood by the side of a moat wounded in the neck, slowly nodding as blood oozed across his white chest, dropping onto the ground. A man in a bicycle carriage seat sat with his feet up in the air, killed in the act of getting out. Another man sat on the ground with an umbrella over his shoulder; his mouth was open, as if when killed he had been trying to say something.

Bombs also struck train cars loaded with oil. The wind spread the flames through the city and the blaze lasted all night. At dawn, people could see oil derricks outside the city wrapped in ribbons of black smoke that seemed to curl out of the ground.

By noon the Japanese infantry had arrived and the city was in their control. Maymyo was next.

For a while in Maymyo, all seemed normal. General Alexander, immaculate in a trim bush shirt and crisp khaki shorts, rode about in a limousine, attending meetings. Stilwell, wearing a khaki shirt and an old pair of trousers, however, stayed at headquarters, studying his maps. He was casting about for a way to stop the Japanese.

But the Japanese drive was inexorable. In the center of the town an hour's worth of incendiary bombing started fires. Soldiers and civilians alike rushed to escape. Stilwell himself realized that he had to retreat. With his British allies heading for the hills and his Chinese units fleeing in mutiny, Stilwell's one concern now was to save his American officers.

But how? By the end of April, the airfield outside Maymyo lay destroyed and a collision had rendered the single-track rail line useless. No highway led out of Burma. As his diary entry for May 1, Stilwell wrote one word: "HELL."

He could wait to be captured by the Japanese or he could walk out of Burma through the jungle. He walked.

5

With the Japanese net closing fast, Stilwell saw only one way of escape: across two hundred miles of some of the thickest jungle, wildest rivers, and steepest mountains in Burma to the border of India. So on the night of May 4, under trees surrounding a temple, he assembled his crew of about 100 persons—American officers, Burmese nurses, Chinese bodyguards, and Indian bearers—and told them that they were going to walk to India. He could make them no promises. Refugees would be on the same route and the Japanese might catch up. The monsoon was about to start. Streams and rivers might be impassable. Rations were nearly gone and the crew might have to live off the land. But if they could reach Homalin, a village high in Burma on the Chindwin River, and then cross that river, they would be in India. A hundred miles farther still, they would be safe.

Before ordering his heavy radio transmitter smashed with hammers, Stilwell beamed a communication westward: "We abandon all transportation. . . . We are running low on food with none in sight. Alert British in India to send food and bearers to Homalin. It is urgent repeat urgent to stock trails with food and medicines as soon as possible. Urgent or thousands will die. . . . This is our last message repeat our last message. Stilwell."

The general did not exaggerate. Roughly a million refugees, sick and starving, were seeking to escape out through the jungle but they had no food. Neither had they water: Retreating Burmese troops had poisoned the wells. They also had burned the ferries. Some of the refugees followed Stilwell's trail that swung to the northwest, others wandered far north over ancient caravan trails and became lost in the mountains. Malaria, cholera, and smallpox took their toll. Corpses of all ages littered the paths. Later estimates put the deaths in the hundreds of thousands.

Stilwell's primary objective was a mountain pass 7,000 feet high and 140 miles away. Along the way the marchers would have to cut through jungle and traverse rivers, making fourteen miles a day. Any slacking off would mean no rations. So from the moment of departure, Stilwell, in superb physical condition, set a fast pace and did not stop.

At half past three in the morning of May 7, about sixty miles out of Maymyo, Stilwell was up and shouting, "Rise and shine!" Slowly, Belden wrote, "everyone rose. Indian cooks started the breakfast bonfire. . . . Over the flames Pinky Dorn, an aide to the general, burned codes. . . . We lined up for breakfast. . . . Plates were washed in a gasoline tin of water; canteens were filled with boiled water. Those who didn't get any used cold well-water, placing a few iodine drops in it to decontaminate it. The lanterns of the muleteers shone on the horse hair covering their mule packs. To those they strapped baggage, the larger of the bedding rolls, and the heavier boxes of food. There were not enough carriers, and some baggage was left over, so that Frank Merrill [a West Point major and formerly a Japanese-language officer] had to shoulder his own large pack. Many of the others were carrying two water bottles, rifles, rucksacks."

Wearing laced boots, khaki trousers, a khaki shirt with the sleeves rolled up to the elbows, a World War I–vintage Boy Scout–type hat, and with a tommy gun slung over his shoulder, the bespectacled Stilwell commanded, "Forward march!" Only the guide preceded him.

General Franklin Sibert, another aide, put a police whistle to his lips and blew a shrill blast. "Fall in," he shouted. Dr. Gordon Seagrave, an American missionary surgeon who had been at Maymyo, got the civilians going.

Stilwell's column soon reached a small river and there the trail disappeared. Without hesitation Stilwell strode into the water and led his followers downstream. Under the hot sunshine and at the general's furious pace the people behind began to collapse. Stilwell wrote in his diary: "Easy pace down the river. . . . Merrill out; heat exhaustion. . . . George Sliney pooped. Nowakowski same. Christ, but we are a poor lot. . . . All packs reduced to ten pounds."

Stilwell refused to stop. British Quakers who had appeared from India in response to Stilwell's message hoisted the fallen onto inflated life rafts, pulling them downstream as fast as possible. They barely could keep up with Stilwell.

A week into the trek and lean with hunger, the marchers sloshed onward. Occasionally, they clambered onto the riverbank, seeking refuge from the sun. Regiments of ants crawled up their legs during these brief rests.

Although Stilwell was about to turn sixty years old, he pushed onward without mercy. His diary showed his intolerance for slackers: "Our people tired. Damn poor show of physique."

Clouds materialized over the jungle and rains descended, turning the trail to muck and signaling the coming of the monsoon. There was also disease: fever, dysentery, malaria.

At one point, members of the party peered through the thickets and a little way off the path saw the big gray hindquarters of an elephant. His head was half-turned and his trunk was pulling at the branches of a tree. The animal stepped into the path and the people backed away. Stilwell ordered his soldiers to hold their rifles at ready, but the elephant merely crossed the trail without even looking at the marchers.

On the evening of May 14, the column reached Homalin, really just a cluster of huts at the edge of the Chindwin River. Members of the party hastily cut wood to make rafts and poles. The first raft with

Stilwell aboard crossed the river at 10:30 P.M. "Nice ride," the general wrote, "but too damn slow." By dawn all were in India. A British officer greeted them on the opposite bank. "Food, doctor, ponies, and everything," Stilwell wrote. "Quite a relief."

But his goal was Imphal, a British military post about fifty miles away. So he put on the pressure again, driving his party as hard as ever up the mountain slope, just inside India.

On May 19, 1942, British officers in their post at Imphal looked out to see a ragtag column of gaunt men and women come marching out of the mountains; the rain was steady. At the head of the column walked a wiry little man with a battered campaign hat. One of the Britons welcomed Stilwell and asked how many people he had lost.

"Not a one," Stilwell answered. "Not a one."

A few days later in New Delhi, Stilwell held a press conference. News of the march had reached the outside world and to many Stilwell was quite the hero. With his usual bluntness, however, he rejected any hint of heroism.

"I claim we got a hell of a beating," he said. "We got run out of Burma and it is humiliating as hell."

9

BUT NOT IN SHAME

1

Barely two weeks earlier, United States forces in the Philippines had suffered far more than humiliation. Corregidor, General MacArthur's headquarters, had surrendered.

Dominating the entrance to Manila Bay and looming like a half-surfaced sea monster whose head scowled out upon the South China Sea, Corregidor was forbidding. Formed by jagged volcanic cliffs that rose straight out of the water to a height of more than 600 feet, from forehead to tail-tip the island measured three and a half miles long. The big end of the island was a mile across. Atop that broad brow, the Stars and Stripes flew over a little white Spanish chapel and huge naval guns menaced any hostile approach from any direction.

Like Singapore, Corregidor was supposed to be invulnerable. But also like Singapore, it had one vulnerability. Its wide, flat beaches were ideal for landing enemy troops.

As commander in chief of the combined Filipino-American colonial army, General Douglas MacArthur had been able to field almost three times as many troops as the Japanese. But his ranks had included 100,000 young Filipinos who were ill-trained, poorly equipped, and indifferently led by native officers. In the immediate prewar months, to be sure, the general had tried to turn the troops into a fighting force, to organize the archipelago into an effective fortress. But poor communications among the twenty-five major islands had made his progress slow. Washington, furthermore, had not sent MacArthur the artillery, planes, and ships he had demanded. Even after the bombing of Pearl Harbor, Army Chief of Staff Marshall, despite his promises, could do little to help.

To make things even more difficult for MacArthur and his staff, the American community in the Philippines had been complacent, treating the islands as if they were the American equivalent of the Indian raj. Even clerks and missionaries had been able to afford servants. Life had been easy. The riding and the golfing had been excellent. Short workdays had been followed by long siestas, then by evenings in the Manila Army and Navy Club, where dance bands had played and the wine had flowed freely.

So when the Japanese invaded the Philippines the defenders were unprepared. Even with excellent fortifications, however, MacArthur and his forces would have had a difficult time. The coastline of Luzon and the other islands were long and indented with innumerable bays and river mouths through which invaders could proceed. Rather than waste resources trying to secure all of Luzon, MacArthur ordered a retreat to Bataan.

2

One of the two biggest of the Philippine islands, Luzon was shaped like a tadpole, with a large head jutting toward the north and a tail that trailed off to the southeast. Facing westward across its bay, Manila lay where the head merged with the tail; across the bay was the heavily forested Bataan peninsula, twenty miles across at the top and twenty-five miles deep. Mariveles, an American base, lay at the very south of the peninsula.

To hold Bataan, MacArthur positioned one corps, under General George Parker, on the swampy eastern shore. Another corps, under General Jonathan M. Wainwright, occupied the steep, overgrown western coast. Between these two positions rose the snarled, wooded, 4,000-foot-high slopes of Mount Natib, whose depth and steepness prevented the two corps from remaining in effective contact.

On January 19, an artillery barrage that shook the northern end of the peninsula announced the start of the Japanese offensive under General Homma Masaharu. Two days later in the early evening, a time when the Japanese often attacked, troops yelling *"Banzai"* ("May the Emperor Live 10,000 Years") charged the barbed wire that protected Parker's location. The first of the Japanese soldiers hurled themselves upon the wire, dying in machine gun fire. But those in the second wave climbed over the backs of the corpses and jumped across and down on top of the defenders.

Two Japanese amphibious attempts to land regiments behind American lines failed. On January 27, however, Homma's troops launched a massive attack on the main battle line.

The fighting ranged from one side of the upper peninsula to the other for the next two weeks. But the defenders lacked adequate air cover. The B-17s had flown to Australia and only a few fighter planes had remained. By the end of the two weeks the Japanese enjoyed complete control of the air. The Singapore debacle was beginning to repeat itself.

Two of General Homma's crack regiments then slipped around Mount Natib and attacked both Parker's and Wainwright's forces from the rear. With their supplies threatened, MacArthur ordered a new retreat, this time halfway down Bataan.

The retreat was pell-mell. The Filipino and American troops were short of food, ammunition, and medicine. The lack of quinine was disastrous. During the retreat soldiers by the thousands came down with the chills and fevers of malaria. Many died.

And the Japanese kept coming. They succeeded in staging an amphibious landing on a narrow spit of land on Bataan's southwestern corner. The defenders were few and the Japanese were able to infiltrate themselves behind the enemy lines.

By the second week of February, General Homma realized that he was on the brink of victory. He radioed Tokyo for new reinforcements and they rushed to the Philippines.

3

MacArthur's own request for reinforcements brought a different response from Washington. Late in the morning of February 23, 1942, in his underground command post at Corregidor, he received a radio order directly from President Roosevelt. MacArthur was to make his way to Mindanao and then proceed to Melbourne. In Australia, FDR indicated, "you will assume command of all United States troops." Perhaps fearing for his reputation as a war hero, MacArthur was reluctant to comply.

A reporter who observed MacArthur at the time thought him "drained of the confidence he had always shown." And no wonder. After locating his wife, Jean, in a lateral of the Malinta Tunnel, he called a staff meeting and read Roosevelt's order. He lamented his predicament. If he refused to go to Australia, he would make himself liable to a court-martial. If he did obey, he would leave his troops abandoned. So he expressed the idea that he should resign, go to Bataan, and fight as a "simple volunteer."

On March 6, however, FDR cabled: "The situation in Australia indicates the desirability of your early arrival there." MacArthur took this to mean that a great American force had gathered down under.

On March 9, after Roosevelt repeated his instruction, MacArthur capitulated. "Jonathan," he said to General Wainwright, who had come down from Bataan, "I want you to understand my position very plainly. I'm leaving for Australia pursuant to repeated orders of the president."

Preparations were made for MacArthur to leave. During the night of March 11, MacArthur and his party—twenty-two in all, including his wife, their small son, Arthur, and Ah Cheu, the nursemaid—would leave Manila Bay on four of the six surviving PT boats. The MacArthur family itself would depart in one of those boats from Cor-regidor; the others would embark at Sisiman Cove and Mariveles, a village by the bay on Bataan. Slipping through the minefields across the mouth of the bay, they would rendezvous in the South China Sea; shortly after dawn they would reach Tagauayan, a deserted islet in the unoccupied Cuyo Islands, about halfway to Mindanao. There they would spend the daylight hours in an inlet. The second night would take them to Mindanao, which was not yet overrun by the Japanese. From the Del Monte airfield, close to the island's northern coast, they would fly by B-17s to Darwin in Australia.

So at dusk on March 11, Lieutenant John D. Bulkeley, a West Point graduate and the swashbuckling, bearded commander of the PT boat flotilla, steered PT-41 out of its hiding place in Sisiman Cove. The crew members thought they were heading for China. To their sur-prise, Bulkeley pulled up to the much-shelled dock at Corregidor. Drums of gasoline lined the edge of the pier. Wainwright was there, supervising a crew that would load them into the boat. He also was waiting to bid MacArthur good-bye.

Just before nightfall, MacArthur's limousine drove up to the dock, its license plate bearing his four-star insignia and, in compliance with the blackout, the top halves of its headlights painted dark. Bulkeley had limited each passenger to no more than thirty-five pounds of bag-gage. So wearing a pantsuit, Jean MacArthur stepped out of the car with one small suitcase. Little Arthur clutched a toy rabbit. Ah Cheu carried all her belongings in a knotted bandanna. MacArthur, dressed in civilian shoes and socks, a worn-out khaki uniform, and a gold-braided cap, carried nothing at all. As his family and a cluster of staff officers climbed down into the boat, he said farewell to Wainwright.

"If I get through to Australia, you know I'll come back as soon as I can with as much as I can," MacArthur said. "In the meantime, you've got to hold." He put Wainwright in charge of the troops still on Bataan. Night fell.

MacArthur looked up. Air intelligence had reported two Japanese warships heading for Manila Bay; as a diversion, the muzzles of the big guns on the cliffs above flashed red, the earth shook, and the odor of gunpowder filled the air. Then the general joined his family in PT-41 and told Bulkeley to cast off.

PT boats then were low and narrow, designed for one purpose—speedy attacks with torpedoes and machine guns. In Commander Bulkeley's words, they were designed "to roar in, let fly a Sunday punch, and then get the hell out, zigging to dodge the shells." But their speed meant that they could carry no weighty armor; if detected and chased down by a destroyer they would be helpless. And Commander Bulkeley's four PT boats were slowed down because with spare parts and mechanics in short supply, their carburetors were choked with carbon. MacArthur's escape was a gamble.

Under the cover of a moonless night, the four boats did rendezvous. But the sea was turbulent. Aboard PT-41, all half-dozen passengers except two became seasick. MacArthur himself was in agony. The boats also became separated. One of them, PT-32, developed engine trouble and headed for Panay Island, midway down the western side of the archipelago and still in American hands, for repairs. PT-41 was running behind schedule; at daybreak Bulkeley's boat still had not reached Tagauayan. Along with PT-34, it put in at a closer island in the Cuyo group. The fourth boat, PT-35, was nowhere in sight.

MacArthur agonized. If they stayed long at this island, little more than an atoll, they risked detection. But to bolt across the sea for Cagayan on the northern coast of Mindanao in daylight seemed suicidal. Yet there was another consideration: At the Del Monte field near Cagayan, Flying Fortresses were supposed to be waiting. If MacArthur failed to reach them by dawn the next day, however, or so he understood, the planes would depart for Australia. At 2:30 in the afternoon, MacArthur's party took off again.

With the passengers from PT-32 divided among them, 41 and 34 cut through the waves. Off Panay Bulkeley yelled a warning and grabbed his binoculars. Ahead, in the circle of the lens, loomed the pagodalike superstructure of a Japanese cruiser. The boats were heading straight for the warship. Since it had a speed that was roughly twice theirs, they seemed doomed.

But the ocean became even rougher than before. "I think it was the whitecaps that saved us," Bulkeley said later. "The Japs didn't notice our wake, even though we were foaming away at full throttle."

Off Negros, the major island just south of Panay and under Japanese occupation, the skippers in the night realized that coastal observers had heard their engines. Spotlights were searching the sky. The PT boats put farther out to sea.

That action, however, took time. When the sun rose again, the boats were still three hours short of Cagayan. With the sun blazing overhead, everyone aboard, ill or not, watched for Japanese ships or airplanes.

None appeared. The two boats entered the Cagayan harbor unscathed. American infantrymen stood at attention on the quay.

After PT-41 had docked, MacArthur helped his wife and son ashore; the others followed. Turning to Bulkeley, the general said, "I'm giving every officer and man here the Silver Star for gallantry. You've taken me out of the jaws of death, and I won't forget it."

PT-35 showed up, but MacArthur's relief soon turned to fear. At the Del Monte airfield, he learned, there were no Flying Fortresses.

MacArthur was incredulous. From Australia the Army Air Corps had sent three old crates, small aircraft that somehow had survived the Battle of the Java Sea. En route to Mindanao, one of them had crashed into the ocean. A second, experiencing engine trouble, had turned back to Darwin. A third now was unfit to fly. And, intelligence reported, the Japanese had landed on Mindanao. They were closing down on the airfield.

Furious, MacArthur fired off a cable to Army Air Corps General George H. Brett in Australia, demanding air transport. (MacArthur, who was claustrophobic, hated submarines.) Brett sent up an old Flying Fortress, which was all he had. When it arrived, it lurched down upon the airstrip and wobbled as it stopped.

"To attempt such a desperate and important trip with inadequate equipment would amount to consigning the whole party to death and I could not undertake such a responsibility," MacArthur radioed to General Marshall. He insisted on airworthy planes and crews that were "completely adequate, experienced."

Within a day of the PT boats landing at Cagayan, three new Flying Fortresses were on the way.

For three and a half days, MacArthur and his party had to stay in Cagayan. When on the last day they heard the buzz of approaching Japanese airplanes, they hid in shacks.

From Cagayan, MacArthur wrote in a letter to Manuel Quezon, the Filipino president who was heading southward aboard a B-17 from Del Monte, en route to establish a provisional Philippine government-in-exile in Washington: "[A]n entirely new situation has developed. The United States is moving its forces into the southern Pacific area in which is destined to be a great offensive against Japan. The troops are being concentrated in Australia which will be used as a base for the offensive drive to the Philippines. President Roosevelt has designated me to command this offensive and has directed me to proceed to Australia for that purpose. He believes this is the best way to ensure the success of the movement. I was naturally loath to leave Corregidor but the Washington authorities insisted, implying that if I did not personally assume command the effort could not be made. As a matter of fact, I had no choice in the matter, being peremptorily ordered by President Roosevelt himself. I understand the forces are rapidly being accumulated and hope that the drive can be undertaken before the Bataan–Corregidor situation reaches a climax."

On the evening of March 16, two Flying Fortresses landed at the Del Monte airfield. MacArthur's party could barely squeeze into the bombers; they had to leave all luggage behind. With his family wedged into the rear of the lead plane, MacArthur took the radio operator's seat behind the pilot, where he could see out the windshield. Ahead of him in the darkness, a single red flare marked the end of the runway and the beginning of the ocean. The pilot started the engines and the bomber lumbered forward. One motor, though, sputtered and missed badly; many of the B-17s were unreliable. As the aircraft approached the red flare, one of the crew yelled: "Our lives aren't worth a nickel!"

But suddenly the faltering engine caught and the plane was airborne. Soon the bomber behind it also was off the ground.

Between Del Monte and Australia, 1,500 miles away, however, lay the Indies, Timor, and western New Guinea, islands of the new Japanese empire. At dawn on March 17, Japanese fighters rose from Timor to intercept the Flying Fortresses. The bombers evaded their pursuers. Then came a radio warning: Darwin in northernmost Australia was under attack and the American planes would have to fly in at an emergency field fifty miles away.

They landed without further incident. As the exhausted party staggered down the steps of the waiting ramp, MacArthur spotted an American officer standing nearby. The general called the man over and asked about the U.S. military buildup.

The officer was puzzled. "As far as I know, sir," he said, "there are very few troops here."

Turning to General Richard Sullivan, one of his party, MacArthur said, "Surely he is wrong."

Boarding an Air Corps C-47, the party flew to Alice Springs in central Australia. There they rode to the train station for the trip to Melbourne.

Reporters gathered on the platform asked MacArthur for a statement and he responded: "The president of the United States ordered me to break through the Japanese lines and proceed from Corregidor to Australia for the purpose, as I understand it, of organizing the American offensive against Japan, a primary object of which is the relief of the Philippines. I came through and I shall return."

A huge crowd was on hand to extend its welcome when MacArthur's train puffed into Melbourne's Spencer Street station. As the train stopped, MacArthur, always the showman, was lounging in a chair on the rear platform. In his ribbonless khaki jacket and gold-braided cap, he looked, in the words of an American reporter, "like business."

But there was no business to conduct. Upon reaching Australia, MacArthur had thought he would find a full-fledged army, navy, and air force. In all Australia there was not even one combat division. Of the roughly 250 military airplanes, only a few could fly. And the American Asiatic Fleet consisted merely of six cruisers and twenty-five submarines, most of which needed serious repairs. When he learned these facts from the Australians, according to a confidant, MacArthur "turned deadly white, his knees buckled, his lips twitched. After a long silence, MacArthur whispered miserably, 'God have mercy on us.'"

4

As MacArthur reached Australia, the Japanese on Bataan withdrew to the peninsula's neck; many were sick and hungry. But even with the pause, a thousand defending troops a day were collapsing with malaria. Rations were down to ten ounces of tinned food per diem plus perhaps an ounce of fish or canned meat. In the south of the Philippines, on Panay, Negros, and Mindanao, furthermore, the Japanese were seizing all port facilities; since the emperor's warships were blockading every sea lane up from the Indies, only three American supply ships got through to Bataan.

The Japanese on Bataan, though, *did* get help: sixty bombers, 150 pieces of artillery, and 21,000 fresh troops. General Homma chose April 3, 1942, to resume the assault. The day bore special significance for both sides of the battle line. For the Japanese it was the anniversary of the death of Emperor Jimmu, son of heaven, god of the sun, and founder of the Japanese imperial line; for the Americans it was Good Friday.

On the morning of April 3, General Nara Akira, a graduate of the Japanese Military Academy, who had arrived the month before, took command of the Japanese Fourth Division on the eastern side of the peninsula. Before him a natural corridor, flanked by two rivers, led to the Filipino and American lines of barbed wire, trenches, foxholes, dugouts, and wooden barricades, laboriously constructed across the lower peninsula to block a Japanese advance. At eight in the morning, General Nara ordered the destruction of those lines. Artillery roared, bombers swooped, and by the end of five hours the line was no more than a heap of junk. At that point the Japanese ground advance got under way.

As infantry, armored cars, and tanks pushed down the corridor, the Filipinos and the Americans fled in terror to the south. The following day the Japanese bombed the next line of defense and turned it into twisted wreckage. On the next day still, the Japanese attained the heights of the 2,000-foot Mount Samat in southern Bataan. Bringing up the rear, General Nara now had a full view of the battlefield; he even could see Manila Bay, where General Parker's troops huddled at the very edge of the water.

On Monday, April 6, Major General Edward King, who had replaced Wainwright (now in command on Corregidor) on the peninsula's western side, tried to counterattack. Hungry, exhausted, and almost out of ammunition, his troops simply could not fight. And as thousands of them fled to the end of the peninsula, bullets from Japanese fighters rained without mercy upon the trails. Hundreds died and the survivors clustered around the small port of Cabcaben, on Bataan's southeastern tip.

Off the eastern shore on the night of April 6–7, the *Mindanao* and the *Oahu*, sister gunboats of the *Panay*, pulled up to the beach at Cabcaben; their skippers hoped to rescue stranded soldiers. Suddenly, however, eleven Japanese vessels appeared. The night lit up with bursting shells, machine gun tracers, and a veritable Fourth of July barrage of skyrockets. Outnumbered, the gunboats withdrew to Corregidor.

Before dawn on April 8, 2,000-some soldiers and nurses paddled boats and barges to Corregidor. That same day, Wainwright passed along to King a radioed order from MacArthur to mount a new attack. King refused to obey.

A quiet, studious-looking man, King was taking matters into his own hands. At "6 O'CLOCK THIS MORNING, GENERAL KING ... WITHOUT MY KNOWLEDGE OR APPROVAL SENT A FLAG OF TRUCE TO JAPANESE COMMANDER," Wainwright cabled MacArthur on April 9. "THE MINUTE I HEARD OF IT I DISAP-PROVED OF HIS ACTION AND DIRECTED THAT THERE WOULD BE NO SURRENDER. I WAS INFORMED IT WAS TOO LATE TO MAKE ANY CHANGE, THAT THE ACTION HAD AL-READY BEEN TAKEN. ENEMY ON EAST HAD ENVELOPED BOTH FLANKS OF THE SMALL GROUPS OF WHAT WAS LEFT OF THE SECOND CORPS AND WAS FIRING INTO THE HOSPI-TAL AREA WHICH UNDOUBTEDLY PROMPTED KING'S AC-TION. IN ORDER TO RELIEVE PRESSURE ON THE RIGHT, LAST NIGHT I ORDERED THE FIRST CORPS TO ATTACK TO THE NORTH ... BUT THE ATTACK DID NOT GET OFF...."

The surrender took place on April 9, on the southern tip of Bataan. A photograph taken at that moment showed General King, lean, craggy-faced, balding slightly at the temples, and wearing trousers, a long-sleeved khaki shirt, and his two major general's stars on his epaulettes, making arrangements with Colonel Nakayama Moto. The Japanese colonel was wearing a plain white tee shirt. The two men, flanked by aides and a translator, were seated in wooden armchairs on opposite sides of a low table covered with maps.

Pointing to the maps, Nakayama demanded to know the location of the remaining American tanks and howitzers.

"We have none," King stated.

Nakayama then asked, "How many troops are there on Corregi-dor?"

"I don't know," King replied.

Holding up one of the maps, Nakayama said, "General King, show me here where the tunnel leads from Mariveles to Corregidor."

"There is no such tunnel."

"There must be a tunnel," Nakayama insisted.

King reiterated his statement.

Nakayama then asked, "Where is the cavern and tunnels where are stored all the large reserves of artillery?"

King denied the existence of such a cavern.

Nakayama exploded. "There *are* such caverns!" On the map he gestured to the Manila Bay side of Mariveles. "There are caverns here where artillery is stored! Do not lie! You must have much artillery! It has been destroyed many times and you bring out additional artillery!"

Walking away, Nakayama shouted for guards to lock up King and his party in a nearby hut. General King was now a prisoner of war. He would remain in captivity until the Japanese surrender. The Japanese did discover a cave used for storing munitions, but no underwater tunnel existed.

Some hours later officers aboard the gunboat *Mindanao* surveying the southern Bataan coastline saw people on shore waving hundreds of flashlights. Filipino and American troops were waiting on the beach, frantic to be rescued. The gunboat had room for about sixty, and no more. About 2,000 of those left on the sand set out for Corregidor. They paddled life rafts or rowed small boats; some even swam. Roughly half of them made it.

Trapped along the southern reaches of the peninsula, however, were 75,000 other troops under General Parker. The Japanese soon captured them. Then began the Bataan Death March.

The march got under way on the morning of April 9 on the parade ground of the camp at Mariveles. The Japanese forced their Filipino and American prisoners, some of them nurses, to stand in long rows for equipment shakedowns. Diminutive Japanese soldiers searched tall Americans, sometimes as many as ten times each. Often a Japanese finished off his search with a rifle butt to the mouth, a kick to the shin, or a knee to the groin. Sometimes the treatment was even worse. Frisking an American captain, a Japanese private discovered some yen notes in a shirt pocket. Without a word, an eyewitness would recall, "he grabbed the captain by the shoulder and shoved him to his knees. He quickly pulled his sword out of its scabbard and raised it high over his head, holding it with both hands. There was a swishing and a kind of chopping sound. The captain's head seemed to jump off his shoulders, hitting the ground in front of him and rolling crazily between lines of horror-struck prisoners."

By this time the sun was blazing like a ball of fire over the treeless Mariveles. Few of the prisoners had hats and those the Japanese removed. This was the sun treatment, a mode of torture at which the Japanese were practiced. As the sun ascended to its noontime high, the guards forced their prisoners to stand at rigid attention. They allowed just enough water to cool the tongue and bring on real thirst. Americans and Filipinos alike became delirious. Shouting and thrashing about while still standing, many collapsed, drifted into comas, and died.

Not until sundown did the Japanese allow their captives to move. Using the tips of their bayonets as prods, they forced the prisoners to walk. The destination was the once American and now Japanese-controlled Camp O'Donnell, sixty-five miles up jungle trails and beyond the Bataan peninsula.

In the night, the procession of thousands passed through a burned-out village; its ruins still gave off an acrid stench. Off to the left in the light of the moon rose the foothills of Mount Natib.

At midnight, the column reached Orani and was shoved into a rice paddy surrounded by barbed wire. A raised pathway along the paddy led to an open latrine slick with feces and crawling with maggots.

At dawn the prisoners received rice mush that tasted like library paste. Then the march resumed. The sun again was brutal. As they passed through villages, the prisoners called out for water. But when Filipino civilians offered cans of water from local wells, Japanese guards knocked the contents onto the pathway. More men collapsed.

John Toland, the writer who interviewed survivors, stated that the "roadside began to be dotted with the dead. They soon became swollen to monstrous size by the heat. Crows tore open these cadavers with their beaks, often fighting each other for the nauseating meat while buzzing hordes of fat, green flies covered the remnants. Most of these men had died of disease, hunger, or exhaustion. Some had been murdered."

An American fell on some stones and cut his face. A Japanese rushed up, "[kicking] him in the ribs to make him get up. The American slowly rose on all fours, then dropped exhausted. The guard kicked harder. The prisoner—blood dripping from his mouth, face covered with bruises—again tried to get up. He extended his right hand to the Japanese in a pleading gesture. The guard slowly, deliberately placed the tip of his bayonet on the side of the American's neck, and quickly jabbed. For a moment, the American squatted in the road suspended like a fly on a pin but when the bayonet was suddenly yanked free, he fell inertly. . . . The Japanese sank his bayonet into the limp figure once more and angrily motioned the horrified onlookers to continue their march."

A Japanese shot a staggering Filipino soldier. When another screamed in delirium, a Japanese pushed him into the bush and shot him to death.

Some of the bodies along the roadway were headless.

Water became an obsession.

The road, pocked by bomb craters, made for treacherous walking. When prisoners stumbled, as they did frequently along the route, they were beaten and jabbed with bayonets.

At a resting place, guards produced shovels and ordered Filipinos to bury an American captain alive. Threatened with death, they complied. Fingers rose from under the dirt, wiggled, then ceased to move.

The road turned to the northeast, out of the Bataan jungle. There were now no trees to provide shade for the prisoners. Men dropped by the hundreds. One group made a dash for an artesian well; Japanese bullets cut them down.

An American staggered away into roadside bushes. A Japanese officer followed. When he returned his bayonet was dripping with blood.

After the town of Lubao, the march reached its final stretch, nine blistering miles to a railroad depot. On the outskirts of San Fernando, on the rail line, military trucks lined the road, creating a narrow corridor. The prisoners had to pass between them single file. As they did so, Japanese soldiers in the vehicles beat them with rifle butts.

At the station, guards herded the prisoners into boxcars, so many men to a single car that they could do no more than stand. Doors slammed shut and the heat inside mounted. Packed tightly, the prisoners could hardly breathe. Many fainted or vomited; dozens died on their feet, crammed upright.

The train lurched forward. Swallowed in darkness, the prisoners could not see where they were going. Finally the train stopped. When the doors opened, those still living stumbled down wooden planks to the ground. Ahead of them was a gate flanked by two wooden towers. Barbed-wire stretched in both directions around rows of ramshackle huts. Inside the fence a Japanese flag hung over a cement block building. The prisoners had reached Camp O'Donnell, their concentration camp.

Of the 75,000 men and women—about 100 nurses—who had started the Death March, only about 54,000 finished it. But the Japanese were not through. Their final target in the Philippines was Corregidor.

5

Having taken Bataan, Japanese artillerymen crowded the peninsula's bay side with more than one hundred big guns, in easy reach of Corregidor. So rapid was the bombardment that the 13,000 American military personnel now crammed into the Malinta Tunnel felt as if they were under fire from giant machine guns. Flames raged outside and from the monster's head to the tip of its tail Corregidor was a blackened cinder. One by one Corregidor's big guns fell silent.

Down in the tunnel beneath the island's crust, the pounding turned fissures in the concrete walls into great gaps. The air was filled with dirt, dust, and the stench of corpses.

On the evening of May 5, the first of General Homma's troops splashed onto the beach; by midnight they were within a mile of the tunnel's entrance. Then tanks rumbled ashore, their guns blasting away at five hundred American sailors sent out to guard the tunnel.

Inside the tunnel, an Army telegraph operator tapped out a last message home: "Everyone is bawling like a baby. They are piling dead and wounded in our tunnel. . . . The jig is up."

Convinced that unless he gave up the tunnel would become a slaughterhouse, General Wainwright agreed. At noon on May 6, he cabled President Roosevelt: "WITH BROKEN HEART AND HEAD BOWED IN SADNESS BUT NOT IN SHAME, I REPORT TO YOUR EXCELLENCY THAT TODAY I MUST ARRANGE TERMS FOR THE SURRENDER OF THE FORTIFIED ISLANDS OF MANILA BAY. . . . WITH PROFOUND REGRET AND WITH CONTINUED PRIDE IN MY GALLANT TROOPS I GO TO MEET THE JAPANESE COMMANDER. GOOD-BYE, MR. PRESIDENT."

On May 6, 1942, the emaciated General Wainwright formally surrendered to General Homma and became a prisoner for the rest of the war. The capitulation at Corregidor marked the lowest point in American morale in World War II.

IO

MIDWAY

1

Spread across a map of Asia and the Pacific, the Japanese Empire in the spring of 1942 looked roughly like a gigantic Ottoman slipper. The pointed toe was Burma; the instep ran up along the China coast through Manchuria; the opening for the foot stretched from the southern half of Sakhalin Island to the tip of the Kurile Islands; the sole ran along the bottom of the Indies; the heel, east of Australia, included the Bismarck Archipelago, the Solomon Islands, Gilbert Island, and Tarawa. The back of the slipper was a north–south line that lay just west of Midway, a thousand miles across the Pacific from Pearl Harbor. Where we can imagine the anklebone, right in the center of Japan's conquests, were the Marshall and Caroline Islands, once German but mandated to Japan in 1919 under the auspices of the League of Nations. And just above the ankle were the Mariana Islands, Guam, Saipan, and Tinian. The outline of this slipper bristled with armaments, forming Japan's defensive perimeter against the eventual American counterattack. With most of the American Pacific Fleet destroyed at Pearl Harbor, and with Japan's own navy possessing twelve battleships (including the new, mighty *Yamato*), ten carriers, and a superb submarine fleet, many Japanese believed their oceanic empire to be invulnerable. Naval planners did not even see a need for the development of an effective antisubmarine warfare force.

Indeed, in the early months of the war, the whole of Japan was in a state of euphoria, celebrating each victory with wild parties and toasts of *sake*. A neutral European war correspondent in Singapore in early 1942 wrote that the "occupation of Malaya and the Dutch East Indies resulted, at least for a short while, in more food and consumer goods in the shops, loot in the form of 'liberated' automobiles and radio sets from Singapore and Batavia, along with rice and other badly needed raw materials, and nearly all Japanese were elated, proud, and on an almost tangible high." According to the diaries of Lord Privy Seal Marquis Kido Koiichi, who had written of the mood inside the Imperial Palace, even the emperor himself shared in the jubilation; if he knew of the Japanese atrocities in China and elsewhere, Hirohito seemed not to care.

The marquis, though, wished that Hirohito would show more caution. He had good reason for concern. Japan's cities, made largely of wood and paper, were vulnerable in the extreme to American firebombing.

2

Claire Chennault, the American aviator who had been in charge of the pre–Pearl Harbor plan for firebombing Japan, was now based in Kunming, in southwestern China. Describing the place early in 1942, he wrote to a friend back in the States that it was "about 6,000 feet above sea level with higher mountains all around—about ten miles away. It is near a very large lake on which thousands of people live all their lives in sampans and small junks. Boys and girls are born and grow up and die on these boats, never having any other home."

Isolated at the edge of the Himalayas, the surrounding province of Yunnan had been China's place of exile for undesirables. It was also backward. Ancient Buddhist and Daoist temples and moss-covered trees dotted the surrounding hills. Kunming itself was built in the old Chinese style, which meant a wall with gates, houses with mud walls and mud roof tiles, and what Chennault called "narrow, dirty, and rough" streets. Living in one of the few modern houses, he managed to be "real comfortable. I have a bath tub and a toilet—very rare conveniences in Kunming." But conditions at the air base by the edge of the lake were primitive. Kunming was short of everything. "No floodlight," he wrote in a small, orange-covered pocket notebook. "Get radio officer. No ammunition. Need cook utensils. No spare parts." And until the airlift over the Himalayas (the "Over the Hump" operation) got under way in 1943, the Japanese closure of the Burma Road pinched supplies even further.

Despite the problems, however, even in the spring of 1942 Chennault's pilots, formerly the American Volunteer Group but now drafted into the Army Air Corps and called the "Flying Tigers," with sinister eyes and rows of sharp white teeth of tiger sharks painted on the sides of their engines, were making a fundamental point. They were outflying the Japanese.

Even over Burma in March and April, 1942, they had shot down fifty Japanese airplanes and lost not one of their own. Back in China they continued to enjoy success. Their coups made headlines back in America and correspondents from all the major journals were making their way to Kunming. The Flying Tigers did not come close to seriously challenging Japanese forces in China, but their tales of derring-do nonetheless contributed to the growing American worship of air power.

3

Yet President Roosevelt wanted more than just harassment. Japan's conquests had deprived the United States of the runways specified in the earlier Chennault plan. Singapore, Hong Kong, Guam, and the

Philippines had all fallen into Japanese hands. The Soviets, not yet at war with Japan, refused to grant American planes access to Vladivostok. And from Kunming, bombers would have to pass over two hundred miles of Japanese-controlled territory, then cross the three-hundred-mile East China Sea, full of watchful Japanese ships, and *then* traverse three hundred more miles of Japan itself before they could strike Tokyo. At this point their fuel would be nearly exhausted. And where were they to put down?

A land-based attack on the Japanese capital seemed out of the question. But FDR was determined to make an early strike. The Navy set out to develop an operation.

On Saturday, January 10, 1942, Captain Francis Low, a submariner stationed at Norfolk, Virginia, had an idea as he glanced at a runway for naval planes. The blue line painted perpendicularly across the strip represented the length of a carrier, about 800 feet, and Navy fighter pilots routinely used the marked-off distance to practice take-offs and landings. The fighters, Low knew, were designed for carrier decks, but their flying range was short. It occurred to him that if bombers with their longer air times also could handle the flight decks, and if a carrier could slip into easy bomber range of Tokyo, *and* if the bombers could land in China, then a raid could succeed. Low made an appointment to see Admiral King.

Admiral Ernest J. King, Chief of Naval Operations, was reserved, austere, and even arrogant. With some trepidation, Low met him in the stateroom of the USS *Dauntless*, a yacht moored in the Anacostia River just off the Washington Navy Yard, and outlined his proposal. To Low's surprise King was enthusiastic.

After the bombing of Pearl Harbor, the Navy engaged in a thorough reevaluation of its strategy and tactics. In their eagerness to sink the American battleships, the Japanese had failed to take out the repair facilities and the oil storage depots—vital ingredients in Pearl Harbor's rapid recovery. They also had missed three aircraft carriers, *Enterprise*, *Lexington*, and *Saratoga*, which had been out at sea. The survival of the carriers gave the Navy the opportunity to rebuild the fleet, not by stressing new battleships, but rather by adding more carriers. Carriers hauling airplanes with a range of 600 miles could strike at Japan from a far greater distance than could battleships. But the Navy needed to test the idea. So in a triumph of patriotism over interservice rivalry, Admiral King referred Low to General Henry A. Arnold, head of the Army Air Force.

Delighted with Low's observations, Arnold called upon Lieutenant Colonel James Doolittle to take charge of modifying and training crews for the mission. Stationed now in Washington, Doolittle went to work immediately, conducting a survey of the Army's various bombers. Most, indeed, would not do. One bomber, however, the B-25, had a wingspan of only sixty feet and would be able to take off from the deck of the *Hornet,* a carrier longer than its predecessors and nearing completion in the Newport News, Virginia, shipyard. Since Doolittle had found the solution, it was decided that he should command the mission.

Operating under strict secrecy, Doolittle assembled pilots and bombers and sent them into training. Practice runs took place primarily at the Elgin Air Base near Pensacola, Florida, and the Columbia Air Base in South Carolina. The pilots learned from U.S. Navy Lieutenant Henry L. Miller how to take off from a carrier deck.

On the morning of March 23, 1942, the bombers and their crews moved out, crossing the Great Plains and the Rocky Mountains to Alameda Naval Base by the San Francisco Bay. With sixteen bombers aboard, on April 2 the *Hornet* weighed anchor, heading for the Golden Gate.

Before the carrier could pass under the bridge, a launch pulled alongside and a sailor handed Doolittle a message; he was to return to shore without delay. Washington was on the line.

Riding the launch back to Alameda, Doolittle decided that if his superiors were going to cancel the mission, he would argue for it as forcefully as possible. When he picked up the telephone and realized that the caller was General Marshall, however, Doolittle knew that to argue would be futile. The decisions of the firm, tight-lipped, and far-seeing Marshall were final.

"Doolittle?" Marshall asked.

"Yes, General."

"I couldn't let you leave without wishing you the best of luck," Marshall said. "Our hearts are with you and our prayers will be with you. Goodbye and good luck, and come back safely."

Accompanied by two destroyers, two fuel ships, and another carrier, the *Enterprise,* the *Hornet* set out across the Pacific. Only away from land did Doolittle announce their destination to the crew: Japan. He had kept the secret from his men and the American public alike.

But not from the Japanese. Early in the morning of April 10, a radio tower outside Tokyo picked up transmissions between the two carriers; Japanese intelligence realized that an American flotilla was on the high seas. Was it heading for the Japanese islands? Taking no chances, authorities in Tokyo ordered the checking of the more than three hundred antiaircraft guns in and around the city, the alerting of fighter pilots who could streak up to stop the invaders, and the positioning of reconnaissance ships 300 miles off the coast. American Navy planes, Tokyo knew, could fly 300 miles from the carriers and then back. Detection surely would be easy.

Out on the Pacific, Doolittle's fleet was steering into trouble. The farther westward it pushed the worse the weather became. According to Quentin Reynolds, journalist and Doolittle biographer, heavy "winds, rains, and high waves buffeted the ships, and visibility was often poor. In one sense, the rough sea was an advantage. It shielded the ships from Japanese observation planes. But it also meant that the *Hornet* could send out fewer air-reconnaissance patrols than before. . . . The pilots were growing concerned about taking off in such storms. One pilot climbed into the cockpit of his plane and was astounded to see the altimeter needle register a two-hundred-foot change in altitude as the carrier's bow rose and fell in the waves."

Then, although few if any aboard knew it, an even greater difficulty arose: the lack of assurance of landing sites in China. With General Stilwell still in India, the task of dealing with Chiang Kaishek fell to his second in command, Brigadier General Clayton Bissell. Bissell's conversations with Chiang were frustrating. Fearing Japanese reprisals if the Doolittle raid was successful, Chiang was reluctant to provide bases as promised. An angry Bissell informed Chiang that the bombers would land in China anyway. On April 15, Chiang gave assurances that the landing strips would be ready.

Bissell cabled the news to Washington and the message went back to Doolittle: "CHINESE AIR FORCE HAS ISSUED ORDERS . . . AND THE FLARE RUNWAY MARKERS YOU REQUESTED WILL BE AVAILABLE AT GUILIN, JIAN, AND LISHUI. SIGNAL TRANSMITTED WILL CONSIST OF FIGURE 57, THEN OFF FOR ONE MINUTE. THIS SIGNAL WILL BE REPEATED CONTINUOUSLY FOR TWO HOURS ON DATE YOU SPECIFY. FLARES WILL BE BURNING DURING SAME TWO HOURS."

Two days later, April 17, Doolittle's fleet was one thousand miles from Japan. Up on the bridge of the *Hornet*, Admiral William F. ("Bull") Halsey ordered a high-speed run toward Japan; oilers and destroyers would have to lag behind. By the next afternoon the *Hornet* and the *Enterprise* were within five hundred miles of Tokyo. The crews fueled the bombers, loaded them with incendiaries, and lined them up on the flight deck. Doolittle's bomber stood first. Two white lines painted along the runway would guide the aircraft on their takeoffs. Their right wingtips would miss the superstructure by only six feet.

At dawn on April 18 as rain, wind, and waves still battered the carriers, Halsey sent three scout planes out on morning patrol. They disappeared into the slate gray sky, then sent back an alarming report: They had spotted three Japanese trawlers. Japanese intelligence, Halsey feared, soon would detect his fleet.

Wanting to withdraw as soon as possible, he ordered the start of the raid. The klaxon screamed: "Army pilots, man your planes!"

Down on the flight deck, sailors pulled the chocks away from the wheels and unfastened the ropes that held the planes in place. Doolittle climbed into the cockpit of the lead bomber and peered out. The sky was murky and wet; the waves were high and salt spray cascaded over his window. The carrier was rolling and the deck was slick.

Nevertheless, he revved his twin engines and the propellers began to turn. Ahead of him a sailor plunged a checkered flag. Doolittle moved forward, following the white lines as he picked up speed. Then he was at full speed, approaching the end of the runway. He was at the edge, in the air. The bomber dipped. It was below the end of the ship.

Then, suddenly, he ascended and circled the carrier. As the men on deck erupted with cheers, the other fifteen bombers followed suit. The time was 8:17 in the morning, four months and eleven days after the Japanese attack on Pearl Harbor.

For the first half hour after takeoff, the bombers practically skimmed the waves, flying single file at a height of a mere two hundred feet. They passed near a cruiser that, as Doolittle could see from the markings, was Japanese. An hour later, a Japanese patrol plane flew overhead at 3,000 feet. Then the sun came out and the American bombers had no cover.

At about noon, Doolittle in the lead plane made out the green coastline of Japan. Yet where in Japan? The navigator thought they were about fifty miles north of Tokyo but the wind had blown them off course and the compass was faulty; so he was not sure. But Doolittle soon saw a lake he remembered from the maps and turned southward, flying just above the treetops.

A squadron of Japanese fighters appeared overhead at 1,000 feet. They descended in attack. Doolittle climbed and lost them.

Then, in the distance, he noticed Mount Fuji and soon, right below, the main landmark: the gray walls and sloped roofs of the Imperial Palace. Just ahead was the target, the smokestacks and factories of Tokyo's principal manufacturing center. Doolittle held his plane level.

The bomb-bay doors opened and a red light on Doolittle's instrument panel blinked four times: Four incendiary bombs were on their way. It was 12:15 P.M. As his airplane ascended, Doolittle could see fires starting to blaze behind and below—beacons for the rest of the American bombers.

The other bombers had also flown off course. Some approached Tokyo from the north, some from the south, and three directly over Tokyo, where Japanese warships stood at anchor in the sparkling water. Amid this hodgepodge of attacks, the defenders, awaiting intelligence from the 300-mile radius, were confused. Disoriented anti-aircraft gunners hardly knew in what direction to fire. Only a few fighter planes took off and to no effect.

As the fires spread across the heart of the Japanese capital, Doolittle's bombers—all intact—had completed their mission. Regrouping, they flew on to China.

One of the bombers, piloted by Captain Edward York, peeled off. It had developed a fuel leak and York realized that he could not keep up with his comrades. His choices were limited. He could crash-land in Japan, where the crew was certain to be taken prisoner and executed. He could ditch in the Sea of Japan and drown or be captured by enemy ships. Or he could proceed to Russia. The air base at Vladivostok, he knew, was closed to Americans. What lay ahead on Russian soil was a great unknown. Captain York set course for Siberia. After the landing, the Soviets impounded the plane and interned the crew for a year.

The other bombers kept going toward China, passing over Kobe, the Inland Sea, and Nagasaki. In the late afternoon the sea still glittered but the pilots and copilots were squinting into the setting sun. At dusk rain began to fall. The crews, enveloped in fog, could barely see their wing tips. In each of the fifteen bombers, strung out in a line over 150 miles long and still needing to traverse the now roughly six hundred miles to China, the pilots checked their gas gauges. Fuel was running low. Later, navigational devices told them that they were approaching the Chinese coast, but it was invisible in the night. They also heard no homing devices. And as, one by one, they neared what were supposed to be the Japanese front lines, they could make out no flares lining the designated airstrips: The Chinese had failed to prepare for the landings. With fuel supplies almost exhausted, each crew captain had to make a quick decision: crash or parachute. They all chose to parachute, most of their planes smashing down into rice paddies.

Eight of the pilots drifted down into Japanese territory. A photograph shows one of them, Lieutenant Robert Hite, wearing his uniform cap and a fleece-lined leather flight jacket, being led blindfolded by two diminutive Japanese soldiers down from a transport plane in Tokyo. Three of the eight were executed; another died in a prisoner of war camp. The others, including Hite, were kept mostly in solitary confinement, somehow enduring until the end of the war.

The rest of the aviators, including Doolittle, dropped to earth in Chinese space. Having been taught to say, as part of their training, *"Wo shi meigwo ren"*—"I am an American"—they were able to make contact with Chinese farmers and soldiers. The reception left them thanking their good fortune. Helped by Chinese peasants, the Americans were able to use boats, ponies, rickshaws, sedan chairs, and even charcoal-burning buses to move inland away from the Japanese lines. Feted as China's potential liberators, Doolittle and his men made their way to Chongqing.

Although Doolittle's attack on Tokyo caused no great physical damage, it gave American morale a great boost. The shock to the Japanese people was also tremendous. The raid led Tokyo's military planners to see that their greatest fear, extensive firebombing, might well come true. They began immediately to consider what they should do next.

4

In the gray stone Naval General Staff Building in downtown Tokyo, Admiral Yamamoto presided over intense discussion. Should Japan act defensively, contenting itself with holding on to what it already had conquered? Or, to prevent an Allied counterassault, should it embark on further offensives?

Yamamoto and his staff thought that they had underestimated the range of Doolittle's bombers, that they must have taken off from a land base—"Shangri-La" as FDR had chortled during a press conference. (This was a magnificent piece of disinformation: "Shangri-La" was the presidential retreat in Maryland's Caroctin Mountains, a bit distant from Tokyo Bay. It is now called Camp David.) Officers of the Imperial General Staff put rulers to their charts. Aside from the Aleutians, where Japanese fleets had seen no sign of a bomber fleet, the U.S. outpost nearest Tokyo was Midway, 2,250 miles away. This, the Japanese concluded, must have been "Shangri-La." Japan's capture of Midway would obviate any further bombing raids of Tokyo, or so Yamamoto concluded.

For an assault on Midway he chose the target date of May 26, 1942. By the end of April, accordingly, the ships chosen for the Midway operation were steaming back from the fringes of the empire and gathering in Hiroshima Bay.

A month later, the *Yamato*, the world's greatest battleship, with Admiral Yamamoto aboard and leading a fleet that in numbers hopelessly outclassed the American fleet, set forth. To Yamamoto the outcome of the voyage was certain: As a Pacific power the United States would be finished.

Only one problem stood in Yamamoto's way. This time the Americans knew he was coming.

To gain entrance to the cellar steps in the Navy's Combat Intelligence Unit at Pearl Harbor one pushed a buzzer and a member of the Sea Patrol would open the door. If one had the highest security clearance, one would tread down a flight of wooden steps to another locked door, this one of steel. Behind the second door was a windowless room.

The room was hardly an example of naval spit and polish. At side-by-side desks, two dozen people sifted through stacks of documents. Piles of paper covered every surface. In charge of the apparent chaos, usually wearing carpet slippers and a red smoking jacket, was Commander Joseph Rochefort. A tall, thin cryptanalyst who knew the Japanese language, he was invaluable to the Navy.

In mid-May, 1942, he scored a significant success by cracking the Japanese naval code. That was a lucky break, for the volume of messages indicated that Tokyo was planning a huge thrust. But where? The Aleutians? Pearl Harbor again? Australia and New Zealand? As Rochefort examined the intercepts, he noticed the frequent use of two back-to-back letters, AF. (Besides the *kanji,* symbols derived from Chinese characters, the Japanese language also uses two systems of spelling, one for foreign sounds and another for native vowels and consonants. In both there are an "a" and a "fu".) Rochefort remembered that for Pearl Harbor the Japanese had employed the letters AH.

But what was AF? Rochefort hazarded a guess. The only American point in the Pacific the Japanese had not attacked was Midway. Was the atoll next?

Approaching Admiral Chester W. Nimitz, the tall, lean, white-haired Texan who was rebuilding the fleet and who was the new Commander in Chief of the Pacific (CINCPAC), Rochefort proposed that the Americans on Midway send out a fake communiqué. They would report in an uncoded message a problem in the water distillation machinery.

Rochefort's scheme worked. Two days after the false broadcast, a Japanese message mentioned a shortage of fresh water at AF. Now Nimitz knew Yamamoto's target.

As designed by Yamamoto, the Midway attack called for a fleet even greater than the one that had attacked Oahu: eight 800-foot-long aircraft carriers, eleven battleships, twenty cruisers, sixty destroyers, fifteen submarines, sixteen troop transports, and seven hundred airplanes, bombers that could be equipped with bombs or torpedoes, and Zeroes, low-winged monoplanes designed for agility. Against this force, Nimitz had just three carriers—*Hornet, Enterprise,* and *Yorktown*—eight cruisers, fourteen destroyers, and not a single battleship. On Midway the Americans possessed only about 100 airplanes. Nimitz was facing disaster.

So at least reasoned Yamamoto. Confident of victory, he felt safe in dispersing his ships. Dividing them into groups, he separated squadrons from each other by 1,000 miles.

The Midway garrison, 1,500 Navy, Marine, and Army men, had been working frantically to prepare the defenses. Surrounded by barbed wire, the atoll was a thicket of guns. Antiboat, antitank, and antipersonnel mines lurked just beneath the surf. PT boats circled the reefs. Submarines guarded the approaches and on the landing strip the few airplanes present stood at ready.

Yet despite these efforts, Midway, an atoll of two islands and a lagoon, would have trouble defending itself. Nimitz knew he had to fortify the ocean.

He divided the ships available into two groups. The *Enterprise* and the *Hornet* with six cruisers and nine destroyers, under Rear Admiral Raymond A. Spruance, made up Task Force 16. The carrier *Yorktown,* two cruisers, and five destroyers made up Task Force 17, commanded by Rear Admiral Frank Jack Fletcher. On June 2, the two groups left Pearl Harbor.

Their rendezvous was "Point Luck," a spot of ocean 350 miles northwest of Midway. Once the two flotillas had reached that location, a light blinked from the *Yorktown* and Spruance's officers made an entry in the log: "TASK FORCE SIXTEEN [is] DIRECTED TO MAINTAIN AN APPROXIMATE POSITION TEN MILES TO THE SOUTHWARD OF TASK FORCE SEVENTEEN . . . WITHIN VISUAL SIGNALING DISTANCE." The next day the log indicated: "PLAN IS FOR FORCES TO MOVE NORTHWARD FROM MIDWAY DURING DARKNESS TO AVOID PROBABLY ENEMY ATTACK."

Yamamoto in the meantime attacked a small American flotilla at Dutch Harbor near the end of the Aleutians. He was trying to lure Nimitz up and away from Midway. Nimitz refused to take the bait.

His refusal was fortunate. Forty minutes before sunrise on June 4, Ensign Jewell Reid took off from the Midway lagoon in a reconnaissance seaplane. As part of a scouting mission that covered 700 miles of the ocean, at nine in the morning he spotted the first column of Yamamoto's ships.

Nimitz ordered both task forces southward. Soon they were 100 miles above Midway. The action was a day away.

Shortly after midnight, the strike force under the aggressive and effective Admiral Nagumo Chuichi, who was aboard the carrier *Akagi,* emerged from a concealing fog. Just before dawn he was astride the International Date Line, 200 miles northwest of Midway. At 4:30 A.M. Nagumo launched seventy-two bombers and thirty-six Zeroes, all heading for Midway.

An hour later Midway learned of the impending attack. All across the atoll pilots raced to their cockpits. A few minutes after six o'clock every plane save one noncombatant utility plane was in the air, hoping to blunt the attack.

Far below the American pilots could see row upon row of Japanese bombers, stretched out in V-formations on a direct course for Midway. The pilots dropped down to attack but, in the words of one reporter, "Zeroes fell on the Americans like wolves, slashing and springing back for another slash. Outclassed and outnumbered, the Americans' only hope of survival was to get back to Midway. Only a few reached the atoll. Zeroes set one American plane after another ablaze, then whirled and machine-gunned two of the pilots in their chutes." Only a dozen American planes and pilots survived.

Down on Sand and Eastern, Midway's two islands, gunners at the anti-aircraft batteries were scanning the sky. The tip of the first V-formation appeared at 10,000 feet. Guns roared and the lead plane exploded. So did another. Even before their remnants hit the sea, however, 500-pound bombs from more than thirty other planes crashed onto the atoll, destroying the barracks and pitting the runway.

More bombers came. The "flight leader dropped his huge 1,770-pounder," an American on the ground wrote, "followed it down, rolled onto his back, and flew across Eastern at fifty feet, thumbing his nose." An antiaircraft crew brought him down, destroying him and his plane.

Other crews sank more bombers, which shot white plumes into the air as they crashed into the blue lagoon. Seventeen minutes after it had appeared, the Japanese air armada returned to its carriers.

Eastern Island had lost its powerhouse, mess hall, and post exchange. But the gasoline dumps and radio facilities had remained untouched. Even so, Midway's defense still depended on the war at sea.

Aboard the *Akagi* and angling down to within 500 miles of Midway, Admiral Nagumo was pleased: not a single American plane had hit his ships. He had not expected his first raid on Midway to bear great results.

At 7:28 A.M. he launched a second assault. On the decks of his carriers bombers revved up for another run at the atoll. But he received discomfiting news from one of his reconnaissance planes: "TEN ENEMY SURFACE SHIPS."

Nagumo's first thought was that the American ships were on their way to Dutch Harbor. Still, he sent out more scouts. At 8:09 a pilot reported: "FIVE CRUISERS, FIVE DESTROYERS." Nagumo was relieved: There was no mention of a carrier. Then, at 8:20, came new intelligence: "ENEMY CARRIER APPEARS TO BE BRINGING UP THE REAR."

Aboard the *Akagi,* Nagumo now was close to panic. The Japanese fleet was too dispersed to offer protection and most of his air wing was heading for Midway. And his bombers, still aboard the *Akagi,* were loaded with bombs, destined for Midway. Nagumo ordered the bombs replaced immediately with torpedoes, better for attacking the

American ships. In their haste, his crews left the bombs stacked on the deck.

Before the planes could take off, a new problem emerged. Back from Midway and low on fuel, Nagumo's pilots were requesting permission to land. The admiral gave permission and with the decks full of bombs his other planes could not depart. With every passing minute, as the scout planes were making clear, the American carrier drew closer.

On the bridge of the *Enterprise,* Admiral Spruance just before seven o'clock had received a seaplane report pinpointing the location of the Japanese strike force. Pushing onward, he was nearing the point at which his planes could reach the Japanese, hit, and return. At 7:02 A.M. he sent off dive bombers, torpedo planes, and fighters from his carrier and the nearby *Hornet.*

Two hours later, aboard the *Yorktown,* Admiral Fletcher sent out his own squadrons, twenty-nine bombers and six fighters. They zeroed in on Nagumo's projected location—and found nothing.

But then Torpedo Eight, a squadron of eighteen planes off the *Hornet,* caught sight of the Japanese fleet. The squadron unfortunately had no fighter protection. A few fired torpedoes, and missed. Refueled from their Midway assault, a swarm of Zeroes shot them all down.

For the Americans the disaster mounted. Torpedo Six rose to 14,000 feet, above the cloud cover. The Zeroes found them; only four American planes escaped. Taking off from the *Yorktown,* Torpedo Three, this time with a fighter escort, located Nagumo's ships and managed to down several Zeroes. But more Zeroes appeared. As James Thach, in charge of Torpedo Three, would recall: "It was like the inside of a beehive." One by one, seven of Thach's planes exploded; others crashed into the ocean. Only two escaped. The American planes were down to fifty-four.

For Admiral Nagumo the great moment was at hand. At 10:24 A.M., with the deck finally cleared, the first of his planes, now refueled, took off for Midway. But in that very moment, lookouts aboard the *Akagi* and the sister carrier, *Soryu,* cried out: "Enemy dive bombers!"

5

Up against the blue of the sky, tiny gray airplanes with white stars on their sides were splitting away from their formations and hurtling straight toward the carriers. Although highly maneuverable, the Zeroes lacked power and could not rise fast enough to meet the attack.

Moments later three bombs hit the *Soryu*. Gasoline blazed across the hangar deck. A magazine exploded. The engines stopped; the steering mechanism was on fire. From the bridge Captain Yanagimoto Ryusaku shouted: "Abandon ship! Every man to safety!" As flames encircled him, crew members made their way to the forward end of the flight deck, which was free of fire and smoke. A new explosion blew them overboard.

Four bombs hit the *Kaga,* another carrier, shattering the bridge and killing everyone there. Explosions jumped from plane to plane and a pillar of fire rose more than 1,000 feet. Shrouded in smoke, the ship zigzagged wildly.

At the same time bombers from the *Yorktown* descended on the *Akagi*. As Nagumo's remaining planes struggled to taxi off, a bomb hit directly among them. Flames from a burning fighter licked up to the bridge. It caught fire. Then the engines ceased to turn: a bomb down the smokestack had killed every man in the boiler room. Up on the flight deck, Fuchida Mitsuo, the first Japanese pilot over Pearl Harbor, learned what it felt like to be on the receiving end of such an attack. "Black objects suddenly floated eerily from [the American planes]," he would write. "Bombs! Down they came, straight toward me!" Leaping away from the bombs, he broke both ankles. The ship's elevator, he recalled, "drooped like molten glass." And the fire had only begun. The wind swirled the flames among the clustered planes; bombs and fuel tanks erupted with stupendous roars. Firemen were blown to pieces. The passageways were all afire. The only way out of the bridge was by a rope tied to a window frame.

Staring down at the fires, Admiral Nagumo was near shock. An aide took him by the hand and led him to the rope. Lowering himself past the burning flight deck, he got to the anchor deck and boarded a waiting launch. As he transferred to a cruiser, he looked back.

His flagship, now a blackened hull, was rolling onto its side. Then it was gone.

The Battle of Midway was not over. At 10:40 A.M. fifteen dive bombers and six Zeroes from the *Hiryu*, the last Japanese carrier in the group, zoomed off its flight deck and followed a cluster of American aircraft back to the *Yorktown*. They struck at the carrier with all their available shells.

At first the *Yorktown* seemed secure. Sprinklers doused the first of the flames. And as a forward elevator exploded, threatening a fuel bin, sluices opened and an inrush of seawater averted the danger for the moment. Another bomb, however, knocked out five of the six boilers. Almost immobilized, the *Yorktown* was on fire fore to aft.

Early in the afternoon Admiral Fletcher transferred to the cruiser *Astoria*. As he did so, repair crews got some of the boilers working again. The *Yorktown* started back to Pearl Harbor. The time was 2:00 P.M.

Just then, the remaining planes from the *Hiryu*, Zeroes and bombers, swooped down. Two torpedoes slammed into the *Yorktown*'s side. Oil gushed forth and seawater poured in, this time uncontrollably. The *Yorktown* was listing. At 3:00 P.M., Captain Elliott Buckmaster issued the order to abandon ship. Soon the *Yorktown* was no more.

Half an hour later, American spotters located the *Hiryu*. From the bridge of the *Enterprise* Admiral Spruance ordered two dozen planes—all he had left—off to the west. After another hour and a half, Lieutenant Earl Gallagher, the flight leader, noticed a ship's wake below. Trailing it, then circling so that he could fly down out of the setting sun, he led the other planes toward the *Hiryu*. A few Zeroes, Admiral Nagumo's last, met them, destroying three of the

American bombers and tearing holes in the fuselages and wings of several others.

Four bombs nonetheless smacked onto the Japanese carrier. Its gasoline tanks blew up and its flight deck caught on fire. Just before midnight its insides burst into flames. Captain Kaku Tomeo ordered all hands into the launches.

As he looked down upon the flames that engulfed the carrier, Admiral Yamaguchi Tanon, considered one of the most brilliant officers in the Japanese Navy and who had overall command of the four carriers, took up a megaphone and addressed the fleeing crew: "I shall remain on board to the end." He went down with the ship.

6

Far to the west, aboard the giant battleship *Yamato*, Admiral Yamamoto read the radio reports and canceled the Midway operation. As he returned to Japan, he tallied up the costs. He had lost 3,500 men, including 100 top-notch pilots, 322 airplanes, one cruiser, and—Japan's most important weapons—four aircraft carriers. The Americans, by contrast (although he did not know the exact figures), had forfeited 307 lives, 150 planes, one destroyer, and one carrier. American code-breaking had saved Midway and stopped the Japanese advance.

After Midway, the initiative in the Pacific passed to the United States. The Germans were advancing deep into Russia, and in Libya General Erwin Rommel's tank division had taken the British fortress at Tobruk. But in the Pacific the Americans were planning their next step, the invasion of Guadalcanal, and from there their island-hopping offensive across the Pacific.

PART III

THE RECEDING
OF THE TIDE

11

AMERICA RISING

1

On September 24, 1941, naval intelligence at Pearl Harbor decoded a message radioed from Tokyo to Consul Kita Nagao in Honolulu: "HENCEFORTH, WE WOULD LIKE TO HAVE YOU MAKE REPORTS CONCERNING VESSELS.... WITH REGARD TO WARSHIPS AND AIRCRAFT CARRIERS WE WOULD LIKE TO HAVE YOU REPORT ON THOSE AT ANCHOR, ... TIED UP AT WHARVES, BUOYS, AND IN DOCK. DESIGNATE TYPES AND CLASSES BRIEFLY. IF POSSIBLE, WE WOULD LIKE TO HAVE YOU MAKE MENTION OF THE FACT WHEN THERE ARE TWO OR MORE VESSELS ALONGSIDE THE SAME WHARF."

President Roosevelt saw a copy of this message. But he saw many messages of many types, and in the constant clamor of communiqués he undoubtedly did not spot this one as forecasting the eventual attack. He did take it seriously enough, however, to authorize Lieutenant Commander Curtis B. Munson, a naval officer in the autumn of 1941 attached to the State Department, to investigate the loyalty of persons of Japanese birth or descent living on the West Coast and Hawaii. After an inquiry carried out in October and the first half of November, Munson delivered a twenty-five page report that testified to the extraordinary loyalty of Japanese-Americans.

It stated:

> 1. The *ISSEI*—First generation Japanese. . . . Probably loyal romantically to Japan. [But they] have made this their home. They have brought up children here, and many would have become American citizens had they been allowed to do so. [*Ozawa v. U.S.*, 1922, had declared persons of Asian birth ineligible for American citizenship.]
>
> 2. The *NISEI*—Second generation who have received their whole education in the United States and usually, in spite of discrimination against them and a certain amount of insults accumulated through the years from irresponsible elements, show a pathetic eagerness to be Americans. . . . In fact it is a saying that all a *Nisei* needs is a trip to Japan to make a loyal American out of him. The American educated Japanese is a boor in Japan and treated as a foreigner.

The Munson report concluded that "there is no Japanese problem." When the war broke out, federal authorities quickly arrested as spies 450 Japanese, most of whom were officials of the Honolulu, Los Angeles, and San Francisco consulates. Japan no longer had an espionage network in the United States.

On February 19, 1942, nonetheless, President Roosevelt signed Executive Order 9066 authorizing the secretary of war to designate certain "military areas" and exile from them "any and all" persons suspected of disloyalty. Some 58,000 Italian and 22,000 German aliens lived in the Pacific states, but the order was clearly aimed at the 127,000 Japanese-Americans in Arizona, Washington, Oregon, and California; three-fourths of these lived in California.

Even before the promulgation of the order, Japanese-Americans were nervous. Typical of them was Charles Kikuchi, a business student at the University of California at Berkeley. A photograph shows him wearing a tee shirt and sporting a crew cut, leaning on an automobile and looking like a typical American collegiate at the time; his diary (preserved in the archives of the University of California, Los Angeles) was couched in ordinary American slang:

> December 7, 1941, Berkeley, California: Pearl Harbor. We are at war! Jesus Christ, the Japs bombed Hawaii and the entire fleet has been sunk. . . .
> December 8, 1941, Berkeley: . . . Maybe I'll go to San Francisco tonight and chase girls. . . .
> December 9, 1941, Berkeley: Holy Christ! San Francisco last night was like nothing I ever saw before and everybody was saying that the Japs are going to get it in the ass. I ran into Jimmy Hong up on Grant Avenue, and he says I'm not allowed to screw Chinese girls anymore. . . .

Kikuchi's deprivations had only begun. Americans in many quarters were demanding the relocation of the West Coast Japanese-Americans, and among them were Associate Justice William O. Douglas (who spoke for the Supreme Court), California's attorney general Earl Warren (who later as the U.S. chief justice would gain renown for his liberal decisions on race), and General John I. DeWitt, commander of the Fourth Army District, that is, the West Coast. DeWitt became responsible for the evacuation to the interior of Japanese-Americans living in his jurisdiction.

Throughout February, in the Bay Area where Kikuchi was going to college and elsewhere, rumors spread that internment was near. *Issei* and *Nisei* alike lost jobs and were attacked in the streets. Grocers, fruit peddlers, and fishermen lost their commercial licenses. Banks refused to cash their checks, insurance companies cancelled their policies, and milkmen stopped delivering their bottles.

Then the blows fell. On March 2, General DeWitt announced that the western halves of California, Oregon, and Washington and the southern portion of Arizona were military areas from which Japanese-Americans could be excluded. On March 21, Congress declared that anyone who refused to go could be imprisoned.

On April 6, the evacuation began. Dragging bedrolls and suitcases, displaced Japanese-Americans were ordered into wire-enclosed assembly centers along the Berkeley and Oakland flats, down by the bay. Charles Kikuchi and his parents were among the crowds. Boxcar trains hauled them all to the Santa Anita Race Track in Los Angeles, where along with thousands of other Japanese-Americans they had to bed down in the stands or even in stalls that reeked of manure. Escorted by military police, they boarded new trains, these headed for ten permanent camps in barren, isolated areas of Nevada, Idaho, Montana, Utah, Arizona, and Arkansas; there they spent the duration of the war in windblown shacks and with barely adequate food and medical care.

Most went without protest, still loyal to an America that was patently disloyal to them. All told, 120,000 Japanese-Americans were now prisoners of war in what President Roosevelt himself acknowledged to be America's "concentration camps."

Why did it happen? The first answer is that the federal government was afraid of espionage. Yet no similar fate befell Italian-Americans or German-Americans. Then, of course, there was racism: Photographs show the evacuation from Los Angeles taking place against the backdrop of billboards with the words "Bye Bye Japs." But no similar roundup took place in Hawaii. The Honolulu telephone book of the time shows that large numbers of doctors, lawyers, accountants, bankers, and the like bore Japanese surnames. But on the West Coast, to which the Japanese had migrated later than Hawaii, future businessmen such as Charles Kikuchi were only students, and their parents on the whole were gardeners, small grocers and restaurant owners, truck farmers—the most vulnerable members of society.

When President Franklin D. Roosevelt asked the Congress to declare war on Japan, he described December 7, 1941, as a "date that will live in infamy." Although the Japanese-Americans were far fewer than the six million Jews who died in the Holocaust, and although the American government engaged in no genocide, they endured years of infamy. Without the slightest regard for their due process rights as guaranteed in the Fifth and Fourteenth Amendments to the U.S. Constitution, the federal government in conjunction with four state governments deprived them of liberty and property, for no cause other than their ancestry. Governments on both state and national levels gave way to racist hysteria as the nation prepared for war.

2

At the War Department early in 1942, Chief of Staff George C. Marshall met with Frank Capra, the movie director who had been drafted into the Army, and asked him to make a series of films for the orientation of American troops. When Capra demurred, saying that he had never made a documentary before, Marshall snapped back: "Capra, I have never been chief of staff before. Thousands of young Americans have never had their legs shot off before. Boys are commanding ships today who a year ago had never seen the ocean before." Capra apologized and promised to make "the best damned documentary films ever made."

Olive-complexioned with thinning black hair, Capra was known as a picture-maker's picture-maker: His credits included *Lost Horizon, You Can't Take It With You,* and *Mr. Smith Goes to Washington.* His name alone got people into the theaters. Capra now proposed documentaries to be shown not just to troops in training but also to American civilians in the cinemas.

Back in Hollywood, he assembled a team of seven screenwriters. In Capra's words, their work was to show that Americans were "fighting for the existence of their country and *at the same time* were carrying the 'torch of freedom' for a better postwar world—a world in which conquest, exploitation, and economic evils had been eliminated, and peace and democracy prevailed."

The first in Capra's series, collectively entitled *Why We Fight,* was a film called *Prelude to War.* Viewers saw the "conquering Jap army" goose-stepping down Pennsylvania Avenue toward the Capitol. "You will see what they did to the men and women of Nanjing, Hong Kong, and Manila," a narrator's voice warned. "Imagine the field day they'd enjoy if they marched through the streets of Washington."

Along with a host of other films, magazine articles, and radio broadcasts, *Why We Fight* in the first half of 1942 mobilized America's righteous anger. At the same time the government with equal success readied the population for war: From a prewar military of about 200,000 men, draftees and volunteers had already swelled the ranks to more than ten times that number.

3

Economic promotion was just as effective. A 1942 wartime poster, put out by the Office of War Information, showed a forest of factories and belching smokestacks receding along the lines of perspective to a distant focal point from which a locomotive steamed straight toward the viewer. The caption was "MORE! MORE! MORE!" The government used posters of women workers to press the nation for more production.

The pressure worked. At the time of Pearl Harbor, the federal government was spending $2 billion a month on the military; by mid-1942, Washington had let out defense contracts for $100 billion, the single greatest boost to the American economy ever. At the end of 1942, military spending alone exceeded the nation's total gross national product in 1933 when FDR took office. Such spending, financed largely by government borrowing, directly or indirectly created 17 million new jobs. Anyone who wanted work could find it. The Great Depression was over.

Coordinating the industrial expansion was former justice and senator James F. Byrnes, head of the Office of Economic Stabilization. Under what the press called his "czardom," all over the country huge factories, tooled for war production, sprang up almost overnight. An example was Plant 2 of the Boeing aircraft company in Seattle. Its roof, built to deceive any Japanese bombers, was an elaborate camouflage. It held a fake village, with trees of green-painted chicken feathers, bushes of green-painted glass, and houses, garages, a grocery store, and a gas station all of white-painted burlap. Cardboard cars stood by cardboard curbs. Shirts and dresses made of paper flapped from clotheslines made of string. Artificial roads of papier-mâché ran down the hillsides to merge with real ones.

When the disguise passed all aerial detection tests, the plant managers and their government contractors were pleased. Underneath the fake town Boeing was making a major contribution to the production of military airplanes.

The great share of aircraft manufacturing, though, was taking place in southern California. In 1942, one-fifth of all government aircraft contracts went to the region, which turned out more airplanes than any other state. With weather that was ideal for test-flying, southern California had a head start on the rest of the nation. Even before Pearl Harbor, while Detroit was still busy churning out cars, plants in southern California already had experience, know-how, and backlogs of orders for building aircraft. By the autumn of 1942, production in Burbank, Long Beach, Inglewood, Santa Monica, and San Diego was increasing even more. The forty-mile radius around Los Angeles contained America's thickest concentration of airplane factories. In streets throughout Los Angeles and Orange Counties, youngsters who once had prided themselves on their knowledge of automobile brands learned to identify Douglas A-20 attack bombers and DC-3 transports, Lockheed P-38 fighters and North American B-25 bombers, and Consolidated's B-24 bombers and PBY flying boats, all being test-flown overhead.

The very numbers bespoke the success. In 1941, American factories had produced 6,600 military airplanes; in 1942, the figure was 47,653, four-fifths of these manufactured on the West Coast. Yet southern California was contributing more than just planes. South Los Angeles was covered with oil derricks. Mills were churning out steel and aluminum. And then there were the ships, the responsibility of the captain of industry, Henry J. Kaiser.

A big-faced, bespectacled managerial genius, "Old Henry," as the newspapers dubbed him, had founded his first shipyard in Spokane just before the First World War. Moving his enterprises to Oakland in the 1930s, he had built a manufacturing empire that included a steel mill, a cement plant, magnesium plants, an artillery shell factory, and, in Richmond, at the northern end of San Francisco Bay, a massive shipyard. Kaiser's enterprises were revolutionary. Using prefabricated sections, an idea then without precedent, his Richmond plant in 1942 slid its first Liberty Ship (the vessel that was to supply American forces all across the Pacific front), the *Robert E. Perry,* into the bay in four days and fifteen hours, start to finish.

To make sure that the work went fast, Kaiser's two most prominent prewar antagonists, Harry Bridges of the Longshoremen's Union and Dave Beck of the Teamsters, radicals turned patriots, frowned on strikes and urged their fellow workers to put forth even greater efforts. The same was true in the aircraft industry.

Propagandists at the Office of War Information lost no time glamorizing the mass production of bombers. At Chicago's Union Station, a colonnaded edifice on Canal Street, with a monumental skylight over its main waiting room, there hung a display of model airplanes. Millions of readers of *Life* saw the same exhibit in the form of a pictogram. The lower fifth of the picture showed the curve of the earth. From out of the left side (representing the American West) a string of dots gradually formed into a row of tanks reaching all the way to the Hudson River; several Manhattan skyscrapers were visible, barely, in the lower right-hand corner. Under a column of tanks a caption read:

"120,000 tanks stretch 2,500 miles from Salt Lake City to New York." Overhead, above a couple of cloud clusters, again out of the West, a stream of bombers arose and spread like the hood of a cobra. Here the words went: "185,000 planes form a mile-wide blanket of bombers under fighters stretching 117 miles."

General Henry Arnold, the air chief, boasted that the Doolittle raid had been "just the beginning of the day of wrath." Arnold already was championing a switch from the B-17 "Flying Fortress" to the B-29 "Superfortress," which would fly higher and faster than the B-17 and be nearly unreachable by Japanese antiaircraft guns. America's bombers would become so fearsome, Arnold prophesied, that "in sixty seconds, the cumulative effect of a hundred years [of Japanese economic growth] can be destroyed."

Two of those eventual B-29s would drop the atomic bombs on Japan. But the Manhattan Project in 1942 was still far from perfecting the weapon. Working in laboratories primarily in Oak Ridge and the University of Chicago, scientists had worked out the theory of nuclear power. But they needed a place to build the bomb in secret, a place far away from civilians.

They chose Los Alamos in northern New Mexico, set in what one of the physicists, Enrico Fermi, called a "beautiful and savage country." Hot and barren, except for the green meander of a river far below, it was situated on a mountaintop. In the valleys all around, and on the adjoining mountain slopes, no vegetation was visible save cacti, sagebrush, and stunted trees. Sunset went from green to red to black. If any locale in the United States was remote, this was it. Here scientists would produce the ultimate weapon against Japan.

4

Well before the advent of the B-29, however, the United States had available another weapon to use against Japan: the submarine. Operating out of Australia and New Zealand, the submarines that had escaped from the Philippines provided the nucleus of a war of attrition against Japan.

The American submarine fleet drew deadly aim against a great Japanese vulnerability. Since the Japanese islands were crowded, with little acreage for farming, Japan needed to import 10 million tons of food a year. Japan's survival thus depended on shipping. And since Japan had paid little attention to the development of an antisubmarine fleet, the shipping lanes were easy targets for American undersea warfare.

Life aboard the submarines was unpleasant; there was no air-conditioning. One crew member wrote:

> [The] bunks beyond the wardroom are filled with torpid, skivvy-clad bodies, the sweat running off the white, rash-blistered skin in small rivulets. Metal fans are whirring everywhere—overhead, at the ends of the bunks, close to my ear. . . . I am playing cribbage with the skipper, because I don't like to wallow in a sweat-soaked bunk most of the day. I have my elbows on the table near the edge and I hold my cards at a slight angle so the sweat will stream down my bare arms . . . without further soaking the pile of cards in the center. Overhead is a fine net of gauze to catch the wayward cockroaches which prowl across the top of the wardroom and occasionally fall straight downward. They live in the cork insulation which lines the insides of the submarine's hull. We've killed over sixteen million cockroaches in one compartment alone. . . . The deck in the control room is littered with towels, used to sponge up the water dripping off the men and the submarine itself. . . . The food is routine—something canned. The dehydrated potatoes, powdered onions, and reconstituted carrots have the same general taste—like sawdust.

Like the rest of the prewar American Navy, the submarines also suffered unending mechanical failures. All had electrical outages, intensified by the tropical humidity. Most of the tanks leaked oil. The sonar was inadequate. Accidents of one kind or another jabbed holes in the sides of the hulls.

But after repairs in Brisbane, on Australia's northeastern coast, they did work. Only a week after Pearl Harbor, an American submarine sank a Japanese tanker off the China coast; on January 1, 1942, another Japanese tanker went under off the shore of Japan itself. And two months after Midway, the "silent service" was regularly attacking the supply chain that had reached Japanese troops abroad. Just as important, they were slipping goods and ammunition to the coast-watchers, a few men on occupied islands who sent radio warnings of Japanese movements in the Solomon Islands. Their warnings would be critical in the battles to come.

5

Masses of green rising out of the sparkling blue sea, the Solomon Islands covered a vast distance; the larger islands formed two parallel chains separated by a 400-mile stretch of ocean nicknamed "The Slot." Along that "Slot," a scattering of Europeans, mostly Australian planters, miners, missionaries, government officials, and criminals, for years had made their homes. When the Japanese came, the whites had escaped by sea, or been caught and imprisoned, or fled to the highlands.

One of those who went upland, Don MacFarlan, an Australian planter of coconuts and rubber on Guadalcanal, was typical. When the Japanese occupied the Solomons in the spring of 1942, he bundled his belongings into a truck and drove inland. At a stream called Bamboo Creek, a dozen hired hands, native islanders, were waiting. Hoisting the gear from the truck, they guided MacFarlan up a trail that wound ever higher. Their destination was Gold Ridge, 2,300 feet up and right in the center of the island. A European company once had prospected for gold at the place and had left behind a comfortable five-bedroom house. A group of other Australian planters had already moved in—so many that on the morning of July 12, 1942, they attracted the attention of two Japanese Zeroes. As the airplanes dived and strafed, the Australians dived into the brush.

Accompanied by his employees, MacFarlan headed southward, then camped for the night. At dawn he was up and out again, down into a dark valley, up over a mountain peak, down again, and up once more. The new encampment was primitive but adequate for MacFarlan's mission.

MacFarlan and other coast-watchers had been recruited earlier by Australian intelligence. Hidden in treetops, jungle camps, and mountain redoubts, and equipped with tele-radios, which could transmit messages up to 400 miles by voice and 600 miles by key, they could observe the vast expanses of the ocean and report what they saw.

From his vantage on Guadalcanal, MacFarlan in particular could see off in the distance to the north and the west two other islands, Savo and Tulagi. Closer at hand was a strait that in time would be called "Iron Bottom Sound," because of all the naval vessels sunk there. On Guadalcanal itself there was a jut of land called Lunga Point. Lunga Point was the key to what happened next.

On August 6, 1942, after studying work on an airstrip the Japanese were building on Lunga Point, MacFarlan relayed a message: "ONE APPROX 6-INCH GUN BEHIND LUNGA STOP AA GUNS ON SAND BEACH LIGHT CALIBER APPROX 2 INCH.... NO ARMED FIGHTING VEHICLES OBSERVED STOP RUNWAY IN POSITION PREVIOUSLY MENTIONED BUT IS GRAVEL AND CLAY FROM NEARBY HILLS NOT CEMENT STOP.... AS NEAR AS CAN BE GAUGED FROM TENT AND HUT ACCOMODATION [sic] FOUR THOUSAND [Japanese] TROOPS OF WHICH HALF LABOR CORPS."

Because of his earlier broadcasts, Washington feared the work would menace communications between America and Australia. Even as Don MacFarlan was tapping out his August 6 reportage, an American task force, under the command of Marine General Alexander A. Vandegrift, was approaching Guadalcanal to launch its first offensive of the Second World War.

6

Sixty miles long and shaped like a kidney bean, Guadalcanal was dominated by mountains that rose to 8,000 feet and by dense tropical forests that descended to the sea. Over the foothills grew a grass called *kunai,* whose tall, stiff blades were as sharp as the edge of a jigsaw blade. Passage through the *kunai,* just beyond the beaches, would prove nearly impossible. At Lunga Point, though, no coral reefs impeded landings on the wide, flat beach. Lunga Point was General Vandegrift's destination.

A dour-faced leatherneck, Vandegrift had no hard intelligence on where the Japanese were on Guadalcanal and his Marine division had been incomplete, some of the men en route from San Diego and others on Samoa. When his force had assembled at the docks of Wellington, New Zealand, furthermore, heavy rains had dissolved ration-loaded cardboard cartons and the weather had contributed to an epidemic of the flu. Finally, Vandegrift had no accurate maps of Guadalcanal. Needing time for aerial photography, he had requested an extension of the scheduled invasion date.

Washington had given him one week; the amphibious assault would take place on August 7, 1942. But there would be no more postponements. As coast-watchers such as Don MacFarlan were reporting, the Japanese had completed most of the Guadalcanal airfield.

Steaming out of Wellington on August 6, an American task force of twenty-three transports, five cargo ships, five mine sweepers, three carriers, and a protective screen of forty-six destroyers and cruisers set out for Lunga Point. As it moved northward past New Caledonia and New Hebrides, French islands in the South Pacific, the vessels communicated only by blinker lights, maintaining radio silence. Scout planes from the decks of three carriers watched for Japanese warships. The pilots had little need to worry: Low clouds and daily downpours hid the fleet from hostile eyes.

Aboard the transports, 19,000 men of the First Marine Division played poker, strummed ukuleles, and endured lectures by officers no more experienced in combat than they. A favorite subject of the classes was "Know Your Enemy." Reading aloud from various manuals, lieutenants droned through descriptions of the Japanese soldier as the "greatest jungle fighter in the world." An imperial warrior could presumably swim for miles underwater, booby-trap the bodies of his fallen comrades, and scamper up to the tops of trees. So, at least, went the myth.

"All right," a lieutenant would ask, "if a Jap jumped from a tree what would you do?"

"Kick him in the balls," came the usual answer.

As the ships neared Lunga Point, the air grew hot. The men's sweat darkened their uniforms. Everyone wondered how he would react in battle.

The tension, wrote Robert Sherrod, a journalist with the Marines, "was almost a living presence. It made voices taut, husky—made the sweat come faster. It was one with the rasp of steel on whetstones, the sound of the Marines sharpening bayonets and sheath knives. . . . Other Marines squatted on the grimy decks blacking rifle sights or applying a last light coat of oil to their rifle bores. Machine-gunners went over long bolts of ammunition coiled wickedly in oblong green boxes, carefully withdrawing and reinserting the cartridges into their cloth loops, making certain that they would not stick and jam the guns. Other men inspected grenade pins or made camouflage nets for their helmets—those exasperating scoops of steel which banged the back of a man's neck at a walk, bumped over his eyes at a run."

At dawn on August 7, 1942, Guadalcanal loomed into view.

Shielded by a tropical rainstorm, several of the troopships scattered to attack the nearby islets of Gavutu, Tanambogo, and Tulagi. The last faced Lunga Point: Its capture would cover the Guadalcanal landing.

At eight in the morning, on August 7, landing craft bearing two Marine battalions of 3,000 men each approached the Tulagi beach and ground to a halt on the coral formations. Splashing into waist-deep water, the attackers made their way ashore. With only a few Japanese on the islands, resistance was minimal. The troops spread out from the beachhead, stopping only to dig in for the night.

Within two days, firing TNT-gasoline explosives, the Marines had secured the outlying islands. Now the offensive against Guadalcanal would begin.

On the morning of August 9, ship guns roared and bombers dived, and the arcs of shells streaked across the water toward Lunga Point. Black smoke billowed up from the beach. Then loudspeakers squawked the order: "Land the landing force!"

Over the sides they went, Sherrod wrote, "clinging to the rough rope nets that swayed out and in against the warm steel sides of the ships. They stepped on the fingers of the men below them and felt their own hands squashed by men above. Rifles clanged against helmets. Men carrying heavy machine-guns or mortar parts ground their teeth in the agony of descending to the waiting boats with thirty or forty pounds of steel boring into their shoulders. And the boats rose and fell with the swells, now close to the ships' sides, now three or four feet away. The men jumped, landing in clanking heaps, then crouched beneath the gunwales while the landing boats churned to the assembly areas, forming rings and circling, finally fanning out in a broad line at a few minutes before eight and speeding with the hulls down" straight on for Lunga Point. Spearheaded by the First Marines, the assault force of 10,000 men waded toward the island.

Once ashore, the Americans found little opposition. The Japanese had not expected the attack and their construction workers at the airstrip fled into the jungle. The first American casualty was a Marine who cut his hand trying to slice open a coconut. About the only movement the Americans could detect was that of wild pigs snorting through the underbrush behind the beach.

But aboard the flagship, General Vandegrift received a warning from Paul Mason, a coast-watcher on Bougainville, up the Solomon chain: Japanese bombers out of Rabaul were headed his way. Stopping the unloading operations, he ordered anchors raised and the ships to disperse. Antiaircraft gunners scanned the sky and fighters from the accompanying carriers *Wasp, Saratoga,* and *Enterprise* (still on duty after the Battle of Midway) gave air protection. The gunners and the pilots did their job well. Although the Japanese sank a transport and a destroyer, they themselves lost forty-two planes and aviators.

While wheeled and tracked vehicles and artillery moved inland, supplies piled up on the beaches in disorder. But by evening, the Marines on Lunga Point had captured the Japanese airstrip. They named it Henderson Field, in honor of Major Lofton Henderson, who had died crash-diving a Japanese warship off Midway. They also seized upon what the Japanese had left behind: gasoline, construction equipment, medical supplies, tons of rice in bags, hundreds of cases of canned food, and, miraculously, an ice-making machine. Soon the shed that housed the machine bore a hand-painted sign: "TOJO ICE FACTORY. Under New Management."

Despite the success of their landing, though, many of the Marines were frightened, especially after nightfall. Lieutenant Samuel B. Griffith captured the mood: "It was darkness without time. It was an impenetrable darkness. To the left and right of the men rose up those terrible formless things of my imagination, which I could not see, but I dared not close my eyes lest the darkness crawl between my eyelids and suffocate me. I could only hear. My ears became my being and I could hear the specks of life that crawled beneath my clothing—the rotting of the great tree which rose from its three-cornered trunk above me. I could hear the darkness gathering against me and the silences that lay between the moving things. I could hear the enemy everywhere about me, whispering to each other and calling my name. I lay open-mouthed and half-mad beneath that giant tree. I had not looked into its foliage before the darkness and now I fancied it infested with Japanese."

Daybreak revealed that the Marine hold on the beachhead was firm. But as the coming events of that August would show, the Japanese had no intention of giving up Guadalcanal. On August 8, Admiral Mikawa

Gunichi, one of Tokyo's most noted naval tacticians and in charge of part of the Japanese Eighth Fleet, made preparations to dislodge the American invaders.

Mikawa's warships steamed southwestward from Rabaul on the night of August 8–9 and entered "Ironbottom Sound." Tulagi and the other Allied-occupied islets lay to the northeast; Guadalcanal to the south. Just at the entrance of the strait stood Savo Island. There the two fleets clashed. At one in the morning, as Mikawa's ships moved around Savo, a Japanese lookout detected an American destroyer, outlined against the stars. It was the *Blue,* doing sentry duty. Aboard the flagship *Chokai,* Admiral Mikawa was incredulous. From the *Blue's* "deliberate, unconcerned progress," a Japanese staff officer would remember, "it was plain that she was unaware of us— or of being watched—and of the fact that every gun in our force was trained directly upon her. Seconds strained by while we waited for the inevitable moment when she must sight us—and then the enemy destroyer reversed course."

Mikawa held his fire and steamed forward. His luck continued to hold. Not until half an hour later, as the last of his ships rounded Savo, did an American destroyer, the *Patterson,* radio a warning. The message went out too late. At 1:45 A.M., flares dropped from Japanese airplanes lit up the American fleet. Mikawa's guns began to fire and his torpedoes were streaking through the water. Forty minutes later, after an immense naval battle, two American cruisers were under the waves and two more had to be abandoned. More than 1,000 American and Australian sailors were dead and another 700 wounded, burned, and exhausted men were floundering overboard. The Battle of Savo was over and the Marines on Guadalcanal stood alone.

Aiming to eliminate the American forces altogether, Japanese destroyers ten nights later landed 10,000 troops twenty miles east of Lunga Point. Hearing the washing of the ships, the Americans in the morning sent out a patrol, which came upon Japanese stringing telephone wires. Information from native Guadalcanal spies indicated that the Japanese were about to march westward.

Japanese units led by Colonel Ichiki Kiyono on the night of August 20–21 indeed set out, pushing away from their own beachhead across the Tenaru River. Fording the stream, they reached the perimeter of Lunga Point before dawn, spread out, and opened fire on the Marine redoubt.

Flush with their victories elsewhere in Asia and the Pacific, however, the Japanese had succumbed to overconfidence. They did not realize that Marines in forward listening posts had detected the advance and had radioed the news back to Lunga Point. The Marines were ready for them. In a dawn attack, they circled up through the jungle and down to the beach to catch the Japanese from the rear. Then, from Lunga Point, American tanks rumbled into action. Terrorized, some of the Japanese fled into the sea and drowned. Others retreated eastward, only to run into American machine gun fire. Still others tried to hide in a coconut grove. But flames from the tanks flushed them out and under the steel treads of the tanks. So many Japanese were mowed down that, as General Vandegrift said, "the rear of the tanks looked like meat grinders."

The immediate crisis over, supplies again began to reach the Americans on Guadalcanal. But the island remained a mass of pestilence, scum-crested lagoons, and swamps inhabited by giant crocodiles. Leeches dropped from trees and centipedes crawling across human skin left tracks of inflamed flesh. Clouds of mosquitoes brought malaria, dengue fever, or any one of a dozen other tropical fevers. Most of the men fell sick and lost weight.

Yet in a hopeful turn of events, early in September fresh pilots and planes, the First Marine Aircraft Wing under Brigadier General Roy S. Geiger, landed on Henderson Field. Conditions for air operations off the landing strip, to be sure, remained primitive. Overlooking the field, though, was a pagodalike structure, an open-air command post. Geiger's men quickly equipped the place with a ground-to-air radio system. By the middle of September, the Marines were ready to mount offensives from the air.

As well as on the ground. About five hundred yards east of the Lunga River, a natural pathway through the jungle led to a series of heights soon to be known as "Bloody Ridge." Sending his troops inland, General Vandegrift captured the hilltops. He even pitched his tent—his divisional command post—on the first of the hilltops. But then, right after dusk on September 12, the Japanese counterattacked.

They seemed unstoppable. As flares etched red streaks in the night sky, they sprinted upward in waves. As they climbed ever higher, the Marines could hear them slapping their rifle butts in cadence.

Then the night fight began. Amid wild shooting, grenades fell among friend and foe alike. Bayonets thrust forward at the sound of a foreign tongue. Men fought with knives, even fists. Gradually, the Japanese got the better of the Americans. Stumbling and mumbling, the Marines at daybreak retreated down "Bloody Ridge."

But the Japanese were no supermen. Guadalcanal was at the very end of their line of supply; they were low on food and ammunition, and just as enervated as the Americans. "Bloody Ridge" was as far as they could go.

In the early hours of September 14, Marine reinforcements recaptured the heights. The battle was over at daybreak. The Marines lost thirty-one soldiers, but in the ravines sprawled the lifeless bodies of some 600 Japanese.

In October the Marines sent out patrols and flew sorties against Japanese strongholds in the area. One pilot flew a few miles up the coast and dropped a bomb into the hold of a beached Japanese transport and blew it apart, flinging hundreds of bodies high into the air. On his return, he passed through antiaircraft fire unscathed.

But starting on the night of October 24–25, the Japanese mounted a concerted effort to overrun Henderson Field. The machine gun fire was incessant. Only at sunrise, as the bodies began to decompose and stink in the heat, were the Marines able to drive the Japanese off.

Another naval battle took place roughly thirty miles northwest of Lunga Point, off Cape Esperance. With the number of ships evenly matched, neither side scored a victory. But Japanese carrier-based attacks damaged Henderson Field so severely that near the end of the month, General Vandegrift directed his staff to prepare a plan for withdrawal into the hills.

In November, Admiral Halsey replaced Admiral Robert L. Ghormley as commander of the American naval forces in the South Pacific. An Annapolis graduate, Halsey at the time of Pearl Harbor had been in charge of the carriers out at sea. The moment he learned of the attack, he ordered all the planes on his decks prepared for fighting: The order was an early example of the aggressiveness that would be Halsey's hallmark throughout the Pacific war. He even looked aggressive, with a bulldog face, brusque manner, and salty speech. But he was always approachable and solicitous, revered by his men. A skin disease kept him from action at Midway. But after treatment in the States, he returned to the fray. News of his South Pacific command spread through the fleet and to the troops on Guadalcanal served like a tonic. They took to heart the slogan he coined on assuming command: "Kill Japs. Kill Japs. Kill more Japs."

Under Halsey's leadership, the ships and airplanes churned out of America's West Coast factories established control of the air and the sea. On the ground, an American Army division, under the command of General Alexander Patch, equipped with B-17 bombers and P-38 fighter planes, relieved the Marines, giving them a much needed rest. Engineers reconstructed Henderson Field.

In late December, the combined Army–Marine units set their sights on Mount Austen, the island's highest peak. Waist-high grass covered the foothills and a dense rain forest enveloped the tops. And Japanese resistance was fierce. Just below the summit, a horseshoe-shaped line on the western slope (the Japanese had named it Gifu, after a prefecture in Honshu) contained a series of interconnecting and mutually supporting pillboxes—a nearly inviolate redoubt. The fighting went on beyond Christmas and into the middle of January, 1943. Finally, after hellish battles, an American tank, supported by sixteen infantrymen, reached the heart of the Gifu and blasted it apart.

Their resistance finished, the Japanese at the beginning of February, 1943, staged an evacuation from Guadalcanal's northwestern tip. The American pursuit was slow and some 6,000 Japanese escaped, surviving to fight on other islands. But Guadalcanal was in American hands. American strategists now could plan their next moves up the Solomon chain.

7

In the remoteness of China's Yanan, Mao Zedong and his comrades at the same time were laying plans for the future. Brush in hand, the chairman at a wooden table issued calls to arms. In the manner of the emperors of old, he alone created the slogans. Communists must penetrate Japanese lines, he urged; Communists must infiltrate the ranks of the *Guomindang;* Communists must subordinate themselves to the will of Mao Zedong.

Mao established a school in Yanan where party cadres corrected thousands of students of "unorthodox tendencies." Outside Yanan, various instruments of propaganda—woodcuts, dance troupes, choruses, opera companies—all stressed Mao's "humanitarian love of the masses." Communist Party officials went into the villages, telling peasants that the red star was rising over China.

Mao was modeling himself on Hong Wu, the peasant leader who in 1368 had overthrown the Mongols and established the Ming dynasty. Members of the Communist Party set him on a pinnacle of adoration; men of rank themselves, Mao's comrades wrote down his free-running speeches, brushing the aphorisms that became the "Thought of Mao." Choruses sang the Maoist anthem:

The East is Red, the sun rises.
In China Mao Zedong is born.
He seeks the people's happiness.
He is the People's Great Savior.

In Yanan in the spring of 1943, shortly after the American victory on Guadalcanal, Mao planted the first millet seeds of the growing season, as in ages past China's emperors had plowed the first furrows. Just as the Ming had overthrown a foreign dynasty, Mao intended to overthrow the American-supported regime of Chiang Kaishek. The seeds of America's conflict with revolutionary China were already germinating.

12

THE HAMMER
AND THE ANVIL

1

Away from the hubbub of the Tokyo streets and beyond the main gate of the Imperial Palace, the arches of the *Niju-bashi* (the Niju Bridge) crossed the moat and led into the emperor's grounds. Official buildings lay scattered about acres of gardens and woods. At the northeastern end of the estate stood the palace itself, a horseshoe of separated, curvilinear rooftops. At the head of the horseshoe was the audience chamber.

Dressed in a morning coat and striped trousers, Emperor Hirohito on February 11, 1943, entered that chamber and sat on his throne. Before him, his ministers wore the pressed khakis and ceremonial whites of the military and naval commands. Their faces were impassive, then stunned.

The emperor was asking a question, and a most embarrassing one at that. Given the losses at New Guinea and Guadalcanal, he wanted to know, what did his warlords plan to do next?

General Tojo spoke for the group: "Stop the enemy's westward advance."

He did not say how. But the thinking of Japan's top officers clearly had shifted from the offensive to the defensive.

2

On January 7, 1943, President Franklin D. Roosevelt "walked" to the rostrum of the House of Representatives. Gripping the edges of the desk, he exuded confidence. "I am going to fight back," he announced to a joint session of Congress. "The period of our defensive attrition in the Pacific is drawing to a close. Now our aim is to force the Japanese to fight. Last year we stopped them. This year, we intend to advance!"

FDR had good reason for optimism. After the gloomy months following Pearl Harbor, a British–American force under General Dwight D. Eisenhower invaded northwestern Africa; the attack, code-named Operation Torch, began on November 8, 1942. Wishing to present the American people with an early victory, Roosevelt and Churchill had chosen the region because its defenses were relatively light: Morocco and Algeria were French colonies, under the control of the government at Vichy, allowed by the Germans to exist because it was collaborationist. So the defenders west of Libya were French, not German. FDR also believed that an opening of the Mediterranean would facilitate the shipment of materiel to the Soviet Union. As Roosevelt hoped, the landings were successful. By November 11, Oran, Algiers, and Casablanca were all in Allied hands.

Pushing eastward, Eisenhower's troops neared Libya, where, the week before at El Alamein, the British under General Bernard Montgomery had defeated the German tank divisions of General Erwin

Rommel. Having thus seized the initiative in the war against Hitler, Roosevelt and Churchill, between January 14 and 24, 1943, held a summit meeting at Casablanca. Staying in the forty-room Hotel Anfa, which overlooked the Atlantic, FDR and Churchill reached several important decisions: They would continue efforts to keep Russia supplied; they would route supplies to China from air bases in British India and over the Himalayas; and later in 1943, they would launch their first joint attack on Hitler's ally, Benito Mussolini's Italy, with an invasion of Sicily.

Overshadowing these decisions, however, was Roosevelt's statement at the concluding press conference on Sunday, January 24: "Peace can come to the world only by the total elimination of German and Japanese war power. . . . The elimination of German, Japanese, and Italian war power means the unconditional surrender by Germany, Italy or [sic] Japan."

Critics cried that FDR's pronouncement would drive the enemy to fight to the last man. But Churchill had refused to invade France then, and Roosevelt needed to show Stalin that he intended to make no deal with Hitler.

Stalin himself was unlikely to strike a deal with Hitler. Having turned back the German advance at Stalingrad on the Volga River in November, 1942, the Soviets now were launching their own offensive. Their war for survival was becoming a war for revenge.

Back in Washington, Roosevelt put into effect his promise of advances in 1943. At his direction, the Joint Chiefs laid plans for the invasion of Sicily and worked out their overall strategy for the defeat of Japan. They described that strategy as a hammer hitting an anvil. The American advance across the Pacific would be the hammer and it would smash the Japanese against the anvil of China; thereafter the American forces would invade the Japanese homeland, compelling an unconditional surrender. But the word "anvil" meant that China would have to mount a serious war of resistance against the Japanese.

3

"The trouble in China is simple. We are allied to an ignorant, illiterate, superstitious, peasant son of a bitch." Thus did General Joseph W. Stilwell describe Generalissimo Chiang Kaishek to *Time*'s young reporter, Theodore H. White. Chiang had studied military science in Japan but Stilwell was giving vent to anger.

Underweight from his ordeal in Burma and exhausted by bouts with malaria and dysentery, Stilwell in mid-1942 returned to Chongqing and checked into his home and headquarters, a dwelling that clung to the side of one of the city's tumbling hills. From its flat roof he could see "directly through the great cleft in the mountains out of which swept the Jialing River from the north." In summer the terraced hillsides were green with rice plants and the lazy muddy waters far below were spotted with junks. Inside his house—concrete, modernistic (then), and built to the taste and order of Chiang Kaishek's wealthy brother-in-law, T. V. Soong—Stilwell was provided with a large staff of servants: seven gatemen, two gardeners, a cook and two kitchenmen, four youths to haul water to the rooftop tanks, three general servants, and several others whose duties were not only to tend to Stilwell's needs but also to keep him under surveillance.

This was nothing new in China's dealings with foreigners. Assistants were also "barbarian handlers," or just plain spies. More than once Stilwell found Chiang Kaishek's agents shuffling through the papers on his desk.

Stilwell's tiny office was on the top floor, adjacent to a sunless bedroom and a toilet that stank. Rickety stairs led to a basement beset with bugs and rats. But at least it had a wall large enough for a large-scale map. Studying that map, Stilwell plotted out what he hoped would be offensives of the Chinese Army under his nominal command against the Japanese.

Such offensives, he believed (as did the War Department in Washington), were essential to the success of the hammer-and-anvil strategy.

Stilwell thought in terms of a syllogism. To be an anvil, China had to be strong. To be strong, China had to have supplies. And to get supplies, China had to reopen the Burma Road.

The map in Stilwell's basement was the canvas upon which he shaped his Burma strategy. His plan called for two assaults. First, Indian divisions would push across the Bay of Bengal and into southern Burma. Second, Chinese units out of Yunnan Province on the southern border would move into northeastern Burma. The object was to trap the Japanese between the two prongs of a pincer. The idea looked good on paper and to coordinate the offensive Stilwell began shuttling between China and India. But the plan fell apart. Lacking resources, the British in India could not launch such a maneuver; and lacking the will, the Chinese under Chiang Kaishek would not do so.

Chiang held back for three reasons. First, he dreaded making direct contact with the better-trained, better-organized, and better-mechanized Japanese: His strategy for survival had been to trade space for time, letting the Japanese overextend themselves. Second, his government was hardly a government at all, merely a coalition of warlords whose major interest lay in looting whatever they could from American Lend-Lease funds. Why should they fight when they could make fortunes? And third, as Chiang knew full well, the implication of the hammer and anvil strategy was that America needed him as much as he needed America: Stilwell had no lever with which to pry Chiang Kaishek into action. Hence Stilwell's frustrated raging against Chiang, whom he dubbed "Chancre Jack" and "Peanut."

Stilwell was no cynic. Rather he had what Theodore White called "an exalted concept of true soldiering, and an impossible ideal of what a true soldier should be." He was also a westerner; and like a long line of earlier westerners—soldiers, teachers, and missionaries—he dreamed of changing China. The problem, as many before Stilwell already had discovered, was that foreigners were not to be the instruments of change.

Stilwell poured his contempt into his journal:

> July 16, 1942: No answer from Chiang Kaishek to any of
> my memos sent during last month. No answer on request
> to see him, a week ago.

After a long hiatus in India organizing the Himalayan airlift, Stilwell in the autumn of 1942 tried to reorganize Chiang's military forces. The millions of troops were starving, sick, and misled by an officer corps hobbled by incompetence and corruption. Some individuals were fine soldiers. As an instrument of war, however, Chiang's army was useless. It could not act. So Stilwell set out to make it active. And Chiang undermined him at every turn.

> September 14, letter to Mrs. Stilwell in Carmel, California:
> We have been marking time. The Peanut is out of town,
> and of course the machinery of government has shut
> down. A one-man dog is a grand institution but a one-man
> government is something else. If I last through this job,
> and get back to Carmel, it will be as an old man of eighty
> and you'll have to push me around in a wheelbarrow. I'm
> getting used to being pushed around. I'm off to a meeting
> with La Grande Dame [Madame Chiang Kaishek]. . . .
> September 21: Dinner at Chiang Kaishek's. . . . Every-
> thing [a plan for training Chinese troops at Rangarh, a
> base in India] approved. . . . The thing that sold Chiang
> Kaishek was the photographs [of Rangarh]. That was a
> brilliant idea—he could actually see what was going on.
> Apparently, he was much pleased with it. Why shouldn't
> he be, the little jackass? We are doing our damnedest to
> help him, and he makes his approval look like a tremen-
> dous concession. . . . [Later, in an about-face, Chiang ve-
> toed the plan.]
> October 2, letter to Mrs. Stilwell: [Wendell] Willkie [the
> Republican candidate for president in 1940 on a world

trip as a presidential envoy to the Middle East, Russia, and China] arrives this afternoon and he has a full schedule for his visit. He has to go to lunch, tea, and dinner every day he is here. They are going to drag him around to see schools and factories and girl scouts and sewing circles and arsenals and keep him well insulated from pollution by Americans. The idea is to get him so exhausted and keep him so torpid with food and drink that his faculties will be dulled and he'll be stuffed with the right doctrines—the idea that China was making a magnificent contribution to the war effort.

October 6: Peanut "directed operations" from Chongqing, with the usual brilliant result. The whole thing was a mess. Peanut ordered two armies to hide in the mountains and attack on flank when the Japs passed. The Japs simply blocked the exit and went on. . . .

Stilwell hoped to launch his Burma campaign in mid-February, 1943. He found the British in India as uncooperative as Chiang Kaishek.

October 10: "Can't have the dirty Chinks" [Stilwell's rendition of the British attitude];. . . fear of Chinese–Indian cooperation; fear of independent operation; or what not. . . . Limeys getting nasty about the [idea of training Chinese at] Rangarh: [General Sir Archibald Percival Wavell, now British commander in India] must have a formal request. . . . How many [Chinese] troops [to come], and what for? WHAT FOR? My God! I told them [the British] to help our allies retake Burma. They are making it difficult; they don't want to be beholden to the Chinese for anything. Same old stuff, like closing the Burma Road. . . . They appear to learn nothing.

But even Washington seemed to thwart Stilwell.

> November 26: From [General] George Marshall: For our
> "war," we are graciously allotted (1) the Lend-Lease stuff
> we already have, (2) the personnel for training, (3) some
> engineer equipment, how much not known! . . . My God.
> So that's the support that we get to put on a campaign. . . .
> Am I to comfort the Chinese with this prospect?
>
> Thanksgiving Day, letter to Mrs. Stilwell: Peanut and I
> are on a raft, with one sandwich between us, so we can go
> right ahead developing our characters and working on that
> shoestring I had presented to me [by Washington].
>
> And November 30: Teevy [T. V. Soong] cautioned me
> this a.m. about pushing too hard. He said Chiang Kaishek
> might resent being pressed because of feeling that he had
> already done a great deal and would take it as critical if
> much more were demanded. Teevy thinks that great prog-
> ress has been made and that we'd do well to let well
> enough alone for a while.

Stilwell would soon realize what Soong meant by "great progress."
Down in Kunming the leather-faced General Claire Chennault had
made a remarkable promise. Claiming to have the ear of President
Roosevelt, he vowed to transform the former Flying Tigers into a
full-fledged air force, powerful and independent of Stilwell. Chiang
would no longer have to tolerate Stilwell's importuning: Chennault
and American air strength alone could give the *generalissimo* his victory. Chennault's pledge made a clash between him and Stilwell inevitable.

An article in *Time*'s February 15, 1943, issue likened the tension
between Chennault and Stilwell to the bursting of a levee. Referring
to the "bitter, burning conflict," it portrayed Chennault as a brilliant, unorthodox genius and miracle worker, and Stilwell came off

as an anachronism. "It's the man in the trenches that will win the war," Stilwell was reported as saying to Chennault, with Chennault snapping back, "Goddammit, Stilwell, there aren't any men in the trenches!"

Chennault was wholly sure of himself. "My entire above plan is simple," he wrote in February in a letter to Roosevelt. "It has been long thought out. I have spent five years [in China] developing an air warning net and radio command service to fight this way. I have no doubt of my success." Chennault was referring to lookouts he had posted near Japanese lines and inland.

Chennault's idea was that if he could receive 105 fighters, 30 medium bombers, 12 heavy bombers, and sufficient stores of spare parts, he could bring about Japan's downfall. He wrote:

> Japan wants to hold Hong Kong, Shanghai, and the Yangzi Valley. They are essential to the defense of Japan itself. But I can force the Japanese Air Force to fight in the defense of these objectives. [I can employ] the best air warning net of its kind in the world. With its use I am confident that I can destroy Japanese aircraft at the rate of between ten and twenty, to one. When the Japanese Air Force refuses to come within my warning net and fight, I will strike out with my medium bombers against the sea supply line to the Southwest Pacific. In a few months the enemy will lose so many aircraft that the aerial defense of Japan will be negligible. I can then strike Japan with heavy bombers. My airplanes can burn up Japan's two main industrial areas, Tokyo and the Kobe–Osaka–Nagoya triangle, and Japan will be unable to supply her armies in her newly conquered empire in China, Malaya, and the Dutch East Indies with munitions of war. The road is then open for the Chinese Army in China, for the American Navy in the Pacific, and for MacArthur to advance from his Australian stronghold all with comparatively little cost.

Rather than send this letter to Roosevelt in the diplomatic pouch (where Stilwell or his staff officers might have seen and destroyed it), he slipped it to Wendell Willkie during the former candidate's visit. On his return to Washington, Willkie dutifully handed the missive to Roosevelt.

When FDR read it he was delighted with Chennault's scheme. It was a bigger and better version of the firebombing plot developed back in late 1940. Chennault's idea, moreover, had the full support of the Army Air Corps chief, General Arnold. And why not? Airpower, as Theodore White wrote, "was so tempting a concept: swoop and strike." To fight from the air was amoral, White contended: Rarely could pilots and bombardiers see the destruction they caused on the ground. Bombing rather was a technical endeavor: Find targets on maps, navigate correctly, and open the bomb bays at just the right time. Airpower appealed to the American technological spirit.

Chiang Kaishek also approved the proposal, for the use of American airpower could rid him of that turbulent General Stilwell. To Chiang, Stilwell's objection—that without supplies Chennault's grandiose plan would burst like a bubble and that without the re-opening of the Burma Road there would be no supplies—was immaterial. Indeed, early in 1943, Chiang dispatched his wife to the United States. Her mission was to sell Congress and the American people on the notion of providing airpower for China.

During her American sojourn of six months in 1943, Madame Chiang Kaishek received an outpouring of admiration that rivaled that heaped on Charles Lindbergh after his trans-Atlantic flight. Her appearance before a joint session of Congress on February 17, 1943, enraptured her audience. Small, delicate, wearing a seductive black *cheongsam,* bejeweled with jade and the wings of the Flying Tigers, she spoke with exquisite diction. And she made her case with the skill of a seasoned actress (she had studied acting at Wellesley College): Making her plea for airpower, she declared that for China it was better "not to accept failure ignominiously but to risk it gloriously."

"Goddamn it," one congressman quoted anonymously in *Time* said later, "I never saw anything like it. Mme. Chiang had me on the verge of bursting into tears."

She went on to speak to a huge crowd in Madison Square and another in the Hollywood Bowl. In raising funds for China, she made broadcasts over all the radio networks. Her appeal was immense.

Not that it was universal. While a guest in the White House she snapped her fingers at the servants and, to Mrs. Roosevelt's disgust, demanded that her bed be made up daily with fresh silk sheets. Piqued, she asked a colonel why he called her "Madam" rather than "Madame"; the former, she pointed out, ran a whorehouse. But "Madam" was the appellation of the queen of England, the officer replied. He said later: "You never saw a facial expression change so fast in your life." And during a White House dinner, at a time which the United Mine Workers were threatening a strike, Roosevelt asked what her husband would do. She sliced a finger across her throat. Laughing, FDR called across the table, "Eleanor, did you see *that?*"

None of this changed the public's perception of her. For the American people, Madame Chiang's visit added a new war aim to their desire to defeat Japan, what she had called the "redemption of China." Few if any realized what she meant by "redemption." She had in mind of course the expulsion of the Japanese invaders. But she also longed for the crushing of Mao Zedong and the Chinese Communist Party. Nor did the public know that, in the hopes of eventually crushing the Reds, her husband's regime was forming an alliance with elements of the U.S. Navy.

Shortly after Pearl Harbor, U.S. Navy Commander Milton Miles went to China, charged by the Navy Department with running "black" or "covert" operations against Japanese fortifications along the coast. By his own later admission, Miles figured that the best way to do the job in an unfamiliar country was to form a link with Chiang Kaishek's secret police boss, Dai Li. A handsome man who spoke passable English and knew how to glad-hand Americans, Dai charmed Miles. He also had been instrumental in purging the Communists in the 1927 Shanghai crackdown. Whether Miles understood Dai's background is unclear. But the outcome of his dealings with Dai Li was the Sino-American Cooperative Organization (SACO—pronounced "Socko"). Under the aegis of SACO, Chinese personnel were to slip Navy men behind Japanese lines. In return, the U.S. Navy was to teach Dai Li's men techniques and instruments of repression, such as the use of cattle-prods and police dogs, for postwar use against the Communists. Commander Miles was lending his position and funds to the support of Chiang Kaishek's regime.

China's propaganda kept most Americans from knowing about the nature of the Chongqing regime. But William Donovan, head of the Office of Strategic Services (OSS, the forerunner to the CIA), saw the truth. During a visit to Chongqing in the spring of 1943 (Donovan traveled constantly to inspect OSS operations), he attended a banquet at which T. V. Soong and Dai Li, who had restricted OSS agents to a camp in Chongqing, were present. Suddenly Donovan accused Dai Li of preventing OSS agents from gathering accurate intelligence. Dai Li, who may have been inebriated, threatened to kill Donovan's men. Donovan replied: "For every one of our agents you kill, we will kill one of your generals."

Such frankness was rare. Hardly anyone in Washington realized that the United States was lending its support to a Chinese regime that would not fight. China was no anvil. It was a trap.

4

That left the hammer. With the victory in Guadalcanal, the Americans in the Pacific had seized the initiative but little more. The naval historian Samuel Eliot Morison would later write that in warfare a

> shift from a defensive to an offensive posture is similar to
> the recovery from a long illness. Bitter memory and lack of
> confidence produce the same timid and uncertain gestures,

a similar reluctance to venture from safety. But with [Guadalcanal] the Allies in the Southwest Pacific found themselves recovering from a year of defeat and retreat, from one illness and relapse after another. Now, they could hardly believe they had the enemy on the defensive—wondered if it were not a hallucination which Tojo would promptly dispel. [For where] was the medicine to continue the cure? Already on its way out from the States but mostly in raw form which would need a lot of stirring and refinement before use. Many moons would wax and wane before the patient could really "go places."

But then came news that rallied the patient. The Navy learned how it could kill Admiral Yamamoto.

At eight in the morning on April 14, 1943, the flags of Pearl Harbor stood at the tops of their poles and the notes of bugles rang through the air. Moments later, Commander Edward T. Layton, an intelligence officer, entered Admiral Nimitz's office suite and pushed a file across the admiral's desk.

Tanned, lean, and fit, with thinning sandy hair, Nimitz sat erect in his chair. As he read the report he grinned with eagerness. Codebreakers had realized that Admiral Yamamoto was heading by air for Bougainville, there to launch a massive counteroffensive against Guadalcanal. The information presented Nimitz an opportunity he could not resist. Decoded from Japanese messages, the report laid out Yamamoto's itinerary.

Nimitz handed the file back. Then he stood and turned to a wall map of the South Pacific. On the chart, a chain of green islands above Australia looped down a thousand miles to Bougainville in the Solomons, down to where Yamamoto was scheduled to land.

Nimitz wheeled back to Layton. "Do we try to get him?" Nimitz asked.

Layton said yes.

"Assuming that we have planes able to intercept him—it would have to be planes—you should first consider what would be gained by killing him," Layton went on. "He's unique among their people. The younger officers and enlisted men idolize him. Aside from the emperor, probably no man in Japan is so important to civilian morale. And if he's shot down, it would demoralize the Japanese Navy."

Nimitz agreed. But he raised a concern. Would getting Yamamoto compromise the code break?

Layton suggested that as a cover the Americans could attribute their success to the Australian coast-watchers.

Nimitz nodded in agreement. Then he wrote out a dispatch for Admiral William Halsey, headquartered then at Noumea on New Caledonia, off eastern Australia and about 1,000 miles below Guadalcanal. The message detailed Yamamoto's flight plan. With FDR's approval Nimitz added: "IF FORCES YOUR COMMAND HAVE CAPABILITY INTERCEPT AND SHOOT DOWN YAMAMOTO AND STAFF, YOU ARE HEREBY AUTHORIZED INITIATE PRELIMINARY PLANNING. GOOD LUCK AND GOOD HUNTING."

Commander Layton had the message coded and sent out.

Two days later, Marc Mitscher, the air commander for the Solomon Islands, was sweltering in his tent beside the Lunga River on Guadalcanal. In his hand he held a message from Halsey: IT APPEARS PEACOCK WILL BE ON TIME. FAN HIS TAIL."

On April 3, Admiral Yamamoto had flown to Rabaul, at the top of the Solomon chain and a major Japanese base since 1942. His mission there was to organize the counterattack back down the chain upon Guadalcanal.

A rugged jumble of rain forests and volcanoes ringed the Rabaul base. Downpours were constant and so were mosquitoes. For the Japanese, though, the locale was invaluable. The base, 2,000 miles south of the home islands, was enormous: It had five airfields, an expansive harbor filled with ships, and a complex of camps and posts in the lowlands that held nearly 100,000 troops.

Yamamoto's own quarters were in a hilltop cottage, but he was rarely up there. Immediately upon his arrival, he began inspecting the hangars and port facilities. He had no time to waste. Delay would give the Americans time to fortify Guadalcanal.

In his tent on Guadalcanal, Commander Mitscher studied a map laid across a footlocker. Straight up The Slot—the 50-mile-wide channel that ran between Santa Isabel and the New Georgia islands—lay Bougainville, only 320 miles away. That route, however, looked dangerous: The Japanese still held the intervening islands. If he picked a longer course, swinging westward away from the Solomons, then northwestward over the open sea, and finally heading back at a right angle toward Bougainville, his P-38s and B-24s might reach their destination undetected. And they would have fuel enough to get back. Yet by taking such a circuitous route, they might not find Yamamoto.

Mitscher decided to chance the longer route. On the night of April 17–18, he ordered his mechanics to prepare two squadrons of four planes each for the flight. At dawn the planes were ready.

Drawn by the smell of coffee at dawn, the pilots climbed from their cots and stumbled into the mess tent. When they reemerged, the morning was fresh and the sky was sparkling. They climbed into the cockpits. As the pilots switched on the ignitions, the engines coughed, fired up and roared, and the propellers began slowly to turn. The lead plane taxied to the end of the Henderson Field runway, then turned back and lifted over the coconut stumps. Its pilot, Major John W. Mitchell, wheeled in a slow circle overhead; the other planes rose and gathered in V-formation. Mitchell led them in a gentle westward curve, out over Cape Esperance, and soon they were beyond sight of land. It was eight o'clock in the morning, by American watches.

In almost the same moment, two time zones to the northwest, Yamamoto Isoroku's twin-engined bomber rose from Rabaul. At the controls himself, he was right on schedule. Accompanied by a squadron of Zeroes, he swept through the smoke from the volcanoes, passed over the ships in the harbor, and started over the open sea. Attaining 5,000 feet, the accompanying planes flew in tight formation, wing tips nearly touching. Yamamoto's bomber was slightly ahead and to the right, steering directly into the morning sun.

An hour and a half after departure, Yamamoto reached the western tip of Bougainville and followed its coastline toward the southeast. The planes descended to about 2,000 feet. Below them they could see Bougainville in detail: a watery island of inlets, palm trees, and mangrove swamps. Off to the north a mountain range rose to 10,000 feet. Mount Balbi, its tallest peak, was trailing smoke. From there his final destination, Buin, a small port at the island's eastern end, was half an hour away. It was 9:30 A.M., American time.

In the American planes, the sunshine coming through the windows made the cockpits feel like overheated greenhouses; to avoid detection, they were flying as low as possible. Some of the pilots were almost skimming the water.

In front of the group, Commander Mitscher was nervous. By 9:33 A.M. he had spotted no sign of Bougainville. Had he led the flight group off course?

But at 9:34 A.M., the mountaintops of Bougainville jutted above the horizon. Moments later, the navigator broke radio silence. "Look eleven o'clock," he barked.

At first all Mitscher could make out were sparkles of light, pale streaks against the dark sides of the mountains. Then he realized that he was looking at a squadron of uncamouflaged Japanese airplanes. Without hesitation, he radioed Lieutenant Thomas Lanphier, in command of the so-called "kill group" right behind, to soar above the Japanese planes.

Suddenly a Japanese plane plunged downward, apparently trying to escape. Three pilots of the "kill group," Lanphier, Besby Frank Holmes, and Rex Barber, dropped with stunning speed. Caught off guard, the Zeroes had no chance to counterattack.

The three pilots opened fire and Yamamoto's airplane exploded by the time it hit the ground, orange flames enveloping its wings and fuselage. Soon black smoke curled up from the jungle at the crash site. Japanese searchers later found the charred body of Admiral Yamamoto Isoroku, the hero of Pearl Harbor.

Not wishing to reveal that it had broken the Japanese codes, the American Navy did not publicize the assassination. But after Japanese scouts discovered the charred corpse in the Bougainville jungle, the Japanese government erected a bronze statue of the admiral at the Kasumigaura Flying School, which he had once commanded. It stood as an inspiration to the Japanese people to fight on for the martyred Yamamoto.

13

GRAND STRATEGY

1

On the day of Yamamoto's death, Tojo Hideki (who served as both premier and defense minister) was working at his desk in the War Office in downtown Tokyo. He was worried. Japanese newspapers and radio broadcasts had told the public nothing about the defeats at Midway and Guadalcanal and the people were not restive. But the Allies were now in a position to advance up the Solomons and their submarines infested the waters all the way from Singapore to Japan itself. The sinking of freighters was causing shortages of meat and rice. To prevent conditions from deteriorating further, Tojo fired out an order to his scientists: Speed up the superbomb project.

Research on the atomic bomb had been taking place in a cream-colored, two-story barrackslike building on the outskirts of Tokyo. Responsibility for the work was shared by Colonel Suzuki Tatsasaburo, who was gifted enough, to Nishina Yoshio, a civilian but Japan's most highly regarded physicist. Once a student of Niels Bohr in Germany, Nishina was well acquainted with the theory of nuclear fission, but he lacked the uranium needed for building a bomb. Japanese officials had had high hopes for uranium imports from Korea, but the mines on the peninsula had turned out to be nearly barren. Gold deposits with twenty percent uranium were available in Malaya, but tankers carrying the ore had trouble getting through the net of submarines; so he lacked the uranium needed for building a bomb.

But Nishina was an expert puzzle solver and he came up with a solution. On July 7, 1943, a coded message reached the Japanese embassy in Berlin: "Please make an immediate investigation of the possibilities of exporting to Japan pitchblende [the principal ore of uranium] from Czechoslovakia." Czechoslovakia was the source of uranium for Germany's own atomic research. The German government agreed to ship the ore aboard a cargo submarine.

Germany had been shipping machine tools and ball bearings to Japan by submarine in exchange for tungsten and copper, and the route was established. Leaving the naval base at Kiel, U-boats would slip through the English Channel and move down the Atlantic to the Cape of Good Hope. British antisubmarine airplanes were thick in the skies off South Africa. But if a submarine reached the expanse of the Indian Ocean, it was fairly secure. The refueling base was built and maintained by German U-boat specialists at Penang, an island just off the western coast of Malaya. The terminus of the route was Japan.

Just when a German cargo submarine bearing uranium left for Japan is unclear. But by October, 1943, Nishina had the uranium he needed.

2

For America's commanders the question in May, 1943, was: What road to victory? In Australia General MacArthur (who by now had adopted his famous props, the sunglasses, the squashed military cap, and the corncob pipe) wanted to proceed immediately to the Philippines. The Navy brass, especially Admiral Nimitz at Pearl Harbor, disliked the idea. A drive up through the rest of the Solomons to

Rabaul, then up from New Guinea and through the eastern Indies, the Navy brass held, would sacrifice lives merely to feed the general's megalomania. They wanted to steam straightaway to Japan.

The general rebutted that by using New Guinea as the jumping-off point, the Allies could dominate the Indies and recapture the Philippines, cutting Japan off from its oil.

Nimitz disagreed. By employing the carriers and landing craft now pouring out of West Coast shipyards, he would blast his way straight across the central Pacific Ocean to hit Japan directly, bypassing the Philippines altogether.

When the debate reached the Joint Chiefs of Staff in Washington, the leaders split predictably along service lines. General Marshall favored MacArthur's proposal, and Admiral King that of Nimitz. The issue went up to Roosevelt. Ever the politician, he said in essence, "Let's do both!"

With FDR's approval, a dual military drive was to go into effect. Nimitz's fleets would put out westward from Pearl Harbor; MacArthur's troops would slog up through the South Pacific. And the Japanese would not know where the next blow would fall.

But to carry out his prong of the advance, MacArthur needed ships. The American ships in the South Pacific lay in the control of the theater commander, "Bull" Halsey. Whether these two military stars, who had never met, would get along was anyone's guess.

A photograph of MacArthur, taken in May, 1942, when he was in Canberra, attending a session of the Australian Parliament, was revealing. In a black robe and powdered wig, the Speaker of the House sat behind a desk on a platform and in a mahogany, ornately canopied chair. Below him two clerks, also bewigged, sat at the end of a long, polished table, solemnly recording the proceedings. Various other officials, dignified in three-piece pin-striped suits, listened to the deliberations. But off to the side of the Speaker's podium, sitting cross-legged in an armchair, was General MacArthur in khaki shirt and trousers, without a regulation necktie.

Obviously he felt no need to don dress uniform for the Australians. He was MacArthur, the American nation's most gifted commander of troops, and, at least in his own estimation, a military genius. No other commander, wrote William Manchester, one of the general's biographers, "on either side of the war would be more jealous of his prerogatives." MacArthur easily could have seen Halsey as a threat.

Another photograph, taken later on a Pacific beachhead, portrayed the essential Halsey. Talking with a clutch of reporters and Marine officers, he sat cross-legged in a captain's chair. He was shirtless in the heat and his right shoulder bore the tattoo of an anchor that dated back to his Annapolis days. His boots were muddy, his trousers were wrinkled, and a sheathed dagger hung from his belt. His forearms were folded peacefully on his lap. But as he listened to a question his heavily browed, jut-jawed face was tilted forward with intensity.

Halsey was not a leader in the sense of saying, "Go!" With Halsey it was always, "Let's go!" His manner was almost wholly opposite to that of the arch-autocrat, Douglas MacArthur.

Early in 1943 Halsey flew to Brisbane from his headquarters in New Caledonia, halfway between Fiji and Australia, to confer with MacArthur. They met in the general's office on the eighth floor of an insurance building, and hit it off immediately. "Five minutes after I reported," Halsey would recall, "I felt as if we were lifelong friends."

Both were sons of officers, MacArthur's father from West Point and Halsey's from Annapolis, and more than forty years before their progenitors had known each other in the Philippines. Beyond that link, Halsey found himself impressed by MacArthur's erect bearing, a "diction I have never heard surpassed," and the "stately way the general paced between his large, bare desk and the facing portrait of George Washington."

The two commanders would quarrel. But their arguments, Halsey wrote, "always ended pleasantly."

They focused on strategy and tactics, their first main goal being to squeeze Rabaul in a vise. MacArthur's troops would go after a few sites the Japanese still held in northern New Guinea, then head across the Vitiaz and Dampier Straits to New Britain, a northeastward-curving island. From beaches on the western point of that island, an air wing would strike at the Rabaul base, on the opposite end. Moving toward Rabaul from the southeast, Halsey's Marines would climb what he called the Solomons ladder, starting up from Guadalcanal. In doing so, Halsey counted on their capturing New Georgia, Kolombangara, and Vella Lavella, in the central Solomons; next would come Bougainville at the western end of the chain. From Bougainville, Rabaul would be only 250 miles away. The campaign, which MacArthur and Halsey code-named "Operation Cartwheel," started rolling on June 30, 1943.

That night MacArthur's 162nd Infantry Regiment reached New Guinea's lightly defended Nassau Bay. The landing was tough: A high surf swamped many of the landing craft, and many others became stuck on coral reefs. But all the troops made it ashore.

Safely, too, for the smattering of 5,000 Japanese near the beach fled into the jungle. The main problem confronting the Americans was that of hooking up with an Australian unit holed up in the mountains. One of the Americans described the trek inland: "If one wished to go from one ridge to another there usually wasn't a high ground connecting link. . . . [O]ne always had to descend into a valley to get on top of an adjacent ridge or mountain. It was covered by rain-forest vegetation, which grew out of red wet clay that turned into grease with the passage of a few feet. . . . If one cut a trail through virgin jungle for a squad of ten men, the last man in the column was ankle-deep in mud. Crawling up a slope was very hard because the footing was so slick. You had to keep a hand free to grasp something. Many men took a tumble."

But the Americans did reach the Australians and together, supported by mortar fire, they ascended a ridge and came upon a squadron of Japanese. "We could see them now and opened fire on their heads as they bobbed up above their foxholes," reported the Australian official history. "Their fire began to slacken off. One of our chaps gave a shrill blood-curdling yell that startled even us, and was partly responsible for some of the Japanese running headlong down the hill in panic. Unable to stop at the edge of the cliff, they plunged to their doom hundreds of yards below."

After capturing Nassau Bay, MacArthur moved forces onto Woodlark and Kiriwana, two barely inhabited islands just off the eastern tip of New Guinea. On both the islands and Nassau Bay about 700 Seabees—the nickname of the men in the Navy's Construction Battalion (abbreviated CBs) who were skilled and speedy builders—quickly constructed airfields. Now for the first time American fighter planes could reach Rabaul and return.

At the same time Halsey started up the Solomons ladder. First he invaded the Russells, small islands between Guadalcanal and New Georgia, equipping them with radar stations, PT boat bases, two new airstrips, and 10,000 Marines ready to jump off to New Georgia.

New Georgia lay roughly 100 miles northwest of Guadalcanal. Samuel Eliot Morison described it as

> forty five miles long in a NW–SE line parallel to the Slot and separated from it by an almost unbroken coral-reef barrier. . . . On the opposite and southwestern side of the island the coral barrier is broken and steep cliffs rise abruptly from Blanche Channel. . . . The rain-forest green of the serrated hills, the calcimine blue of the still lagoons, and the lazy foam around the reefs, as seen from the ocean, suggest a tropical paradise; and ashore there is some substance to that elusive dream. Wild orchids bloom in extravagant profusion, bird-winged butterflies fly about, nearly as large as the screaming white cockatoos which keep them company; friendly natives ply graceful canoes along the quiet shores.

But New Georgia was no paradise. At Munda Point, on its southwestern extremity, the Japanese had built an airstrip that was only thirty minutes flying time from Guadalcanal. Stringing cables along the tops of nearby coconut trees and covering the cables with fronds, the Japanese had camouflaged the field. Pilots could not make it out from the air.

Thanks to Donald C. Kennedy, an Australian coast-watcher, the Allies nonetheless knew the airstrip's location. Hiding in a transmitting station at Segi Point—on the eastern tip of New Guinea and forty miles from Munda Point—Kennedy had tracked Japanese planes to the airfield.

Kennedy's intelligence was invaluable. As long as Japan held Munda Point and had airplanes there, it could stop Halsey's progress at the Russells. So on June 30, an Allied task force of 5,000 men under the command of Admiral Richmond Kelly Turner, an expert on amphibious warfare, started out from the Russells for Munda Point. It ran into near disaster.

The troops went ashore first on Rendova, a small island six miles across the water from Munda Point that was to serve as a staging area for the attack on Munda itself. Resistance on Rendova was light. But out from under their camouflaged airfield on Munda Point, the Japanese hit hard with air attacks for several days, the planes flying low, many of then at treetop level.

Even under such attacks, though, the Seabees kept working. And when they finally had constructed a roadway from the landing beach to a hilltop from which artillery could reach Munda Point, they stopped working and cheered.

Still, the Allied command realized, a straight approach to Munda Point would be dangerous. The coral reefs were impenetrable and the shore bristled with Japanese guns. Halsey decided to hit New Georgia at Zanana, a beach four miles east of Munda Point and beyond the range of the Japanese big guns. The troops would take Munda from the rear and two weeks later the Allies would have the Japanese airfield. Such at least was the idea.

But the jungle was dense and the Japanese were all around, especially at night. They "plastered bivouacs with artillery and mortar barrages," Morison wrote, "crawled silently into American foxholes and stabbed or strangled the occupants. Often they cursed loudly, in English, rattled their equipment, named the American commanding officers, and dared the Americans to fight. . . . For sick and hungry soldiers who had fought all day, this unholy shivaree was terrifying. They shot at everything in sight—rotting stumps, land crabs clattering over rocks, even comrades."

The four miles of jungle felt like four hundred. Banyan trees blocked mortar shells. Hand grenades hit branches and bounced back. A stream was flooded. For three days one Japanese patrol firing from out of the brush held up the progress of an entire American division. Supplies were running low; the bulldozers intended to clear pathways for roads became stuck in mud and their operators came under steady Japanese fire. Each bulldozer had to be sent back to the Zanana beachhead to acquire protective steel plates on the cabs. Everything that could go wrong did go wrong. Halsey sent in reinforcements, but so did the Japanese.

The U.S. troops under General Oscar W. Griswold inched ahead. Only 3,000 yards from Munda Point, they used flamethrowers to take out a series of Japanese pillboxes. One regiment got to within 1,000 yards of the airstrip. Supported by soldiers with flamethrowers, tanks pushed even closer. By August 1, an American patrol had reached the end of the Munda airfield, and by that same date the constant bombardment from Rendova across the strait had taken its toll. The camouflage was long gone and the Japanese survivors in their bunkers were starving. Four days later, Griswold radioed Halsey: "Our ground forces have wrested Munda from the Japs and present it to you . . . as the sole owner."

Almost all the Japanese on New Georgia were dead, for neither side took many prisoners. The Americans lost 600 men.

Despite the victory, the New Georgia campaign had required four divisions and set Halsey's timetable back by a month: He had advanced only 200 miles up The Slot toward Rabaul. A few miles ahead lay the next island of some size, Kolombangara, guarded by 10,000 Japanese. An attack on Kolombangara promised further American deaths.

The "undue length of the Munda operation and our casualties made me wary of another slugging match," Halsey was to write. "But I didn't know how to avoid it. I could see no victory without Rabaul, and no Rabaul without Kolombangara."

To take Kolombangara, Halsey needed reinforcements. Yet in mid-July, 1943, the Allied invasion of Sicily was just starting and Washington could spare no troops or ships. Halsey therefore decided to skip ahead to the next island, Vella Lavella.

The strategy of leapfrogging was nothing new. The Navy brass had already proposed the bypassing of many Japanese-held islands and leaving them to "wither on the vine." Admiral Nimitz had been using the tactic successfully up in the Aleutians, where the Japanese had seized several islands. Besides, Halsey realized, Vella Lavella was blessed with large, flat stretches of land from which airplanes could turn around and bombard Kolombangara. Halsey gave the order to take Vella Lavella.

On August 15, 1943, Marines waded up to the island's beach. The attack caught the Japanese, encamped inland, by surprise, and almost all were killed. By September, Seabees had constructed a new airfield and bombers began to drop their loads on Kolombangara.

Seeing that the defense of that island was hopeless, Admiral Kusaki Jinichi, the Japanese commander at Rabaul, ordered an evacuation. On the moonless night of September 28, a convoy of barges out of Bougainville, protected by a destroyer escort, went down The Slot to rescue the stranded Japanese troops. The rescue mission went on for two weeks amid fierce naval battles, mostly under the ceiling of stars. The Japanese got out of Kolombangara but at the cost of 1,000 troops lost on sunken barges.

Japan was still 3,000 miles away. But the leapfrog had succeeded and would prove a major element in the American forward drive. Now it was MacArthur's turn to move.

In Tokyo, Emperor Hirohito cautioned War Minister Tojo to take care not to let "Lae and Salamaua become another Guadalcanal." By tradition, the emperor was to remain above politics and transcend factional feuds, for he represented all the Japanese people. But, although a modest and studious man, Hirohito now broke with that tradition. He was giving Tojo military advice. Tojo ignored the advice.

Lae and Salamaua indeed were MacArthur's next objectives. They were ports on the Huon peninsula.

If the end of New Guinea resembled a lizard's tail, then the Huon peninsula, on the eastern coast, was the rump, jutting out into the Vitiaz and Dampier Straits. MacArthur wanted this jut of land for the jump over to New Britain. For taking the peninsula, Lae, a port with an airfield and anchorage, was the key to success.

MacArthur's attacks on September 4 came from three directions: by sea from the south to draw the defenders' attention, then overland from east and west to hit the port from the back. The land-based columns were Australian. The two commanders bet each other twenty cases of whiskey on who would get to Lae first. The winner accepted the booze, but found the town "indescribably and thoroughly wrecked" by American bombs.

Sick and starving, the surviving Japanese in the port fled to the mountains. By September 16, MacArthur was poised for the drive on New Britain.

At the end of September, 1943, the momentum went back to Halsey. Wishing to reduce Rabaul to rubble, he set his sights on the last rung of the Solomons ladder, Bougainville.

Bougainville was about 130 miles long and thirty miles wide. Dense jungle hillsides extended from the beaches to heights of over 10,000 feet. But on its southern end, Bougainville also possessed a major anchorage, Empress Augusta Bay. Halsey's staff estimated that the Japanese troop strength there numbered 35,000 to 40,000 men, under General Hyakutake Haruyoshi. Even with Admiral Yamamoto dead, Hyakutake presented a threat to Guadalcanal. Halsey wanted the anchorage.

Halsey moved with stealth. In the last week of October, he sent reconnaissance planes to photograph the Shortlands, islets just southwest of Bougainville. Their presence lured Japanese troops into the southern area.

Halsey then went north. In the predawn of November 1, 1943, a flotilla of American cruisers and destroyers opened a bombardment targeting two northern Japanese airfields. At about noon, two new carriers, *Saratoga* and *Princeton*, showed up. Their bombers smashed the remaining Japanese planes.

That same morning, Halsey staged a landing at Empress Augusta Bay. Resistance was light and the Seabees quickly repaired the bombed airstrips. But a Japanese task force was on the way.

On November 2, Admiral Kusaki at Rabaul dispatched three heavy cruisers, a light cruiser, and six destroyers to Bougainville. Forty-five miles from the island, however, Admiral A. Stanton Merrill, a Naval Academy graduate who had been in action off Guadalcanal, appeared with four light cruisers and eight destroyers. In a savage three-hour exchange of gunfire and torpedoes, Merrill drove the Japanese away. He had sunk a Japanese light cruiser and a destroyer; four of his own destroyers were damaged, but he had not lost one ship.

With the Japanese fleet in retreat, a flotilla of carriers, *Saratoga, Princeton, Essex, Bunker Hill,* and *Independence,* gathered in Empress Augusta Bay. On November 5, they sent ninety-seven planes to bomb Rabaul.

On Bougainville itself, General Hyakutake had made a fundamental mistake. Believing the American presence in Empress Augusta Bay to be a feint, he had held his troops back, thus allowing the Americans time to expand the beachhead. Soon the American line of defense, a horseshoe-shaped perimeter more than ten miles long, looked like a pincushion of mortars, machine guns, and howitzers. U.S. troops had mined the approaching trails and chopped away at the jungle, so that from the shoreline they could look out on a clear field of fire. The Americans were ready.

The Japanese came the day after Thanksgiving. The battle lasted seventeen days, often tree to tree and hand to hand. But the Japanese were outnumbered and outgunned. They lost 7,000 soldiers to 1,000 Americans killed.

Christmas Day, 1943, brought the American victory. Now the Americans could strike Rabaul at will.

MacArthur had been waiting for this moment. The day after Christmas, he ordered the First Marine Division ashore at Cape Gloucester, the western tip of New Guinea: The cape overlooked the channel through which his attack on the Philippines would have to pass. A photograph of the landing showed helmeted men waiting on the beach as the front flaps of a landing craft opened to release a tank. Although prone to bogging down in swamps, the tanks soon proved indispensable in demolishing Japanese pillboxes. And while seventy or eighty Japanese bombers flew down from Rabaul, American P-38s shot down almost all of them. Cape Gloucester was MacArthur's.

At this point he and Halsey decided not to bother taking Rabaul. With American planes up from Cape Gloucester blasting away at the air base and port, the general and the admiral felt free to let the 100,000 Japanese dug in at the base "wither on the vine." MacArthur now could begin his push to the Philippines—and Admiral Nimitz his drive across the central Pacific.

So the Pacific hammer was raised to strike. The Chinese anvil, however—if it had ever existed—was falling to pieces.

3

Up on a crest above Chongqing stood the stone mansion of Generalissimo and Madame Chiang Kaishek. On a ridge at the end of the crest a few hundred yards away, lived H. H. Kong, banker and China's prime minister, and his own wife, Soong Ailing, one of Madame's two sisters. T. V. Soong, the women's brother, lived half a mile down the road. General Stilwell lived another half a mile away. As Stilwell observed his wealthy neighbors, who treated ruling a country as if it were a family affair, he concluded that they represented all that was wrong with China.

Although Madame Chiang Kaishek had always struck many Chinese as greedy and vain, she once had sympathized with the plight of her people. After Japan's invasion of China in 1937, she had worked hard for those whom she called the nation's "warphans." But even before Pearl Harbor, she had spent much of her time in the Soong mansion on Victoria Peak, looking down upon Hong Kong's harbor. There her chief interest, many thought, had seemed to be gaining publicity abroad.

Stilwell thought her real disintegration had set in during her trip to the United States. In his judgment, the adulation there had turned her conceit to corruption. Certainly unaccounted millions of American aid dollars had flowed into the hands of those around her.

Back in her grand house on the edge of Chongqing, she spent most of her time on clothes and makeup. On one occasion she did fly to Kunming. Not expecting a reception, as the American Graham Peck observed, "she got out of the plane in the natural state of a traveler: dress wrinkled, hair untidy, lipstick chewed. The first thing she saw was a GI with a camera, grinning irreverently as he snapped a candid record of her. She hustled back into the plane and into a rage which lasted until an officer ordered the soldier to destroy the film. [But] she was [still] mad. . . . She refused to get out again. The generals and colonels uneasily standing about could see her dimly through one window, her chin cupped in her palms as she glared at them."

Stilwell heard the story and found it disturbing. Madame Chiang, he thought, was manifesting an arrogance typical of the Chongqing regime as a whole. He considered the government, mired in corruption, altogether out of touch with the Chinese people. Stilwell likened himself to a jockey riding a dead horse.

In the China–Burma–India theater, General Stilwell's bailiwick, the first half of 1943 was quiet. Along thousands of miles of trench, foxhole, and jungle outposts, emaciated Chinese soldiers just sat. Little had changed. Japanese bombers still droned over Chongqing and dropped their lethal loads. From Kunming, Claire Chennault's Flying Tigers still sallied forth to hit the Japanese-held ports. Ramshackle cargo planes still appeared from over the Hump, each time landing in China with a couple of tons of war goods.

Stilwell could not resist penning a bit of doggerel:

Lyric to Spring

I welcomed the spring in romantic Chongqing,
I walked in her beautiful bowers.
In the light of the moon, in the sunshine at noon,
I savored the fragrance of flowers.
Not to speak of the slush, or the muck and the mush
That covers the streets and alleys.
Or the reek of the swill, as it sweeps down the hill,
Or the odor of pig in the valleys.
The sunset and dawn, and the dew on the lawn,
And the blossoms in colors are rare.
The jasmine in bloom, the magnolia's perfume,
The magic of spring's in the air.
The garbage is rich, as it rots in the ditch,
And the honey-carts scatter pollution,
The effluvium rank, from the crap in the tank,
Is the stink of its scummy solution.
Aromatic Chongqing, where I welcomed the spring,
In a mixture of beauty and stenches,
Of flowers and birds, with a sprinkling of turds,
And of bow-legged Sichuan wenches.
Take me back to the Coast, to the place I love most,
Get me out of this odorous sewer.
I'm in _____ to my neck, but I'm quitting, by heck!
And I'll never more shovel manure.

Yet there was more shoveling in store for Stilwell. Whether in British Delhi or in Chinese Chongqing, he found himself repeating the same arguments so frequently that, as Theodore White, who was often with Stilwell, put it, "a commander's authority was reduced to the status of a housewife's nagging."

The more Stilwell nagged, the more intransigent Chiang Kaishek became. He even began to question Stilwell's strategy. Why, he insisted on knowing, should there be a rush to liberate Burma? Why not double and redouble the flights over the Himalayas? Instead of stressing ground war, why not build up Chennault's air force?

The last line of questioning left Stilwell infuriated. For reasons of personality and interservice rivalry alike, he and Chennault loathed each other. So bitter was the Stilwell–Chennault conflict, in fact, that in May, 1943, Roosevelt summoned them both to the White House.

The State Department had kept the president fully abreast of the Stilwell–Chennault dispute. But Roosevelt was hardly neutral. Still espousing the idea of China as the anvil and enamored of American airpower, he sided with Chennault and wanted Stilwell to stop his sniping.

The Washington conference left Stilwell even more embittered. "Nobody," he wrote in his journal, "was interested in the humdrum work of building a ground force [in China] but me." Stilwell recognized that the person who had Roosevelt's ear was Chennault. He could drive the Japanese out of China in six months, the aviator boasted, and all he needed was the equipment.

Stilwell left Washington in a foul mood. "So everything was to be thrown to the air offensive," he lamented. "FDR [whom he called 'Blah-blah'] pulled 7,000 tons [monthly over the Hump, the Himalayas] out of the air when told that 10,000 was impossible, and ordered that tonnage for July. . . . They will do the Japs some damage but at the same time will so weaken the ground effort that it may fail. Then what the hell use is it to knock down a few Jap planes?"

But Roosevelt, being Roosevelt, also authorized Stilwell to open the Burma campaign. Back in India, Stilwell oversaw the attempts by American officers to teach Chinese soldiers, peasant boys, how to load howitzers, build sanitary camps, and handle the wounded. Despite the language barrier, the troops made some progress. By the late autumn, Stilwell was ready to lead thirty Chinese divisions into Burma—if Chiang Kaishek would not be obstructive.

Then, at the end of November, 1943, Roosevelt summoned Chiang, Madame, and Stilwell to Cairo. FDR wanted to make sure that Chiang was actively in the war.

4

When the Americans and British under General Eisenhower landed on the southern coast of Sicily in mid-July, 1943, a combined German–Italian force at first put up a vigorous resistance. But the resistance soon crumbled. Yet roughly 230,000 enemy troops, mostly Italian, were still in Sicily and Eisenhower was determined that they would not escape to Italy. So he sent the British General Montgomery and the American General Patton to Messina, only three miles from the toe of Italy. Although the Italians were left behind, the Germans succeeded in moving most of their own personnel and equipment over to Italy. At the beginning of September, the Allies invaded Sardinia and Corsica, and the mainland of southern Italy—the toe, shinbone, instep, and heel. On October 1, the Americans entered the ruined port of Naples and the British, having crossed the peninsula to the east, overwhelmed the German airfields at Foggia. On November 8, Eisenhower ordered the assault on Rome.

On the eastern front, the Soviets by November had pushed beyond Kiev on the Dnieper. The city of Smolensk, near the border of Latvia and Lithuania, was about to fall to the Red Army.

Given the gains in Italy and eastern Europe, Roosevelt, through the embassy in Moscow, proposed a meeting with Stalin. FDR hoped that he and the Soviet dictator could establish a constructive relationship that he considered necessary for postwar cooperation. The two leaders agreed to meet in Tehran starting on November 28. Churchill would also attend.

But first, Roosevelt would meet with Churchill in Cairo. They had met several times already and had exchanged scores of messages.

FDR had yielded to Churchill on postponing the invasion of France. But Roosevelt wanted Churchill to meet Chiang at Cairo and to let both know that he, as the American president, was now in charge of the war effort.

Official photographs showed the major participants, Churchill in a white linen suit, Roosevelt in a dark business suit, Chiang in a high-collared khaki uniform, and Madame Chiang (who translated) in a white silk jacket and black slit skirt, sitting in side-by-side chairs under the Egyptian sunshine. The pictures presented a scene of apparent amity.

To Churchill the conference was anything but amiable. FDR let him know that, after the war, he intended to treat China, along with Britain, America, and the Soviet Union, as one of the world's "four horsemen." Churchill's reaction was explosive. He protested that the Chinese in general and the Chiangs in particular were weak, corrupt, and attractive to Americans only because the United States planned in the postwar era to replace Great Britain as the dominant power in China.

Roosevelt brushed off Churchill's concerns. China, he informed Churchill, would become America's worthy junior partner.

Churchill growled that Chiang would pretend to support whatever Roosevelt wanted. Then, back in China, he would slip back into his corrupt ways.

But Roosevelt was certain that he could handle Chiang Kaishek. The Chinese leader, the president informed him bluntly, was to work with Stilwell and get the Burma campaign to succeed. Back in Chongqing on December 20, Stilwell wrote: "Off to Burma again. Under better auspices than last time. CAN WE PUT IT OVER?"

Was Roosevelt realistic about China? In the Chongqing of 1943, John King Fairbank, a Harvard professor of Chinese history serving at the time with the OSS, observed that "our ally the Nationalist regime [of Chiang Kaishek] was self-destructing and on the way out of power."

According to the Confucian classics, Fairbank explained later in a book about the United States and China, "the wickedness of the last ruler of the Shang [the first Chinese dynasty], who was a tyrant, caused Heaven to give a mandate to the Zhou [the succeeding dynasty]. . . . Heaven withdrew its mandate and the people were justified in deposing the dynasty." Three thousand years later, Heaven was withdrawing its mandate from Chiang Kaishek, and giving it to Mao Zedong.

14

UNANSWERABLE
STRENGTH

1

The Japanese public knew nothing of the atomic bomb project or the desperation it reflected at the highest levels of government. Even by the time of the Cairo Conference, when the Allies were beginning to consider the look of postwar Asia, the populace had little inkling of impending disaster.

The people of Japan were walled off from their own war. The government controlled all the newspapers, the airwaves, and the speeches given to labor associations, youth and women's groups, and organized neighborhood units. Families usually were not notified that their sons had been killed. Meals were sparse, and to conserve leather and rubber the government urged people to wear wooden clogs *(geta)* rather than shoes or sneakers. But no one was starving and the Japanese traditionally had worn wooden clogs. Besides, from the start of the

"China Incident" onward, wall posters and loudspeakers had exhorted the populace to "make do." All along the patriotic duty of the citizenry had been to sacrifice for the emperor and the war effort.

Still, a scene photographed by a news cameraman in November, 1943 [the photograph was made public by the *Mainichi* (Daily) newspaper chain only in 1976], was revealing. In the Meiji Gaien stadium in Tokyo, hundreds of women aligned in rows were wearing black peasant pantaloons and hooded shrouds and moving in unison, perhaps as ordered by a drill instructor. In their extended left hands all the women were holding empty buckets and relaying them along.

They were practicing passing water to douse fires. The government was preparing for the incendiary bombing it knew was to come.

2

Economic realities were grinding Japan down. Even in the decade before Pearl Harbor, America's gross national product had measured roughly ten times that of Japan; and the population of the United States was commensurately larger. Now, with seemingly inexhaustible numbers of airplanes, carriers, and other vessels of war, America was reducing the very idea of a Japanese "defensive perimeter" to a fiction. American submarines were ranging as far as Japan's home islands. And at Pearl Harbor, Nimitz was preparing to take full advantage of Japan's vulnerability.

A map of the Pacific covered all of one wall in Nimitz's office. Inked-in lines divided the ocean into a series of roughly rectangular zones.

The top zone lay above the 42nd parallel, a line that ran from just above San Francisco to the strait between Honshu and Hokkaido. Above the line rose the Great Circle route of the northern Pacific— the sweep of the American and Canadian coastlines up toward Alaska, then along the Aleutian Islands and pointing back down like a long curving finger toward Japan.

Below the line was the "Central Pacific Area" between the 42nd parallel and the equator. It included Hawaii, Midway, and, much farther to the west, the Marshalls, the Marianas, and finally Taiwan.

To form the third area, the line drawn along the equator turned northward at a right angle just beyond New Guinea, then westward again above the Philippines to the Gulf of Tonkin. Another north–south line ran down from Java past the western coast of Australia to finish the zone. Shaped like Utah, this was the "Southwest Pacific Area." Including the Solomons and New Guinea, it was the MacArthur–Halsey domain.

Finally, a line ran along the 40th parallel from western Australia to the coast of Chile. In this rectangle, the "South Pacific Area," were several Japanese-controlled atolls, the most important of which were the Gilbert Islands near the northwestern corner of this zone and about five hundred miles southwest of Hawaii.

The heart of the Nimitz strategy was the central zone, where the Marshalls and the Marianas opened a broad avenue to the west. Taking them would enable American air and naval power to strike ever closer to Japan.

Before he could proceed, though, Nimitz wanted to control the Gilberts. With two main atolls, Makin and Tarawa, these islands lay athwart communication lines between Hawaii and MacArthur's Southwest Pacific Area; from the airstrip on Tarawa, especially, Japanese planes would be able to harass the rear of Nimitz's cross-Pacific drive.

So the Gilberts were his first target. Nimitz thought he could grab them with ease.

His attack fleet was formidable. Vice Admiral Raymond A. Spruance, a hero of Midway, led ships from Pearl Harbor, New Zealand, and elsewhere in the Pacific—twelve battleships, twelve cruisers, sixty-six destroyers, three dozen transports carrying 35,000 Marines and soldiers, and seventeen carriers loaded with more than 900 airplanes.

Assembling where the equator crossed the international date line, on November 20, 1943, they headed for the Gilberts.

Spruance divided his fleet into three parts: a shield of ten fast new carriers to protect the operation from Japanese airplanes; a task force for Makin atoll; and another group for the Tarawa atoll, 100 miles south of Makin. Rear Admiral Richmond Kelly Turner, also of Midway fame, commanded the Makin ships and Major General Holland M. Smith, nicknamed "Howlin' Mad," took charge of the landing.

As black smoke from oil dumps hit by naval gunfire billowed beyond the beach, 6,500 Americans waded ashore on Butaritari, a tiny island in the atoll. Butaritari was shaped like a hammer. Along the handle of the hammer, Japanese defenders were nowhere in sight.

But the landing went awry. The surf splashed onto radios, hampering communications. Flamethrowers got soaked and were useless. Most of the Americans, Army men who had done garrison duty in Hawaii, had never seen combat. They wasted time and ammunition firing at what they thought were Japanese snipers but actually were coconuts up in the palm trees. Soldiers did not know how to set up artillery. The slow pace of the advance gave a Japanese submarine time to sink an American carrier. General Smith was indeed howlin' mad.

The capture of Makin took four days and cost nearly 700 American lives. But the Japanese and a battalion of conscripted Koreans lost about 2,000. The victory message radioed to Washington was "Makin Taken."

The Tarawa atoll was shaped roughly like an isosceles triangle. From the top left to the bottom right ran a coral hypotenuse about thirty miles long. Enclosing a lagoon was another reef, the vertical leg of the triangle. Just above the base was an island called Betio. Half the size of Central Park, Betio was another South Pacific lizard, with a head on the west and a long tail descending to the southeast. The American objective was the midsection, where a Japanese airstrip crisscrossed the belly. The battle to get it was one of the bloodiest of the Second World War.

Before the battle, the opposing commanders indulged in extravagant boasting. Taking command of 2,500 experienced troops stationed on Betio, Rear Admiral Shibasaki Keiji bragged that a "million men cannot take Tarawa in a hundred years." In command of the landing, Rear Admiral Howard F. Kingman assured the Second Marine Division: "Gentlemen, we will not neutralize Betio. We will not destroy it. We will obliterate it."

Kingman was speaking prematurely. Japanese artillery covered Betio's every beach and every avenue of approach. Concealed behind a wall of tree trunks, more than 100 machine guns guarded the lagoon. And belowground, dug into the coral, reinforced with steel and concrete, covered with sand so they showed up in no aerial photographs, and connected by a network of tunnels that allowed troops to move quickly to points under attack, were Admiral Shibasaki's pillboxes. Out on the beaches concrete pillars and barbed-wire entanglements created pathways that led invaders straight toward the pillbox guns. Under the surf and beaches explosive mines encircled the atoll. And the surrounding reef opened at two points only—both within easy range of Betio's artillery.

Even before the landing, however, new American B-24s, which had greater range than the B-17s and could fly lower over targets, roared up from the New Zealand–occupied Ellice Islands, about 400 miles to the south, and smashed Betio with tons of bombs. Off the decks of *Essex, Bunker Hill,* and *Independence,* dive-bombers came in low to hit the pillboxes. A flotilla of destroyers, cruisers, and battleships, *Tennessee, Maryland,* and *Colorado,* pulled in close, hurling upon Betio approximately ten tons of shells per acre.

On November 21, 1943, the Second Marine Division landed on Betio. Organized Japanese opposition ended two days later.

In the early morning of November 20, 1943, a half-moon above Tarawa flitted in and out of fleecy clouds. On the ocean below ships slid into position. Near the lagoon entrance closest to Betio, an American fleet stood ready to send its shells high over the heads of the landing force and onto the island. Just a few miles north of Betio, the troop transports gathered together and moved ahead.

Robert Sherrod, a *Time-Life* correspondent aboard an LST (for Landing Ship, Tank—a big, flat-bottomed vessel designed to haul tanks, trucks, and bulldozers directly to the beaches), described the approach. "After making last-minute adjustments of my gear," he wrote, "I went up on the flying bridge. . . . It was cool up there, with a brisk breeze on the rise. It was possible to make notes when the moon was out. A calm voice came over the loudspeaker: 'Target [Betio] at 112 true, 26,800 yards ahead.' '*Blackfish* 870 yards.' The *Blackfish* was the lead transport and the *Blue Fox* was next. The first red signal light of the lead ship slowly flashed on and off as we followed her to Tarawa."

At 3:30 in the morning the transports halted. Outside the ward room now, Sherrod watched as the "first and second waves [of Marines] walked through and out to their boats. . . . They were a grimy . . . lot. Under the weight, light though it was, of their combat packs, lifebelts, guns, ammunition, helmets, canvas leggings, bayonets, they were sweating in great profusion. Nobody had shaved for two or three days. . . . [Then] at 0505, we heard a great thud in the southwest. We knew what that meant. The first battleship had fired the first shot. We all rushed out on deck. The show had begun. The show for which hundreds of thousands of men had spent months of training, scores of ships had sailed thousands of miles, for which Chaplains Kelly and MacQueen had offered their prayers. The curtain was up on the theater of death."

The curtain rose on bedlam. At dawn, transport captains saw that they had located their ships right in the path of the battleship bombardment. Japanese shells were also splashing ever closer. So just as the landing craft were scheduled to move forward, the transports had to move backward. The Marines had to go ashore in full daylight.

According to Sherrod:

> [I] tried to count the number of salvos—not shells, salvos—the battleships, cruisers, and destroyers were pouring in the island. A Marine who had a waterproof watch offered to count off the seconds up to one minute. Long before the minute had ended I had counted over one hundred, but then a dozen more ships opened up and I abandoned the project. I did count the number of planes in sight at one time. It was ninety two. These ships and these planes were dealing out an unmerciful beating on the Japs. . . . As we came within two miles of the island [Sherrod by this time was aboard a landing craft] we could get a better view of what was happening. There were fires up and down the length of the island. Most of them would be the barracks, the power plant, the kitchens, and other above-ground installations we had studied time and again in the photographs. Once in a while a solid mass of flame would reach for the sky and the roar of an explosion could be heard from our position in the water. That would be an oil tank or an ammunition dump.

After one round of explosions, another Marine private said to Sherrod, "It's a wonder the whole goddam island doesn't fall apart and sink."

But as American amphibian tractors ("amtracks," adaptations of "swamp buggies" used in the 1930s to rescue hurricane victims in the Everglades) inside the atoll reached the sand, Japanese guns opened fire. "They were knocking boats out right and left," Private Newman Baird in the first assault wave recounted. "A tractor'd get hit, stop, and burst into flames, with men jumping out like torches. . . . Our boat was stopped, and they were laying lead on us from a pillbox like holy hell. . . . I grabbed my carbine and an ammunition box and stepped over a couple of fellows lying there and put my hand on their side so's to roll over into the water. . . . Only about a dozen of twenty five men went over the side with me."

Hit in their fuel tanks, dozens of the amtracks exploded. Others sank. Some reached the beach but not at the assigned spots.

Following the amtracks came a wave of LSVPs (Landing Craft, Vehicle and Personnel), nicknamed Higgins boats after Andrew Jackson Higgins, their New Orleans creator. Although of shallow draft, many became hung up on the coral, easy marks for Japanese gunners.

Robert Sherrod went ashore on a Higgins boat. When it stalled, he jumped over the edge and waded on in. He wrote:

> [No] sooner had we hit the water than the Jap machine-guns really opened up on us. There must have been five or six of these machine-guns concentrating their fire on us— there was no nearer target in the water at the time—which meant several hundred bullets per man. . . . It was painfully slow, wading in such deep water. And we had several hundred yards to walk slowly into that machine-gun fire, looming into larger targets as we rose onto higher ground. . . .
>
> I do not know when it was that I realized I wasn't frightened any longer. I suppose it was when I looked around and saw [an] amtrack scooting back for more Marines. Perhaps it was when I noticed that bullets were hitting six inches to the left or six inches to the right. I could have sworn that I could have reached out and touched a hundred bullets. I remember chuckling inside and saying, "You bastards, you certainly are lousy shots."

Sherrod and his Marine comrades were able to make their way to the end of a 500-yard-long pier that jutted out into the lagoon. Built on coral, its coconut-log stanchions afforded protection.

They were lucky. Of the first group of attackers, under the direct command of Colonel David M. Shoup (later commandant of the Marine Corps), only thirty percent got onto Betio unharmed. The ratio of the next two waves was little better. With no evidence that his troops had harmed the Japanese, Shoup knew that he had to take drastic action.

At the outbreak of the war, Shoup had been serving in Iceland. During the Battle of the Atlantic in the summer of 1941, the American Navy had taken command of the Azores, Greenland, and Iceland, as bases from which to track German submarines. By late 1942, however, the U-boat menace had receded and Shoup was transferred to the Pacific. He was a tough Marine, bull-necked, red-faced, and given to bellowing orders like a drill sergeant. With Japanese fire disrupting the American assault waves at Tarawa, he needed all his toughness.

The only way his Marines were going to take Tarawa was by standing up, climbing over the seawall, and charging right into Admiral Shibasaki's pillboxes. They needed Shoup to get them moving.

At high noon he was crouching under the pier. When a Higgins boat drew near, he waded out and climbed aboard. Most of the men on the deck were dead. Those alive were immobilized by fear. Shoup was determined to press on.

Jumping off a Higgins boat and wading to the beach, Shoup took a hit on a leg but kept going. Others followed. Then, despite heavy fire, tanks came ashore. So did heavy artillery. Shoup directed the fire. But the shielded pillboxes seemed impervious to the attack. The sun went down. Ignoring his wounds, Shoup kept up the barrage, still to little effect. But at dawn he realized that one of the pillboxes was silent. They had demolished all its exposed weapons.

On the second day of the fighting, the tide flooded in. Higgins boats were able to come across the reef and pick up the wounded and deliver fresh supplies. An infusion of 400 new Marines seized a section of the island's south shore and from all units Shoup began to receive reports of Japanese soldiers committing suicide.

Admiral Shibasaki, from his steel and concrete bunker, radioed Tokyo for help, but American air strikes at Rabaul had sunk ships that might have come with reinforcements and food. Shibasaki was abandoned by his helpless superiors. Three days after the American landing, he radioed Tokyo again: "Our weapons have been destroyed. From now on everyone is attempting a final charge. May Japan exist for ten thousand years!"

Seventy-six hours after it had begun, the struggle for Tarawa was over. With hardly a Japanese survivor of the original 2,600, the atoll was in American hands.

Along with Robert Sherrod, who filed reports sympathetic to the American command, a number of American correspondents taken to Tarawa sent back hostile stories, likening the attack on Tarawa to the Charge of the Light Brigade, citing the loss of 1,000 American lives for a few acres of coral. Editorialists in U.S. newspapers used the phrase "tragic Tarawa." Even General Holland Smith, writing in *The Saturday Evening Post* after the war, declared that the United States could well have leapfrogged the Tarawa atoll. It is hard to escape the conclusion that at Tarawa the American commanders were bent on displaying American mastery.

Tarawa nonetheless provided lessons. In reconstructing the Tarawa defenses, Navy planners in Hawaii found that if fired high enough to fall almost straight down, shells could penetrate the Japanese pillboxes.

So on February 1, 1944, with new tactics and refurbished ships, Admiral Nimitz turned his attention to the rectangle across the middle of his big wall map. His next targets were Kwajalein and Eniwetok, atolls way out in the Marshall Islands. Nimitz was on his way—and MacArthur too was now on the move.

3

As in the First World War, Australia in the Second fought loyally alongside Great Britain. In 1941 and 1942, the "Aussies" made major contributions against Rommel's *Panzerkorps* in North Africa. After the fall of Singapore, however, the Labour government of Prime Minister John Curtin realized that Britain could not help with Australia's defense. London had few resources to expend in the Pacific. Meeting in the white, square Parliament Building in Canberra, Curtin and his ministers, upon the arrival of MacArthur, had decided to place their forces under the American's command.

Headquartered from early 1942 to the autumn of 1944 in Brisbane, MacArthur commanded a combined force of Americans and Australians. During those two years, the force grew from a few thousand men to nearly 750,000, as against about 350,000 Japanese stationed in New Guinea and its nearby islands. Added to the troops were a scattering of remaining Dutch ships, American and Australian air squadrons, the Australian Navy, and the American Seventh Fleet under Admiral Halsey. Infantry training took place under a single command, but out in the field U.S. General Walter Krueger directed the American men and General Sir Thomas Blaney, commander in chief of the Australian Army, led his own troops.

Presiding over thoroughly cooperative units, MacArthur was confident that he could leapfrog and envelop—he used the term "loops of envelopment"—all the way across the New Guinea lizard's back until he reached the Indies.

His next major goal was Hollandia, a port that lay midway along the lizard's back. Before the war, Hollandia had been the capital of western New Guinea, a Dutch territory. Upon seizing it in 1942, the Japanese had used the anchorage as a transshipment point for eastern New Guinea and Rabaul. MacArthur wanted Hollandia as his own launching pad for the drive to the Philippines.

He would approach the port in the spring of 1944 by sea and by land. While Halsey's ships came to dominate the Bismarck Sea, west of Rabaul, MacArthur's American and Australian units would proceed across the mountainous, rain-forested New Guinea terrain and spring upon Hollandia from the rear.

The going proved tough. The year before, the Imperial Headquarters in Tokyo had decided to establish a new defensive line from the Marianas in the central-western Pacific down through Dutch New Guinea and the former Netherlands East Indies. The Japanese high command said it would defend this line to the bitter end. And when the Allies landed on the New Guinea beaches, front-line Japanese soldiers fought back fanatically.

But the Japanese had taken few precautions to protect their planes. On March 25, Allied fliers in a daylight raid caught Japanese aircraft parked wing-to-wing on the Hollandia airfield and wiped them out.

By March 26, Hollandia was besieged. MacArthur got together with Nimitz to plan the rest of the Pacific campaign.

Late in March, 1944, MacArthur and Nimitz met for the first time, in Brisbane. Before the session, reporters wrote of potential conflict between the two. No collision took place. Nimitz flew in with gifts of orchids and silks with Polynesian prints, and MacArthur gave a banquet in the admiral's honor. Nimitz also agreed to lend MacArthur ships for the northward drive and MacArthur consented to provide planes for Nimitz's trans-Pacific push.

MacArthur soon issued the go-ahead for the completion of the Hollandia operation. At dawn on April 22, 1944, the Marines went ashore at Humboldt Bay, Hollandia's anchorage. As usual, a coral reef blocked their way; only a narrow opening let them attain the white-sand beach. There was no resistance. In dugouts just beyond the sand, the first Americans found bowls of rice and still-boiling teapots. The Japanese defenders had been taken by surprise and fled into the surrounding hills. But of some 3,000 defenders, to the Allies' surprise, this time 611 Japanese surrendered.

"Not only did the majority [of Japanese] flee without a show of resistance," General Walter Krueger, the commanding officer, later told Samuel Eliot Morison, "but those who remained to fight failed to offer any type of resistance we have come to regard as characteristic of the Japanese."

Around the anchorage lay an extensive network of useable roads, barracks, and supply dumps that connected three airfields. Four days after the landing, MacArthur's troops were turning the airstrips to Allied use. Hollandia, MacArthur proclaimed in a communiqué, "reverses Bataan." With that statement he began his race to finish off New Guinea.

After making more landings farther west along the coast, then at two nearby islands, he was ready to take on the Vogelkop (Dutch for Bird Head) peninsula, New Guinea's final westward extremity. He scheduled the attack for July 30, 1944.

Then came a delay. From Washington, General Marshall ordered MacArthur to be at Pearl Harbor on July 26.

At Oahu, MacArthur guessed correctly, he and Nimitz would be expected to confer with President Roosevelt. Just nominated for reelection, FDR wanted to show the voters that he himself, and not the top officers, was in charge of Pacific strategy. So as MacArthur flew to Hawaii in a B-17, he paced the aisle of his plane muttering to General George C. Kenney, his top aide, about having to waste time at a "political picture-taking junket."

There was picture-taking. One photograph showed MacArthur and Nimitz flanking Roosevelt at a banquet. All three, seated at a white-clothed table, were dipping spoons into hollowed-out pineapples. Wearing a white dinner jacket and a black bow tie, and talking to Nimitz on his left, Roosevelt already had the gaunt, slack-jawed look that presaged his death. Nimitz was giving the president his full attention. MacArthur, on FDR's right, looked bored.

Perhaps he was just calculating how best to deal with Roosevelt. In the session at Pearl Harbor, certainly, he won FDR to his side.

The Joint Chiefs still had not given MacArthur permission for the Philippine landing. In Washington, Admiral Ernest J. King, the chief of naval operations, preferred Taiwan, and Nimitz dutifully, although now with reservations, was pressing that point on the president. But up in Nimitz's office, looking at the map of the Pacific, Roosevelt said, "Douglas, where do we go from here?"

MacArthur seized a bamboo pole and pointed to Mindanao in the southern Philippines: "Leyte, Mr. President, and then Luzon!"

The general then played the political card: "You cannot abandon seventeen million loyal Filipino Christians to the Japanese in favor of first liberating Formosa and returning it to China. American public opinion will condemn you, Mr. President, and it would be justified."

Flying back to Brisbane, MacArthur was ecstatic. FDR had approved the Philippine landing.

As MacArthur was returning to Australia on July 30, the First Infantry of the U.S. Sixth Division was landing on the northern tip of the Vogelkop and on two offshore islands, Amsterdam and Middleburg. Two weeks later, the Seabees completed a PT boat base on Amsterdam and a fighter field on Middleburg. On September 3, with the Japanese defenses on Vogelkop completely subjugated, the Sixth Division prepared to move out to the Philippines.

On September 11, MacArthur flew from Brisbane to Hollandia. The next day he went aboard the cruiser *Nashville,* heading for the Philippines. That same day, Halsey bombarded Mindanao. On September 13, the admiral reported to the general that the central Philippines were "wide open."

Two days later, MacArthur took a launch to Morotai, the main island in the Moluccas at the eastern end of the Indies; the Sixth Division had just taken the island. MacArthur stood on the beach and looked out in the direction of the Philippines. An aide who was with him said it was almost as if MacArthur could "see through the mist the rugged shapes of Bataan and Corregidor."

"They are waiting for me there," MacArthur said. "It has been a long time."

4

A long time had passed for General Stilwell as well. In September, 1944, two and a half years had gone by since he had last seen Burma. For Stilwell, retaking Burma was a strategic necessity. It was also a psychological one: A victory in Burma, he believed, would redeem his reputation.

On the much-marked maps in his own offices, both in Chongqing and in Ramgarh on the India–Burma border, the route back was clear enough. Between Myitkyina in northern Burma and Rangoon in the south, the Japanese had built a 250-mile railway to improve their communications. If Stilwell could take Myitkyina and the British somehow could move up from Rangoon, then the Allies could use the rail-line to recapture Burma and once again open its supply link to China.

Ignoring jibes from some commentators about his being the "best three-star company commander in the US Army" and about the "platoon war in Burma," Stilwell sought to do what many thought impossible. He would show the world that, with proper training and equipment, the Chinese soldiers could outfight the Japanese.

Stilwell's method was audacious. He would take "raw recruits," as Theodore White was to write in his memoirs, "divorce them completely from the possibility of retreat, abandon fixed supply lines as completely as did Sherman in Georgia, make them dependent on air drops alone, [and] drive them two hundred miles through jungle, swamp, and mountain to conquer a skillful, entrenched, and desperate enemy."

The advance through China's Yunnan Province commenced at the end of October, 1943. "We have to go into a rat hole," Stilwell said in his diary, "and dig the hole as we go."

"Rat hole" was apt. A wide dirt path, constructed by Stilwell's engineers and called the Ledo Road, extended part of the way to Myitkyina; covered by P-40 fighters, American-trained Chinese troops proceeded to march along this course. But soon the road ended and the jungle began. Hacking through a half-mile of undergrowth could take a day. The rivers, fed by the snows of the Himalayas, were torrential. The monsoon descended. Insects and blood-sucking leeches abounded. The few existing trails were littered with the skeletons of many who, two and a half years before, had tried to escape from the Japanese.

Under the command of Brigadier General Haydon L. Boatner (like Stilwell a former Chinese language intelligence officer) while Stilwell was attending the Cairo Conference, the column of 3,000 men finally hacked their way through the jungle to within twenty miles of Myitkyina. Then machine gun fire from a Japanese division, well dug in around a series of villages, impeded the advance. By the time Stilwell had returned from Egypt on November 28, 1943, progress had stopped altogether.

Two weeks later, Chiang Kaishek formally acknowledged Stilwell's leadership of the Burma operation. FDR at Cairo had practically demanded that Chiang do so.

In a letter to his wife, Stilwell wrote:

> Put down December 18, 1943, as the day, when for the first time in history, a foreigner was given command of Chinese troops with full control over all officers and no strings attached. Can you believe it? . . . I have a letter to the [Chinese] army and division commanders to take orders from me as though I were Peanut himself. This has been a long uphill fight and when I think of some of our commanders who are handed a ready-made, fully-equipped, well-trained army of Americans to work with, it makes me wonder if I'm not working out some of my past sins. They gave me a shoestring and now we've run it up to considerable proportions: the question is, will it snap when we put the weight on it?
>
> I've had word from Peanut that I can get away from this dump [Chongqing] tomorrow. That means I'll spend Christmas with the Confucianists in the jungle. "Jungle Bells, Jungle Bells, jungle all the way. O what fun it is to ride in a jeep on Christmas Day."

Once near Myitkyina with Boatner and the Chinese troops, Stilwell lived like one of his men. He slept on a cot that crawled with bugs.

He used a packing crate for his desk. He washed from his helmet. He ate Chinese chow. And he hiked regularly to join his forward units. Progress was still almost nonexistent. "Yesterday," he wrote to his wife on January 12, "on a cut trail I took 3½ hours to do three miles, tripping and cursing at every step. It takes a long time even to locate the Japs, a lot more to dig them out."

By keeping up the pressure on his Chinese troops, he attained some minor victories, overrunning some Japanese outposts. "They are full of beans," he wrote his wife about his troops, "and tickled to death at beating the Japs."

Yet the Japanese resistance was determined and fierce. Stilwell's troops could do no more than take a few steps forward and at times he verged on despair.

And then a new fury. In February, 1944, a British unit, led by Brigadier Orde Wingate, parachuted into Burma far behind enemy lines. Wingate, an eccentric aristocrat out of the tradition of Gordon at Khartoum and Lawrence of Arabia, was not fighting Stilwell's war. Fighting a guerrilla war away from the front, he offered Stilwell little direct help. Stilwell held him in contempt.

But General Frank D. Merrill, who had walked out of Burma with Stilwell, brought in from India a group of 3,000 Americans soon to be known as "Merrill's Marauders." The Marauders were no ordinary troops. Some had served at Guadalcanal and, addicted to danger, had volunteered for a Burma mission. Others had been volunteered: Their ranks included the Army's worst drunks, psychopaths, and jailbirds. They had trained with Wingate in India and had expected to fight alongside imperial troops. Stilwell, though, had successfully lobbied Lord Louis Mountbatten, who had replaced Wavell as commander of the forces in India, to get the Marauders under his own control. Stilwell sent the Marauders parachuting directly behind the Japanese Myitkyina lines. He called the action a "left hook."

On March 1, in a pitched battle that took place about two-thirds of the way from the Indian border to Myitkyina, the Marauders matched Japanese cries of *"Banzai"* with howls and screams of their own. They killed 800 Japanese and lost only eight Americans. Although the Japanese division slipped away, Stilwell could claim his first major gain in Burma.

On May 11, 1944, 72,000 Chinese troops entered into Burma. Their sheer numbers overwhelmed the 20,000 Japanese on the outskirts of Myitkyina, and on August 1, with American bombers from India demolishing supply trucks, the Japanese had to withdraw. Stilwell's strategy of opening Burma had started to work.

On August 4 he noted in his diary: "Myitkyina—over at last. Thank God. Not a worry in the world this morning. For five minutes anyway."

Stilwell's reconquest of Burma took two and a half more months. By the middle of October, 1944, after a British fleet under Mountbatten had landed at Rangoon and with American armored vehicles overran enemy defenses, the Japanese in Burma were finished.

5

But on October 19, 1944, only days after the victory, Stilwell's journal read: "THE AXE FALLS."

While Stilwell was moving down through Burma, General Claire Chennault had launched an air offensive against the Japanese in China. The Japanese in retaliation launched a drive to capture Kunming. The effort failed, but hundreds of thousands of Chinese refugees fled westward away from the Japanese; during their escape the only food, shelter, and medicine they received were from Chiang Kaishek's old enemies, the Communists. Chiang blamed the turn of events on Stilwell's having taken the Chinese troops into Burma.

Chiang's attitude only exacerbated the earlier tensions between him and Stilwell. Stilwell's mission had been to win the war; Chiang's imperative had been to hold together the political coalition that had supported him in his rise to power. But rather than fight, the warlords around Chiang were content to steal from American aid programs

Stilwell walking out of Burma
(Hoover Institution)

James H. Doolittle
(UNITED STATES AIR FORCE)

Doolittle's take-off from the deck of the U.S.S. *Hornet* (UNITED STATES AIR FORCE)

Henry J. Kaiser inspecting his shipyard at Richmond, California, 1943 (ACME PHOTOS)

Liberty Ship launched at Long Beach,
January 31, 1942 (ACME PHOTOS)

Entrance to the Boeing Aircraft
Company, 1941 (U.S. Signal Corps)

B-17s off the assembly line at Seattle (Boeing Company)

Joseph J. Rochefort
(U.S. NAVAL HISTORICAL CENTER)

The Yorktown listing in the Battle of Midway (NATIONAL ARCHIVES)

The deck of the Yorktown
(U.S. Naval Historical Center)

Chester W. Nimitz at Midway Island shortly
after the battle (U.S. NAVAL HISTORICAL CENTER)

Richmond Kelly Turner, *left,* and Alexander A. Vandergrift, *right,* planning the invasion of Guadalcanal (U.S. NAVAL HISTORICAL CENTER)

William F. Halsey (U.S. NAVAL HISTORICAL CENTER)

Douglas MacArthur, *left,* Franklin D. Roosevelt, *center,* and Chester W. Nimitz, *right,* at Pearl Harbor (FRANKLIN D. ROOSEVELT LIBRARY)

Left to right, Chiang Kaishek, Franklin D. Roosevelt, Winston S. Churchill, and Madame Chiang Kaishek (Soong Meiling) at the Cairo Conference (FRANKLIN D. ROOSEVELT LIBRARY)

Franklin D. Roosevelt, *center,* in cap
(GEORGE C. MARSHALL FOUNDATION)

Douglas MacArthur going ashore
at Leyte (MACARTHUR FOUNDATION)

Left to right, Edward R. Stettinius (bareheaded), Vyacheslav Molotov, Winston S. Churchill, and Franklin D. Roosevelt after landing on the Crimean Peninsula (FRANKLIN D. ROOSEVELT LIBRARY)

John S. Service working at Yanan (COURTESY AMBASSADOR ROBERT E. SERVICE)

Patrick J. Hurley, *left*, and Mao Zedong, *right*, at Yanan (WESTERN HISTORY COLLECTIONS, UNIVERSITY OF OKLAHOMA LIBRARIES)

Mount Suridachi,
Iwo Jima
(National Archives)

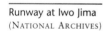

Runway at Iwo Jima
(National Archives)

Kamikazes off
Okinawa
(U.S. Naval
Historical
Center)

The destruction of the Yamato (U.S. Naval Historical Center)

A shrine standing amid fire-bombed Yokohama (National Archives)

Tokyo firebombed (National Archives)

Kamikaze damage off Okinawa
(NATIONAL ARCHIVES)

Winston S. Churchill, *left,* Harry S. Truman, *center,* and Josef Stalin, *right,* at Potsdam (HARRY S. TRUMAN LIBRARY)

MacArthur taking the Japanese surrender
(U.S. Army Military History Institute)

George C. Marshall, Madame Chiang Kaishek, Chiang Kaishek in Shanghai at the start of the Marshall Mission
(George C. Marshall Foundation)

and let the regime sink ever further into corruption. Clashes between Stilwell and Chiang intensified.

In September, 1944, Chiang had informed Patrick Hurley, the new American ambassador to China, that he wanted Stilwell recalled. On October 19, President Roosevelt complied. Stilwell returned to his home in Carmel and was forbidden to tell his side of the story to the American public.

Lacking in tact, Stilwell without question had provoked Chiang over the years. But Stilwell's problem went beyond his contempt for Chiang. Through the influence of T. V. Soong and Madame Chiang, Chiang Kaishek by now had powerful allies in Washington. Both *Life* and *Time,* magazines of the China-born press magnate Henry R. Luce, supported the Nationalist cause; so did many other journals of mass circulation. Chiang's wartime friends were the nucleus of what would become known as the China Lobby. President Roosevelt's newly appointed ambassador to China, Patrick Hurley, was a Republican ally of those China lobbyists. In flying to wartime Chongqing, Hurley's mission was to bring about the unification of China under Chiang Kaishek.

But to all who would listen, "Vinegar Joe" insisted that Chiang could not unify anything. The general thereby ran afoul of official American doctrine—that the United States was committed to Chiang Kaishek as one of the "four horsemen" of the postwar world. Many officials in the Chongqing embassy, to be sure, had reported that Chiang had lost touch with the bulk of the Chinese people. In Washington, nonetheless, Chiang held out the promise that under his leadership China would be strong, unified, and allied with America. It was a masterful illusion on his part, and a momentous delusion on the part of America's government.

15

TURNING POINTS

1

On June 15, 1944, the mightiest armada in history was preparing to descend on a thirteen-mile-long island at the head of the Marianas in the western Pacific. With Admiral Nimitz aboard the *Lexington,* a new, fast aircraft carrier and flagship of the fleet, the armada included seven battleships, twenty-one cruisers, fifteen carriers bearing nearly 900 airplanes, scores of destroyers, and transports crammed with more than 125,000 Marines and soldiers. The island, Saipan, was key to the next phase of the naval war.

Admiral Nimitz was confident of success. His captains had learned from the Tarawa battle how to deliver firepower more effectively. The amtracks bore more armor than before. The troops now carried waterproofed radios. And Nimitz had raced through the Marshall Islands, taking some and ignoring others. The central Pacific belonged to Nimitz and now he wanted the western part of the ocean, starting with Saipan.

During the First World War, Japan had taken possession of the German Marianas (right in the middle of the chain, Guam was a United States territory) and had populated most of them with settlers from the home islands. The Marianas thus had a Japanese look. Saipan's lowlands were a checkerboard of sugarcane and corn fields interspersed with groves of hardwood. On the hillsides, red-flowering trees framed the curved eves of wood and paper houses. In the center of the island, Mount Tapotchau was a miniature Mount Fuji without the snowcap.

Saipan, though, was more than a picture postcard. Japan had held it under a League of Nations mandate, which prohibited fortifications on the island. Nevertheless, Japanese engineers on the southern end had constructed an airfield—for "cultural purposes"—that had become the most valuable landing zone between Japan and the Philippines. If Nimitz could take Saipan, and then reclaim Guam, he could jump down the rest of the Marianas toward the Philippines.

At dawn on June 15, 1944, the American armada neared Saipan. That morning, 20,000 Marines walked ashore. The beachhead established, they spent the night easily hurling back a Japanese assault. The next morning, some 700 Japanese corpses lay at the edge of the sand.

In the night, though, Admiral Raymond Spruance, once described as a "cold-blooded fighting fool" and second only to Nimitz in the fleet, learned that a Japanese carrier fleet was approaching. At two in the morning, when his radar showed that Japanese bombers were only 150 miles away, he ordered a flotilla of his own bombers to fly the 100 miles south to Guam. They demolished the airfield there, making it impossible for the oncoming Japanese to land for refueling. Then Spruance's carriers sent fighters to meet the approaching enemy.

Of the first wave of seventy-nine Japanese planes, forty-two went down; the rest scored no hits. Of the next 128 planes, seventy hit the water, leaving the surface of the nighttime sea covered with burning debris. American submarines sank two Japanese carriers.

In one night, the Japanese Navy had lost a major part of its air fleet. Americans called the event the "Great Marianas Turkey Shoot."

On July 9, the Japanese on Saipan surrendered. As they did so, the civilian population engaged in mass suicide. Whole families jumped into the sea to drown. A group of them bowed to American Marines on a cliff above; then they held hand grenades against their bellies and pulled the pins. Robert Sherrod observed a solitary suicide: "On the edge of the slippery, tide-washed rocks a Japanese boy of perhaps fifteen, attired in knee-length black trousers, walked back and forth. He would pause in meditation, then he would walk on, swinging his arms. He sat on the edge of the rocks, then he got up. He sat down again, waiting. When a high wave washed the rock, the boy let it sweep him into the sea. At first he lay face down, inert on the surface of the water. Then his arms flailed frantically, as if an instinct stronger than his will power bade him live. Then he was quiet. He was dead."

Three miles south of Saipan, Tinian Island came next. On its flat, gentle terrain, a narrow-gauge railway connected two sugar mills with cornfields. The Japanese had nearly completed three airstrips. Those airstrips would take on an immense significance when a year later the *Enola Gay* took off from them, heading for Hiroshima.

On July 24, 1944, American warships appeared off Tinian Town, on the island's southwestern coast. Landing craft used full daylight to stage a landing. The action was a feint. The major American force hit from the north, where there was no coral reef. Within a week, Tinian was in American hands.

The jungle on Guam was nearly as thick as that on Guadalcanal and to the invading Marines its ravines and ridges gave rise to the gripe, "Here we go again!" But the fight for Guam did not last long.

On the night of July 25, the Marines could scarcely believe their ears. Having captured the main coastal road, they had set up a line around a mangrove swamp. From inside the swamp the Marines heard Japanese soldiers laughing, shrieking, and smashing bottles. "It sounded," a Marine later recalled, "like New Year's Eve in the zoo." Soon after midnight the drunken Japanese rolled out of the swamp across open ground toward Marine lines, the officers waving flags and swords, the enlisted men brandishing empty bottles and even baseball bats. The Americans let loose devastating artillery fire on the charging Japanese. Arms and legs flew through the air. Running amok, most of the Japanese screamed in terror until they died. The survivors fled back into the swamp, where they were wiped out by readjusted artillery fire.

With the Marianas won, in the middle of September Nimitz ordered the armada to the Palaus. Flanking the Philippines, the Palau Islands were an important part of Japan's main defense line. Peleliu, the main island, was dominated by a long, precipitous ridge honeycombed with caves and masked by dense jungle growth. Backed by mangrove swamps, a coral reef surrounded the entire island. There the Japanese were determined to hold on.

As they landed, the Marines stepped on underwater mines, then ran into intense fire from heavily fortified concrete pillboxes. The carnage on both sides was frightful. "The human wreckage I saw," remembered Captain George P. Hunt, "was a grim and tragic sight. Wounded and dying [Japanese] littered the edge of the coconut grove where we landed. As I ran up the beach I saw them lying shoulder to shoulder. I saw a ghastly mixture of bandages, bloody and mutilated skin; men gritting their teeth, resigned to their wounds; men groaning and writhing in their agonies;. . . men with their entrails exposed or whole chunks of body ripped out of them."

The fighting on Peleliu was vicious and Army units had to come in to relieve the Marines. But by mid-October, just as MacArthur was landing in the Philippines, the Japanese resistance was over. And from the islands just captured, the B-29s began to fly to the Philippines and even to Japan.

2

As American airplanes in September, 1944, began to appear in Philippine skies, Filipino guerrilla units that had been in communication with MacArthur demolished bridges, passes, and culverts; they cut telegraph wires and blew up supply dumps.

Especially on Mindanao, the island farthest from the Japanese centers of control, the guerrillas took their toll, lobbing Molotov cocktails through the windows of Japanese outposts, placing plastic explosives on the bellies of Japanese airplanes, and cutting through the barbed wire of Japanese camps to allow prisoners of war to escape. And they repaired roads in the expectation of the arrival of General MacArthur.

So it came as a surprise to the Japanese when MacArthur first hit the Philippines, for the initial assault was not on Mindanao. The invasion took place just to the north, where Admiral Halsey believed the Japanese defenses to be the weakest, on the island of Leyte.

In Europe, the Allies had liberated Paris on August 25 and the Red Army of Stalin was moving into Poland. And fully confident that at Leyte the Japanese position was a "hollow shell with weak defenses and skimpy defenses," Halsey pressed for a straightforward attack. Nimitz and MacArthur, then Roosevelt and Churchill, who were meeting at Quebec, agreed. On October 17, 1944, after the minesweepers had cleared Leyte Gulf, the first Americans went ashore.

In an article datelined October 20, 1944, the *New York Times* carried a promise from President Franklin D. Roosevelt to the people of the Philippines:

> The suffering, humiliation, and mental torture that you have endured since the barbarous, unprovoked, and treacherous attack upon the Philippines nearly three years ago have aroused in the hearts of the American people a

righteous anger, a stern determination to punish the guilty
and a fixed resolve to restore peace and order and decency
to an outraged world. . . . On this occasion of the return of
General MacArthur to Philippine soil with our airmen, our
soldiers, and our sailors, we renew our pledge. We and our
Philippine brothers in arms—with the help of Almighty
God—will drive out the invader; we will destroy his power
to wage war again, and we will restore a world of dignity
and freedom—a world of confidence and honesty and
peace.

FDR had timed his proclamation to coincide with the landing. On
the clear, bright morning of October 20, MacArthur stood on the
bridge of the cruiser *Nashville;* in the surf beyond Marines and
troops of the Sixth Army were splashing ashore.

The greatest moment of MacArthur's life had arrived. Accompanied by his subordinate generals, Sergio Osmeña (who, following the
death of Manuel Quezon in 1944, had succeeded as the Philippine
president-in-exile), and a coterie of reporters and news photographers, he boarded a landing craft. About thirty yards from the beach
it ground to a halt and the photographers went ashore, followed by
MacArthur.

"It took me only thirty or forty long strides to reach dry land,"
MacArthur stated later, "but that was one of the most meaningful
walks I ever took."

Once on the beach, he returned the salutes of his shore commanders. Turning to a Signal Corps microphone, he then broadcast the
good news.

"People of the Philippines, I have returned," he broadcast in a
shaky voice. "By the grace of Almighty God our forces stand again
on Philippine soil. . . . The hour of your redemption is here. Your patriots have demonstrated an unswerving and resolute devotion to the
principles of freedom. . . . Rally to me. Let the indomitable spirit of
Bataan and Corregidor lead on. As the lines of battle roll forward to

bring you within the zone of operations, rise and strike. . . . For future generations of your sons and daughters, strike! In the name of your sacred dead, strike! Let no heart be faint! Let every arm be steeled!"

MacArthur's words thrilled those on the land. But the great battle—what Samuel Eliot Morison called the "Battle for Leyte Gulf, the greatest naval battle of all time"—was about to take place on the sea.

In Tokyo, Admiral Toyoda Soemu, who had succeeded Yamamoto as commander of the Imperial Combined Fleet, had perceived the danger of the MacArthur landing. If the Americans took the Philippines, then they could block the Japanese fleet's north–south route. Toyoda's ships would not be able to get above the archipelago for supplies from the home islands or below it for oil from the Indies. Either way, Japan's naval forces would be useless. And if the Japanese Navy could not fight, Japan itself was doomed.

Admiral Toyoda therefore adopted a radical tactic that he called *Sho Go,* or Victory Operation. It was a huge gamble. Risking the destruction of his fleet, he would hurl all the warships at his disposal at the Americans around the mouth of the Leyte Gulf.

In doing so, he would divide the ships of his already much diminished Navy into three parts. The first two would trap the Americans in a vise. A column under the Command of Vice Admiral Kurita Takeo, which included the *Musashi* and the *Yamato,* the world's most potent battleships, would steam out of Singapore, round Borneo, pass through the Mindanao Sea, and swing north of Leyte. At the same time, a row of carriers and destroyers from Taiwan would cut through the Philippines below Luzon and reach Leyte from the south. From Japan itself the so-called Northern Fleet under Vice Admiral Ozawa Jisaburo, while weaker than the other two, would serve as a decoy. By luring some of the U.S. ships to the north, Toyoda hoped to divide and conquer the American fleet.

The strategy at first seemed to work. Halsey did take the bait, on October 25 moving part of his own fleet to the north; just after dawn,

Admiral Ozawa sank the American aircraft carrier *Gambier Bay*. That same day Admiral Kurita's column from the south came out through the San Bernardino Strait, right above Leyte.

In the Battle for Leyte Gulf, however, the superior numbers, speed, and power of the American naval force simply overwhelmed the Japanese. After hitting it many times with torpedoes and shells, the Americans tore the *Musashi* to pieces. "The big battlewagon was momentarily lost under the towering fountains of near misses and torpedo hits, soaring puffs of white smoke from bomb hits, and steaming black smoke from recalcitrant fires," a reporter wrote. "Then the long dark bow slid out of the cauldron, slowing. *Musashi* stopped, burning. Then it sank." Although remaining afloat, the *Yamato* also took disabling hits. And as the carrier *Zuikaku* went down, its crew of 1,700 men gathered on the deck to raise their arms and voices in a farewell *"Banzai."*

The battle ended at dusk on October 25, with a Japanese retreat. The Americans had lost one fast carrier, two escort carriers, two destroyers, one destroyer escort, and just under 3,000 men. The Japanese, however, had lost a total of four carriers, three battleships, six heavy cruisers, four light cruisers, nine destroyers, and 10,000 lives. The Japanese Navy was shattered. Never again would it be an effective fighting force.

3

The victory of the American Navy had been spectacular. But the United States possessed a weapon even more devastating than its ships. The B-29 Superfortress, produced by the Boeing aircraft company, was ninety-nine feet long with a wingspan of 141 feet. It had a pressurized cabin that enabled the crew to function at altitudes of more than 30,000 feet, eight fifty-caliber machine guns in remotely controlled turrets, twenty-millimeter cannon in manned rear turrets, and the capability of carrying up to ten tons of bombs and of flying for 5,830 miles. The B-29s would be decisive factors in the Pacific war, and by the time MacArthur landed at Leyte beach, they were already reaching Japan out of the Marianas.

From early 1944 onward, when the first B-29s rolled off the Boeing production lines, the American government had been developing a chain of bases, in the Azores and along the North African coast up into Italy, then from India into southwestern China. Under the leadership of Air General Curtis E. LeMay, a skillful navigator of the B-29s, the Americans ordered the construction of new runways in China: So heavy were the Superfortresses that Chennault's old airstrip at Kunming would not suffice. A third of a million Chinese laborers went to work, pulling giant hand-pulled rollers to pack the runways; coolies who fell before the rollers were simply crushed underneath.

To pay for the work, Chiang Kaishek's demands for money were so imposing that an Air Force historian in 1945 wrote that one "does not speak of blackmail on the part of an ally, but at best this was very shrewd trading," so much so that B-29 operations from China were "among the most costly of the war."

The operations out of China were also costly because of distance. Just to get to China, the pilots and other crew members of LeMay's Twentieth Air Force had to go to India and fly over the treacherous heights of the Himalayas. Then came the long flight to Japan, where air defenses were still strong. Takeoff itself involved peril, for the B-29s were so heavily loaded with bombs and gasoline that any mechanical or human failure could lead to disaster. And on flights of some fourteen hours from China to Japan and back, winds of 150 miles per hour or more could confound all calculation of speed, altitude, and fuel consumption. Dozens of pilots had to ditch their Superfortresses in the Yellow Sea between Japan and the Shandong peninsula; downed fliers were rarely found and rescued.

Ernie Pyle, the American journalist who specialized in reporting the personal side of war, wrote that the B-29 airmen were over Japan "for only twenty minutes to an hour. . . . What gave the boys the willies was 'sweating out' those seven or eight hours of ocean beneath them on the way back," often at night.

Conditions aboard the B-29s created a sense of unreality. From high altitudes, the crews could see the strings of their bombs fall and the white puffs of explosions arising from their Japanese targets. But they had no sense of the devastation wreaked by their bombs below, of the cities and villages destroyed and the mutilated corpses strewn about the streets. The B-29s were cocoons. Aboard a bomber, a thirty-foot tunnel, just wide enough for a person to crawl through, was the only way to traverse the length of the plane, adding to the claustrophobia felt on the long missions. The sense of isolation was further exacerbated by the public relations policy of the Twentieth Air Force. Pyle wrote that crews were "picking up news on their radios, when only halfway home, that their bombing mission had been announced in Washington. All the world knew about it, but they still had a thousand miles of ocean to cross before it was finished."

Then, if they were lucky, they landed safely back in China. After the American victory at Peleliu, the B-29 operations shifted from China to the Marianas, much closer to Japan. But Washington's determination to see China as a strong and unified ally under the leadership of Chiang Kaishek persisted, in spite of growing evidence that Chiang's regime was in serious trouble.

4

Mao Zedong's anti-Japanese guerrilla tactics were proving successful and the Communists were proving equally successful in winning the hearts and minds of the peasantry. "Of course," Mao wrote, "the plains [of northeastern China] are less suitable than the mountains, but it is by no means impossible to develop guerrilla warfare or establish base areas . . . there. The widespread guerrilla warfare in the plains of Hebei [around Beijing] and of northern and northwestern Shandong proves that it is possible to develop guerrilla warfare in the plains. . . . It is definitely possible to conduct seasonal guerrilla warfare by taking advantage of the 'green curtain' of tall crops in summer and of the frozen rivers in winter."

Mao's analysis was correct: The Japanese in China were increasingly vulnerable to attack from Communist guerrillas. The Japanese positioned garrisons in important cities, such as Beijing, Tianjin, Shanghai, Hangzhou, and Guangzhou, which were well defended. But the Japanese also stationed troops in towns, along railways, at bridges and road crossings, and in isolated pillboxes. The farther the Japanese garrisoned their troops beyond the cities, the farther they ventured into the stubble of the Chinese countryside, terrain across which uncounted peasant guerrillas could harass, kill, and retreat to their native villages.

How had the Communists mobilized the peasantry? Mao again provided the answer: "By word of mouth, by leaflets and bulletins, by newspapers [hence the stress on literacy and the development of simplified Chinese characters], through plays and films, through schools, through mass organizations and our cadres."

Communist propaganda was relentless. But it fell upon willing ears and eyes. In a China where traditionally a peasant knew little or nothing of anything beyond the village or perhaps the nearby market town, the Japanese had created waves of refugees, people removed to the hinterland where for the first time they began to recognize each other as citizens of a nation. The Japanese had managed to brutalize the people into a sense of national unity. And Mao made sure that, to the populace, the Communists were seen as the rightful heirs of the mandate of heaven.

Even in the remoteness of Yanan, the Communist Party was acting as if it already were the people's government. It organized villages. It routed the most oppressive of the landlords. It coined money. It set up small arsenals and police stations. And it expanded its influence to small scattered Communist armed forces all over northern China: It was putting together a national army.

Thus by 1944, the northern part of the country had become a checkerboard of intermixed Japanese and guerrilla positions. Chiang Kaishek's Nationalist divisions occupied only the edge of the playing board.

Between mid-July and October, 1944, half a dozen or so American journalists received invitations to visit Yanan. Among them were Brooks Atkinson, later a theater critic with the *New York Times*, and Theodore White, Henry R. Luce's *Time* and *Life* correspondent in China. Their reports stressed the high morale at Yanan—Atkinson wrote admiringly of the quality of the plays, operas, and puppet shows—and the simple fact that in northern China Mao led a popular government waging an active guerrilla campaign against the Japanese. Chongqing censors soon refused to let such stories out of China, but not before President Roosevelt found the reportage intriguing.

Roosevelt had been committed to a China under Chiang Kaishek. But the president was also flexible: He was no ideologue. Back in the early part of the New Deal he had been famous for saying that if a certain program does not work, try another, "but above all try something." In that spirit, FDR pressed for an official mission that would send him first-hand reports from Yanan. So in June, 1944, Vice President Henry A. Wallace, visiting China in the hope of stimulating the government actually to go to war, demanded that an American delegation be permitted to meet the Communists.

Reluctantly bowing to the pressure, Chiang authorized the dispatch of a small American mission to Yanan. Called the United States Army Observer Group, the unit was nicknamed the "Dixie Mission" after the large number of participants from the American South. In charge of the mission, whose members were mostly military men, was Colonel David D. Barrett, an Army officer who spoke Chinese. Also attached to the group as political officer was John S. Service from the State Department. Born in China as the son of missionaries, Service had grown up speaking a Chinese dialect with playmates; he then graduated from Oberlin College, entered the Foreign Service, and learned to speak Mandarin, as well as becoming literate in the Chinese language. Joining him was a sprinkling of other Foreign Service and OSS officers, also conversant in Chinese. Their task was to examine the ways and means of the Communist prowess. Early in the morning of June 22, 1944, the first nine members of the mission that would last half a year boarded a C-47 cargo plane at Chongqing and took off for Yanan.

As the airplane ascended to 10,000 feet and swung northward, those aboard could see below the muddy rivers that carried the silt of eroded hills and fields. Villages appeared to be built entirely of earth. Fields of green, interrupted by brown pathways, extended up the sides of mountains in terraces to the very peaks. Then the airplane crossed the loess hilltops and descended toward Yanan. Colonel Barrett, in a memoir of the mission, described the landing:

> As we neared the Yanan airfield, the pagoda on a hill close by . . . had come into plain sight. Visible on the field below was a large crowd, evidently gathered to greet the plane. The field lacked a control tower to guide approaching planes, but some of the crowd were giving signals to indicate where we were to land. . . . We felt the wheels touch down. . . . Suddenly the plane lurched and settled to the left. Immediately there came a terrific blow on the left side of the pilot compartment as if someone had struck it with a sledge hammer, and we came to a sudden stop. As soon as we could unhook our belts, those of us nearest the door jumped out, and we could see at once what had happened. As the plane was rolling to a stop, the left wheel of the landing gear had crashed into an old grave, no sign of which was visible above ground.

After some confusion, Zhou Enlai, second to Mao in the Communist Party, walked forward in greeting. He introduced the Americans to Mao and other important Communists. Then the members of the Dixie Mission climbed into the back of a truck that conveyed them to the caves where they would stay.

Fitted blocks of hewn stone lined their quarters. The floors were of gray brick. Rough tables, wooden chairs, planks set on sawhorses for beds, enameled wash basins and towel racks were the only furnishings. Running water did not exist; the Americans had to relieve themselves at an outdoor latrine. Aside from the ditch, though, Barrett commented, everything was "clean and ample for the requirements of anyone not expecting soft living."

Life for the Communists was anything but soft. They had enough to eat—thanks to the fertile loess soil nearby—but their drills were exacting and their conditioning was rugged. And their morale was high. The atmosphere in Yanan was wholly different from that in Chongqing, mired as the capital was in grime, corruption, and night-soil. "We have come into a different country," John Service wrote, "and we are meeting a different people." Instead of the class distinctions practiced in Chongqing, people in Yanan enjoyed relaxed and informal relations. Party leaders, most of whom were of peasant origins, walked about without noticeable protection. Chairman Mao would appear frequently at weekend dances to which all would come. Dressed in trousers and a white shirt without a jacket, he would stand with the other guests on terms of perfect equality. Girls with pigtails would ask him to dance.

Was it all a display to win the Americans' goodwill? To a point, perhaps; Barrett later confessed that he had fallen for the "agrarian reformer guff," but they did display high spirits.

The military discipline was strict. And the Americans, Zhou Enlai was convinced, would look to the Red Army for help in fighting Japan.

Such, at least, was the recommendation of John Service after the Dixie Mission returned to Chongqing in August. Service had spoken with nearly everyone at Yanan, from Chairman Mao down to the most junior Communist cadre members. Perhaps coached, all had pressed one point upon him: The Communist Party fervently wished to cooperate with the United States in the struggle to defeat Japan and to build a new China. Service considered that the Communist revolutionaries were well suited to conditions in China and that Yanan was deserving of American support. In his capacity as political officer of the Dixie Mission, Service wrote an official report dated October 10, 1944. Among his observations were the following:

> Our dealings with Chiang Kaishek continue on the unrealistic assumption that he is necessary for our cause. It is time, for the sake of the war and also for our future interests in China, that we take a more realistic line.
>
> The *Guomindang* [Nationalist] government is in crisis. . . .
>
> With the glaring exposure of the *Guomindang*'s failure, dissatisfaction within China is growing rapidly. The prestige of the [Nationalist] Party was never lower, and Chiang is losing the respect he once enjoyed as a leader.
>
> In the present circumstances, the *Guomindang* is dependent on American support for survival. *But we are in no way dependent on the Guomindang* [emphasis in the original, and other Foreign Service officers in Chongqing were making the same point]. . . .
>
> Our policy toward China should be guided by two facts. First, *we cannot hope to deal successfully with Chiang without being hard-boiled.* Second, *we cannot hope to solve China's problems* (which are now our problems) *without consideration of the opposition forces*—Communist, provincial, and liberal. . . .
>
> More than ever, we hold the aces in Chiang's poker game. It is time we started playing them.

Service prefaced this analysis with an introductory letter to General Stilwell: "You have allowed me as a political officer . . . to express myself freely," he wrote. "I trust that you will permit the continued frankness which I have assumed in the attached memorandum."

But Stilwell never received the report. He had already left China.

Stilwell's immediate successor in Chongqing as American commander of the Chinese armies was Major General Albert C. Wedemeyer, a six-footer with a gray pompadour and a quiet, friendly manner. A West Pointer, he had done a tour of duty between 1930 and 1932 in Tianjin, where he had studied Mandarin. So he was a natural to go to Chongqing. He did so with optimism. In his first press interview, Wedemeyer described the military situation as "unfavorable but not irretrievable." Although he would soon appreciate the Stilwell–Service point of view, he refrained from humiliating Chiang face-to-face.

His civilian counterpart was General Hurley, tall, erect in bearing, white-haired with a handlebar mustache, and pompous. His military rank was an honorific, conferred by Roosevelt to impress the Chinese. The Chinese were less than impressed. When Hurley's plane landed at Chongqing, he stood at the top of the ramp and, to the bafflement of the waiting Chinese dignitaries, let out a Choctaw war whoop. His Chinese nickname was "Big Wind."

Chiang Kaishek nonetheless welcomed Hurley with warmth. And no wonder. Hurley knew so little of China that he addressed the first lady as "Madame Shek": He never saw behind the screens of deception raised by the Nationalist government. So taken was Hurley with the wealth around Chiang Kaishek that he declared "the United States armed forces, China, and the American embassy today are united as one and we have one common objective—the defeat of Japan."

But Chiang and Hurley also shared another objective, the defeat of the Communists. Hurley accordingly refused to forward the Service report to Washington and engineered the transfer out of China of Service and John Paton Davies, John K. Emmerson, and other "China Hands" in the embassy, who had held him in the utmost contempt.

Hurley made plenty of American enemies. Theodore White wrote scathingly of the corruption in Chongqing. OSS operatives shared Service's views of the trends in Chinese politics and Solomon Adler, a Treasury Department representative, warned Secretary Henry Morgenthau of the looming disaster. Adler wrote that Chiang possessed a death wish to precipitate a civil war with the Communists.

But Hurley had his own allies. Back in the United States, Henry Luce fired White, and in China itself the legacy of SACO (Milton

Miles had returned to America for medical treatment and his organization near the war's end was disbanded) continued as a secret American war against the Communists.

A cooperative relationship between the United States and the Chinese Communist Party might have come into being. Hurley killed off any such possibility.

5

On January 9, 1945, U.S. Army Major Ray Cromley, assigned as an observer in Yanan, radioed a message to the embassy in Chongqing, to be forwarded to President Roosevelt: "YANAN GOVERNMENT WANTS DISPATCH TO AMERICA AN UNOFFICIAL RPT UNOFFICIAL GROUP TO INTERPRET AND EXPLAIN TO AMERICAN CIVILIANS AND OFFICIALS INTERESTED THE PRESENT SITUATION AND PROBLEMS OF CHINA. NEXT IS STRICTLY OFF RECORD SUGGESTION BY SAME: MAO AND ZHOU WILL BE IMMEDIATELY AVAILABLE EITHER SINGLY OR TOGETHER FOR EXPLORATORY CONFERENCE SHOULD PRESIDENT ROOSEVELT EXPRESS DESIRE TO RECEIVE THEM AT WHITE HOUSE AS LEADERS OF A PRIMARY CHINESE PARTY."

Cromley's message revealed the Reds' faith in their cause. If they could get to Washington, they believed, they would have a chance of convincing President Roosevelt that they, not Chiang Kaishek, represented the future of China. Time was in their favor, they believed; the mandate of heaven would soon be theirs. And if Roosevelt would recognize this, he might cut America's ties with Chiang Kaishek.

But the frail and dying Franklin D. Roosevelt did not even receive the message. It reached Chongqing on January 10, 1945. Acting on his authority as ambassador, Hurley refused to send it to Washington.

PART IV

RECASTING THE IMPERIAL FAR EAST

16

YALTA

1

Saturday, January 20, 1945, the day of the fourth inauguration of President Franklin D. Roosevelt, dawned gray and cold over Washington; the wind off the Potomac penetrated the warmest of clothing. Putting up with the elements, several thousand persons left their homes and hotel rooms and, because of gasoline rationing, walked to the White House.

Because of the exigencies of war and his own increasing frailty, FDR had decided to take the oath of office not at the Capitol but rather at the White House. With the view of the Ellipse and the Washington Monument behind them, the onlookers gathered on the hard snow on the White House lawn and waited.

Shortly before noon, the Marine Corps Band, resplendent in uniforms of red and blue, appeared on the South Portico and played "Hail to the Chief." The doors opened and, supported by a cane and the arm of his son, James, Roosevelt emerged. Despite the frigid weather, he wore no cloak or overcoat. Lurching ahead, he reached a padded chair and sat. Exactly at noon, James and a Secret Service man bent over the chair, lifted Roosevelt and carried him forward until, standing, he could grip the edge of the podium. There he shook hands with Harry S Truman, just sworn in as vice president. Facing Chief Justice Harlan Fiske Stone, Roosevelt renewed his own oath of office. Then he turned to address the crowd waiting below.

"We Americans of today, together with our allies, are passing through a period of supreme test. It is a test of our courage—of our resolve—of our essential democracy," he began. "If we meet that test—successfully and honorably—we shall perform a service of historic importance—of historic importance which men and women and children will honor throughout all time. . . ."

2

The wintry weather, Roosevelt speaking in public, even his sense of history, all were reminiscent of that day, just over three years before, when he had asked Congress to declare war upon Japan. But how America had changed in those three years. Between 1943 and 1945 American industrial production had risen ninety percent, agricultural output twenty percent, and the total gross national product of all goods and services sixty percent. Most other economies, including that of Great Britain, were casualties of the war. Financially and commercially, as never before the United States stood like a colossus among nations.

Such might had a profound effect on the thinking of the administration. Will Clayton, formerly a Texas cotton merchant and by the time of FDR's fourth inaugural the State Department assistant secretary for economic affairs, advised the president that America's financial interests demanded an open, orderly world. Henry Grady, another government economist, advised President Roosevelt forcefully that "the capitalist system is essentially an international system. If it cannot function internationally, it will break down completely." Secretary of the Treasury Henry Morgenthau agreed; a full year before the inaugural he had urged Roosevelt to turn his attention from problems of military strategy to those of the economic and political postwar world.

In response to the advice, in July, 1944, Roosevelt called a conference of the world's nations, excluding Germany and Japan, at Bretton Woods, New Hampshire. As they met for two weeks in the huge old Victorian-era hotel at the foot of Mount Washington, Morgenthau persuaded the delegates to create three new institutions: the International Bank for Reconstruction and Development (the World Bank—a source of American-provided capital for the economic recovery and development of the nations outside North America); the International Monetary Fund (IMF—for the maintenance of currency stability); and the General Agreement on Tariffs and Trade (the GATT—a treaty and later an institution designed to encourage worldwide free trade). Capital infusions, currency stability, and free trade were the hallmarks of the Bretton Woods system.

For Roosevelt, Morgenthau, and other educated Americans of their generation had learned from teachers and historians that these principles also had been the major features of Great Britain's nineteenth-century dominance of the world's economy. These men were well aware of the abuses, extortions, and inhumanities of the imperial practices of Britain and other European countries and, taking it as an article of faith that America was the exceptional country, morally superior to the Old Countries, they believed fervently that an American-led global economy could eliminate the inequities of the century before. But they also intended to resurrect the benefits: As the pound sterling once had done, the dollar could stabilize currencies and thus trade everywhere; as the banks of London had done, so would the Treasury in Washington and the commercial houses of New York provide investment funds; and as Britain had done by passing the Corn Laws of the 1840s, the United States would stand as a beacon of free trade.

In the nineteenth century, the world was Europe-centered, Britain-protected, and London-financed. By 1945, the world had become North America–centered, United States–protected, and New York-Washington–financed. In the three years since Pearl Harbor, not only the United States but also the world had undergone a great transformation: The British Empire had been replaced by what in effect was the American Empire.

When President Roosevelt appeared before the Congress to ask for the declaration of war, he was healthy, as strong and robust as a man with crippled legs could be. When he appeared on the South Portico of the White House on January 20, 1945, he was dying; he looked gaunt, shrunken, with dark circles under his eyes, and his doctors had diagnosed him with acute hypertension and congestive heart failure.

Because of his illness, his critics after his death charged that at the Yalta Conference, held in February, 1945, he sold out American interests. This was simply not true. Despite his infirmity, Franklin D. Roosevelt, as he had done before the war and during it, above all else upheld American interests as he saw them. How he understood those interests can be summed up with the German word *Realpolitik*.

Literally "realist politics," *Realpolitik* refers to a usually expansionist foreign policy having as its primary purpose the advancement of the national interest. Originally the term pertained to the way the European rulers divided the continent and settled differences through balances of power, spheres of influence, and buffer zones. *Realpolitik* as used by supposedly cynical Europeans of old had never been a part of democratic America's vocabulary. Indeed, as in his 1945 inaugural address, FDR consistently spoke in terms of democratic values. But only a month after his inauguration, Roosevelt took measures that embodied *Realpolitik* in its Old World meaning. At the Yalta Conference he in effect granted Marshal Josef Stalin an empire in eastern Europe in return for acquiescence in United States dominance of the Far East.

3

The road to Yalta had been rocky. After the Cairo Conference in late 1943, he and Churchill had flown to Tehran to talk for the first time with Stalin. The meeting had accomplished little—one historian called it "a kind of diplomatic papering over of cracks in the wall"—because while the Soviet army at the end of 1943 was pushing the German forces ever westward, the Americans and the British had yet to open a second front in France. Stalin had complained bitterly about the lack of help from the West.

In the Normandy invasion of June, 1944, General Eisenhower had presided over a joint Anglo-American army. But at Tehran, FDR and his advisers already had begun to think of the Soviet Union, not the declining British Empire, as the major power with which the United States would have to deal once the war was over. And at the Bretton Woods Conference, American officials had made clear to their British counterparts that London would have to open up the empire and the commonwealth to United States trade and investment. Secretary Morgenthau simply had steamrollered over the objections of the main British delegate, the economist John Maynard Keynes.

Roosevelt and Churchill had met again in September, 1944, in Quebec. Churchill had demanded trade protection for the British Empire and Commonwealth, but Roosevelt had so brutally brushed aside British concerns that the prime minister finally had blurted out: "Do you want me to beg, like Fala [Roosevelt's Scottie]?"

His faith in Roosevelt diminished, in October, 1944, Churchill had flown to Moscow to have a private talk with Stalin. They worked out a deal: In return for Soviet control of Romania, Bulgaria, and Hungary, Britain would have influence in Greece. Along the Aegean, the British-supported monarchy was trying to put down a coalition of leftist rebels. Churchill wrote later that Stalin uttered not "one word of reproach" when Britain, in October, 1944, moved a force into Greece partly to chase the retreating Germans and partly to suppress the rebels. Churchill and Stalin had been playing the imperial game of divide and conquer, with no regard for American interests.

In mid-December Roosevelt had received another blow. Although the Allies had liberated France, Hitler counterattacked with 250,000 troops in Belgium. In the ensuing Battle of the Bulge, only a last-ditch Allied resistance and an empty German supply line averted defeat.

Before pushing the *Wehrmacht* back into Germany, the British and the Americans together lost 100,000 men.

On the eve of Roosevelt's inauguration, the Soviet forces were well into Germany from the east, roughly fifty miles from Berlin.

With Germany on the verge of collapse, Roosevelt, Churchill, and Stalin agreed to meet once more and to sketch out the elements of the postwar settlement. This time they would gather at Yalta, a resort on the Black Sea. Worried about the effect of the long trip on his health, Roosevelt hoped to convene somewhere else, but Stalin was adamant about not leaving his own country in the time of war. So Roosevelt consented to go, with a stopover at British Malta, from where he and Churchill would fly to the Soviet Union.

4

At about 9:30 on the sparkling morning of February 2, 1945, the American cruiser *Quincy* steamed into the harbor at British Malta. Overhead, guns at Fort St. Elmo, guarding the promontory, boomed out their salute. The bay itself bristled with the superstructures of ships of the Royal Navy. As Roosevelt's ship passed HMS *Orion*, Churchill's own vessel, the two leaders waved to each other across the water. Two hours later Churchill and a small party went over by launch to join Roosevelt for luncheon.

"My friend [FDR] has arrived in best of health and spirits," the prime minister cabled to his wife in the evening. "Everything going very well. Lovely warm sunshine." Then he added: "We are on the wing at dawn."

That evening some 700 British and American conferees made their way by taxi and jeep to Malta's Luqa airfield, ready for a predawn flight. Their destination in the Soviet Union was the Saki airport on the Crimean peninsula, near the resort city of Yalta. Lined up on the tarmac and waiting for the passengers were twenty American Skymasters and five British Yorks. Seeing the size of the fleet, Sarah Churchill, the prime minister's daughter, wondered aloud if the Soviets would think they were being invaded.

All through the night, at ten-minute intervals, the airplanes took off on their 1,400-mile journey. In a steady stream they adhered to the same route: straight east across the Mediterranean; a southward swing around Crete; then up across Turkey and the Black Sea—making radio contact with the tower at Saki to indicate that the Allies were not coming to attack—and down upon the newly built concrete-block runway.

Once Roosevelt's airplane, the "Sacred Cow" (the early version of Air Force One) had landed, and FDR had been carried to the ground, Soviet soldiers lining the runway snapped to attention. The Red Army Band struck up the "Star-Spangled Banner," "God Save the King," and the Communist *"Internationale."* Then Roosevelt was lifted into a jeep, and headed off to inspect an honor guard. Churchill accompanied the jeep on foot and Sir Alexander Cadogan, a high-ranking British official, recorded the scene: "The PM walked by the side of the president, as in her old age an Indian attendant accompanied Queen Victoria's phaeton. They were preceded by a crowd of cameramen, walking backwards as they took snapshots."

The procession stopped before the honor guard. Then the Soviet welcoming committee—principally Foreign Minister Vlacheslav Molotov, his deputy Andrei Vishinsky, and Andrei Gromyko, the ambassador to the United States—led the foreigners to a tent for lavish and classically Russian refreshments: "hot tea with lemon and sugar, vodka, brandy, and champagne, caviar, smoked sturgeon and salmon, white and black bread, fresh butter, cheese, and hard- and soft-boiled eggs."

Churchill, being Churchill, indulged himself to the fullest. But Roosevelt, a light eater and drinker, started out almost immediately through the snowy mountains for the six-hour, ninety-mile drive to Yalta.

Around the Yalta resort, pine-covered mountain slopes descended into parks and gardens where stood the cedars, magnolias, and olive trees of a Mediterranean climate. In their retreat, the Germans had laid waste to many of the buildings and the red tile roofs and French windows that once had opened onto balconies and the promenade below were largely demolished. But the Soviets had worked frantically to restore Livadia, Tsar Nicholas II's fifty-room-plus palace; huge numbers of painters, plasterers, and plumbers had come down from Moscow to restore the interior. Trucks had hauled furniture and lamps all the way from hotels in the capital.

Roosevelt stayed in a first-floor bedroom, surrounded by orange velvet panels; next door, the tsar's old billiard room of oak and red velvet served as the president's private dining room. Alone among the Americans, Roosevelt enjoyed a private bathroom. On the same floor, Secretary of State Edward R. Stettinius (a former chairman of the board of United States Steel who, after four years in the State Department in late 1944, had replaced the ailing Cordell Hull) had a two-room suite that overlooked the Black Sea. Others in the American delegation, including Harry Hopkins, FDR's close adviser, Charles Bohlen, a Russian-speaking official in the State Department, and Alger Hiss, the State Department official later accused of espionage, had more cramped quarters upstairs.

Stalin's and Churchill's villas were not so grand. Stalin's was in considerable disrepair. The British establishment looked a mixture of Scottish and Moorish. "It's a big house," Cadogan wrote to his wife, "of indescribable ugliness ... with all the furnishings of an almost terrifying hideosity." As Churchill discovered, his rooms were infested with bedbugs.

Stalin and Churchill agreed to hold the meetings in the ballroom of the Livadia Palace, on the first floor and convenient for Roosevelt in his wheelchair. The room was in the grand style, with a handsome molded ceiling, marble columns along its length, windows that gave onto an interior courtyard, and at one end of the chamber a huge fireplace.

A photograph taken during the weeklong Yalta Conference portrayed the Big Three seated side-by-side in three wooden armchairs. Churchill sat on the left, bareheaded and swathed in a double-breasted, military-style greatcoat. Stalin wore a beaked marshal's cap and a heavy coat with epaulettes. Roosevelt, the palm of his right hand resting on a wasted thigh and the fingers of his left hand holding a cigarette, wore a dark cape. Unsmiling, each appeared to be encased in his own thoughts.

Churchill at Yalta maintained his routine of sleeping late, orating over dinners about anything at anyone who would listen, and working until two or three in the morning. His daughter Sarah, though, noticed that he seemed depressed; for years he had suffered from what he called his "black dog." But now he had an especially good reason to be downcast. "I did not become the king's first minister," he had declared in 1942 to an audience in Mansion House, the Lord Mayor's official residence in the City of London, "to preside over the liquidation of the British Empire." But at Yalta he was doing just that, for clearly Roosevelt was rejecting Churchill's Balkan deal with Stalin.

On January 21, 1945, just a week before the conferees had left for Yalta, the *New York Times* on its first page ran a banner headline: "U.S. AIM FIRM PEACE, CHURCHILL IS TOLD." The following article stated that American public opinion would not accept the possibility that "a discredited old order [the British Empire] rise from the ashes of the old or to see the tyranny of Nazi occupation [in Greece] replaced by some catspaw totalitarianism masquerading behind a native name [the British behind George II, King of the Hellenes]. Roosevelt, the article stated, believed that "liberated people should choose for themselves." At Yalta, much to Stalin's amusement, Roosevelt teased Churchill mercilessly about Britain's decline. Churchill said later to Mary, his other daughter, that he had felt crushed between the American buffalo and the Russian bear.

Josef Stalin, small, swarthy, yellow-eyed, and from Russian cigarettes yellow-toothed and yellow-fingered, knew precisely what he wanted and was sure that he could get it: an expansion of the Soviet perimeter. "All through its history," Harold Macmillan, heir to the publishing fortune and British political adviser to Eisenhower, wrote in his memoirs, "the landlocked Russian Empire has sought two main objectives: outlet to the warm seas and a defensive ring around its western borders. The [Communist] government pursued the same aims as its predecessor."

Macmillan saw clearly the link between the past and the present. The tsars had sought access to the Mediterranean; Stalin would do the same. In 1907 Russia's rulers had acquired from Great Britain a sphere of influence in northern Iran; Stalin would cite the agreement as justification of a Soviet presence in the region. The last Romanov, Nicholas II, had dreamed of Russian power in northeast Asia, and had seen that dream shattered; now Stalin would revive it.

Roosevelt expected no less. He was dying, although he made no mention of it. People around him at Yalta noticed that, his mouth agape, he often dozed off in discussions. But his mind was still acute; he still understood reality. And the reality was that the impending defeats of Germany and Japan were opening power vacuums, west and east, that Stalin intended to fill. The Soviets were moving through eastern Europe and Roosevelt would not be able to dislodge them: The American people wanted victory, and then they wanted to bring their boys home. So Roosevelt would sacrifice eastern Europe for what he considered the greater good—a peace based on Russia's joining America in running the world. And nowhere was FDR's idea of a co-dominion clearer than in East Asia.

5

The Yalta Conference brought one issue to a quick resolution. There would be a United Nations with a Security Council and General Assembly: The UN would be the first international congress dominated not by Europe but rather by America and Russia. Several other problems, however, raised tempers and fears.

Stalin demanded control of Poland and rule of his "Lublin Poles," Communist anti-German underground fighters, in Warsaw. Fully in agreement on this point, Roosevelt and Churchill objected. They wanted a "more broadly based" Polish government that would include Poles who had taken refuge in London (and who presumably were pro-Western). As was his wont, Stalin exploded. Since Germany had attacked the Soviet Union across the plains of Poland, the establishment of Poland as a buffer zone, he screamed, was for the Soviet Union "a question of both honor and security." In the end he did agree to a "broadly based" regime and to "free elections." But neither Roosevelt nor Churchill pressed him for a definition of those terms; nor did he offer any clarification.

The Big Three fought over the new borders of Germany and over Stalin's demand for $20 billion in reparations from whichever authorities would succeed Hitler in Germany. Churchill wanted a share for Great Britain of any wealth that remained in Germany. But being close to the center of Europe, the Red Army was in a position to remove remaining farm animals, machine tools, vehicles, anything of economic significance. Churchill got nothing of the sort.

Roosevelt brought up a favored State Department project and one pushed by Stettinius, a Declaration of Liberated Europe. The proposal would have pledged the Americans, the British, and the Soviets with regard to eastern Europe to "act in concert." Such action, the declaration read, would enable those peoples liberated from the Nazis "to create democratic institutions of their own choice." This, the declaration stated, "is a promise of the Atlantic Charter—the right of all peoples to choose the form of government under which they will live—the restoration of sovereign rights and self-government to those people who have been forcibly deprived of them."

At these words, Molotov interjected himself into the discussion. The phrase, he pointed out, well might mean an Anglo-American veto over Soviet actions. He insisted that "act in concert" be replaced by "mutual consultations." Powerless to impose any kind of "concert," Roosevelt yielded and the Soviets gave the meaningless statement their approval.

But Churchill, too, had been uneasy about the Declaration on Liberated Europe. He wanted it understood that the reference to the Atlantic

Charter "did not apply to the British Empire." The Atlantic Charter had pledged America and Britain to respect the self-determination of nations, a principle that went back to President Woodrow Wilson and his Fourteen Points of World War I. Mindful, however, of the Indian independence movement and indeed the restiveness of non-Britons throughout the colonies, Churchill claimed that "as far as the British Empire was concerned the principles already applied": Britain had already extended self-government to subject peoples.

Dismissing such concerns, Roosevelt and Stalin henceforth ignored Churchill almost altogether. They needed to chat between themselves about the war with Japan. Churchill spent the rest of the conference in his chambers, brooding.

Retiring to the dark wood-paneled study beside his bedroom in the Livadia Palace, Roosevelt, through his interpreter, Charles Bohlen, explained to Stalin the state of the Pacific war. America held the Marianas and waves of American bombers were starting to fly northward, dropping incendiary bombs on the wood and paper cities of Japan. Bombing alone could win the war, Roosevelt told Stalin; with even more bases, American troops would not have to invade the Japanese islands.

Although he had previously forbidden American airplanes the use of the base at Vladivostok, Stalin conceded that Roosevelt was right. He even offered to provide the Americans with new air bases.

Yet Roosevelt wanted more than bases. He looked forward to Soviet–American joint military planning for the Far East. Stalin in turn wished to talk about "the political conditions under which the USSR would enter the war against Japan." He desired the recovery of the territories lost under the tsardom.

Roosevelt agreed that Russia was entitled to the southern half of Sakhalin and to the Kuriles, the chain of islands that reached northward from the tip of Hokkaido to Russia's Kamchatka peninsula. The Soviets also should get the use of the rail-line that in the nineteenth century Nicholas II had built through Manchuria to Port Arthur.

Roosevelt confided in Stalin that so far he had not discussed such arrangements with Chiang Kaishek. But he had little doubt that the *generalissimo*, having no choice and still wanting American aid, would give his consent. Actually, Roosevelt thought that Port Arthur and Dairen should be internationalized, perhaps under the control of the United Nations. FDR ignored the fact that Manchuria once had been Chinese and that its internationalization would fly directly against the principles of the Atlantic Charter.

Then, to twist the tail of the British lion, he suggested that Hong Kong, too, should be placed under an international regime. Learning of Roosevelt's proposals over before-dinner drinks, the British at Yalta were outraged. Anthony Eden, the foreign secretary, considered Roosevelt's idea "discreditable" and seriously suggested that Churchill not sign any agreement.

Ignoring British sentiments, Roosevelt turned to Korea. America, Russia, and China, he indicated to Stalin, might be able to manage the peninsula jointly. Since Korea had been the staging ground for Japan's assault on Russia in 1904, Stalin agreed.

And China. Since well before Pearl Harbor, Roosevelt told Stalin, the United States had been "trying to keep China alive." China would "remain alive," Stalin assured Roosevelt; the Soviet Union had hardly lifted a finger to help the Chinese Communists. In fact, Stalin proposed, Chiang Kaishek should bring the Communists into his government (just as the Nationalists and the Communists had been united before Chiang's 1927 Shanghai massacre). Stalin did not hesitate to undercut his fellow Communist, Mao Zedong.

Nor was Stalin predisposed to help the Communists led by Ho Chi Minh in Vietnam. Like Mao in China, Ho had led a successful guerrilla campaign against the Japanese, albeit without Soviet aid. To Roosevelt's embarrassment, General Charles de Gaulle, who had led the French resistance from exile in London and now was the provisional president of France, wanted American ships to transport his troops to Indochina. Stalin wondered where de Gaulle would even get enough troops to fill the ships. Roosevelt responded that he himself did not even seem able to find the vessels to transport the French. Roosevelt and Stalin assumed that, like Great Britain, France would be excluded from the postwar Far East.

So in the Far East, the leaders of the Soviet Union and the United States cut their deal. Roosevelt recognized the return of the Russian Empire: Sakhalin, Outer Mongolia, and parts of Manchuria would revert to the Soviet Union. Stalin accepted America's taking over French, British, and Japanese imperial interests. Korea would serve as a buffer, for there American and Soviet power would be roughly balanced. The arrangement, signed by a Churchill who had come to recognize Great Britain's dependency on the United States, was the diplomatic climax of World War II.

6

The Far East portion of the Yalta Agreement read: "The leaders of the three Great Powers—the Soviet Union, the United States, and Great Britain—have agreed that . . . after Germany has surrendered and the war in Europe has terminated the Soviet Union shall enter into the war against Japan."

Stalin would come in and be entitled to a share of the spoils on condition that:

"1. The *status quo* in Outer Mongolia (The Mongolian People's Republic) shall be preserved."

Outer Mongolia had been a Soviet client state and would remain such; Mongolia had been a Russian client state since the Chinese revolution of 1911.

"2. The former rights of Russia violated by the treacherous attack of Japan in 1904 shall be restored, viz:

"(a) the southern part of Sakhalin as well as all the islands adjacent shall be returned to the Soviet Union.

"(b) the commercial port of Dairen shall be internationalized, the pre-eminent interests of the Soviet Union in this port being safeguarded and the lease of Port Arthur as a naval base of the USSR restored."

The clause about Port Arthur had nothing to do with internationalization. It would entitle the Soviet Navy to a position in Chinese waters.

"(c) the Chinese Eastern Railroad and the South Manchurian Railroad which provides an outlet to Dairen shall be jointly operated by the establishment of a joint Soviet–Chinese Company, it being understood that the pre-eminent interests of the Soviet Union shall be safeguarded and that China shall retain full sovereignty in Manchuria."

This meant a return to the status quo of the late nineteenth century, minus the British.

"3. The Kurile Islands shall be handed over to the Soviet Union."

Here lay a guarantee against another Japanese invasion of Siberia; in the wake of the Russian Revolution, the French and the Poles had invaded the Bolshevik state from the west, the British and the Americans from Archangel in the north, and the Japanese along the trans-Siberian railroad from the east.

"It is understood that the agreement concerning Outer Mongolia and the ports and railroads referred to above will require the concurrence of Generalissimo Chiang Kaishek. The president will take measures in order to obtain this concurrence on advice from Marshal Stalin."

The pipeline to the *Guomindang* was to stay open.

"The heads of the three Great Powers have agreed that these claims of the Soviet Union shall be unquestionably fulfilled after Japan has been defeated.

"For its part the Soviet Union expresses its readiness to conclude with the National Government of China a pact of friendship and alliance between the USSR and China in order to render assistance to China with its armed forces for the purpose of liberating China from the Japanese yoke.

JOSEF STALIN
FRANKLIN D. ROOSEVELT
WINSTON S. CHURCHILL
February 11, 1945"

17

RETURN TO
THE COLONIES

1

Three hundred miles short of the Kunming air base, the Japanese thrust by early 1945 had come to an end. They had outrun their supply lines and now retreated to their garrisons; their last offensive had failed.

In Burma, too, the Japanese were in retreat. The previous October, General Daniel I. Sultan started a new drive. Sultan had gone to Burma to replace Stilwell but he had retained Stilwell's strategy. In a giant pincers movement, units out of China and India would converge on Mandalay. Then an amphibious British force under Lord Mountbatten, in charge of the Southwest Asia Command, would move from the easternmost tip of India down the Bay of Bengal and up into the delta of the Irrawaddy to Rangoon.

The effort to connect at Mandalay in November led to near-catastrophe. On seeing yellow-skinned soldiers, Sultan's forward American units from India thought they had come upon Japanese and they opened fire. Only when an American brigadier raced up and down the front line in a jeep, explaining that the soldiers in question were Chinese, did the shooting stop. Then the combined columns began their march toward Mandalay.

At the same time, a British–Indian–Australian force under the command of Lieutenant General William J. Slim (who had used antimalarial inoculations that at last had got his troops in shape) was marching on Mandalay; they reached a plain that lay along the west bank of the Irrawaddy. The lack of Japanese resistance puzzled Slim. Then he learned from reconnaissance pilots that General Kimura Hoyotaro, fresh from Tokyo, had withdrawn to the east bank. Rather than fight in the open, where British armor and artillery would have the advantage, Kimura would use the river as his line of defense and the British crossing the flow would be vulnerable to gunfire.

To evade the trap, Slim resorted to a ruse. Establishing a radio post and sending out fake messages, he created the illusion that he indeed would cross at Mandalay. Actually, most of his force went over the Irrawaddy well below the city and, keeping radio silence, reached Kimura's positions from the rear.

Early in March, 1945, General Slim led his columns past the buffalo wallows and brick pagodas on the outskirts of Mandalay. Before he could proceed, he needed to take Fort Dufferin, the Japanese stronghold in the heart of the city. Blocking the way was a Buddhist center called Pagoda Hill. It rose some 700 feet and its numerous temples gave cover to Japanese snipers. After three days of intense fighting, a company of Gurkhas commanded the hill.

From the height, Slim had a panoramic view of Mandalay. The city was laid out like a grid. Paralleling a canal, tree-lined streets ran straight from Pagoda Hill to a moat behind which an earthen embankment footed huge crenellated walls. This was Fort Dufferin.

Slim opened the bombardment with 500-pound bombs that hit the walls but did little damage. A week's barrage of 2,000-pound bombs opened a few breaches. The thunder of explosions continued. Finally, on March 20, 1945, half a dozen Burmese collaborators emerged from the fort. Most of the Japanese inside were dead, a few having escaped through a sewer, and the Burmese were waving a white flag.

The same month an amphibious force under Admiral Lord Mountbatten headed for the Irrawaddy delta. And at the beginning of May, 1945, the combined Allied forces closed the ring on Rangoon. Japanese in the capital fled pell-mell toward Thailand. In June, after several mopping up operations, the Burma Road was operative and Burma itself was back in British hands.

It would not remain so for long. In May, 1945, Churchill issued a White Paper claiming the right to restore Burma to the British Empire. But British rule in Burma had been highly unpopular. George Orwell, the novelist who had been born in Bengal, been educated at Eton, and served with the Indian Imperial Police in Burma, in a 1930s memoir illustrated the Burmese hatred of the British by quoting an article from the *Rangoon Gazette,* an underground journal:

> In these happy times, when we poor blacks are being uplifted by the mighty western civilization, with its manifold blessings such as the cinematograph, machine guns, syphilis, etc., what subject could be more inspiring than the private lives of our European benefactors? We think therefore that it may interest our readers to hear something of events in the upcountry district of Kyauktada. And especially of Mr. Macgregor, honoured Deputy Commissioner of said district. Mr. Macgregor is of the type of the Fine Old English Gentleman, such as, in these happy days, we have so many examples before our eyes. He is "a family man" as our dear English cousins say. Very much a

family man is Mr. Macgregor. So much so that he has already three children in the district of Kyauktada, where he
has been a year, and in his last district of Shwemyo he left
six young progenies behind him. Perhaps it is an oversight
on Mr. Macgregor's part that he has left these young in-
fants unprovided for, and that some of their mothers are in
danger of starvation, etc., etc., etc.

Burmese hatred of the British went beyond matters of sexually
predatory behavior. Taxes had been onerous, the plantation system
had exploited labor, and Indian moneylenders who had entered
Burma under British protection had been blatantly usurious. During
the time of the Japanese occupation, the British and Indians had fled.
But when the British returned, they discovered that an organized
Burmese nationalist guerrilla movement that had taken up arms
against the Japanese was ready to go to war again, this time against
the Britannic overlords.

Seeing little point in expending perilously scarce resources in trying
to hold on to Burma, which had little or no strategic value, the Labour
government of Prime Minister Clement Attlee, who won the British
general election at the end of July, 1945, revoked the Churchill White
Paper. Burma went free, soon choosing not even to join the British
Commonwealth.

2

Early in 1944, about a year before his return to the Philippines, General MacArthur gave thought to the future of the archipelago. The
Tydings-McDuffie Act of 1934 had pledged that in a dozen years the
islands would attain their independence. But after liberation from
Japan and the promised emancipation of 1946, how would the
Philippines be governed? As an American territory the prewar Philippines had fallen under the jurisdiction of the Department of the Interior, led by the crusty "Old Curmudgeon" Harold L. Ickes. Although

RETURN TO THE COLONIES

often churlish, Ickes was a staunch New Deal liberal, believing that after liberation the Filipinos should enjoy popular sovereignty.

MacArthur loathed Ickes, who, he charged, "seemed to think of the islands as one of his national parks." Should Ickes assign a new, civilian, liberal high commissioner to Manila (just before the war, the high commissioner had been Francis Sayre, son-in-law of Woodrow Wilson and not known for any democratizing tendencies), the general would "put him on a boat and send him home." MacArthur would not tolerate a "cloud of carpetbaggers."

The allusion to the American South before the Civil War (and after Reconstruction) was apt. A handful of wealthy Filipino families, descended from the Spanish and bearing names such as Soriano, Marcos, and Aquino, had long dominated the economy. These people, the *Illustrados,* the landowning elite, had derived their riches from coffee, sugar, cattle, and the like; as the oligarchs of Philippine society, that had enjoyed the benefits of American rule that allowed them their privileges. MacArthur had courted them and they him. Indeed, two of MacArthur's closest aides in the Pacific war were General Courtney Whitney, before the war a Manila lawyer for the rich, and Colonel Andres Soriano, controller of gold mines, real estate, and the San Miguel beer conglomerate. They buttressed MacArthur's conviction that in the Philippines true independence would mean revolution. In their eyes, and MacArthur's, Sergio Osmeña, a middle-class, nationalistic lawyer who had won election in 1935 as vice president and then become the president-in-exile, was a revolutionary.

While MacArthur was crossing the Pacific toward the Philippines, Osmeña, who was residing in Washington, believed it his proper role as president to go ashore with MacArthur. Meeting with Osmeña, however, Ickes had counseled him not to do it. The "country will be entirely under military command," Ickes predicted, "and you as a civilian leader will be powerless."

But Secretary of War Henry L. Stimson interceded, demanding that Ickes not "gum up the game by his own hostility to MacArthur." Perhaps pressured by Roosevelt, Ickes gave way and Osmeña had prepared to fly across the Pacific to join MacArthur. "But," Ickes added, "don't blame me later."

3

After MacArthur's landing at Leyte, amphibious units of his Sixth Army moved both north and south to capture Japanese airfields. Over the next few days the American footholds expanded steadily inland.

On October 26, 1944, MacArthur moved his headquarters from the *Nashville* to a spacious two-story stucco house in the coastal town of Tacloban. Vincent L. Powers, an Army sergeant, observed the general in the first days in the "Big House":

MacArthur, Powers wrote, "as was his habit could be seen at all hours walking up and down the veranda, smoking his elongated corn-cob pipe, strolling alone, or with an aide, or conferring with high-ranking military leaders. . . . At night the fluorescent lights of his inner office threw his easily recognizable figure into sharp relief. Should the air alert sound, he would knock the glowing ashes from his pipe, stand by the rail in the center of the porch, peer into the sky, watching the red tracers and the 90-mms blast at the enemy. The raid over he would resume his pacing."

From that oceanfront porch near the northeastern corner of the island, MacArthur directed the Leyte campaign. He set his sights on Leyte Valley, a watery land that lay between the beachheads on the east coast and the island's central mountain range. With five airstrips and a thoroughly anti-Japanese population, the plain seemed to be an ideal location for major air facilities. From those runways MacArthur could send his bombers to smash the Japanese throughout the archipelago, sink oil tankers heading up from Sumatra, and even hit enemy positions on Taiwan and the Chinese coast. MacArthur planned that the bombers would be taking off no later than early December, 1944.

The plan went awry. In November, the monsoon turned streams into torrents and washed out bridges and roads to the interior. The "rains came in 11-day downpours," the reporter Allen Raymond radioed the *Saturday Evening Post*. "It rained, for change of pace, in gusts and gales that blew with typhoon velocity, so that water was like horizontal gunfire, mercilessly pounding men, knocking over tents, reducing unwaterproofed material to shapeless, sodden masses. It rained all day and it rained all night."

Keeping the troops supplied became a nightmare. Constant exposure to water afflicted the men with skin diseases. Jeeps bogged down in fender-deep mud. The American troops and their Filipino bearers were wading across Leyte.

Tokyo, moreover, had decided to throw all the force it could muster into the defense of Leyte. The Japanese command had transferred its remaining aircraft from Taiwan and Luzon to airfields on Biliran and Samar, Philippine islands just above Leyte. Since several American carriers, battered in the battle for Leyte Gulf, had withdrawn for repairs, Japanese planes for the moment enjoyed control of the air. Forty-five thousand imperial troops also went onto Leyte as reinforcements.

But Leyte would demonstrate the might of American industry, which was now running at full throttle. The Japanese simply were outnumbered and outgunned. Early in December, an American amphibious force hit Ormos, the Japanese landing and supply center on Leyte's western coast. Tanks rumbled up the beach and ship-propelled missiles pounded the center of the town. Soon, in the words of an Army operations report, Ormoc turned into a "blazing inferno of bursting white phosphorus shells, burning houses, and exploding ammunition dumps, and over it all hung a pall of heavy smoke from burning dumps mixed with the gray dust of destroyed concrete buildings blasted by artillery, mortar, and rocket fire." By midafternoon, December 10, the Japanese in Ormoc surrendered.

In the fight for Leyte, the Japanese had lost 60,000 troops to 3,500 Americans dead. Luzon came next.

4

At about the time of MacArthur's landing at Leyte beach, Vice Admiral Onishi Takijiro, in charge of the Japanese air wing on Luzon, called a meeting of his staff. Onishi was blunt.

"As you know, the war situation is grave," he said. "There is only one way of assuring that our meager strength will be effective to a maximum degree. That is to organize suicide attack units composed of fighters armed with 550-pound bombs, with each plane to crash-dive into an enemy carrier."

With Onishi's address, a special Japanese air corps came into being. It took the name of *Kamikaze*, "divine wind," named after the thirteenth-century typhoon off Korea that was believed to have saved Japan from a Mongol invasion. Now *Kamikaze* pilots were to save Japan from an American invasion. But most of Japan's trained pilots were dead. So in the home islands thirteen- and fourteen-year-old boys, too young to have been inducted into the military, volunteered for the mission in large numbers. To show their fervor, many filled out their applications in blood. One wrote: "How I appreciate the chance to die like a man."

After receiving only the barest training, the pilots gathered in Tokyo before a tall, marble national monument that honored those who had lost their lives in war. Carved in the marble were huge *kanji* (characters) that read, "Patriotic Ghosts." Then the youths were off to the Philippines.

Once at bases on Luzon, the pilots performed traditional Japanese rituals. They partook of seaweed, rice, and *sake*. Some gave belongings to friends. Most wrote epistles to their families, sometimes enclosing fingernail clippings and locks of hair. One brushed a letter to his parents: "Please congratulate me. I have been given a splendid opportunity to die. This is my last day. The destiny of our homeland hinges on the battle in the seas to the southwest where I shall fall like a blossom from a radiant cherry tree. . . . May our deaths be as sudden and clean as the shattering of crystal."

Gathering on Luzon runways, the pilots tied on traditional *hachinaki*, white headbands worn by the *samurai* of old to symbolize courage. Then they attended final briefings and, decked out in their flight uniforms, raised gloved right hands in salute to their commanders. Passing rows of cheering comrades, they strode to their airplanes. Each carried into the cockpit a lunch box with *tofu*, rice, and chopsticks: It was the last meal. Gunning their motors, they went up in groups of three. As they headed southward, the pilots kept in mind the "First Order to the *Kamikazes*": "Do not be in too much of a hurry to die. If you cannot find your target, turn back; next time you may find a more favorable opportunity. Choose a death which brings about a maximum result." Their mission was to stop MacArthur's invasion of Luzon. He was sending the huge naval force that had gathered off Leyte toward Lingayen Gulf, about midpoint on the western coast. Just off the gulf, the ships and hundreds of *Kamikazes* collided.

Most of the *Kamikaze* pilots were shot down by American fighters and shipboard gun crews and so never reached their targets. Yet some got through. In a stupendous detonation, one American oil tanker simply disappeared. A munitions ship blew up with such force that its debris fell on other vessels a quarter of a mile away. Several destroyers received hits and aboard the *Nashville,* MacArthur's flagship, 137 seamen lost their lives. More attacks were to come.

Against the advance of MacArthur's armada upon Lingayen Gulf, however, their hits were no more than pinpricks. Nor could the regular Japanese land and naval forces mount a sure defense. On Leyte Japan had lost thousands of troops and more than half its supply ships. There the Americans had broken almost every valve and piston of the Japanese war machine. And by mid-December, 1944, the Japanese on Luzon possessed no more than 200 aircraft, most in disrepair; the Imperial Navy there was down to nineteen patrol boats, ten midget submarines, and 200 one-man suicide boats. Against MacArthur's assault, the Japanese on Luzon were nearly helpless.

At 9:30 on the morning of January 9, 1945, 70,000 Americans went ashore at Lingayen Gulf on Luzon. To the surprise of many, the town of Lingayen welcomed the Americans by unfurling long-buried United States flags. The crowds were Filipino: The Japanese had vanished.

Lieutenant General Yamashita Tomuyuki was in charge of the Japanese forces on Luzon. He had led the Japanese drive down through Malaya and was a realist: He knew they were going to lose Luzon. But he might be able, he calculated, to stop MacArthur from using the island as a stationary aircraft carrier for bombing Japan. So he had withdrawn his troops to the hills, from where, he hoped, they could harass the American air forces. In so doing he left the road to Manila open.

Some Japanese did resist. At Clark Field, an air base about fifty miles north of Manila, groups of Japanese pinned down American columns with heavy fire. "The Japanese," an American soldier recollected, "were using their anti-aircraft guns as anti-personnel and that's how I got wounded. They were using 40mm stuff, striking the trees near us, splintering the trees and the splinters dug right into us."

But after a week of fighting, American firepower prevailed. By nightfall on January 30, 1945, Clark Field and the ridge that overlooked it were controlled by the Americans. MacArthur pushed on immediately toward Manila, sending ahead an advance guard on a most special mission.

Pushing southward, the tanks and armored cars in two columns beat the Japanese to a string of bridges; Marine Corps dive-bombers swooped low to offer protection. By Saturday, February 3, the columns had reached a bridge at Novaliches, five miles above Manila. The bridge spanned a deep gorge and the Japanese had attached dynamite to the pilings. The fuses were burning. But a Navy bomb-disposal expert dashed through Japanese bullets and snipped the wires. The American columns crossed the gorge.

Late the same afternoon, a squadron of fighters buzzed the Santo Tomás camp in Manila. Since the fall of Corregidor the camp had held American prisoners of war and civilian internees. As the planes came low, a black object dropped from one of the cockpits. It was a pair of goggles. A note was attached. "Roll out the barrel," it said. "Santa Claus is coming Sunday or Monday."

The internees did not have to wait until Sunday. They had hardly passed the note around when they heard the roar of tanks and an American voice shouting, "Where the hell is the front gate?" A tank smashed through the barbed wire.

Carl Mydans, a newsman and photographer for *Life,* accompanied the lead tank. Captured by the Japanese in Manila when the war broke out, Mydans had been incarcerated in Santo Tomás; later he had been freed in a prisoner exchange. Now he was coming back, he wrote, for the "liberation of my own prison camp."

Mydans was "astonished . . . to see that gate, which had stood so long between me and freedom, fall over like a painted illusion." The prisoners rushed up to the tanks. "A woman threw her arms about me. Hands grabbed me and lifted me and carried me, equipment and all, onto the stairs of what had been the Administration Building" (the camp had been a Filipino university).

As they reached the steps, the troops heard cries of prisoners at the windows of the nearby Education Building. "Let us out! The Japs won't let us out! They're holding us in here! Let us out!"

Rather than blast his way into the building and cause casualties, Brigadier General William Chase, in charge of the rescue columns, chose to bargain. He sent Lieutenant Colonel Charles E. Brady and Ernest Stanley, a Canadian missionary who spoke Japanese, to work out an agreement.

Inside the Education Building, Brady found Hayashi Toshio, a lieutenant colonel, blocking his way, straddling the entrance with his hands on his holstered pistols. Hayashi said that he would release his prisoners only if his men could leave under a safe conduct fully armed. Brady refused. Then they negotiated a compromise: The Japanese could leave but bear only personal arms.

At dawn on Monday, February 5, a procession formed at the main door of the Education Building, led by Brady in a helmet, Hayashi in a uniform cloth cap, and Stanley, the translator, in a civilian white shirt. About 100 Japanese soldiers, three abreast, followed Hayashi, chanting to the rhythm of their own footsteps. Flanking them on both sides, Brady's men held rifles, ready to fire. They did not have to shoot. After the Japanese had crossed the campus, marched out along the streetcar tracks on the street beyond, and neared their own fortifications in the city, Mydans wrote, they "broke ranks and scrambled in terror."

Two days later, dressed in khaki and his beaked and braided cap, MacArthur paid a visit to Santo Tomás. As he stepped into the entrance hall of the Administration Building, a host of hollow-cheeked internees, their arms and legs as thin as broomsticks, and their wrists and ankles swollen from beri-beri, swarmed around him. He recognized many of them, spoke to them by name. "It was wonderful," he said later, "to be a life-saver, not a life-taker."

But more lives remained to be taken. The battle of Manila was in its opening phase.

5

While General Yamashita was up in the hills trying to slow the American southward advance, Admiral Iwabushi Sanji had taken over the defense of Manila. He had ringed the city with barbed wire, placed machine guns in houses (carpenters had sawn slits in walls for the barrels), and ordered artillery from his ships in the harbor cemented onto street corners. When the first of MacArthur's infantry entered Manila on February 4, he implemented his scorched earth policy. Retreating along the Pasig River, which bisected the capital, the Japanese troops dynamited each bridge they passed. The explosions set off fires and the wind carried the flames toward bamboo houses along the waterfront. Soon most of Manila was on fire, with huge dense black clouds billowing toward the sky.

The fires did not stop the Americans. After bulldozing buildings to create firewalls, on February 7 they began to ford the Pasig. From the city's eastern edge, the columns that had advanced so swiftly to Santo Tomás regrouped and pushed their way toward the government sector. As they did so, still other U.S. units moved across the bay to Corregidor. MacArthur was bent on revenge.

On the morning of February 10, 1945, American paratroopers landed on the Corregidor beach. Some died in the landing but many others were fortunate. Most of the Japanese had squeezed down into the Malinta tunnel. Thus the airborne troops were able to clear the plateau quickly. After nailing an American flag to the top of a pole, the paratroopers set up guns to cover the coming amphibious attack.

The landing went smoothly and the Americans swung into action. The Japanese had loaded the rabbit warrens carved into the rock with blasting powder: of this U.S. intelligence was sure. So the troops worked their way ever closer to the sealed-up tunnel entrances, then blasted holes open and went to work dropping in hand grenades.

At 9:30 on the night of February 21, the tactic bore fruit. The innards of Corregidor exploded. Flames shot forth from all orifices, blazes of light in the darkness. Rock and debris flew up everywhere, and cracks split open all over the hillsides.

Five days later, trapped and starving, the Japanese in the Malinta tunnel engaged in mass suicide by setting off an explosion that lifted the top off a knoll on the eastern end of Corregidor. An American described the scene as "utter carnage, bodies lying everywhere, *everywhere*." The tunnel entrance was nothing more than a crater. Witnessing the dead Japanese, an American medic said: "I sat down on a rock and burst out crying. I couldn't stop myself and didn't even want to. I had seen more than a man could stand and still stay normal."

After the fall of Corregidor, MacArthur went ashore. This time he did not wade. Ever aware of the value of symbols, he and his officers landed in four PT boats. "We went back to the Rock," he said, "the same way we had left it."

On March 4, 1945, MacArthur's troops flushed the Japanese altogether from Manila; the rest of the Philippines would fall with the Japanese surrender. Most of the city was in rubble. But at last it was free.

To celebrate, MacArthur summoned an assembly of Filipino notables to the Malacañan Palace, the traditional site of authority in Manila. As they gathered in the dust of the ruined building, the general proclaimed the reestablishment of the Philippine Commonwealth, with the promise soon of independence. "My country has kept the faith," he declared. "Your capital city, cruelly punished though it be, has regained its rightful place—citadel of democracy in the East." He went on to say that "America buried imperialism here today." He was referring to Japanese imperialism.

18

THE NEW TAIPANS

1

With the end of the war in sight, the British found the American presence in China alarming, for they once had seen the country as part of their own empire. A telegraph from the embassy in Chongqing to the cabinet in London dated January 1, 1945, stated: "The reasons why an effort on our part to help China seems desirable are (a) it is in the general Allied interest to avoid a collapse in China;... (b) to continue in the role of passive spectator cannot fail to have an adverse effect on our prestige and future standing, not only in China but elsewhere in Asia."

But Britain's prestige and future standing remained in jeopardy and four months later G. E. Price, the Chongqing representative of Swire and Sons, before the war one of the leading British companies in China, complained to the Foreign Office: "The aggressive American salesmen in and out of uniform are having things very much their own way. They can talk about first finance and early large-scale delivery.

They seem to have an unlimited supply of technicians and planners unengrossed by the war to put at Chinese disposal. The Chinese have been made to realize that they [the Americans] are in a hurry and they [the Chinese] turn first to the eager continent with an intact economy, not to Britain with a smashed one to repair."

But although the British longed for the restoration of their former hegemony in China, the Americans were hostile to their return. On Christmas Eve, 1944, Ambassador Patrick Hurley cabled the State Department: "Foreign influence, composed of a group of imperialist nations now fighting for reconquest and reestablishment of their colonies in . . . Asia presents the greatest opposition to the unification of China."

The British wanted to keep China disunited so that, as in the nineteenth century, they might divide and conquer. The American strategy, however, was to strive for a unified China: Confident of being able to reach every corner of the China market, the United States reverted to its old policy of the Open Door. In January, 1943, the United States had pressured the British into signing a treaty with China whereby the former rulers relinquished their treasured extraterritoriality. In 1944, Ambassador Hurley visited Mao Zedong in Yanan, hoping to persuade the chairman to join with Chiang Kaishek in a unified Chinese government. Mao suspected that by participating in such a government the Communists would be placing themselves in jeopardy, as in the Shanghai crackdown of 1927, and that in any case an all-China regime simply would enable the Americans to subject the country again to colonialism. Mao refused to cooperate.

For a 1943 United States agreement with China allowed *American* extraterritoriality. By 1945, some 60,000 U.S. troops who had finally gone to China were free of Chinese criminal jurisdiction. There were now numerous American bases, transport services, military radio stations, and post exchanges, and American personnel acted with as much impunity as any of the Europeans in the days of the unequal treaties. In the summer of 1945, the streets of Chongqing were filled with roistering American soldiers and sailors just as the Victorian-era treaty-ports had been filled with the British.

Saul Steinberg, the famous cartoonist with *The New Yorker,* captured the feel of American-occupied Chongqing. In a line drawing published near the end of the war, he portrayed a teeming Chinese street. Curving tile roofs frame the top of the picture. Latticework covers the upper stories of the buildings. In the open shops on the ground level hang chicken carcasses and padded jackets for sale. Under an umbrella on the street a wok is steaming away. And scattered throughout the mass of Chinese humanity—people wearing conical hats, riding water buffalo, carrying shoulder poles, and peddling trinkets laid out on mats—American soldiers gawk, leer, and bully. And right in the focal point of the picture, one of them rides arrogantly in that classic symbol of European imperialism, a rickshaw.

Steinberg's picture belied Washington's claim of China's status as a great power. Indeed, by the summer of 1945, the Chinese Communists were inveighing against what they saw as the new American imperialism. And in Washington John Service, who believed that the United States should recognize the Communists' popularity in China, was under arrest for treason.

2

A double shock awaited Service upon his return from China. First, his airplane landed at the National Airport on April 12, 1945, the day of Roosevelt's death. And second, when he finally reached the State Department, he learned that he was officially in disgrace.

The State Department then shared offices with the Bureau of the Budget in the State, War, and Navy Building (now the Old Executive Office Building), just west of the White House. With a mansard roof and pillared porticoes, it dated back to the nineteenth century. Dean Acheson, in 1945 an official in the department and later secretary of state, described his offices as consisting "of two large, high-ceilinged rooms in the southwest corner. . . . A corridor between the rooms had been enclosed to provide space of sorts for secretaries. Together we stifled under the full blast of the summer sun aided by its reflection from the roof of the portico and unabated by any such new-fangled contrivance as air-conditioning."

Things were hot for Service too. He had returned to State just in time to get caught up in bureaucratic warfare.

The man in charge of the Far Eastern Division was Stanley K. Hornbeck. Earlier in the war, some of the China hands charged that he had withheld from Secretary of State Cordell Hull information unfavorable to Chiang Kaishek and the Nationalist Chinese. Then, by April, 1945, with victory over Germany assured and victory over Japan probable, a new issue had swept over the State Department: Communism. Hornbeck, who was a political ally of Ambassador Hurley, suspected Service of leftist leanings.

With his pregnant wife and two children across the continent in Berkeley, his family's home, Service settled in behind a desk in the Division of Chinese Affairs. But he was assigned almost no duties, so he had plenty of time to think. It was a shame, he thought, that with the Communists in a strong position in China, the American embassy in Chongqing was in the hands of Hurley.

Service took it upon himself to publicize his views. Only six days after FDR's death, Mark Gayn, a reporter with *The Saturday Evening Post,* telephoned him and they had lunch. The next day Service also accepted an invitation to a party at the Arlington apartment of Andrew Roth, naval intelligence liaison officer to the State Department; Roth suggested that Service go first to the Statler Hotel and meet Philip Jaffe, the publisher of *Amerasia,* a strongly anti-Chiang magazine.

At six o'clock on the afternoon of April 19, 1945, Service went to Jaffe's room at the Statler. Unknown to him, Gayn, Roth, and Jaffe were left-wingers interested in using him for propaganda. Also unknown to him, Jaffe's room was bugged and FBI agents were listening to the conversation from the next room.

Before driving down to the Arlington party, Jaffe and Service talked about an article that Gayn recently had published about China. Service expressed surprise that the wording had come almost verbatim from one of his own reports. He was concerned, he added, that someone was leaking his work.

After the party, Service himself sent several of his China reports (some of which he himself had classified secret) to the New York offices of *Amerasia*. Leaking was an integral part of Washington's culture, as it still is, and part of Service's job in China had been to give briefings to the press. He was neither passing along military secrets nor engaging in espionage. But, with the arrogance and naiveté of a young man who knew his subject better than anyone else, he *was* taking a risk.

On June 5, 1945, Service noticed several FBI men hanging about in the black-and-white-tiled corridor outside his office. They were there when he left for lunch and when he came back. In the afternoon, Service had a visit from an emissary of General Donovan, who wanted Service to work in the OSS. When the visitor left, the FBI agents opened Service's door, put him in handcuffs, and searched his office. They found nothing incriminating. The same was true in his apartment. The agents nevertheless whisked him to the federal courthouse. Before arraignment, Service, wearing a white shirt, a necktie, a dark suit, and a fedora, was seated in the waiting room beside Emmanuel Larson, another China hand. Larson spoke to Service in Chinese.

Reporters were nearby.

"Speak English," Service snapped, fearful that he would be taken for a spy.

Slapped in a jail cell until his wife and sister-in-law could raise bail, Service felt, he said later, "overwhelmed with disgrace and shame." But even after his release the next day, he found that State Department colleagues treated him as a pariah. He grew increasingly bitter. Around the office he had made no secret of forwarding documents to *Amerasia*. Why, he asked himself, had no one in State warned him of

Roth's and Jaffe's radical connections? Was Hornbeck, or someone else in the department, trying to set him up as a scapegoat?

From California, General Stilwell offered support. Ever since his own recall from China, Stilwell had been prohibited from going public with his distrust and assessment of Chiang Kaishek. A subpoena to testify as a defense witness for Service, however, would give the general a platform.

Yet Service's lawyer, Thomas Corcoran, who was renowned for getting things done, did not call on Stilwell. The former White House aide whom FDR had called "Tommy the Cork," Corcoran had been the principal attorney for China Defense Supplies, the dummy corporation established to route pilots and planes to Chennault's earlier planned firebombing of Japan. That connection had led to his becoming a Washington lobbyist for Chiang Kaishek and the Chinese Nationalist government. The last thing Corcoran wanted was Stilwell on the stand, trumpeting the failure of his Chinese clients.

As it happened, a federal grand jury voted unanimously not to indict Service of anything and he resumed his diplomatic career, although he was never again assigned to China. In fact, by his count, nine State Department loyalty boards later gave him full clearance. A Senate committee also exonerated Service, declaring that he should not be branded as "disloyal for writing what appears to have been the true facts as he saw them."

The *Amerasia* case nevertheless had profound consequences. East Asia experts in the State Department learned not to protest American alignments with reactionary regimes. And to the Chinese Communists the episode was proof positive of animosity from imperial America, even as America was on the verge of destroying Japan.

3

With the capture of the Marianas, Leyte, and Luzon, and the quick repair of their airfields, American bombers were within range of Japan. But Iwo Jima stood in the way. Admiral Nimitz had the assignment of organizing its conquest.

Six hundred and fifty miles south of Japan lay the Bonin, or Volcano, Islands. The largest of them was a pork chop–shaped islet called Iwo Jima. In Japanese, *Jima* meant "island" and *Iwo* meant "sulfur"; bubbling, hissing deposits of the mineral often filled the air with the stench of rotten eggs. Most of the thousand or so residents worked in a refinery that shipped processed sulfur to Japan's main islands. Japan had claimed the place in 1861 and, despite its remoteness, regarded Iwo Jima as part of the sacred homeland. As such, it was to be defended to the death.

Nowhere else in the Pacific theater in World War II did American airplanes so blanket a target with bombs. Starting in November, 1944, the American carriers *Chester, Pensacola,* and *Salt Lake City* shelled Iwo Jima all day, every day.

By the turn of 1945, the assault plan was in place. Steaming out of Hawaii, Task Force Fifty-Two, under the command of Admiral W. H. P. Blandy and made up of battleships, cruisers, aircraft carriers, and support vessels, would pound the black beaches of Iwo Jima. Then Task Force Fifty-Three, a fleet of seventy-three transport ships under Rear Admiral Harry W. Hill, would haul 80,000 Marines, and for each of those Marines 1,000 pounds of supplies, across the Pacific to Iwo Jima. General Holland Smith would lead the men off the landing craft of the latter fleet onto the island. The first landing took place at dawn on February 19, 1945.

Just before going ashore, many of the Marines read a prayer passed out by the chaplains. Composed in England in the 1640s, it read:

> *Lord! I shall be verie busy this day.*
> *I may forget Thee,*
> *But do not Thou forget me.*

After a two-hour bombardment from the ships, Navy aircraft took over. In screaming dives, squadrons of Corsairs and Hellcats hit the pillbox fortifications. After the aircraft withdrew, the naval bombardment resumed, first focusing on the areas just behind the beach, and then up higher, striking inland. During the bombardment, landing craft that had been circling a few miles out headed for the shore.

Just after nine in the morning, the landing began. First to reach the black sands were seventy amtracks, each manned by a crew of three and carrying several machine guns and a 75-millimeter howitzer. They raced up the beach and opened fire.

Japanese return fire was light. Lieutenant General Kuribayashi Tadamichi was in charge of the island's defense. He was an audacious officer chosen to defend Iwo Jima to the end, and had ordered his troops to refrain from shooting until the beaches were packed with Marines. Although he was doubtful that he could hold the island ("The United States," he had written to his wife, "is the last country in the world Japan should fight"), he had adopted a new tactic. Sooner or later, he knew, their pillboxes would crumple. So he had planned to have his forces burrow down in the hardened volcanic rock of Mount Suribachi, at the southern end of the island. But thirty feet below the surface the heat was intense. Rather than sacrifice Japanese troops, he had ordered hundreds of drafted Koreans to dig tunnels. He had brought engineers from Japan to lay out concrete and iron underground reinforcements. Assisting the engineers, construction workers had cut down every tree and wooden structure on the island to serve as beams. By the beginning of 1945, they had completed a subterranean network of hospitals, bunkers, and command posts connected by eighteen miles of tunnels. Protected by concrete barriers, tunnel openings ringed the mountain. Their guns covered every point of the compass and the deforestation seemed fortuitous. The Americans would have no place to hide.

Despite such precautions, General Kuribayashi had given way to gloom. "I have lost much weight," he wrote to his wife from under the mountain. "I look like Gandhi, the great Indian. The meals consist mostly of dried vegetables, so that I often have a sour feeling in my stomach. We sweat a lot; unfortunately there is no clear water available here. There are so many flies and mosquitoes that we sometimes cannot open our mouths and eyes." The privation, he had believed, had been an omen of disaster. "It really does not matter much to me where my grave will be. If there really is such a thing as a soul, then it will stay with you and our children."

He was going to die on Iwo Jima, he was sure. But he was going to make the Americans pay. Once the Americans landed, he ordered, every Japanese soldier "will resist until the end, making his position his tomb." So Kuribayashi held his fire until just the right moment.

A few minutes after the amtracks were ashore, the first tide of landing craft hit the beaches; their ramps dropped and 1,400 Marines surged onto Iwo Jima. Following them at five-minute intervals, row after row of still more landing craft stopped in the surf, dispatching 12,000 more Marines. Watching from headquarters in Mount Suribachi, General Kuribayashi kept his guns silent.

The Marine advance went slowly. The volcanic sand clogged weapons and in some cases explosions caused temporary blindness. In the dense sand, digging foxholes was almost impossible. Because each man was loaded down with equipment and ammunition, his mobility was restricted. So many men were on the beach that the Marines were virtually elbow to elbow and without cover. Now the Japanese general sprang his trap.

At 10:00 A.M. the Japanese opened fire. Hidden machine gun pits blazed to life, spraying the beach in a deadly cross fire. From concealed concrete pits, hundreds of mortars hurled their shells onto the massed Marines. Artillery tucked away in the recesses of Mount Suribachi blasted away at the beach and the landing craft offshore. The beach was two miles long and every bit of it was under attack. With no place to hide, the Marines took hideous casualties. Dozens of landing craft were under water, blocking access to the beach. But others kept coming with more men, tanks, bulldozers, and supplies. The beach was in chaos. For the Marines there was no room to maneuver; retreat was impossible. They could fight or fall.

Shortly after noon, Admiral Richmond Turner, in charge of the landing, ordered his craft to hold back until the situation on land improved. By late afternoon, however, the beach was still jammed and under steady assault. One unit of nearly 1,000 men suffered a death rate of seventy percent. Only slowly and under constant fire were Marines able to shove some of the wrecked vehicles into the surf, dig supply dumps in the sand, and clear pathways up from the beach. Even so, thousands of men had to spend the first night trapped on the shoreline. Yet by the end of the day several Marine units had made their way across the southern tip of the island, the small end of the pork chop. Iwo Jima's main airfield was on their right and Mount Suribachi was on their left. The dome-shaped mountain was their critical objective.

But the objective posed problems. Manned by 2,000 Japanese troops, Mount Suribachi was an immense, self-contained fortress with hundreds of concrete blockhouses, mortar installations, and machine gun nests. Its defenders were quite prepared to sacrifice their lives, as long as they could kill enough Americans.

On the morning of the second day of the Iwo Jima invasion, the Marines started toward Mount Suribachi. As they did so, the Navy in a coordinated move blasted away at the mountain. The defending guns answered. Soon both sides let loose so much explosive power that in the smoke the base of the rise was almost invisible.

The view from the summit, though, was unimpeded. As the Marines crept toward the slope, spotters at the peak directed fire with horrific accuracy. Bodies of Marines littered the ground.

The Marine plan for the capture of Mount Suribachi was almost simple-minded. "A frontal assault," one officer had asserted. "Surround the base, locate a route up, then climb it!"

But the defenders could detect the Marines' every move. As they advanced, squads of Japanese staged ambushes. Not until the end of the second day were the Marines able to bring tanks and howitzers into the action. At nightfall on February 20, they finally ringed the base of the mountain.

The third day brought ferocious hand-to-hand combat. In this the Marines excelled and gradually won the advantage. Led by Lieutenant John K. "Genghis Khan" Wells, a Marine platoon started up the slope. This platoon, the Third of Easy Company, Second Battalion, Twenty-Eighth Regiment, Fifth Marine Division, would become the most decorated in the history of the Corps. As night fell, the platoon was ready for the final assault of Mount Suribachi.

Under rain-filled clouds on the morning of February 22, the Marines broke camp. On the western side of the mountain, a patrol found a path and climbed partway up the slope. The rest of the Third Platoon followed right behind.

By this point, more than half the Japanese on and in Mount Suribachi were wounded or dead. Their fire had become sporadic. By the end of day four, though, the Marines themselves had suffered some 4,500 casualties.

The early morning of the fifth day brought the final attack. Leading the drive, Lieutenant Harold Schrier, who had replaced the wounded "Genghis Khan" Wells as head of the platoon, carried an American flag. His orders were to climb all the way up, secure the peak, and plant the Stars and Stripes. While the American naval guns remained silent, Schrier and twenty-seven other Marines scraped and crawled their way to the crest. Although their guns were at ready, they met no resistance. As the rest of the platoon joined the advance guard, someone saw and shot a Japanese. A few more Japanese then emerged from nearby caves, hurling hand grenades. After a brief firefight, the defenders retreated to their holes. A Marine found a long piece of pipe. He tied a flag to it and as he and three other Marines drove the pipe into the ground on the top of Mount Suribachi, Joe Rosenthal, an Associated Press photographer, was on hand to take his famous photo. The picture did not satisfy him and he asked the Marines to hoist a larger flag. *Then* he was satisfied.

At 10:20 A.M., February 23, 1945, the new American *taipans* had captured their first piece of Japan.

The Japanese still held the northern part of the island, the meaty part of the pork chop. On February 24, the Marines took the main airfield and a B-29 made a landing. But then the *Kamikaze* attacks begun in the battle of Leyte resumed. A fleet of suicide airplanes smashed into the American invasion fleet, hitting five vessels that included two carriers. The USS *Saratoga* suffered serious damage and the USS *Bismarck* went down. More than 500 American seamen lost their lives.

In the last days of February the infantrymen pushed onward; at last they had the support of Sherman tanks. And by the beginning of March, the American forces had taken a second airfield and about half the island. Navy Hellcats and Army P-51s flew low in air-support missions, strafing Japanese strongholds. Loaded with rifles, bayonets, grenades, and flamethrowers, the troops finally reached the northern end of the island, but losses again were heavy.

Not until March 26, after five weeks of battle, did the Marines finally secure Iwo Jima. The victory was militarily significant, for it provided the United States with a base from which bombers could reach Japan easily; Iwo Jima deservedly occupies an eternal place in the annals of American military history. Yet it also served well as propaganda. As Joe Rosenthal's little manipulation of his flag photograph shows, America, like all imperial powers dating back to Rome, was ready and willing to trumpet its triumphs to the public at home and abroad.

In April, Seabees and Army engineers made the airstrips ready for full-scale operations. Escorted by accompanying P-51s, by the end of the month B-29 Superfortresses were taking off to firebomb the cities of Japan.

On a dank night late in February, 1945, Felix de Weldon, a swarthy Navy artist born in Austria and assigned to the Patuxent air station in Hampton Roads, Virginia, was at work on a Pacific war mural. But his assignment was about to change. As soon as the Rosenthal photograph came off the wire, his executive officer brought it over to him.

What a great statue the picture would make, de Weldon's boss said. The artist agreed and rushed to his studio. Throwing together hunks of wax, he shaped a two-foot-high model of Marines formed into a triangle. From the midst of the straining men-in-miniature a stick of balsa help up a toy American flag. The wax figure was rough but de Weldon had outlined the basic idea.

He labored on. On the weekend of the fall of Mount Suribachi, he finished his preliminary effort. He had seen in the Rosenthal photograph the ideals of European classical statuary in which he had been schooled in Vienna.

Even on a small scale, his piece was impressive. Marine Commandant Alexander A. Vandegrift, who went to de Weldon's studio for a look, was overwhelmed. He practically stole de Weldon from the Navy, setting the artist up in a studio in the Marine headquarters in Quantico, Virginia. There de Weldon worked on his model until it was ready for its first official showing.

On the afternoon of Monday, June 4, 1945, de Weldon, decked out in Navy whites, wheeled his clay sculpture into the Oval Office. Joining him and uniformed in the Army's dress "pink" trousers and drab olive jacket was the bespectacled Joe Rosenthal. President Truman, natty in a dark suit and polka-dotted bow tie, strode in. Cameras flashed. Photographs showed a diminutive version of what would become the Iwo Jima Memorial.

Empires win victories. They also erect monuments to commemorate those victories.

4

Another photograph, taken on June 21, 1945, showed a triangular cluster of helmeted Marines standing on a hillock, raising another American flag. Using the imagery of Iwo Jima, the men were laying claim to the final island in America's Pacific war, Okinawa.

A rugged, mountainous island sixty miles long and two to eighteen miles wide, Okinawa is the largest island in the Ryukyu chain, which stretches between Kyushu, the southernmost of the four main Japanese islands, and Taiwan. The Ryukyus had provided a shield against an American advance toward the coast of China. Okinawa itself was Tokyo's last Pacific base. Since it was only 350 miles from Japan's main islands, its capture would enable the United States to cut off supplies to the Japanese Empire, as well as to bomb it without mercy.

So even as the fighting raged on Iwo Jima, Admiral Nimitz was preparing Operation Iceberg, the code name for the invasion of Okinawa. More than 1,500 warships were to be involved; Admirals Spruance and Turner would oversee the landings. Led by Army General Simon Bolivar Buckner, 180,000 soldiers and Marines would go ashore.

As a leader Buckner was fearsome. Once commandant at West Point, he had exhausted his cadets by taking them on thirty-five-mile forced marches. He did not hesitate to take on the Japanese. At the outset of the Okinawa invasion, he toasted his men with bourbon and water, saying, "May you walk in the ashes of Tokyo." The landing took place on April Fool's Day, 1945.

The Americans went ashore on the southern and western flanks of the elongated island, then established a defensive line across the narrow waist, advancing almost unopposed. As on Iwo Jima at first, their big question was, "Where is the enemy?"

They soon found out. Pocking limestone cliffs along the southern lump of the island were hundreds of caves, hideouts for Japanese snipers. Surrounding hills also concealed artillery and nearly 100,000 troops. Pillboxes overlooked every path and roadway in the south. Lieutenant General Ushijima Mitsuru, the Japanese commandant, had ordered all his forces to remain quiet until they had the Americans in their sights.

On April 3, as two American divisions moved south, the island erupted in gunfire. Trapped among the Japanese fortifications, the Americans endured heavy losses. At the same time, *Kamikaze* strikes against the American fleet damaged twenty-eight ships and sank three. And then the giant battleship *Yamato*, escorted by destroyers, acted as a decoy to draw the American ships within range of a carrier and its suicide pilots.

The *Yamato* itself was on a suicide mission. On April 6, American submarine spotters made out its profile in Okinawan waters and the next day at noon a U.S. fighter-bomber group descended upon it from above a cloud cover. The monster ship greeted the American planes with thunderous gunfire. Its high-powered transmitters jammed the pilots' radios. Unable to communicate with each other directly, the fliers were confused. But recovering their wits, torpedo plane pilots dropped right down on the water's surface and delivered their parcels.

Hit by two bombs and a torpedo, the *Yamato* steered westward, then to the south, trying to escape to the protection of stormy weather. But the bombing had destroyed the battleship's radio system and the American pilots were able to coordinate their attacks by voice. At two in the afternoon, while the geysers of near misses showered up all around the *Yamato,* five torpedoes slammed into its hull. Eight bombs exploded on the ship's main deck. The *Yamato* was zigzagging. It was listing, too, exposing its thinly armored underbelly.

Four more torpedoes penetrated the ship's bottom, and the *Yamato* began to go under. Flame and smoke from the powder magazines billowed high above the water. Three Japanese destroyers stood by to pick up survivors. Then, after a sea battle of 105 minutes, the once mighty *Yamato* disappeared from sight.

The battle on Okinawa continued for eight more weeks. In the final assault on Naha, the capital, General Buckner lost his life; 26,000 of his men died or lay wounded.

But the Japanese had sacrificed fully half of their contingent, and on June 20, 1945, their troops began voluntarily to surrender: Japanese morale was cracking. A few days later, knowing that he was defeated, General Ushijima committed *hara-kiri.*

19

THE MASTERS

1

Beginning in late 1944 and into the spring of 1945, the momentum of the war in China was changing. American submarines in the South China Sea had reduced to almost nothing the petroleum that Japan could ship from the Indies. Japan's armored warfare in China had nearly ground to a halt.

Under General Albert Wedemeyer's leadership, furthermore, China had begun to take steps against the Japanese. Under Wedemeyer's guidance, the air base at Kunming had been fortified. With substantial American resources at his disposal, he provided the Chinese soldiers with adequate food and medicine. The general also planned a large-scale effort to open China's seaports. And the American Fourteenth Air Force, flying out of a string of runways, had started to pound away at Japanese coastal garrisons.

By June, 1945, with the Japanese on the defensive, Chiang Kaishek allowed himself to gloat. Had he not, he asked his people over the radio, predicted the current course of events? Had he not been correct in his belief that American airpower would win the war? Had he not, by surviving, earned anew the right to rule?

A photograph taken close to the war's end and reproduced in *The National Geographic Magazine* portrayed Chiang as China's rightful ruler. Standing erect behind a long table, and trim in his high-collared tunic, Chiang was speaking to an audience. On the wall behind him was a photograph of Sun Yatsen. The caption read: "Flags of country and *Guomindang* flank the portrait of Sun Yatsen, founder and even in death the spiritual leader of the Chinese Republic. He is the George Washington of China."

This implied that Chiang Kaishek was the Abraham Lincoln of China. Unlike Lincoln, however, Chiang was unknowingly presiding over impending defeat.

Early in June, 1945, President Truman agreed to meet in the White House with China's foreign minister, T. V. Soong. Soong was worried. He had learned of the Yalta accords. Stalin had promised to recognize the existing Chinese government, but the Soviet dictator and President Roosevelt also had agreed that the Soviet Union would regain the lost tsarist territories. Soong wanted to know if Truman would guarantee China's borders.

When Truman assumed the presidency on April 12, 1945, he said he felt that the sun, the moon, and the stars had dropped upon him. All he knew of foreign policy was what he read in the papers and he had none of Roosevelt's grasp of world geopolitics. But he was determined to be decisive. Through the thick lenses of his eyeglasses, Truman looked across the desk at Soong. Unlike Roosevelt, Truman was direct. He said no. Although a dedicated anti-Communist, Soong resolved to get Stalin to change his mind.

The next month Soong was at the Kremlin. He and Stalin haggled. Soong refused to acknowledge the independence from China of

Outer Mongolia, in reality a Soviet satellite; he also demanded the restriction of Soviet influence in Manchuria to two ports and railroads and to joint Chinese–Russian management.

Stalin would not submit to such limitations. He even raised the ante. At the tip of Manchuria, at Dairen and Port Arthur, he wanted to establish special Soviet military zones—the treaty-ports and extraterritoriality of previous times reborn.

Impossible, said Soong. The United States sees China at last as a great power.

Like a good Turkish rug dealer, Stalin lowered his price. He would offer Chiang Kaishek a "Treaty of Friendship and Alliance" and China's legal sovereignty in Manchuria. And if he could have economic control of Manchuria, he would disown Mao Zedong and the Chinese Communist Party.

The Soviet Union under Stalin was reentering the imperial Far East. And as of old, a crumbling China was incapable of resistance.

At about the time of Soong's sojourn in Moscow, Chiang Kaishek gave a radio speech. The "*Guomindang*," he declared in his staccato manner, "is the historical party of national revolution. It overthrew the Manchu Dynasty. It destroyed Yuan Shikai [the general who in the second decade of the century for a time seized power], who wanted to be emperor. It utterly defeated the warlords and overcame Yuan Shikai. It brought about national unification. It achieved the removal of the [British-imposed] unequal treaties. It led the country in the eight-year-old struggle with the Japanese. Finally, it is the party of liberation and progress."

If any of Chiang's claims had been true, he might have remained in power. But the Manchus had fallen through their own ineptitude, shortsightedness, and corruption. Yuan Shikai had died unmolested by the nascent *Guomindang*. Chiang Kaishek never did fully subdue the warlords. As Stilwell had pointed out repeatedly, Chiang throughout most of the war had led no one anywhere. And, like the Manchu dynasty, Chiang's regime during the war had grown so incompetent, myopic, and engorged with corruption that any notion of its representing "liberation and progress" was farcical.

Yet myths have lives. As President Truman in July, 1945, prepared to meet with Churchill and Stalin at Potsdam, just outside Berlin, for the last of the wartime summit conferences, official Washington clung to the belief that Chiang Kaishek was America's man in China, and that China would be both a great power and America's ward. Hardly anyone in America, certainly not President Truman, saw the contradiction. For America's attention was riveted elsewhere. The United States was firebombing Japan into extinction.

2

Official American policy had forbidden U.S. pilots to bomb cities of no military worth. Scientists under Dr. Vannevar Bush, in charge of military research, had invented, manufactured, and tested the M-69, an incendiary bomb especially crafted for the paper and wood structures. At first the Army Air Force, set in its ways, showed no interest in the incendiaries. But Bush had lobbied the Joint Chiefs and eventually air chief General Henry H. ("Hap") Arnold recommended dropping the devices from the new B-29s. The United States thus possessed the ability to burn Japan to the ground.

Early in 1945, taking command of the American air forces in the Pacific theater, General Curtis E. LeMay was dissatisfied with conventional bombs dropped from high altitudes; he believed that they were not destroying enough Japanese factories. By flying in daylight his bombers were also encountering fighter resistance.

LeMay's solution was to send the B-29s, loaded with incendiaries as well as other bombs, over Japan at night and much closer to the ground. His decision led to an attack on the night of March 9–10, 1945.

That night, Richard Gerdau saw a sight he would never forget. The copilot of a B-29 Superfortress, he was flying along in the midst of a river of bombers that stretched for more than 300 miles. Based in the Marianas, the bombers were heading toward Tokyo. At about one in the morning, Captain Raymond Tutten, commander of Gerdau's B-29, wheeled to the left and steered straight for the Japanese capital, now only thirty miles away. As the plane turned, Gerdau had a view before him of countless yellow-orange streaks cutting down through the darkness. Along with heavy conventional bombs, the B-29s ahead of him were releasing their loads of incendiaries. More than 1,500 six-pound incendiaries blended into a 2,000-foot-long swath of spreading flame.

The next day, the *New York Times* reported the attack: "Why flames spread so fast and leaped so high in Tokyo Saturday was made clear today when the Army's Chemical Warfare Service released a limited description of the M-69 incendiary bomb, designed especially for use in Japan. At about 5,000 feet the cluster bomb opens, releasing individual six-pound bombs filled with jellied gasoline. Each small bomb spreads burning gasoline for some thirty yards around upon exploding."

When those bombers first appeared, a Tokyo woman for a moment thought they looked beautiful. "In the eastern sky loomed a flight," she was quoted as saying, "another flight, and yet another of B-29s. . . . Trailing white streamers of exhaust gas, they sailed in perfect formation . . . riding through the seas of the universe."

Horror broke her reverie. "The process of splashing the earth with showers of incendiary bullets in rhythmic rumbles of ocean breakers, and hurling heavy bombs, each pounding with a fatal thud into the depths of the globe, was repeated by each flight of planes. Almost every raid, it seemed to us, brought over new kinds of sound effects from those used the last time. The unaccustomed noises intensified the terrors . . . of each new invasion."

The terrors indeed intensified. The wind swirled individual fires into towering yellow, red, and white furnaces. Everywhere was the crackling sound of houses collapsing. Soon most of eastern Tokyo was ablaze and the winds were sweeping the flames westward. Residents fled their homes en masse.

"People panicked," a woman would recall in an interview with the journalist John Toland. "Running, screaming. 'We're all going to die! The fire is coming!' The sound of incendiary bombs falling, 'Whizz,' the deafening reverberations of the planes, and the great roar of the fire and wind overwhelmed us. 'If we stay here we'll die! Let's run!'"

Another interviewee recounted that people's "clothes were on fire. . . . Some people were writhing about in torment and no one had time to help them. . . . Intense heat was coming from the firestorm. My eyes seemed about to pop out. Yoshikawa-san cut her way through the mob and I followed along the road, seeking some respite from the flowing heat of the terrible fire. We ran. We saw fleeing shapes, but little else. A telephone pole collapsed and twisted electric wires snaked out along the ground. The road on both sides was full of people's possessions, burning up. My eyes hurt. Breathing was difficult and I felt that life was escaping me. I found a broken hydrant and soaked my *zukin* [air-raid turban] and put it on my head, almost unconsciously. Finally, I fled as far as the Kiyosu bridge."

The impulse to head for water was natural. But the fire was sucking up the oxygen; those who did not drown in the river suffocated. Many roasted to death.

After dawn an Army captain wrote: "The entire river was black as far as the eye could see, black with burned corpses, logs, and who knew what else, but uniformly black from the immense heat that had seared it way through the area as the fire dragon passed. It was impossible to tell the bodies from the logs at a distance. The bodies were all nude, the clothes had been burned away, and there was a dreadful sameness about them, no telling men from women or even children. All that remained were pieces of charred meat. Bodies and parts of bodies were carbonized and absolutely black."

In the full light of day, much of Tokyo was charred black, intermixed with the gray of broken tile and the reddish-black of roasted sheet metal. For Tokyo, the air attack on the night of March 9–10 was an even greater disaster than the earthquake of 1923, which had destroyed all the downtown buildings except the Imperial Hotel.

Reaching far beyond the purported industrial targets, the flames had consumed more than fifteen square miles, destroying more than 250,000 houses and leaving 1.5 million homeless and an estimated 100,000 dead.

"No Jap," *Newsweek* declared in the week after the bombing, echoing widespread press commentary in the United States—"and for that matter few Americans—had ever expected that such attacks could be mounted . . . The vital center of Japan's greatest city [is] burned out . . . [This represents] an entirely new technique of bombing for the Army Air Forces." Letters to editors revealed overwhelming American public support.

For Tokyo and almost all other Japanese cities, though, even more was to come. Once LeMay could operate out of Iwo Jima and Okinawa, 200 more Japanese cities would be within his bombers' flight range.

During an incendiary raid over Tokyo on May 26, 1945, more winds whipped the flames far beyond the original targets. In the middle of the night flames were leaping up from the capital's most important and even sacred buildings: the Kabuki Theater; the Yasakuni Shrine to the War Dead; the once yellow stonework of the Frank Lloyd Wright–designed Imperial Hotel; the Transportation, Foreign, War, and Navy Ministries; Tokyo University; most of the foreign embassies; the official residence of the prime minister; and, finally, the Imperial Palace.

Around midnight, flaming embers from outside the palace moat blew across the water and landed in the eaves of the front edifice. Soon the roof and the ceiling were on fire. Attempts to put the fire out with hoses were in vain for the ancient cypress wood burned like kindling. Flames spread rapidly, melting the copper roof shingles and threatening the rear building of the palace complex.

During the night, Japanese Army engineers tried to dynamite the passageways that connected the front and back parts of the compound, hoping to create a firewall. But the flames just kept spreading.

Resorting to crowbars and sledgehammers, soldiers went to work. Again they could not do the job in time. So while troops hauled out truckloads of furniture, paintings, and scrolls, firemen poured water onto the menaced residential palace.

Thirty-four soldiers and imperial retainers died in the onrushing flames. Although the imperial family, including the present Emperor Akihito, survived in an air raid shelter, the Imperial Palace lay in ruins.

In Japan there had been something like a religious faith, wrote Alvin D. Coox, an American historian of the country, "held even among those at the top of the government, that the Imperial Palace was immune from the foe. . . . The actuality was an immense shock, 'like the fall of a castle in the days of old.'"

A week later, Emperor Hirohito appeared in public. He wished to see the destruction for himself.

As the imperial motorcade left the bomb shelter, it headed north to the Asakusa ward, where the great fires had started. Along the way it passed people who were poking about in the ashes. Sometimes they turned and looked up, startled and then bowing when they saw the imperial pennant fluttering from the hood of the car. Upon reaching Asakusa, the procession halted. The emperor stepped out from his limousine. He was aghast. For block after block around him, where houses and shops and office buildings had once stood, nothing remained but gutted walls, scorched automobiles, blackened rubble. At the Kototoi, one of a dozen bridges that spanned the Sumida River, the emperor saw the bank where thousands, fleeing the fires, had jumped into the water, only to drown. At a police station, the final stop of the inspection tour, the emperor learned that almost all the ward's 13,000 houses had disappeared. Hirohito wondered how long Japan could endure.

With a mid-June bombing raid on Osaka, the B-29s completed the demolition of factories in thirty-nine of what Washington had designated "Selected Urban Industrial Concentrations." The Pentagon had ruled out raids on Kyoto (the ancient Japanese capital, and considered the possible locale of a postwar Japanese government under American auspices) and Hiroshima, selected for the ultimate horror. And until engineers could make Iwo Jima and Okinawa flight-ready, the northernmost Japanese cities were out of range. But that left the rest of the cities and towns to be leveled—not because of any military importance but rather because they were there. Dresden had provided the precedent.

On the nights of February 13–15 and again on March 2 and April 15, 1945, Allied bombers had laid waste to Dresden, a city about 150 miles south of Berlin and of no military significance. No one knows the extent of the casualties, but some estimate that 35,000 persons of the city's population of one million died in the February raids alone. American newspapers referred to the attacks as "deliberate terror bombing." Churchill himself had qualms about the wisdom of the attacks. On March 28, he told his military advisers that the "destruction of Dresden remains a serious query against the conduct of Allied bombing." He warned against the folly of any "bombing of German cities simply for the sake of increasing the terror" and as a result coming into possession "of an utterly ruined land." The prime minister, however, did not publicize these words and the final attack on Dresden took place, as did the American policy of "simply . . . increasing the terror" in Japan.

As the terror spread in Japan, President Roosevelt, the overseer of American strategy, passed away. Afflicted by hypertension and congestive heart failure, he had become shrunken and wasted. Death came while he was in his cottage, known as the Little White House, in Warm Springs, Georgia, where for two decades he had sought recovery for his paralyzed legs in the supposedly curative mountain waters. When he died of a cerebral hemorrhage on April 12, 1945, he was sitting in the living room, having his portrait painted. All America mourned. But the mighty military machine he had set in motion did not pause. His successor, Harry S Truman, only presided over the inexorable destruction of Japan.

The expansion of the incendiary bombing over Japan began on the night of June 17–18: B-29s dropped more than 3,000 tons of incendiaries on four small cities. No Japanese fighters rose in defense. As at Dresden, no one can calculate the number of deaths. But American flyers became so brazen that they took to dropping leaflets specifying their next targets, like Babe Ruth's famous gesture toward the center field fence.

Back home in America, the press portrayed the destruction in percentages: eighty percent of Hachioji, twenty-three miles west of Tokyo; sixty-five percent of Nagaoka; sixty-five percent of Mito; and at Toyana, on the west coast of Honshu, ninety-five percent of the town.

But the B-29 incendiary raids were only part of the story. American submarines and carrier-based bombers had reduced food shipments from abroad to a trickle, and in July the Americans began mining Japan's major harbors. Japan was on the verge of starvation. In the words of an official American report, "the success of the mining program cannot be assessed alone on loss or damage to vessels. The reduction of efficiency of shipping caused by closed channels, the diversion to poorly serviced and ill-equipped harbors, are effects inherent in mining which do not equally apply to attacks by other agents." Soon, the report concluded, "the enemy will find his merchant marine inadequate to carry the minimum of [food] imports necessary for the prosecution of the war." The code name of the mission was Operation Starvation.

Then came Admiral "Bull" Halsey. The need for repairs and resupply, combined with a late July typhoon, had kept his ships away from Japan. But then he struck. Cryptanalysts had discovered that, in a last, desperate effort, the Japanese military was assembling about two hundred remaining transport planes in northern Honshu; their goal was to carry 30,000 troops on a suicide mission to the Marianas. Operation Damocles, the code name for Halsey's aerial counterattack, wiped out the transports as they sat on the ground.

"It is my intent," Halsey stated, "to tighten the blockade and keep pressure on the enemy by throwing light force sweeps against Empire coast and outlying islands at every opportunity. Objective denial of coastal sea lanes to enemy, destruction of shipping and bombardment of shore targets."

Halsey left no doubt that Japan could look forward to nothing less than destruction. American conventional weapons alone were eliminating whatever was left of Hirohito's empire.

After Halsey's assault, General LeMay believed that Japan could not hold out for long. "I am influenced by the conviction that the present stage of development of the air war presents the Army Air Force for the first time with the opportunity of proving the power of the strategic air arm," he wrote to General Lauris Norstad, the deputy chief of the Air Staff. "I consider that for the first time strategic air bombardment faces a situation in which the strength is proportionate to the magnitude of the task. I feel the destruction of Japan's ability to wage war lies within the capability of this command." At the same time the American government had evidence that Japan had lost the race to build an atomic bomb.

3

In midsummer, an American patrol plane over the North Atlantic spotted a German submarine 500 miles from Cape Race, Newfoundland, and directed the destroyer *Sutton* to give chase. At 11:30 that night, the submarine, *U-234*, surrendered and an American crew went aboard, ordering the captain to make for the navy yard at Portsmouth, New Hampshire, where under the guidance of Theodore Roosevelt (FDR's distant cousin) Russia and Japan had signed the peace treaty of 1905. Portsmouth had submarine docks and a military prison.

According to *Surrender at Sea,* a collection of reports broadcast over WHEB radio in Portsmouth, a news bulletin stated:

> A German submarine which was headed for Japan with three high *Luftwaffe* generals aboard has surrendered. . . . Admiral Jonas Ingram, commander in chief of the Atlantic

Fleet, reveals . . . [that] two dead Jap[anese] aboard . . . committed *hara-kiri,* probably to avoid capture by the Americans. There are no details at this hour on [their] identity . . . or what they were doing aboard. . . . Neither is there any clue to the strange drama which must have been enacted aboard . . . when it was learned that Germany had surrendered and when [the ship] decided to give up rather than continue the long trip to Japan. Admiral Ingram says charts and aviation equipment of the German Air Force were found in the Japan-bound U-boat. This indicates that the German officers may have planned to carry on their air war against the Allies from Japan.

Japanese scientists working to construct an atomic bomb had been desperate for more uranium. Because they had no access to American atomic research, their experiments had been wasteful, using up their uranium reserves. Nonetheless, by early 1945, Susuki Tatsusaburo had made some progress, developing five uranium separators in a hangarlike building at the Sumitomo plant just outside Osaka. But a March 12 B-29 raid had knocked out all the electricity and water lines to the plant. The research team had decided to find a new location. They chose Seishin (Japanese for Chongjin) in Korea; Korea, Susuki had believed, might be safe from the bombing. So according to Jerome Cohen, a Harvard law professor and East Asian expert, the Osaka plant "was completely dismantled in the spring of 1945—part of the equipment reached Seishin, some was sunk, and at the end of the war some remained in crates at the old site waiting to be shipped." Still hopeful of success, the Japanese government again sent a request for uranium to Berlin.

In command of the *U-234,* on March 25 Lieutanant Johann Heinrich Fehler steered out of the Kiel naval base. All around were signs of the destruction wrought by Allied bombing: Docks and warehouses were in splinters; tall cranes were bent and blackened; vessels of war were listing or partly submerged. One of the few survivors was Fehler's ship, which carried products of Germany's end-of-the-war research and development: new armor-piercing antiaircraft shells; blueprints and parts for rockets; and, in ten containers marked only "Japanese Army," more than 1,000 pounds of uranium oxide, enough for a fully equipped laboratory to make two atomic bombs.

For more than two weeks, the U-234 crossed the North Sea, running on the surface at night and submerged by day. As it entered the English Channel, it had almost collided with a British steamer and was forced to plunge to unusual depths. Only after reaching the Atlantic did the submarine resurface again.

The ship's radio brought bad news: On May 2, Berlin fell to the Soviets. Submerging again, the U-234 proceeded for several days without information from Germany. Well out into the North Atlantic but not yet having turned southward, Fehler surfaced again. Word came that Hitler was dead and that Germany on May 8 had surrendered. Then, on May 10, the radio crew of the U-234 picked up the order from Admiral Karl Donitz, the last commander in chief of the Nazi Navy, to surrender.

After consulting his crew, Fehler considered making a run for Argentina. But he was spotted by the American scout plane and without putting up a fight he consented to dock at Portsmouth.

War Department officials met the U-234 at the Portsmouth pier and feverishly examined its cargo. All news reports of the submarine's capture thereafter ceased. But the War Department, suspecting since even before Pearl Harbor that Japan was engaged in nuclear research, had learned the truth. The United States had won the race to build the atomic bomb—knowledge that President Harry Truman took with him as he left the United States for the last wartime summit conference.

4

"I am getting ready to go see Stalin and Churchill," President Truman wrote to his mother from the White House on July 3, 1945, "and it is a chore. I have to take my tuxedo, tails, high hat, top hat, and hard hat as well as sundry other things. I have a briefcase all filled up with information on past conferences and suggestions on what I'm to do and say. Wish I didn't have to go but I do and it can't be stopped now."

Born in 1884 into a farming family near Independence, Missouri, Truman had seen himself as a little man. A farmer himself and a World War I veteran, he had opened a men's clothing store in Kansas City in the immediate postwar period, only to go into bankruptcy. He then had tried politics, being made a local judge by Tom Pendergast, the notoriously corrupt Kansas City boss. In 1934, the political machine had elevated Truman to the U.S. Senate, but he had reached Washington under the cloud of being the "Senator from Pendergast." During Truman's obscure first term in the nation's capital, Pendergast had gone to prison, leaving Truman to fend for himself in the 1940 election. Truman had eked out a victory and, on his return to Washington, had finally made a name for himself by investigating waste in military spending, an issue popular with the public. Because he had become a known, yet uncontroversial senator and a moderate Democrat from Missouri, a border state during the Civil War, the bosses of his party in 1944 had selected him over South Carolina's racist and anti-union James F. Byrnes as FDR's vice presidential running mate.

During Truman's three months as vice president, Roosevelt never shared with him any confidences about the war, and not until he took the oath of office in the White House late in the afternoon of April 12, 1945, did Secretary of War Henry L. Stimson tell him about the atomic bomb. Unprepared to be president, Truman found himself overwhelmed by the job, largely subservient to decisions made by the Roosevelt-era officials around him. But he was a hard worker and read extensively in the then-classified accounts of the previous wartime summit conferences. He was determined to master the knowledge he would need to deal with Stalin in Potsdam.

At six in the morning on July 6, 1945, the presidential train reached Newport News, pulled into Pier Number Six, one of the row of covered docks that bristled into the James River, and puffed to a stop. Stepping forth briskly, Harry Truman mounted the wooden-railed gangplank and crossed to the deck of the cruiser *Augusta*. After breakfast in the mess, the new president climbed to the bridge. Under the clear sky, the profiles of the ships by the docks at Norfolk, on the opposite side of Hampton Roads, stood out clearly. At 6:55 A.M. President Truman gave the order to go.

Steaming past the main landmark of Tidewater Virginia, the huge brick Chamberlin Hotel on Old Point Comfort, the *Augusta* passed through the mouth of the James River into Chesapeake Bay. Then it steered through a gap in the blue-painted buoys of the submarine net that stretched between Cape Charles to the north and Cape Henry to the south, and sailed into the Atlantic Ocean.

On the afternoon of July 15, as the USS *Augusta* was docking at Antwerp, Churchill's airplane put down at an airport close to Berlin. The demolished German capital lay deep in Soviet-occupied territory. Lord Moran, Churchill's personal physician, wrote, there "were Russian soldiers everywhere, lining the road, behind bushes, knee deep in the corn. We drove to where a substantial stone house [in Potsdam] which was said to have belonged to [Hjalmar] Schacht, the banker, had been reserved for the prime minister. I followed him [Churchill] through two bleak rooms with great chandeliers to the opposite side of the empty house, where French windows that had not been cleaned for a long time opened upon a balcony, and there, without removing his hat, Winston flopped into a garden chair, flanked by two great tubs of hydrangeas, blue, pink, and white. He appeared too weary to move."

Facing the 1945 British general election, at the end of July, Churchill must have had a foreboding of defeat. He must have realized also that Britain's years of imperial power were over.

Stalin, whose revolutionary code name meant the Man of Steel, was afraid to fly. For his trip to Germany he had ordered up a special train with eleven coaches, four of which workers had extracted from a museum and given a thorough dusting. Ironically, they had belonged to the very nemesis of the Soviet Communist Party, Tsar Nicholas II. As Stalin passed through the moonscapes of war-leveled Russia, Lithuania, and East Prussia, he was able to look out upon his newly overrun domains from the cushioned comfort of Russia's imperial past.

As his train puffed westward over the vastness of the Soviet Union, Stalin surely experienced a degree of satisfaction: He had outdone even his tsarist predecessors. Although Poland was not yet fully secure—hence the northern route to Berlin along the Baltic—the Red Army already had forged a column of satellite states, the Baltic countries, Hungary, Romania, and Bulgaria, along Russia's western border. To the south, he was in a better position than any of the rulers of old to link the Black Sea through the Bosphorus and the Dardanelles to the warm waters of the Mediterranean. The 1936 Convention of Montreux, drafted by the British and the French to contain Russia, had given Turkey control of the inland waterway. But, as demonstrated in his dealings with T. V. Soong, Stalin knew how to bargain.

What Stalin wanted most was an eastern European buffer against invasion from the west. To get it he would lay claim to far-flung cities such as Tripoli and Tangier, controlled by the Allies; then, showing himself to be reasonable, he would drop those demands. He would even sacrifice Russia's historic "right" of access to the Mediterranean. Ever solicitous of human life, or so he would appear, he would remind his counterparts at Potsdam that in the war the Soviet Union had lost 20 million lives. Therefore client states in eastern Europe that could serve as buffers against further invasion from the West, he would contend, were vital and legitimate Soviet interests. And if the American president still did not grant Stalin that zone of defense, then the Soviet leader, like a chess master, would bring out his queen.

As part of the Yalta deal, Stalin had promised FDR that three months after the German surrender the Soviet Union would enter into the war against Japan. That date was August 8, 1945. And even as Stalin's train chugged westward into Germany, Soviet troops were moving into position in eastern Siberia; Stalin intended to live up to his pledge. But did Truman know about the promise? Stalin was unsure. He would bring the matter up again, this time to extract concessions from Truman on eastern Europe. Indeed, as Stalin would discover, Truman felt no great need to have the Soviets in the war against Japan: Stalin would raise the matter to keep the Yalta accord intact.

Truman met Stalin for the first time on July 17, while working in the "Berlin White House" in the suburb of Babelsburg. "Promptly a few minutes before twelve I looked up from the desk," the president wrote in his diary, "and there stood Stalin in the doorway. I got to my feet and advanced to meet him. He put out his hand and smiled. I did the same, we shook, I greeted [Vyacheslav] Molotov [the Soviet foreign minister], and we sat down. . . . After the usual polite remarks we got down to business. . . . [Finally Stalin] got on the Chinese situation. . . . Most of the big points are settled."

On Monday, July 18, 1945, the Big Three convened in plenary session in Potsdam's *Cecilienhof,* once a rural residence of the German emperor. Charles Mee, an historian of the Potsdam gathering, described the palace thus: "It was a 176-room ersatz Tudor country house, with swatches of stucco here and there interrupted by mock-Elizabethan windows and stone portals that appeared embarrassed by their lack of moats and drawbridges. Topping it all off was a collection of chimneys, one vaguely Italian in inspiration, some reminiscent of the columns of the *baldachino* of St. Peter's Cathedral, and all of them together resembling nothing so much as the rooftops of nineteenth century Nottingham."

Into this architectural jumble the Russians had moved furniture scavenged from around Potsdam: faded French carpets, clunky German chairs, and second-rate (at best) Italian paintings of mountains and village squares. For consultations, the three principals and their advisers could retire to outlying rooms. The conference room itself lay on the ground floor. Surrounded by dark-paneled walls—except for French windows that opened onto a lake below and let in mosquitoes—the conferees sat around a circular oak table. There, for two hot weeks, with Truman taking charge like the chairman of the board, the statesmen deliberated on the shape of the postwar world.

Churchill played a minor role in the discussion. He may have succumbed to depression, but he also lost the election to the Labour leader, Clement Attlee, who arrived at Potsdam on July 28. Replacing Churchill at Potsdam, Attlee knew little of foreign affairs. Truman, too, was inexperienced in diplomacy, but his advisers, headed by the new secretary of state, James F. Byrnes, had been with Roosevelt and informed Truman of FDR's worldviews.

The talks focused largely on the problem of Germany and a question that had surfaced at both the Tehran and Yalta conferences: Should postwar Germany be united or divided? Here Stalin got the better of Truman, who wanted the Soviets out of eastern Europe altogether. A united Germany would fall under the control of all the occupying powers, including the Soviet Union. Such an arrangement possibly would spread Stalin's influence throughout central Europe. A divided Germany would limit the Soviets to one zone, in the eastern part of Germany, which they already possessed. Truman chose a divided Germany. Once he had made that choice, he had to settle for a Communist regime in what became East Germany.

With regard to East Asia, Stalin and Truman came quickly to an understanding. The Soviet leader complained that in Manchuria Chiang Kaishek's government still did not want to allow "the preeminent interests of the Soviet Union." Truman promised to take care of the matter. As agreed upon at Yalta, the United States would adhere to the Soviet Union's demand for the restoration of the Russian imperial holdings in China. Stalin in turn would proceed with his recognition of the *Guomindang* government, abandoning the Chinese Communists and joining the war against Japan.

Then, just before departure, came the Potsdam Declaration, broadcast so that Japan could pick it up. The Declaration repeated FDR's unconditional surrender statement at Casablanca: "We call upon the government of Japan to proclaim now the unconditional surrender of all Japanese armed forces and to provide proper and adequate assurances of their good faith in such action. The alternative for Japan is prompt and utter destruction."

5

On the morning of August 2, 1945, satisfied with his foray into diplomacy, President Truman left Potsdam for Antwerp. As America once had been to Great Britain, the Soviet Union now was to the United States—a junior partner in the Far Eastern empire. Truman even thought he had scored a triumph in not telling Stalin about the atomic bomb (Stalin had not revealed that in fact he did know about it). Only the formality of the Japanese surrender remained.

Or was it just a formality? In Truman's presence, Stalin had told Molotov of a telegram from Hirohito asking for peace. But the Japanese leadership then flatly rejected the Potsdam Declaration, which had been broadcast by radio. Truman as commander in chief thereupon had authorized the use of the atomic bomb any time after August 3, 1945. The consensus among Truman and his advisors was to compel Japan's surrender quickly and they had no hesitation about dropping atomic bombs to do so.

At Antwerp, Truman again boarded the *Augusta*. Four mornings out to sea, on Monday, August 6, the president was sitting in a deck chair enjoying the Atlantic sunshine and listening to the strains of the ship's band. Just before noon, Truman and James Byrnes went below for lunch. Truman sat down at a table with six enlisted men and was just starting to eat when Captain Frank Graham, an officer from the map room, gave Truman a telegram: "HIROSHIMA BOMBED VISUALLY WITH ONE TENTH [CLOUD] COVER. . . . THERE WAS NO FIGHTER OPPOSITION AND NO FLAK. . . . RESULTS CLEAR-CUT SUCCESSFUL IN ALL RESPECTS. VISIBLE EFFECTS

GREATER THAN IN ANY TEST. CONDITION NORMAL IN AIRPLANE FOLLOWING DELIVERY."

Excitedly, Truman shook Graham's hand. "This is the greatest thing in history," the president exclaimed.

Then a second wire arrived, cabled by Secretary Stimson from Washington: "BIG BOMB WAS DROPPED ON HIROSHIMA. . . . FIRST REPORTS INDICATE COMPLETE SUCCESS WHICH WAS EVEN MORE CONSPICUOUS THAN EARLIER TEST [at Alamogordo, New Mexico]."

To the mystification of the diners in the mess, Truman leapt from his chair and, followed by Byrnes, dashed to the officer's wardroom. Clutching the telegrams, he asked those present to keep their seats. Then, since they knew nothing about atomic research, he explained: "We have just dropped a bomb on Japan which has more power than 20,000 tons of TNT. It was an overwhelming success. We won the gamble!"

The officers stood and cheered. They realized that the end of the war was near.

20

THEY CALL IT PEACE

1

At the time the Americans landed on Tinian Island in June, 1944, the Japanese had completed three runways and were at work on a fourth. But after the invasion some five hundred surviving Japanese troops literally had headed for the hills. Lacking food, they had made it a practice to climb Mount Lasso, the highest peak on the island, at dusk to see where the Americans were pitching their garbage. Then they would sneak down in the darkness to paw through the leftovers.

On the evening of August 5, 1945, the Japanese foragers were again peering down from their perches. This time, however, they stayed on the mountain. The airfields below were ablaze with light.

Soon after nightfall, the crew of a B-29 named the *Enola Gay*, after the chief pilot's mother, made preparations for a flight. Paul Tibbets, the captain, Thomas Ferebee, the bombardier, and Theodore van Kirk, the navigator (all regarded as the best in the American Air Force), went to the mess hall for a late dinner. Some of the other airmen in the crew retreated to their bunks. A few napped. One or two read. Then, just before midnight, the twenty-six men of the crew headed for a final briefing in the crew lounge off Broadway.

Tinian was about the size of Manhattan and the streets had acquired names from New York: Broadway, Canal, 42nd, Riverside Drive, and the like. Aside from Tibbets, an Ohioan known as America's best pilot, however, no one on the crew knew of the Manhattan Project itself. Never once had he let out the words "atomic" or "nuclear." Even now, during the final briefing, he referred only to carrying a bomb that had "the potential to end the war." That much said, he simply reminded his crew of the rules: "Do your jobs. Obey your orders. Don't cut corners or take chances."

The weather officer stepped forward and gave his report. No storms were in the offing and by dawn the sky over Japan would be clear.

At 12:15 A.M., all those assembled bowed their heads as William Downey, a chaplain, read a prayer: "Almighty Father, Who wilt hear the prayer of them that love Thee, we pray Thee to be with those who brave the heights of Thy heaven and who carry the battle to our enemies. . . . May the men who fly tonight be kept safe in Thy care, and may they be returned safely to us."

Then all rose. Slowly they gathered their gear and lined up on the sidewalk outside.

At 1:12 A.M., trucks gathered up the crews of the two B-29s scheduled to accompany and protect the *Enola Gay*. Three minutes later the crew of the *Enola Gay* climbed into another truck. At 1:37 A.M., three weather-scout planes took off from North Field, heading for southwestern Japan. In that same moment, the truck transporting Captain Tibbets and his crew entered North Field and pulled up at the *Enola Gay*. A dozen spotlights illuminated the bomber.

Brigadier General Leslie Groves, military commander of the Manhattan Project, had told Tibbets to count on a "little publicity." As Tibbets stepped from his truck and faced photographers, film crews, and a hundred reporters, he saw that Groves had understated the case. "This," he said, "was full-scale Hollywood premier treatment. I expected to see MGM's lion walk onto the field or Warner's logo to light up the sky."

As the crew walked to the plane, the crowd applauded. Waving back, Tibbets mounted the steps of the *Enola Gay*, followed by the rest of the crew. Inside he opened the cockpit's left side window. As he peeked out, grinning over the painted words *Enola Gay*, cameras flashed and bystanders on the ground shouted their farewells.

Then he called down, "Okay, fellas, cut those lights. We've gotta be going."

Tibbets ordered Wyatt Duzenbury, the copilot, to switch the engines on. The propellers slowly began to turn. Robert Lewis, a reserve pilot, noted in his logbook, "Started engines at 2:27 A.M." Then Lewis radioed the tower for taxi and takeoff instructions. A jeep led the *Enola Gay* to the beginning of the mile-long runway. The beams of the jeep's headlights flashed along a line of ambulances and fire trucks parked facing the tarmac. Then the jeep wheeled aside.

At 2:45 A.M., after receiving an all-clear weather report, the *Enola Gay* began to inch forward. With twenty-six men, 7,000 gallons of gasoline, and a five-ton bomb aboard, the airplane was overweight. Tibbets decided that to build up the takeoff speed, he would keep the bomber on the ground until the last possible moment.

Duzenbury grew nervous when, two-thirds down the runway, the wheels were still on the pavement. Lewis reached for his own controls but Tibbets ordered him to hold still. Lewis obeyed, but his worry was turning to fright. Just ahead the runway ended at the edge of a cliff. Lewis once again reached for his controls.

But at just that moment, Tibbets lifted the nose of the *Enola Gay* and the airplane sailed upward on its way to Hiroshima.

2

As the *Enola Gay* rose in the darkness, its aluminum shell crackled from the pressure of the weight inside. Several loose cans skittered along the floor and clattered against the walls. Every member of the crew was tense. But the four 2,000-horsepower engines thundered away without pause and as the blue-red flames streaked back from the exhausts, those aboard relaxed.

Flying out over the Pacific, Tibbets climbed to 4,000 feet and throttled back to cruising speed. Overhead, the moon seemed to move in and out of cumulous clouds. With the B-29 droning on through the night, crew members ate sandwiches and drank pineapple juice. The eastern sky began to lighten around four o'clock, and as the *Enola Gay* reached Iwo Jima fifteen minutes later, shafts of the rising sun touched the cockpit windows.

Followed by the support planes, Tibbets took the *Enola Gay* to 9,000 feet. Flying almost straight northwest, he soon spotted Shikoku, the large island off the southeastern coast of Honshu. The bomber was on target for Hiroshima, chosen, like Dresden, not for any strategic value but simply for its large population.

At 6:40, Tibbets descended to 3,100 feet, six miles above the Inland Sea, where Shikoku nestled into the curving arm of lower Honshu. When Honshu itself came into sight, the air was so clear that the pilots could see patches of green grass. No Japanese fighter planes appeared. At 8:13, Tibbets recognized the outskirts of Hiroshima. Then he could see the features he had memorized from maps: three oblongs of land pushing into the bay; the seven fingers of the Ota River; and the principal streets that crisscrossed the city. The target, the center of the main bridge over the Ota's largest branch, slid beneath the bombardier's sight.

At 8:15 plus seventeen seconds, the bomb-bay doors fell open and a second later the *Enola Gay* lurched upward, 10,000 pounds lighter. The first atomic bomb was plummeting toward Hiroshima. As it did so, Tibbets used the intercom to congratulate his crew on a job well done.

3

Dr. Hachiya Michihiko, a physician living in Hiroshima, later wrote in his diary:

> [The] hour was early, the morning still, warm, and beautiful. Shimmering leaves, reflecting sunlight from a cloudless sky, made a pleasant contrast with shadows in my garden as I gazed absently through wide-flung doors opening to the south. Clad in drawers and undershirt, I was sprawled on the living room floor exhausted because I had just spent a sleepless night on duty as an air warden in my hospital. Suddenly a strong flash of light startled me—and then another. So well does one recall little things that I remember vividly how a stone lantern in the garden became brilliantly lit and I debated whether this light was caused by a magnesium flare or sparks from a passing trolley. Garden shadows disappeared. The view where a moment before all had been so bright and sunny was now dark and hazy. Through swirling dust I could barely discern a wooden column that had supported one corner of my house. It was leaning crazily and the roof sagged dangerously.

Other accounts of the bomb were equally appalling. Mrs. Nakamura Hatsuyo, a tailor's widow, was laboring at her sewing machine, for she did piecework to support herself and her children: Rising from the machine for a moment, she found that something had picked her up, so that she seemed to fly into the next room pursued by parts of her house, and her youngest daughter, five years old, was buried in debris, unable to move. Dr. Fujii Masakazu was seated cross-legged on his porch matting, reading the morning newspaper: The print suddenly turned brilliant yellow and before he knew it two timbers of the house squeezed him up into the air, as if he were a piece of fish suspended between two giant chopsticks. Father Wilhelm Kleinsorge of the Society of Jesus was on his cot when he was knocked unconscious: When he came to he was wandering through the mission's vegetable garden and heard the Japanese housekeeper murmur *"Shu Jesusu, awaremi tamai!"* ("Lord Jesus, have mercy on us!").

Moments after the bomb dropped, the fires erupted. No one in Hiroshima had ever seen such flames. Out of the heavy dust that lay close to the ground throughout the city, clumps of dust were beginning to rush upward.

Although there had been no morning breeze, winds started to blow every which way, igniting buildings and bridges so that blasts of hot air and showers of cinders fell upon thousands of people who had rushed from their houses. Kimonos and tee shirts were on fire; eyebrows were burned off, and scorched skin hung from faces and hands. Bare of leaves, charred trees were uprooted in whirlwinds. From all over the city, flat things such as pieces of paper, doors, and mats flew about as the wind convulsed into a twisting tunnel. The dust clouds and flames formed a mushroom cloud that reached for miles into the sky.

Thousands of people lay dead in houses that were no longer houses, in parks to which they had fled and that had become infernos, and in all the seven rivers where many had drowned. The still living staggered about dazed, bleeding, arms and legs broken, skulls smashed, some trying to make their way to vomiting doctors and nurses who were as ill as their patients. Hiroshima had been the victim, as President Truman broadcast the next day, of "the largest bomb ever yet used in the history of warfare."

On August 9, with Japan not having surrendered immediately, Major Charles W. Sweeney captained another B-29 loaded with the only other atomic bomb then available. The principal target was Kokura, the site of a Japanese military arsenal, with Nagasaki at the western extremity of Kyushu as an alternative. The weather over Kokura was stormy and so Sweeney flew to cloud-banked Nagasaki; there the bombardier found a hole in the overcast and released the bomb.

Because of the mountainous terrain surrounding the city, Nagasaki received less structural damage than had Hiroshima. The Japanese government nonetheless estimated that the two blasts killed 240,000 people and injured close to 1 million.

Were the atomic bombs necessary? The old and standard claim, still heard today, is that the bombs eliminated the need for an invasion of Japan; at the time of the atomic bombings, Operation Coronet, code name for an invasion of Japan, was in the planning stages, with two American armies and three Marine divisions, both covered by the Third and Fifth Fleets, scheduled to go ashore in March, 1946, to crush opposition in the central Honshu plain. But "when the atomic bombs were dropped and news began to circulate that [an invasion of Japan] would not, after all, be necessary," Paul Fussell, author of *The Great War and Modern Memory,* wrote in 1981 in *The New Republic,* "when we learned to our astonishment that we would not be obliged in a few months to rush up the beaches near Tokyo assault-firing while being machine-gunned, mortared, and shelled, for all the practiced phlegm of our tough façades we broke down and cried with relief and joy. We were going to live." Such was the point of view of the ordinary troops at the time.

And not just ordinary troops: Secretary of State Byrnes had strongly urged Truman to authorize the use of atomic bombs on the grounds that doing so would deter the Soviet advance down through Korea.

But, among others, General MacArthur after the bombing saw no military need for using the atomic bombs. "The Japanese were beaten and seeking peace before the bombs were dropped," he wrote to former President Herbert Hoover in 1959. Of course this was said fifteen years after the event. But even at the time, as the historian Kai Bird has revealed: "Numerous peace feelers [from Japan] had been received. OSS director William Donovan, for example, had reported on May 12, that Japan's minister to Switzerland . . . had communicated his wish 'to help arrange for cessation of hostilities.'. . . President

Harry S Truman . . . referred to one . . . intercept [of Japanese cable traffic] as the 'telegram from [the] Jap Emperor asking for peace.'. . . [And Secretary of War] Stimson [believed] that the Pacific war would end without an invasion of the Japanese home islands." And in April, 1946, a then top-secret War Department study, "Use of Atomic Bombs and Japan," found that "the Japanese leaders had decided to surrender and were merely looking for a sufficient pretext to convince the die-hard Army Group that Japan had lost the war and must capitulate." Russia's entry into the war, the study concluded, "would almost certainly have furnished this pretext, and would have been sufficient to convince all responsible leaders that surrender was unavoidable."

And the modern assessment? Summarizing reams of research, J. Samuel Walker, chief historian with the U.S. Nuclear Regulatory Commission and thus no radical, contended in 1990 that "the consensus among scholars is that the bomb was not needed to avoid an invasion of Japan and to end the war within a short time. It is clear that alternatives to the bomb existed and that Truman and his advisers knew it." Another expert has added that recently discovered documents have been "devastating" to the old view of the bomb's necessity in saving American lives.

Then, again, why were the bombs dropped? The papers of President Truman are of little help. "I've gotten what I came for—Stalin goes to war on August 13 [sic] with no strings on it," he wrote Bess, his wife, from Potsdam on July 18. This was before he knew any details of the atomic test at Alamogordo. He added: "I'll say that we'll end the war a year sooner now, and think of the kids who won't be killed." Did Truman actually think that the fighting would go on for another year? If so, the old argument that he authorized dropping of the atomic bombs to save lives makes sense. But the same day Truman wrote in his diary: "Believe Japs will fold before Russia comes in. I am sure they will when Manhattan appears over their homeland." Truman may have seen the bomb as a way to contain the Soviets, but his jottings are inconclusive. In any case, Truman as a nonscientist could have had only the haziest notion of what atomic power entailed and he gave his authorization to a project of which he knew practically nothing.

To American leaders who had seen the war progress from Doolittle's raid to crippling of the Japanese fleet, the massive use of incendiaries, and the deliberate effort to starve the Japanese people, the bomb was different only in degree, not in kind. At the time American officials recognized no restraints, military or moral, that might have impeded their dropping the atomic bombs on Japan and deriving whatever benefits ensued. Nothing could stop the might and resolution of the American military.

The atomic bombs thus symbolized the triumph of the American Empire over the Japanese. As Tacitus, the first-century Roman historian wrote of his own empire, *"Ubi solitudinem faciunt, pacem appellant"* ("Where they make desolation, they call it peace").

4

After the bombing of Hiroshima and Nagasaki, events in northeastern Asia moved fast. On August 8, 1945, the Soviet Union declared war on Japan. Just after midnight the next day, Soviet ships moved from Vladivostok to take over the Kurile Islands, the 1,350-island chain that stretched from the Kamchatka peninsula to Kunashimi, just off the northeastern tip of Hokkaido. On the same day, armored vehicles proceeded from Manchuria down into Port Arthur and Korea.

How far would the Soviets go in Korea? In Washington no one knew. Despite American conversations with Stalin on his entry into the war, neither Washington nor Moscow had even raised the matter of a demarcation line in Korea.

With peace at hand, however, the Pentagon saw the Korean issue as urgent. On the night of August 11–12, the State–War–Navy Coordinating Committee (SWNCC—created early in the war to reduce bureaucratic squabbling) met in the Pentagon to consider Korea. Wishing to put as much of the peninsula as possible in the hands of Syngman Rhee, a Korean nationalist with close ties to Chiang Kaishek, State Department representatives wanted American forces to accept the Japanese surrender halfway up into what is now North Korea. But Dean Rusk, a former Rhodes Scholar from Georgia and a young colonel on the staff of General Marshall, pointed out that the American ground troops closest to Korea were in Okinawa, 600 miles away. John J. McCloy, who had risen from boyhood poverty in Philadelphia to excel at the Harvard Law School, make a fortune on Wall Street, and serve as assistant secretary of war under Henry Stimson, told Rusk and another colonel, C. H. Bonesteel III, to retire to a map room and locate a feasible point of surrender.

Rusk and Bonesteel chose a 190-mile line along the 38th parallel. The line was arbitrary and made no economic sense. Below it lived 21 million people, two-thirds in farm villages; above were 9 million people working in an economy with steel, cement, chemical, and fertilizer plants that under the Japanese had complemented the agricultural production of the south. Neither half of the peninsula had been self-sufficient.

Nonetheless, Washington wanted the Soviets to stop at the Rusk line, as it came to be called. By the time of the August 11–12 Pentagon session, scattered Soviet units had crossed the parallel, moving down a highway toward Seoul. But SWNCC authorized a cable to Stalin and to the surprise of everyone in the group, he accepted the 38th parallel. When told of the demarcation line, the Soviet troops quickly withdrew.

To make sure they stayed withdrawn, MacArthur chose General John R. Hodge, who had led the invasion of Okinawa, to organize a military occupation of South Korea. The appointment of Hodge, who was brave but tactless and racist, proved to be the first step toward the Korean War and the direct military confrontation between America and China.

On August 11, 1945, Mao Zedong, the leader who five years hence would send Chinese troops into battle against America, appeared before a crowd on the parade ground at Yanan. He wore a thick brown

Sun Yatsen tunic; it was tight around the waist because, like the emperors of old, he was starting to be portly. Quiet as a Buddha, he displayed no mannerisms, no motion. Standing behind a microphone on a wooden platform, he made a terse announcement: On that day the Chinese Communist Army, 100,000 strong, would abandon Yanan and set off for Manchuria. Mao had just launched a civil war for mastery of the Middle Kingdom.

On the evening of August 14, fires flared all over Tokyo. These were not the "flowers of Edo" (the old name for Tokyo), the popular euphemism for the flames ignited by the American incendiary bombs, but rather bonfires. Even in the ash heaps of what had been governmental buildings, officials were burning their files.

In the safety of his underground shelter, Emperor Hirohito waited to tape a radio address to his people.

Until now no one outside the Imperial Palace had heard his voice before.

One official bowed to another, who bowed to the emperor and handed over a prepared text. The chamberlain spoke into the microphone, making sure that it was working. Hirohito leaned forward and spoke.

At noon the next day, all Japan, and those listening from abroad, heard his words: "To Our good and loyal subjects. After pondering deeply the current trends of the world and the actual conditions obtaining in Our Empire today, We have decided to effect a settlement of the present situation by resorting to an extraordinary measure. We have ordered our Government to communicate to the Governments of the United States, Great Britain, . . . and the Soviet Union that Our Empire accepts the provisions of their joint declaration [at Potsdam]."

5

Shortly after dawn on Sunday, September 2, a cool mist hung over the waters of Tokyo Bay. The air was moist and low-hanging clouds obscured any view of the rising sun, appropriately. For representatives of Japan, the Land of the Rising Sun, were about to sign the instrument of surrender.

In celebration of that event, nearly 260 warships of all the nations that had fought against Japan were gathered in an immense stationary armada. Standing at anchor in the midst of the fleet was the American battleship *Missouri*. Fluttering from the superstructure, as a reminder of the earlier occasion when the United States had humbled Japan, was the thirty-one-starred American flag that had flown over the flagship of Commodore Matthew Calbraith Perry in 1853.

Down on the main deck, admirals and generals, British, Russian, Dutch, Australian, New Zealander, Chinese, French, Canadian, and American, talked excitedly. Suddenly, they went silent and everyone snapped to attention.

Just after 8:00 A.M., two destroyers pulled alongside and the top brass of the Pacific theater, Halsey, Nimitz, and MacArthur, boarded the battleship. They retired to a cabin. While they were out of sight, a delegation of Japanese appeared on the gangway: four officials from the Foreign Office and seven high-ranking officers from the Army and the Navy. All wore striped trousers, morning coats, and silk tophats. In view of the sailors and cameramen who packed every inch of the quarterdeck, and the now stony-faced Allied admirals and generals arranged in a great semicircle, they formed a straight line. Then Halsey, Nimitz, and MacArthur reappeared.

They strode to a wooden mess table covered with green baize and sat, MacArthur in the middle. Just behind them stood the skeletal figures of Generals Jonathan Wainwright, defender of Corregidor, and Arthur Percival, British commander at Singapore, both recently released from a Japanese prison camp in Manchuria.

MacArthur read a short speech from a piece of paper: "It is my earnest hope, and indeed the hope of all mankind, that from this solemn occasion a better world shall emerge out of the blood and carnage of the past—a world dedicated to the dignity of man and the fulfillment of his most-cherished wish for freedom, tolerance, and justice." Then, putting the paper down, he beckoned Foreign Minister Shigemitsu Mamoru and General Umezu Yoshijiro, chief of the Imperial General Staff, to sign the document of surrender. After they had done so, the Allied representatives added their signatures.

The time was 9:25 A.M. At that moment, the *New York Times* reported, "a mighty host of airplanes paraded into sight sweeping over the warships. Four hundred B-29s and 1,500 fighter planes joined in an aerial pageant in a final salute."

With that salute, the Second World War in the Pacific came to an end. But the long struggle that had led to it, the struggle for the mastery of Asia, was hardly over.

EPILOGUE:
WORLD WAR II AND
THE ROAD TO VIETNAM

1

Throughout East Asia, the old order had receded and a new order had taken its place. When the Japanese surrendered, the Union Jack rose again over Hong Kong and Mark Young, the prewar governor now emaciated from his imprisonment, returned to Government House. But Man-Kan Lu, leader of the Legislative Council, made clear that henceforth the resident Chinese would receive just and equitable treatment.

On September 5, 1945, British reoccupation forces, headed by Lord Mountbatten, landed at Singapore, but they found a largely Chinese local population unwilling again to accept colonialism. Lee Kuan Yew, formerly a brilliant student at Cambridge University and later prime minister of independent Singapore, stated in a talk given in 1961 that "My colleagues and I are of that generation of young men who went through the Second World War and the Japanese occupation and emerged determined that no one—neither the Japanese nor the British—had the right to push and kick us around." When in 1945 the Dutch tried to reenter the Indies, they found themselves confronted by a full-fledged and successful nationalistic revolutionary organization headed by Sukarno. But America's experience in postwar Asia was different.

2

As the major island in the Ryukyu chain, Okinawa at the time of the Perry visit had been the head of an independent kingdom, closer culturally to China than to Japan. Japan had overrun the islands in 1895, the same year that Tokyo colonized Korea and Taiwan. Now, in the summer of 1945, Okinawa was in the control of the United States.

It has remained so ever since. In the years to come, Okinawa became the site of a multitude of American military bases. The United States also commanded the surrounding seas and the airspace over the Ryukyus. And in Okinawa, only American courts have jurisdiction over Americans. Like the British treaty-ports along the China coast in the nineteenth century, Okinawa became and remains an American zone of extraterritoriality. From time to time Okinawans protested against their status, but they protest in vain. And the Filipinos hardly protested at all.

3

The Philippines did gain formal independence in 1946. But informally the archipelago reverted to its colonial dependence on the United States and MacArthur played a crucial role in making certain that it did so. "I can't work with Osmeña," the general told a visitor soon after the war's end, thus fulfilling Harold Ickes's prophecy. MacArthur wanted to cast himself alone in the part of the islands' savior and saw Osmeña as too independent a spirit. He proceeded to withhold food from civilians and back pay from soldiers, blaming the shortfalls on Osmeña. MacArthur championed instead a favorite, Manuel Roxas.

In his forties, Roxas was a scion of the old order. His parents were Spanish and he married into a wealthy Luzon family; he owned three

Manila newspapers and MacArthur late in the war had anointed him with the rank of colonel in the United States Army. There was just one problem: Roxas had collaborated with the Japanese.

So had some 5,000 of the other *illustrados*, the Filipino landowning elite. Having profited hugely under prewar American colonialism, during the war they had switched their allegiance to the Japanese overlords. But many had served as officials in the previous American administration and MacArthur deemed them necessary in restoring the islands' postwar government. So with a stroke of a pen in August, 1945, he exonerated them of all collaborationist crimes. The next year, he used his influence to make Roxas the first president of the Philippine Republic.

If MacArthur reestablished the old Philippine political system, other Americans recolonized the islands commercially and militarily. American investment again dominated all commerce. Negotiators from Washington forced the Philippine government to accept United States control over the Clark airfield and the Subic Bay naval yard, then America's largest overseas bases, almost free of rent. Americans on the bases enjoyed immunity from Philippine courts: Like Okinawa, Clark and Subic Bay were modern versions of extraterritoriality.

Before the war, the *illustrados* participated in their own country's economic exploitation. In sharing the wealth with the American rulers, they had been content with the colonial status quo. And after the war, they were content with the neocolonial status quo—quite unlike revolutionaries on the mainland of Asia.

4

On the day of the Japanese surrender, Chiang Kaishek entered a sound studio in Chongqing and sat in a chair behind a microphone. Dressed in simple khaki, with no insignia or ribbons, he adjusted his horn-rimmed glasses. Then he spoke, pronouncing his words slowly in halting Mandarin (his native dialect was that of coastal Zhejiang Province, just south of Shanghai): "Our faith in justice in the black and hopeless days and eight years of struggle today have been restored. . . . We have won the victory. But relaxation and pride are not the results of victory that we seek. Peace presents us with stupendous and difficult problems. . . . We must march forward on the great road to unity."

Loudspeakers carried Chiang's words to crowds gathered outside. From inside, even as he spoke, he could hear shouts and the popping of firecrackers.

His speech lasted only a few minutes, but when he finished he slumped with exhaustion. Then pulling himself together, he strode out of the studio and stepped into a Cadillac sedan. As his car moved off he found himself engulfed in a tide of joyous humanity. People were yelling from rooftops, leaning over balconies, crawling through police lines, holding children on shoulders, and packing the streets so tightly that some of them could gawk right through the rear windows of the sedan: His lean, ascetic face for once bore a smile. As the automobile passed through central Chongqing, hands thrust upward in victory salutes to the chant of *"Chiang . . . Zhongguo . . . wan sui . . . wan wan sui!"*—"Chiang . . . China . . . live ten thousand years . . . live ten thousand ten thousand years!"

This picture, conveyed to American readers in the familiar, red-bordered Henry R. Luce newsweekly, *Time,* was accurate, as far as it went. It just did not go very far. Nowhere did the Luce press (or for that matter the rest of the mainstream American press) convey a sense of the corruption, inflation, malnutrition, and violence that were besetting China. For high in the Time-Life Building in midtown Manhattan, Luce's editors, under his orders lobbying for Nationalist China, were busy substituting image for reality. And the reality was that Chiang Kaishek's "ten thousand years" were destined to last but four.

Shortly after noon on November 27, 1945, President Truman conducted a brief ceremony in the courtyard of the Pentagon. Presenting General Marshall, who was retiring, with an Oak Leaf Cluster, he read aloud this citation: "In a war unparalleled in magnitude and in horror, millions of Americans gave their country outstanding service. General of the Army George C. Marshall gave it victory." Marshall, the wartime chief of staff, and Katherine, his wife, then drove to their new home in northern Virginia.

Even more than MacArthur, Marshall had been the star of the U.S. Army. Born in 1880 in Pennsylvania, he had graduated first captain from the Virginia Military Institute. He later finished first in his class at the Fort Leavenworth infantry and cavalry school. During the First World War, his immediate commander had urged that Marshall be promoted to "brigadier general . . . and every day this is postponed is a loss to the Army and the nation." It was done, and Marshall climbed steadily through the general ranks. In time he earned President Roosevelt's respect and on September 1, 1939, the day Hitler invaded Poland, he became full general and chairman of the Joint Chiefs of Staff. His reputation during the war was one of impeccable integrity and Harry Truman regarded him as the greatest living American. But the time had come to retire.

Mrs. Marshall looked forward to the quiet years ahead. So as they turned in through their manor house gate, from inside she heard a record player blaring out the "Hallelujah Chorus," and she hummed along with the music. But as they entered the front door, the telephone rang. The general answered quietly. Mrs. Marshall went upstairs for a nap. When she came down again, her husband was listening to the radio. Marshall explained that the telephone call had been from President Truman. "I could not bear to tell you," the general said, "until you had had your rest."

President Truman, the announcer was saying, had called Marshall back into service. He was to leave immediately as the president's special ambassador to China. There he was to mediate an end to the most explosive unresolved issue of World War II—the Chinese civil war.

On August 11, 1945, three days before the Japanese surrender, Chinese Communist army units had left their base in northwestern China and moved into Manchuria. Alarmed, Chiang Kaishek had sent a message to Mao Zedong, asking him to come to Chongqing to discuss "internal problems." Mao had grudgingly accepted the invitation and, on August 27, Ambassador Patrick J. Hurley had flown to Yanan to serve as escort. The next day, Mao and Hurley had reached the wartime Chinese capital.

After six weeks of talks, the Communists and the Nationalists had issued a joint communiqué, expressing a vague agreement on troop unification. Upon Mao's return to Yanan, however, fighting had erupted.

The civil war had broken out in earnest. By the end of October, Communist troops had cut the rail-lines from Beijing to the Yangzi, attacked Datong in the north, and continued their buildup in Manchuria. On November 2, *Guomindang* troops had landed in Manchuria, ferried in by American transport planes.

Almost immediately, the Communist-run Radio Yanan had denounced the American action. Indeed, on November 8, General Wedemeyer had admitted that American troops had been engaged in small-scale fighting against the Reds.

Then a diplomatic bombshell exploded. On the morning of November 27, Ambassador Hurley, who had returned to Washington, had given a press conference to announce his resignation. He also had flayed the Truman administration: "A considerable section of our State Department," he had declared to reporters, "is endeavoring to support Communism generally as well as specifically in China."

At a luncheon cabinet meeting that day, Clinton Anderson, the secretary of agriculture, had suggested to Truman that to head off criticism he might send General Marshall, who could keep his feelings to himself, to China. Animosities in China were mounting. The Communists on November 30 invaded Shandong Province; and on December 1, General Wedemeyer acknowledged that the Chinese government still was receiving aid under the wartime Lend-Lease program. Against this backdrop, General and Mrs. Marshall flew to China. On December 22, 1945, they reached Chongqing. The ill-fated Marshall mission was under way.

Through Marshall's disinterested mediation, on January 10 the Communists and the Nationalists had agreed to a cease-fire; a month and a half later they had agreed to the gradual unification of their forces. But in the middle of March, with the Red position in Manchuria stronger than ever, Marshall had informed Truman that the state of affairs in China's northeast was "extremely critical." A month later, Soviet troops had evacuated Changchun, then the Manchurian capital. (Pursuant to the Yalta accords, the Soviets had been "holding" Manchuria for Chiang Kaishek; having looted the region of its "Japanese" machinery, however, they had now withdrawn.) The Nationalists and the Communists immediately had raced to the city and, on April 17, the Reds had made it theirs. And Nationalist–Communist talks were breaking down over the makeup of a national assembly. So Marshall's mood was disconsolate.

General Marshall, the journalist John R. Beal wrote in his diary on May 4, 1946, "is occupying the home of the former German ambassador. It is Chinese style outside, and modern, comfortable, and spacious inside—probably the best in Nanjing [the prewar capital to which Chiang Kaishek's government had just returned]. The general invited me out on the terrace and we dragged a couple of wicker chairs near the edge, overlooking the lawn and garden."

Marshall, who was normally reserved, poured out his fears. By delaying their departure, he believed, the Soviets had allowed the Chinese Communists to seize virtual control of Manchuria. Yet by "stirring up anti-Communist demonstrations, by breaking into and sabotaging the Communist radio in Guangzhou"—Marshall's words—elements of the *Guomindang* were his worst enemies.

On June 7, Marshall managed to negotiate a fifteen-day truce and even got it extended to the end of the month.

But then, as this cease-fire collapsed, the American involvement in the Chinese civil war became plain. On July 28, Communist troops near Beijing ambushed a Marine convoy, killing three and wounding twelve; on August 5, Washington announced that it had no intention of withdrawing U.S. forces from China. At the end of the month, the United States signed an agreement for sale to the Nationalists of surplus military supplies; and the Communists denounced Marshall for pretending to mediate between the two sides while furnishing one of them with materiel.

Two weeks later, perhaps as a publicity ploy, Chiang Kaishek ordered his troops to cease hostilities and invited the Communists to attend the national assembly, scheduled to meet on November 15. Believing themselves to be militarily superior and the forum illegitimate, the Reds boycotted the meeting. On November 19, Zhou Enlai, the Communist foreign minister, returned to Yanan. China braced for all-out war.

On January 6, 1947, President Truman announced that he was recalling Marshall from China. Indeed, the United States soon announced the end of its effort to bring about a settlement in China. Born of wartime diplomacy, the Marshall mission had collapsed. Ironically, Marshall immediately became secretary of state.

Why did Marshall's efforts fail? Undoubtedly rivalries in China were too deep for any honest broker to resolve.

But to the Communists, Marshall was no more than a representative of the latest imperial power that supported Chiang Kaishek. In China, the American wartime agencies, SACO, the OSS, the Navy, and the Marine Corps, all had remained for a good year after the war, trying to contain Communist power, and American aid for Chiang continued even longer. To the Communists that aid was nothing more than the imperialist intervention of old. And Mao Zedong had no intention of seeing the Chinese nation subjected ever again to the forces of imperialism.

The Communists went on to win the civil war. On October 1, 1949, Mao Zedong stood on a balcony high over Tiananmen Square and proclaimed the creation of the People's Republic of China.

Earlier in the year, Chiang Kaishek and two million adherents of the old *Guomindang* fled to Taiwan, which they called the "Republic of China," and maintained the pretense that Taipei, the island's principal port, was the capital of all China. The claim that Taiwan was an independent country, however, was spurious. Well into the 1960s, Taiwan remained reminiscent of the British treaty-ports, Shanghai, Tianjin, and Giangzhou. When the Communists took over the mainland, all American extraterritorial rights in China ended. In Taiwan, however, a 1954 mutual security treaty with the United States ratified the presence of American bases and made them subject exclusively to American jurisdiction. Under the American protective umbrella, Taiwan, like the treaty-ports of old, emerged as a center of trade and technology, far more advanced economically than the hinterland of mainland China.

Yet that hinterland, unconquered and defiant, continued to bedevil the United States. Early in 1950, Mao Zedong and an entourage of Chinese Communist leaders went to Moscow to sign a Sino-Soviet mutual defense treaty; and then China intervened in the Korean War.

5

Chalmers Johnson, an academic specialist on East Asia, has commented that the "end of World War II . . . proved no more of a 'liberation' day for Korea than for Czechoslovakia or other nations of eastern Europe." Hardly was the war over when Kim Il Sung, a Communist who had led a Mao-like guerrilla war against the Japanese along the Soviet–Manchurian border, imposed his rule on North Korea.

His alignment with China was clear. Some 400 Korean Communists had joined Mao Zedong on the Long March to Yanan. Kim even used Maoist imagery: During the war Mao had been the "Red Sun of Our Hearts" and Kim the "Beautiful Red Star in the Sky." Immediately after the Japanese surrender, the 2,000 members of the Korean Emancipation League, a military-political school organized at Yanan with Chinese assistance, reentered the homeland to set up the Korean People's Republic.

Even before Mao's victory in China, American observers in South Korea saw the rule of Kim Il Sung as an extension of the Chinese Communist revolution. Led by General John Hodge, who transferred his conviction that the Japanese were subhumans to the North Koreans and to all revolutionaries and reformers in South Korea, the occupying U.S. military launched a large-scale campaign of repression. A staunch Korean nationalist, Syngman Rhee was appointed as South Korea's leader, and General Hodge and his aides prosecuted for treason—not in Korean courts but rather in American courts-martial—thousands of South Koreans suspected of leftist views.

When in the autumn of 1946 labor strikes and rural protests arose, American troops and tanks played a role in the suppression. Hugh Deane, an American journalist on the scene, reported: "It was a full-scale revolution. . . . The railroad workers at Taigu [in southeastern South Korea] followed by the phone and metal, textile and electric workers went on strike. As each strike was suppressed by the police, another took its place. Students went out into the streets to demonstrate, and then the whole city was aflame. From the city, the revolution spread into the countryside and was taken over by the sharecroppers. The farmers refused to surrender their rice to the police. They attacked the homes of the landlords, and then the police stations. They tore off jail doors to release arrested sharecroppers, they burned the records and stole the weapons."

Like the Mao-led peasant uprisings that took place in 1946 and 1947 in China, the Korean disturbances seemed to American authorities to presage a spreading of Chinese Communism all the way through South Korea. The ensuing crackdown was savage. In the spring of 1947, Roger N. Baldwin, director of the American Civil Liberties Union, visited South Korea and publicized his findings at a New York press conference. Describing South Korea as an American-imposed "police state," he stated that he had "found political leaders who were afraid to sleep in the same bed two successive nights, trade union leaders with whom he had appointments unable to keep the dates because they had been thrown in jail, and another important figure lying in a bed in an American hospital because he was, as he put it, 'politically ill.'"

Elected president of South Korea in 1949, Syngman Rhee, the beneficiary of the U.S.-led repression, made the statement that the "artificial" barrier of the 38th parallel "must and will be torn down." Attending the inaugural ceremony, General MacArthur promised to defend the new regime.

By tearing down the "artificial" barrier and by defending the new regime, both Rhee and MacArthur meant using Japan as a base from which to roll through North Korea and overturn the Chinese revolution. When the "China Incident" of 1937 set into motion the slide into World War II, the Roosevelt administration had looked to Chiang Kaishek's China to replace Japan, once favored by Theodore Roosevelt, as America's ally in Asia. Washington had poured money and arms into China and President Truman had sent General Marshall to China to negotiate a peace that would bolster Chiang's regime.

But by 1948 and 1949, it had become obvious that China was not going to be America's ally. In October 1949, a National Security Council policy statement (NSC-48) described the island chain of Japan, Okinawa, Taiwan, and the Philippines as "our first line of defense and, in addition, our first line of offense from which we can seek to reduce the area of Communist control, using whatever means we can develop, without, however, using sizable US armed forces." If not American forces, the United States would use the South Korean military to initiate the rollback.

In a 1972 article entitled "How Did the Korean War Begin?" Karunakar Gupta, an Indian scholar, noted that, according to the *New York Times*, on the day of the outbreak of the Korean War, June 25, 1950, South Korean units were found north of the 38th parallel and "that there must have been an element of surprise in this attack."

Did South Korea initiate the war? The evidence is inconclusive, but the possibility remains.

The North Korean forces drove through South Korea as far as the southeastern port of Pusan, but MacArthur's autumn amphibious landing at Inchon forced them back. With the North Koreans in retreat, in October MacArthur met President Truman at Wake Island, and said to reporters: "Come on up to Pyongyang [the capital of North Korea]. It [the victory] won't be long now." And if the Chinese intervened, he would deal them a blow that would "rock Asia and perhaps turn back Communism."

In the autumn of 1941, *US News* had carried a pictogram of the Pacific, with arrows from various U.S. bases pointed at Tokyo and indicating the flight times required for American bombers. In October, 1950, *US News* printed a similar pictogram, only this time the target was Beijing. At the end of October, in response to such published threats as well as to MacArthur's push up the Korean peninsula, Chinese troops crossed the Yalu River and intervened in the Korean War, forcing the United States into a stalemate. Many Americans feared the beginning of World War III.

6

For the United States leadership, World War II had taught three great lessons. First, the Munich Conference when the British prime minister, Neville Chamberlain, had appeased Hitler: The moral was to stop aggressors, or alliances of aggressors, in their tracks. Second, Pearl Harbor: Any country that would attack United States forces in an unprovoked manner—such was the memory—was just such an aggressor. And third, America the "can-do" nation: The massive military production during the war, the bombing of Japan, and the ability and valor of the American troops as they crossed the Pacific meant that, even without using atomic bombs again, the United States could win.

To those Americans who came to maturity during the Second World War, these lessons were articles of faith. But the Chinese intervention in Korea, which was successful in forcing the United States into a stalemate, challenged each article of the catechism.

If generals always fight the last war, so do politicians. Rather than learn from the stalemate in Korea, American leaders sought another way to throw back, or at least contain, Mao's China. Fearing links between Communists in Vietnam and those in China, the Truman administration had given so much funding and equipment to the French, who sought by force to recapture their Indo-Chinese colony, that by 1954 Washington was paying ninety percent of the cost of the French–Vietnamese colonial war. When the French effort failed at Dienbienphu in May, 1954, Washington made formal commitments to the defense of South Vietnam and President Dwight D. Eisenhower, with Japan's southward thrust in mind, justified the commitment by invoking the domino theory. And when, after various American-sponsored South Vietnamese attacks on North Vietnam in the summer of 1964, a North Vietnamese PT boat attacked the U.S. destroyer *Maddox* in the Gulf of Tonkin, President Lyndon Baines Johnson likened the episode to Pearl Harbor, calling the attack "unprovoked."

In the summer of 1966, Senator J. William Fulbright, Democrat of Arkansas and chairman of the Committee on Foreign Relations, staged a series of televised hearings on America's role in Vietnam. Fulbright called in his star witness, Secretary of State Dean Rusk. Rusk was reluctant to appear, but a subpoena brought him out of his office in Foggy Bottom. The exchanges between Fulbright and Rusk were bitter. Fulbright questioned the very need for the war. Rusk in turn was contemptuous, contending that in Vietnam the United States had to stop aggression and that it had the will, the might, and the wealth to do so.

For the members of the Johnson administration and many other Americans, the lessons of World War II in Asia and the Pacific seemed directly applicable to Vietnam. But they misapplied the lessons. No evidence, then or now, has shown that outside the Indo-Chinese peninsula, China, North Vietnam, or both were on the march toward vast conquest in the manner of Nazi Germany and Imperial Japan. The Chinese intervention in Korea and the North Vietnamese attack on the *Maddox* clearly were far from unprovoked. While American airpower had destroyed Japanese factories and cities, the U.S. bombing raids deterred the economically underdeveloped peasant society of North Vietnam not at all. And while local populations across the South Pacific and in the Philippines had welcomed and helped the American liberators, in Vietnam the United States was fighting the same kind of unpopular war that the Japanese had waged in China, and had lost to the same kind of guerrilla opponents.

For the American empire, like the Japanese before it, pitted itself against the forces of Asian nationalism and lost. We Americans, to be sure, do not think of ourselves as possessing an empire. Throughout our history, we have regarded our country as the "shining city upon the hill" and ourselves as the exceptional people, not at all like those depraved and corrupted European and Japanese imperialists. In 1898, of course, we took over the remnants of the Spanish Empire, but that was back then; and America certainly ruled no formal colonial system in the manner of the British: there was no Colonial Office in Washington. But if by "empire" we mean wealth, power, and the will to mold the world to one's wishes—if it walks like a duck, and quacks like a duck—then World War II in Asia and the Pacific saw the emergence of an American empire. As the Japanese had arisen to sweep away the imperialism of the Dutch, the French, and the British, so did we Americans struggle to master Japanese imperialism, to bring the Pacific and the Asian mainland under our own control. Nothing symbolized that control more vividly than the dropping of the two atomic bombs.

But our mastery was not what we thought. An America that during World War II had believed itself in control of its own destiny and fighting for democracy with moral righteousness, in Vietnam discovered itself tragically out of control and struggling in the murky waters of military and moral uncertainty. World War II in Asia and the Pacific had created the illusion of mastery. The Vietnam War—an unpopular, ill-conceived campaign against ideologically committed and locally recruited guerrilla fighters—shattered that illusion.

NOTES

Prologue: Washington, December 8, 1941

Pages:

xi The declaration of war speech: *New York Times, Washington Post, Chicago Tribune*, December 9, 1941.

Chapter 1. The Fall of Imperial China

Pages:

4 The Macartney mission: Peyrefitte, passim; Cranmer-Byng, passim; Coates, 83–92.

5 Letter from George III: Cranmer-Byng, 189.

5 Imperial response: ibid., 196.

6 "Do not say . . . ": Coates, 90.

6 Macartney's judgment: Cranmer-Byng, 212–213.

7 The secret societies: Naquin, passim.

7 Opium problem: Fairbank, *Trade and Diplomacy*, passim.

8 Opium War: Collis, *Foreign Mud*, passim.

9 Burning of Summer Palace: Oliphant, 289–300.

9 Treaty-ports: Fairbank, *United States and China*, 167.

10 *Taiping* defeat: Spence, 305–328.

12 Self-strengthening movement: Teng and Fairbank, 50–61.

12 "Today our country . . . ": ibid., 54.

13 The imperial landgrab: Fleming, 23–34.

14 Kang's conversation: Teng and Fairbank, 117.

15 Liang Qichao: quoted in Dicks, 67.

15 The Boxers: Fleming, 60–62 and 195–210.

17 Morrison: *The Times*, March 30, 1911.

17 Abdication: Behr, *Last Emperor*, 69.

18 Chiang's rise: Crozier, 1–94.

19   Long March: Payne, *Mao*, 148–149.
19   Yanan: Snow, *Red Star*, 26–28.

Chapter 2. Japan's Response to the West

Pages:
23   Perry visit: Robert L. Reynolds, passim, and Wiley, passim.
23   "gospel of god": quoted in Bergamini, 240.
25   "squadron was full . . . ": quoted in Robert L. Reynolds, 83.
26   "thus closed . . . ": Perry, *Journal*.
27   "It was an imposing . . . ": ibid.
27   "We have in our country . . . ": ibid., 85.
28   "Circumstances may lead . . . ": ibid.
29   Japan's growth: Beasley, 56–57.
30   Japan's war with China: Michael and Taylor, 156.
32   The Russo-Japanese war: Warner and Warner, passim.
33   Portsmouth conference: Nathan Miller, 446–448.
36   Twenty One Demands: LaFeber, *American Age*, 276–277.
37   Washington Conference: Vinson, passim, and Pusey, 466–470.
38   Manchurian incident: Toland, *Rising Sun*, 5–9.
39   Stimson Doctrine: Elting Morison, 332.

Chapter 3. The Open Door

Pages:
42   *Empress of China*: P. C. K. F. Smith, 1–3.
42   Early China trade: Tamarin and Glubok, passim.
42   Caleb Cushing: Fuess, 397–454.
44   Treaty of Guadalupe Hidalgo: Graebner, 1–5.
44   Trans-Pacific expansion: LaFeber, *American Age*, 178–183.
47   Rockhill and Open Door: Varg, *Open Door Diplomat*, passim.
48   Open Door language: LaFeber, *American Age*, 276–277.
49   Manchuria: Courtney.
50   Japan in Manchuria: Snow, "Fate of Manchuria."
50   Japan below Manchuria: Snow, "Japanese Juggernaut."
52   Kidnapping: Payne, *Chiang Kaishek*, 199–219.
53   Marco Polo Bridge: Lu, 16.
55   Palace Hotel: Baum, 409.

Chapter 4. New Order in East Asia

Pages:
57   Harbor scene: *New York Times*, August 21, 1937.
59   Yangzi River war: ibid., December 4, 1937.
60   Rape of Nanjing: *New York Times*, December 18, 1937.
61   *Panay*: Gale, Koginos, and Perry, passim.
64   Byas's account: Byas, 17–18.

66   Japanese problems: *New York Times*, January 13 and 27, 1938.

66   Johnson's cable: quoted in Schaller, *U.S. Crusade*, 18.

67   Yarnell: quoted in Pelz, 199.

67   Leahy's proposal: Pearson and Allen.

68   Passage of bill: *Washington Star*, March 29, 1938; ORANGE: Morton, 247–248.

68   State meeting: Burns and Bennett, 198–216.

70   Konoye's speech: Heinrichs, *American Ambassador*, 262.

71   Arita: quoted in Iriye, *Second World War*, 68–69.

72   Johnson's trip: Buhite, *Nelson T. Johnson*, 135–142.

Chapter 5. The Road to Pearl Harbor

Pages:

75   *New York Times*, June 8–10, 1939.

76   Tianjin: *New York Times*, July 3, 1939.

77   Tokyo: *New York Times*, June 23, 1939.

78   Grew's speech: U.S. Department of State, *Japan*, 19–29.

79   Reactions to Grew: Heinrichs, *American Ambassador*, 293; *New York Times*, November 3–20, 1939.

80   Abend's report: Abend, 49–51.

81   Japan's threats: U.S. Department of State, *Japan*, 281.

82   Squeeze on Japan: Akashi, 24.

82   Japan's defenses: Wilcox, 51–52.

83   Arita's press conference: Morley, 129–130.

84   Hanoi: Feis, *Road*, 66.

85   *Life*, March 24, 1941.

87   Tojo: Bergamini, 754–756; Williams and Wallace, passim.

87   Callender reports: *New York Times*, September 3 and 12, 1940.

89   Burma Road: *Time*, October 28, 1940.

90   Bombing plan: Morgenthau Diary, Book 342a, 18–27.

91   Elements of the plan: Corcoran papers, China Defense Supplies.

92   Embargo: Anderson.

93   Pearl Harbor preparations: Farago, 216.

94   Orders to MacArthur: "The Problem of Defeating Japan," MacArthur Foundation Archives.

95   Kurusu's trip: *Time*, November 24, 1941.

96   Ultimatum: Sherry, 108–109; Baldwin letter, Marshall Foundation.

Chapter 6. The Onslaught

Pages:

101   The test run: Prange, *At Dawn*, 314–319.

106   Chongqing: White, *In Search of History*, 67–68.

107   Stilwell: Tuchman, *Stilwell*, 299.

108   Doolittle: Thomas and Jablonski, 154.

108   Donovan: Troy, 114–116.
109   Churchill's reaction: Gilbert VI, 1268.
110   Japanese reactions and motives: Bergamini, 898.
111   Wake: Schultz, *Wake Island*, passim.
112   Hong Kong: Gilbert VII, 7.
113   Brereton and MacArthur: Manchester, 196–198.
114   Threat to Philippines: Toland, *But Not in Shame*, 58–64.
120   Singapore: ibid., 90.

Chapter 7. The Singapore Debacle

Pages:
124   Japanese advance: Attiwill, 1–30.
125   Bar scene: Barber, 97–98.
126   Christmas in Singapore: Cecil Brown, 397–415.
127   Churchill's outrage: Gilbert, 45–60.
128   Japanese training manual: Zich, 123.
129   Johore: Tsuji, 227–229.
131   "Good morning . . . ": quoted in Attiwill, 81.
133   "There must be no . . . ": quoted in Toland, *Rising Sun*, 312.
134   "All ranks . . . ": quoted in ibid., 161.
136   Hospital scene: ibid., 217–220.
137   "No Dunkirk . . . ": quoted in ibid., 222.
139   Surrender scene: Stein, 178.

Chapter 8. Warriors of the Rising Sun

Pages:
141   "After dark . . . ": quoted in Winslow, xvii.
144   "I strained . . . ": quoted in ibid., 113–114; "my heart pounds . . . ": quoted in Zich, 127.
145   "It seemed as though . . . ": quoted in *loc. cit.*
146   View of Rangoon: Collis, *First and Last*, 116.
149   "lieutenant generals and . . . ": quoted in White, *Stilwell Papers*, 15.
149   Stilwell on the British: quoted in ibid., 45.
150   Stilwell on Chiang: quoted in ibid., 49.
151   Stilwell's gloominess: ibid., 49–51.
152   "Extrawdinery . . . ": quoted in ibid., 52; "Your Excellency . . . ": quoted in Tuchman, *Stilwell*, 345.
153   "glittered beneath . . . ": Belden, *Retreat*, 63.
155   "We abandon all . . . ": quoted in Moser, 32.
156   "everyone rose . . . ": Belden, *Retreat*, 308–309.
157   "Easy pace . . . ": quoted in White, *Stilwell Papers*, 99; "Our people tired . . . ": quoted in Moser, 33.
158   "Nice ride . . . ": White, *Stilwell Papers*, 100–102.
158   "I claim . . . ": quoted in Moser, 33.

Chapter 9. But Not in Shame

Pages:

162 FDR to MacArthur: James, 98; "simple volunteer": Huff; FDR's renewed effort, Manchester, 250–256.

162 MacArthur's capitulation: James, 98–99.

163 "If I got through . . . ": Blair, *MacArthur*, 73.

164 "to roar in . . . ": quoted in Manchester, 258.

165 "I think it . . . ": Manchester, 261.

166 "To attempt such . . . ": quoted in Willoughby and Chamberlain, 54.

166 "[A]n entirely new . . . ": quoted in Eyre, 90–91.

167 "Our lives . . . ": quoted in Beck, 157.

167 "As far as I know . . . ": quoted in ibid., 159.

167 "The president . . . ": quoted in Blair, *MacArthur*, 76–77.

168 "turned deadly white . . . ": quoted in ibid., 79.

169 The Japanese advance: Zich, 477.

170 Wainwright to MacArthur: quoted in ibid., 584.

170 "We have none . . . ": quoted in ibid., 588–589.

172 "he grabbed . . . ": quoted in Young, 327.

173 "roadside began . . . ": Toland, *But Not in Shame*, 198–201.

173 "him in the ribs . . . ": E. B. Miller, 223.

175 "We asked only . . . ": quoted in Zich, 97; "Everyone is bawling . . . ": quoted in *loc. cit.*

175 "WITH BROKEN HEART . . . ": quoted in Toland, *But Not in Shame*, 376.

Chapter 10. Midway

Pages:

178 "occupation of Malaya": quoted in Guillain, 96–97.

178 "about 6,000 feet . . . ": quoted in Byrd, 9; "narrow, dirty, and rough . . . ": quoted in ibid., 94.

180 Low and King: Schultz, *The Doolittle Raid*, 80–81.

181 Doolittle's departure: ibid., 91.

182 "winds, rains . . . ": quoted in ibid., 113.

183 "CHINESE AIR FORCE . . . ": ibid., 116.

184 Scene over Tokyo: ibid., 118.

188 Rochefort decoding: Lord, *Incredible Victory*, 19.

189 "TASK FORCE SIXTEEN . . . ": quoted in Zich, 178.

190 "Zeroes fell . . . ": quoted in Bryan, 117.

191 "flight leader dropped . . . ": quoted in *loc. cit.*

191 Nagumo's intelligence: Zich, 180.

192 "It was like the inside . . . ": quoted in *loc. cit.*

193 "Abandon ship . . . ": quoted in Bryan, 180.

193 "Black objects . . . ": Fuchida and Masatake, 26.

195 "I shall remain . . . ": quoted in Zich, 183.

Chapter 11. America Rising

Pages:

199   "HENCEFORTH . . . ": quoted in Weglyn, 33.

200   Munson report: quoted in ibid., 41–42.

201   Charles Kikuchi: Kikuchi Papers.

203   Capra's promise: quoted in Capra, 372.

204   "Why We Fight": Dower, *War Without Mercy*, 16.

205   West Coast production: Albright, passim; Blum, 91.

206   Union Station display: reproduced in Sherry, 146–147.

207   Arnold's boast: Arnold, August 15, 1942.

208   "Metal fans are . . . ": quoted in Blair, *Silent Victory*, 297.

210   MacFarlan's message: quoted in Lord, *Lonely Vigil*, 36.

211   Guadalcanal description: Morison, *Struggle*, 5.

212   "All right . . . ": Leckie, 5.

213   "The tension . . . ": ibid., 4.

213   "Land the landing force": quoted in Steinberg, *Island Fighting,* 19; "clinging to the . . . ": Leckie, 18.

214   "TOJO ICE . . . ": quoted in Steinberg, *Island Fighting,* 25; "It was darkness . . . ": quoted in Richard P. Frank, *Guadalcanal,* 70.

215   "it was plain . . . ": quoted in Steinberg, *Island Fighting,* 27–28.

Chapter 12. The Hammer and the Anvil

Pages:

222   Answer to the emperor: quoted in Steinberg, *Island Fighting,* 72.

222   "I am going to fight back . . . ": quoted in Burns, 305.

223   "unconditional surrender": quoted in Gregg, 73.

224   "The trouble in China . . . ": quoted in White, *Stilwell Papers,* 134.

224   Stilwell's house: ibid., 111.

225–26   "an exalted concept . . . ": quoted in Tuchman, *Stilwell,* 387; "No answer . . . ": quoted in White, *Stilwell Papers,* 126; "We have been . . . ": quoted in ibid., 147.

226   "Dinner at Chiang . . . ": quoted in ibid., 148.

226   "Willkie arrives . . . ": quoted in ibid., 150.

227   "Peanut 'directed operations' . . . ": quoted in ibid., 158.

227   "can't have the . . . ": quoted in ibid., 161.

228   "From George Marshall . . . ": quoted in ibid., 171; "Peanut and I . . . ": quoted in ibid., 171–172.

228   "Teevy. . . .": ibid., 172.

228   Chennault: Chennault, 212.

229   "Japan wants to hold . . . ": quoted in Heiferman, 84–85.

230   "was so tempting": White, *In Search of History,* 143.

231   "Goddam it . . . ": quoted in *New York Times,* February 18, 1943.

231   "You never saw . . . ": quoted in Tuchman, *Stilwell,* 449; "Eleanor . . . ": quoted in Roosevelt, 249.

232   "Shift from a defensive . . . ": Morison, *Breaking*, 51.
233   Decoded Japanese messages: quoted in Davis, 3–4.
233–34   Nimitz and Layton: quoted in Davis, 4; "Assuming that we . . . ": quoted in ibid., 5; "IF FORCES YOUR . . . ": quoted in ibid., 8.
235   On Yamamoto's plane: Agawa, 351.

Chapter 13. Grand Strategy

Pages:
239   The Japanese bomb: Wilcox, 56–110.
242   "on either side . . . ": Manchester, 284.
242   "I felt as if . . . ": quoted in Steinberg, *Island Fighting*, 75.
243   "If one wished . . . ": quoted in Bergerod, 363–364.
243   "We could see them . . . ": quoted in ibid., 364.
244   "forty five . . . ": quoted in Morison, *Breaking*, 147.
        "hit Rendova hard . . . ": quoted in Bergerod, 457.
245   "plastered bivouacs . . . ": quoted in Steinberg, *Island Fighting*, 83.
247   "but I didn't know . . . ": Halsey, 70.
248   "indescribably . . . ": quoted in Steinberg, *Island Fighting*, 87.
251   "she got out . . . ": quoted in Peck, 469–470.
252   "Lyric to Spring . . . ": quoted in White, *Stilwell Papers*, 199–200.
253   "a commander's authority . . . ": ibid., 188.
253   "Nobody . . . ": quoted in ibid., 204; "FDR pulled . . . ": quoted in *loc. cit.*
256   "Confucian classics . . . ": Fairbank, *United States and China*, 57.

Chapter 14. Unanswerable Strength

Pages:
257   Conditions in Japan: Havens, 2.
258   Nimitz's map: Potter, 46.
260   The landing: Steinberg, *Island Fighting*, 104–106.
261   "Gentlemen . . . ": quoted in Gregg.
262   "After making . . . ": quoted in Sherrod, 57–58.
262   "first and second . . . ": quoted in ibid., 58–60.
263   "They were knocking . . . ": quoted in Steinberg, *Island Fighting*, 110.
264   "sooner had we hit . . . ": quoted in Sherrod, 110.
268   Krueger's statement: quoted in James, 470.
269   "reverses Bataan": quoted in ibid., 471.
269   "political picture-taking . . . ": quoted in ibid., 480.
269   MacArthur–FDR: quoted in ibid., 482.
270   "They are waiting . . . ": quoted in ibid., 490.
271   Ignoring jibes: Tuchman, *Stilwell*, 531; "take raw recruits . . . ": quoted in White, *Stilwell Papers*, 268.
271   "We have to go . . . ": quoted in *loc. cit.*; also Wilson, 223.
271   On the trek: Collis, *First and Last*, 202; Anders, passim.

272 "Put down December . . . ": White, *Stilwell Papers*, 266–267.

273 "Yesterday . . . ": quoted in ibid., 274; "They are full": quoted in ibid., 257.

273 Merrill's Marauders: Ogburn, passim.

274 "Myitkyina . . . ": quoted in White, *Stilwell Papers*, 311; "THE AXE FALLS": quoted in ibid., 345.

275 · Chiang's influence: Franklin D. Roosevelt Presidential Library, assorted files.

Chapter 15. Turning Points

Pages:

278 MacArthur's peroration: quoted in Manchester, 368.

278 Toyoda's hope: Field, 64.

278 Japanese on Saipan: Morison, *New Guinea*, 152.

279 "Great Marianas . . . ": quoted in F. C. Jones, 272.

279 "On the edge . . . ": quoted in Sherrod, 278.

279 Tinian: Morison, *New Guinea*, 152.

280 "It sounded . . . ": quoted in Steinberg, *Island Fighting*, 173.

280 "The human wreckage . . . ": Hunt, 192–193.

284 "The big battlewagon . . . ": Fahey, 271.

285 "for only twenty . . . ": quoted in Sherry, 211–212.

286 "Of course . . . ": quoted in Boorman, 109.

287 Communist gains: Chalmers Johnson, *Peasant Nationalism*, passim.

288 Dixie Mission: Barrett, passim.

289 "As we neared . . . ": ibid., 14.

290 "We have come . . . ": quoted in Service, 684.

290 Service's report: ibid., 162–166.

291 Service's preface: ibid., 161; "unfavorable but . . . ": quoted in Feis, *China Tangle*, 259.

293 "YANAN GOVERNMENT . . . ": quoted in Tuchman, "If Mao," 44.

Chapter 16. Yalta

Pages:

297 Inaugural: *Washington Post*, January 21, 1945.

298 "the capitalist system . . . ": quoted in LaFeber, *Clash*, 431.

301 "not one word . . . ": quoted in ibid., 433.

302 Arrival at Malta: Gilbert, 1167–1168; "My friend . . . ": quoted in *loc. cit.*

303 "hot tea with lemon": quoted in Clemens, 112.

304 "It's a big house . . . ": quoted in *loc. cit.*

305 "All through its history . . . ": Macmillan, 15.

306 "broadly based": quoted in LaFeber, *Clash*, 440.

307 Declaration: U.S. Department of State, *Malta and Yalta*, 977–978.

310 Yalta agreement: ibid., 968–984.

Chapter 17. Return to the Colonies

Pages:

314 Slim's offensive: quoted in Moser, 160.

315 White Paper: Cady, 505.

317 "put him in . . . ": quoted in Karnow, *In Our Image*, 328.

317 "country will be . . . ": quoted in ibid., 330.

318 "rains came in . . . ": Raymond.

320 *Kamikazes*: Bernard Miller, passim.

322 "The Japanese . . . ": quoted in Steinberg, *Return*, 111.

322 "Where in the hell . . . ": quoted in Morison, *Liberation*, 195.

323 Mydans's astonishment: Mydans, 175.

323 Brady scene: ibid., 177.

325 "utter carnage . . . ": quoted in Steinberg, *Return*, 120.

326 "My country has kept . . . ": quoted in Willoughby, 268.

Chapter 18. The New Taipans

Pages:

327 "The reasons why . . . ": quoted in Xiang, 14–15.

327 "The aggressive American . . . ": quoted in ibid., 30.

329 Steinberg's drawing: reproduced in Fairbank, *United States*, 339.

329 State Department: Acheson, 40.

330 State Department politics: May, 93.

330 Service, Gayn, and Jaffe: Klehr and Radosh, 1–46.

331 "Speak English," quoted in ibid., 95.

332 Corcoran's defense: ibid., 109–135.

334 "The United States . . . ": quoted in Wheeler, 40.

334 "I have lost . . . ": quoted in ibid., 44.

335 "will resist . . . ": quoted in *loc. cit.*

336 "A frontal assault . . . ": quoted in Black and Blashfield, 24.

338 Felix de Weldon: Marling and Wetenhall, 90–91.

340 "May you walk . . . ": quoted in Wheeler, 109.

Chapter 19. The Masters

Pages:

344 "Flags of country . . . ": *National Geographic Magazine*, March, 1944.

344 Stalin and Soong: Harriman to Truman, July 3, 1945, U.S. Department of State, *1945*, 911–914.

345 Chiang's speech: quoted in Payne, *Chiang Kaishek*, 249.

346 Incendiaries: Kerr, 5–6.

347 "In the eastern sky . . . ": quoted in Toland, *Rising Sun*, 757.

348 "People's clothes . . . ": quoted in Werwell, 68–72.

349 *Newsweek*, March 15, 1945.

349 Raid of May 26: Kerr, 212.

350 Hirohito's inspection: ibid., 218–219.

352 "It is my intent . . . ": Halsey to Truman, July 26, 1945, Harry S Truman Presidential Library, Berlin Conference, Naval Aide File, Map Room, Box 6; Walker, 97.

353 "I am influenced . . . ": quoted in Kerr, 228–229.

353 Journey of the *U-234*: Wilcox, 147–160.

355 "I am getting . . . ": quoted in Daniel, 265; the departure: Presidential Logbook, July 7, 1945, Truman Presidential Library.

357 "were Russian soldiers . . . ": Gilbert, 1204.

357 "afraid to fly": Mee, *Meeting*, 53.

359 "Promptly a few minutes . . . ": The President's Diary, July 17, 1945, Truman Presidential Library.

360 "the preeminent interests . . . ": quoted in *Congressional Quarterly*, 78; Potsdam Declaration: quoted in Feis, *China Tangle*, 333.

361 Hirohito's telegram: The President's Diary, July 18, 1945.

361 Messages to Truman: quoted in McCullough, 454.

Chapter 20. They Call It Peace

Pages:

363 View from Mount Lasso: Thomas and Witts, 151–152.

365 Takeoff: ibid., 237–238.

366 The flight: Knebel and Bailey, 158–165.

367 "hour was early . . . ": Hachiya, 1.

367 Other accounts: Hersey, 13–55.

369 MacArthur on bomb: MacArthur Archives, VIP File, RG 10.

369 "Numerous peace feelers . . . ": Bird, 84–85.

370 The modern assessment: Walker, passim.

370 Truman's comments: Ferrell, *Dear Bess*, 519; Ferrell, *Off the Record*, 53–54.

372 The Rusk line: Goulden, 19–21.

373 The Japanese surrender: Behr, *Hirohito*, 301–307; Mosley, 330.

374 Aboard the *Missouri*: *New York Times*, September 2, 1945.

Epilogue: World War II and the Road to Vietnam

Pages:

377 Lee Kuan Yew: quoted in Chew and Lee, 117.

381 "I could not bear . . . ": quoted in Pogue, 3; "internal problems": quoted in *Congressional Quarterly*, 79.

382 "A considerable section . . . ": quoted in *loc. cit.*

383 "extremely critical . . . ": quoted in *Congressional Quarterly*, 80; Marshall's residence: Beal, 22; "stirring up . . . ": *Congressional Quarterly*, 81.

386 "police state . . . ": *New York Times*, June 23, 1947.

387 "artificial barrier . . . ": quoted in Tewksbury, 95.

387 "How Did . . . ": Gupta; "Come on up . . . ": quoted in Cumings, 715.

Sources

Archives

Air Force Historical Office, Bolling Field, Washington, D.C.
Army War College, Carlyle, Pennsylvania
Bancroft Library, Berkeley, California
Hoover Institution, Stanford, California
Library of Congress, Washington, D.C.
MacArthur Foundation, Norfolk, Virginia
Marine Corps Archives, Washington Navy Yard, Washington, D.C.
George C. Marshall Foundation, Lexington, Virginia
National Archives, College Park, Maryland
Naval Historical Center, Washington Navy Yard, Washington, D.C.
Public Record Office, London
Franklin D. Roosevelt Presidential Library, Hyde Park, New York
Richard B. Russell Library, Athens, Georgia
Harry S. Truman Presidential Library, Independence, Missouri
University of California–Los Angeles Library, Los Angeles, California

Individual Paper Collections

Henry H. Arnold: Library of Congress
Hanson Baldwin: George C. Marshall Foundation
David D. Barrett: Hoover Institution
Jack Belden: Hoover Institution
Haydon L. Boatner: Hoover Institution
Evans Carlson: Marine Corps Archives and Franklin D. Roosevelt Library
Claire L. Chennault: Hoover Institution
O. Edmund Clubb: Hoover Institution
Thomas Corcoran: National Archives
Lauchlin B. Currie: Hoover Institution

William Donovan: Army War College
James Doolittle: Air Force Historical Office
Frank Dorn: Hoover Institution
Stuart Gilbert: Hoover Institution
Stanley Hornbeck: Hoover Institution
Charles Kikuchi: University of California–Los Angeles
Milton E. Miles: Hoover Institution
Henry Morgenthau: Franklin D. Roosevelt Library
Dean Rusk: Richard B. Russell Library
John S. Service: Bancroft Library
David M. Shoup: Hoover Institution
T. V. Soong: Hoover Institution
Edward Stettinius: National Archives
Joseph W. Stilwell: Hoover Institution
Robert A. Theobald: Hoover Institution
John Carter Vincent: National Archives
Albert C. Wedemeyer: Hoover Institution
Raymond A. Wheeler: Hoover Institution
Carlton de Wiart: Public Record Office

Published Papers

Joseph W. Esherick, ed., *Lost Chance in China: The World War II Dispatches of John S. Service* (New York, 1971).

Robert E. Ferrell, ed., *Dear Bess: The Letters from Harry to Bess Truman, 1910–1959* (New York, 1983).

_____, *Off the Record: The Private Papers of Harry S Truman* (New York, 1980).

Government Economic Research Institute, *Nihon no Zengyo* [*Japanese Shipbuilding*] (Tokyo, 1959).

Francis L. Loewenheim, Harold D. Langley, and Manfred Jonas, *Roosevelt and Churchill: Their Secret Wartime Correspondence* (New York, 1975).

John Medell, ed., *The Kikuchi Diary: Chronicle from an American Concentration Camp* (Urbana, Ill., 1973).

Matthew C. Perry, *The Japan Expedition, 1852–1854: The Personal Journal of Commodore Matthew C. Perry* (Washington, D.C., 1968).

Donald G. Tewksbury, compiler, *Source Material on Korean Politics and Ideologies* (New York, 1950).

U.S. Department of State, *Foreign Relations of the United States: The Conference at Malta and Yalta, 1945* (Washington, D.C., 1955).

_____, *Foreign Relations of the United States: Japan, 1931–1941*. 2 volumes (Washington, D.C., 1944).

_____, *Foreign Relations of the United States, 1944* (Washington, D.C., 1950); *1945* (Washington, D.C., 1951).

U.S. Strategic Bombing Survey, *The Campaigns of the Pacific War* (New York, 1969).

Theodore H. White, ed., *The Stilwell Papers* (New York, 1948).

Dissertation

Susan Naquin, "Millenarian Rebellion in China: The Eight Trigrams Uprising of 1813," Yale University, 1974.

Articles

Gar Alperovitz, "Hiroshima: Historians Reassess," *Foreign Policy,* Summer, 1995.

Irving H. Anderson, "The 1941 De Facto Embargo on Oil to Japan: A Bureaucratic Reflex," *Pacific Historical Review,*" May, 1975.

Henry H. Arnold, "America Takes the Offensive," address of June 8, 1942, in *Vital Speeches of the Day,* August 15, 1942.

O. Atsushi, "Why Japan's Anti-submarine Warfare Failed," *United States Naval Institute Proceedings,* June, 1952.

Josephine A. Brown, "6,000 Miles over the Roads of Free China," *National Geographic Magazine,* March, 1944.

J. Bryan, "Never a Battle Like It," *The Saturday Evening Post,* March 26, 1949.

W. B. Courtney, "Blueprint for Empire," *Collier's,* April 22, 1936.

Anthony Dicks, "Treaty, Grant, Usage, or Sufferance? Some Legal Aspects of the Status of Hong Kong," *The China Quarterly,* September, 1983.

Roger Dingman, "Farewell to Friendship: The USS *Astoria*'s Visit to Japan, April, 1939," *Diplomatic History,* Spring, 1986.

T. G. Fraser, "Roosevelt and the Making of America's East Asian Policy, 1941–1945," in T. G. Fraser and Peter Lowe, *Conflict and Amity in East Asia: Essays in Honor of Ian Nish* (New Hampshire, 1992).

Paul Fussell, "A Soldier's View," *The New Republic,*" August 22, 1981.

Essen M. Gale, "The Yangtze Patrol," *U.S. Naval Institute Proceedings,* March, 1955.

Karunakar Gupta, "How Did the Korean War Begin?" *The China Quarterly,* 1972.

Fraser Harbut, "Churchill, Hopkins, and the 'Other' Americans," *International History Review,* May, 1986.

He Di, "*Kangri Zhanzheng Houqi Meiguo Dihua Zhengce de Yanbian* [The Evolution of U.S. China Policy in the Late Period of the War of Resistance]," *Jindaishi Yanjiu,* 1981, no. 4.

Sid Huff, "My Fifteen Years with MacArthur," *The Saturday Evening Post,* September 22, 1951.

Robert A. Lewis, "How We Dropped the Bomb," *Popular Science,* August, 1957.

Chin-tung Liang, "The Sino-Soviet Treaty of Friendship and Alliance of 1945: The Inside Story," in Paul K. T. Sih, *Nationalist China During the Sino-Japanese War, 1937–1945* (Hicksville, N.Y., 1977).

Louis Morton, "War Plan ORANGE: Evolution of a Strategy," *World Politics*, January, 1959.

Drew Pearson and Robert S. Allen, "Washington Daily Merry-Go-Round," *Washington Herald*, March 25, 1938.

Allen Raymond, "The Japs Had Allies on Leyte," *The Saturday Evening Post*, February 3, 1945.

Michael M. Sheng, "America's Lost Chance in China? A Reappraisal of Chinese Communist Policy Toward the United States," *The Australian Journal of Chinese Affairs*, January, 1993.

Edgar Snow, "Fate of Manchuria," "Coming Conflict in the Orient," *Saturday Evening Post,* January 4, 1936.

_____, "Japan Digs In," *The Saturday Evening Post*, January 4, 1936.

_____, "The Japanese Juggernaut Rolls On," *The Saturday Evening Post*, June 6, 1936.

Barbara Tuchman, "If Mao Had Come to Washington: An Essay in Alternatives," *Foreign Affairs*, October, 1972.

J. Samuel Walker, "The Decision to Use the Bomb," *Diplomatic History*, Winter, 1990.

Journals

The Christian Century
Current Biography
The Economist
Life
Newsweek
The New York Times
Time
The Times
United States News
The Washington Post
The Washington Star

Biographies and Autobiographies

Dean Acheson, *Present at the Creation: My Years at the State Department* (New York, 1969).

Hiroyuki Agawa, *The Reluctant Admiral: Yamamoto and the Imperial Navy* (Tokyo, 1979).

John Robinson Beal, *Marshall in China* (Garden City, N.Y., 1970).

Edward Behr, *Hirohito: Behind the Myth* (New York, 1989).

_____, *The Last Emperor* (London, 1987).

Jim Bishop, *FDR's Last Year, April, 1944–April, 1945* (New York, 1974).

Clay Blair, Jr., *MacArthur* (Garden City, N.Y., 1977).

Michael Blankfort, *The Big Yankee: The Life of Carlson of the Raiders* (Boston, 1947).

Russell D. Buhite, *Nelson T. Johnson and American Policy Toward China, 1925–1941* (East Lansing, Mich., 1968).

James MacGregor Burns, *Roosevelt: The Soldier of Freedom* (New York, 1970).

Martha Byrd, *Chennault: Giving Wings to the Tiger* (Tuscaloosa, Ala., 1987).

Frank Capra, *The Name Above the Title* (New York, 1971).

Caleb Carr, *The Devil Soldier: The American Soldier of Fortune Who Became a God in China* (New York, 1992).

Claire Chennault, *Way of a Fighter, 1941–1945* (Silver Bay, Minn., 1982).

Robert Conquest, *Stalin: Breaker of Nations* (New York, 1991).

Margaret Truman Daniel, *Harry S. Truman* (New York, 1972).

Robert J. Donovan, *Conflict and Crisis: The Presidency of Harry S Truman* (New York, 1977).

James K. Eyre, *The Roosevelt–MacArthur Conflict* (Chambersburg, Penn., 1950).

John King Fairbank, *Chinabound: A Fifty Year Memoir* (New York, 1982).

Ladislas Farago, *The Broken Seal: The Story of Operation Magic and the Pearl Harbor Disaster* (New York, 1967).

Benis M. Frank, *Halsey* (New York, 1974).

Claude M. Fuess, *The Life of Caleb Cushing* (New York, 1923).

General de Gaulle, *Memoires de Guerre: L'Appel, 1940–1942* (Paris, 1954).

Martin Gilbert, *Winston S. Churchill*, Vols. VI and VII (Boston, 1986).

Michihiko Hachiya, *Hiroshima Diary: The Journal of a Japanese Physician, August 6–September 30, 1945* (Chapel Hill, N.C., 1995).

Edward Haggerty, *Guerrilla Padre in Mindanao* (New York, 1946).

William Halsey, *Admiral Halsey's Story* (New York, 1947).

D. Clayton James, *The Years of MacArthur*, Vol. II, *1941–1945* (Boston, 1975).

Don Jones, *Oha: The Last Samurai* (Novato, Calif., 1986).

George C. Kenney, *The MacArthur I Knew* (New York, 1951).

Warren F. Kimball, *The Juggler: Franklin D. Roosevelt as Wartime Statesman* (Princeton, 1991).

Eric Larrabee, *Commander in Chief: Franklin Delano Roosevelt, His Lieutenants, and Their War* (New York, 1987).

William Manchester, *American Caesar: Douglas MacArthur, 1880–1964* (Boston, 1978).

Carl Mann, *Lightning in the Sky: The Story of Jimmy Doolittle* (New York, 1943).

Gary May, *Scapegoat: The Diplomatic Ordeal of John Carter Vincent* (Washington, D.C., 1979).

David McCullough, *Truman* (New York, 1992).

Milton Miles, *A Different Kind of War* (New York, 1967).

Nathan Miller, *Theodore Roosevelt: A Political Biography* (New York, 1992).

Elting E. Morison, *Turmoil and Tradition: A Study of the Life and Times of Henry L. Stimson* (Boston, 1960).

Samuel Eliot Morison, *"Old Bruin": Commodore Matthew C. Perry* (Boston, 1967).

Leonard Mosley, *Hirohito: Emperor of Japan* (New York, 1966).

Robert Payne, *Chiang Kaishek* (New York, 1969).

_____, *Portrait of a Revolutionary: Mao Tse-tung* (New York, 1950).

E. B. Potter, *Nimitz* (Annapolis, Md., 1976).

Merlo J. Pusey, *Charles Evans Hughes* (New York, 1951).

Quentin Reynolds, *The Amazing Mr. Doolittle: A Biography of Lieutenant Colonel James H. Doolittle* (New York, 1953).

D. D. Rooney, *Stilwell* (New York, 1971).

Elliott Roosevelt, *As He Saw It* (New York, 1946).

Michael Schaller, *Douglas MacArthur: The Far Eastern General* (New York, 1989).

Philip Short, *Mao: A Life* (New York, 1999).

Jonathan D. Spence, *God's Chinese Son: The Taiping Heavenly Kingdom of Hong Xiuquan* (New York, 1996).

Lowell Thomas and Edward Jablonski, *Doolittle: A Biography* (Garden City, N.Y., 1976).

Barbara W. Tuchman, *Stilwell and the American Experience in China, 1911–1945* (New York, 1971).

Paul A. Varg, *Open Door Diplomat: The Life of W. W. Rockhill* (Urbana, Ill., 1952).

Theodore H. White, *In Search of History: A Personal Adventure* (New York, 1978).

Charles A. Willoughby and John Chamberlain, *MacArthur, 1941–1945* (New York, 1945).

Secondary Histories

Hallett Abend, *Japan Unmasked* (New York, 1941).

Yoji Akashi, *The Nanyang Chinese National Salvation Movement, 1937–1941* (Lawrence, Kans., 1970).

Donald Albright, ed., *World War II and the American Dream: How Wartime Building Changed a Nation* (Cambridge, Mass., 1995).

Joseph H. Alexander, *Utmost Savagery: The Three Days of Tarawa* (Annapolis, Md., 1995).

Gar Alperovitz, *Atomic Diplomacy: Hiroshima and Politics* (New York, 1995).

Leslie Anders, *The Ledo Road: General Joseph W. Stilwell's Highway to China* (Norman, Okla., 1965).

Raymond Aron, *The Imperial Republic: The United States and the World, 1945–1973* (Cambridge, Mass., 1973).

Kenneth Attiwill, *The Singapore Story* (London, 1959).

Kenneth T. Bainbridge, *Trinity* (Los Alamos, N. Mex., 1945).

Hanson W. Baldwin, *Battles Lost and Won* (New York, 1969).

Noel Barber, *The Singapore Story: From Raffles to Lee Kuan Yew* (London, 1978).

A. J. Barker, *Midway: The Turning Point* (New York, 1971).

———, *Suicide Weapon* (New York, 1971).

Pat Barr, *The Coming of the Barbarians: A Story of Western Settlement in Japan, 1853–1870* (London, 1967).

David D. Barrett, *Dixie Mission: The United States Army Observer Group in Yenan, 1944* (Berkeley, 1970).

Vicki Baum, *Shanghai '37* (New York, 1940).

W. G. Beasley, *The Meiji Restoration* (Stanford, 1972).

John Beck, *MacArthur and Wainwright* (Albuquerque, 1974).

Jack Belden, *China Shakes the World* (New York, 1949).

———, *Retreat with Stilwell* (New York, 1943).

David B. Bergamini, *Japan's Imperial Conspiracy* (New York, 1971).

Eric Bergerod, *Touched with Fire: The Land War in the South Pacific* (New York, 1996).

Kai Bird, *The Color of Truth: McGeorge Bundy and William Bundy, Brothers in Arms* (New York, 1998).

Wallace B. Black and Jean F. Blashfield, *Iwo Jima and Okinawa* (New York, 1992).

Clay Blair, Jr., *Silent Victory: The U.S. Submarine War Against Japan* (Philadelphia, 1975).

Larry I. Bland, ed., *George C. Marshall's Mediation Mission to China, December 1945–January 1947* (Lexington, Va., 1998).

John Morton Blum, *V Was for Victory* (New York, 1976).

Scott A. Boorman, *The Protracted Game: A Wei-ch'I Interpretation of Maoist Revolutionary Strategy* (New York, 1969).

Cecil Brown, *Suez to Singapore* (Garden City, N.Y., 1943).

Russell D. Buhite, *Patrick J. Hurley and American Foreign Policy* (Ithaca, 1973).

Robert J. Bulkeley, *At Close Quarters: PT Boats in the United States Navy* (Washington, D.C., 1962).

W. G. Burchett, *Trek back from Burma* (Allahabad, n.d.)

Richard Dean Burns and Edward M. Bennett, eds., *Diplomats in Crisis: United States–Chinese–Japanese, 1919–1941* (Santa Barbara, Calif., 1974).

Hugh Byas, *Government by Assassination* (New York, 1942).

John F. Cady, *A History of Modern Burma* (Ithaca, 1958).

Kate Caffrey, *Out in the Midday Sun: Singapore, 1941–45: The End of an Empire* (New York, 1976).

Oliver J. Caldwell, *A Secret War: Americans in China, 1944–45* (Carbondale, Ill., 1972).

Tim Carew, *The Longest Retreat: The Burma Campaign, 1942* (London, 1969).

Ernest C. T. Chew and Edwin Lee, eds., *A History of Singapore* (Singapore, 1991).

Diane Shaver Clemens, *Yalta* (New York, 1970).

Austen Coates, *Macao and the British: 1673–1812: Prelude to Hong Kong* (Hong Kong, 1966).

Jerome Cohen, *Japan's Economy in War and Reconstruction* (Minneapolis, 1949).

Stan Cohen, *Destination: Tokyo* (Missoula, Mont., 1983).

Maurice Collis, *First and Last in Burma* (London, 1952).

_____, *Foreign Mud: Being an Account of the Opium Imbroglio at Canton in the 1830s & the Anglo-Chinese War That Followed* (London, 1946).

Congressional Quarterly, China: U.S. Policy Since 1945 (Washington, D.C., 1979).

Charles Cook, *The Battle of Cape Esperance: Encounter at Guadalcanal* (Annapolis, Md., 1992).

Haruka Taya Cook and Theodore F. Cook, *Japan at War: An Oral History* (New York, 1992).

Alvin D. Coox and Hilary Conroy, *China and Japan: A Search for Balance Since World War I* (Santa Barbara, Calif., 1978).

Wanda Cornelius and Thayne Short, *Ding Hai: America's Air War in China, 1937–1945* (Gretna, La., 1980).

John Costello, *The Pacific War* (New York, 1981).

J. L. Cranmer-Byng, ed., *An Embassy to China: Being the Journal Kept by Lord Macartney During His Embassy to the Emperor Ch'ien Lung, 1793–1794* (London, 1962).

Russell S. Crenshaw, Jr., *South Pacific Destroyer: The Battle for the Solomons from Savo Island to Vella Gulf* (Annapolis, Md., 1998).

Brian Crozier, *The Man Who Lost China: The First Full Biography of Chiang Kai-shek* (New York, 1975).

Bruce Cumings, *The Origins of the Korean War*. Vols. I and II (Princeton, 1990).

John Paton Davies, *Dragon by the Tail: American, British, Japanese, and Russian Encounters with China and One Another* (New York, 1972).

Burke Davis, *Get Yamamoto* (New York, 1969).

Gavan Daws, *Prisoners of the Japanese: POWs of World War II in the Pacific* (New York, 1994).

Beth Day, *Manila Hotel: The Heart and Memory of a City* (Manila, 1978).

Richard Deacon, *The Chinese Secret Service* (New York, 1974).

Hugh Deane, *The Korean War: 1945–1953* (San Francisco, 1999).

Donald De Nevi, *The West Coast Goes to War, 1941–1942* (Missoula, Mont., 1998).

Gerard M. Devlin, *Back to Corregidor: America Retakes the Rock* (New York, 1992).

J. Henry Doscher, *Little Wolf at Leyte* (Austin, 1996).

John W. Dower, *Embracing Defeat: Japan in the Wake of World War II* (New York, 1999).

_____, *Empire and Aftermath: Yoshida Shigeru and the Japanese Experience, 1878–1954* (Cambridge, Mass., 1979).

_____, *War Without Mercy: Race and Power in the Pacific War* (New York, 1986).

Edward J. Drea, *MacArthur's ULTRA: Codebreaking and the War Against Japan, 1942–1945* (Lawrence, Kans., 1992).

Foster Rhea Dulles, *China and America: The Story of Their Relations Since 1784* (Princeton, 1946).

Richard Dunlop, *Behind Japanese Lines: With the OSS in Burma* (Chicago, 1979).

_____, *Donovan: America's Master Spy* (Chicago, 1982).

Robert B. Edgerton, *Warriors of the Rising Sun: A History of the Japanese Military* (New York, 1997).

Joseph W. Esherick, ed., *Lost Chance in China: The World War II Dispatches of John S. Service* (New York, 1974).

Raymond A. Esthus, *Theodore Roosevelt and Japan* (Seattle, 1966).

James J. Fahey, *Pacific War Diary: 1942–1945* (Boston, 1963).

John K. Fairbank, *China Perceived: Images and Policies in Chinese–American Relations* (New York, 1974).

_____, *Trade and Diplomacy on the China Coast: The Opening of the Treaty Ports, 1842–1854* (Cambridge, Mass., 1954).

_____, *The United States and China*, 4th ed. (Cambridge, Mass., 1983).

Stanley L. Falk, *Liberation of the Philippines* (New York, 1971).

Herbert Feis, *The China Tangle: The American Effort in China from Pearl Harbor to the Marshall Mission* (Princeton, 1953).

_____, *The Road to Pearl Harbor: The Coming of War Between the United States and Japan* (Princeton, 1950).

Eric A. Feldt, *The Coast Watchers* (Garden City, N.Y., 1979).

A. B. Feuer, ed., *Coast Watching in the Solomon Islands: The Bougainville Reports, December 1941–July 1943* (Westport, Conn., 1992).

James A. Field, *The Japanese at Leyte Gulf* (Princeton, 1947).

Peter Fleming, *The Siege at Peking* (Hong Kong, 1983).

Simon Foster, *Okinawa 1945: Assault on the Empire* (London, 1994).

Benis M. Frank, *Okinawa: Touchstone to Victory* (New York, 1969).

Richard P. Frank, *Downfall: The End of the Imperial Japanese Empire* (New York, 1999).

_____, *Guadalcanal: The Definitive Account of the Landmark Battle* (New York, 1990).

I. J. Galantin, *Take Her Deep! A Submarine Against Japan in World War II* (New York, 1987).

Carroll V. Glines, *The Doolittle Raid: America's Daring First Strike Against Japan* (New York, 1988).

Joseph C. Goulden, *Korea: The Untold Story of the Korean War* (New York, 1982).

Norman A. Graebner, *Empire on the Pacific: A Study in American Continental Expansion* (New York, 1955).

Charles T. Gregg, *Tarawa* (New York, 1984).

Samuel B. Griffith, *Sun Tzu: The Art of War* (New York, 1963).

Robert Guillain, *I Saw Tokyo Burning* (London, 1981).

Eric Hammel and John E. Lane, *76 Hours: The Invasion of Tarawa* (Pacifica, Calif., 1985).

Thomas R. H. Havens, *Valley of Darkness: The Japanese People and World War II* (New York, 1978).

Grace Pearson Hayes, *The History of the Joint Chiefs of Staff: The War Against Japan* (Annapolis, Md., 1982).

Ron Heiferman, *Flying Tigers: Chennault in China* (New York, 1971).

Waldo Heinrichs, Jr., *American Ambassador: Joseph C. Grew and the Development of the United States Diplomatic Tradition* (New York, 1966).

_____, *Threshold of War: Franklin D. Roosevelt & America's Entry into World War II* (New York, 1988).

John Hersey, *Hiroshima* (New York, 1946).

Gary R. Hess, *The United States' Emergence as a Southeast Asian Power, 1940–1950* (New York, 1987).

W. J. Holmes, *Double-Edged Secrets: U.S. Naval Intelligence Operations in the Pacific During World War II* (Annapolis, Md., 1979).

Townsend Hoopes and Douglas Brinkley, *FDR and the Creation of the UN* (New Haven, 1997).

Frank O. Hough, *The Assault on Peleliu* (Washington, D.C., 1950).

Edwin F. Hoyt, *Storm over the Gilberts: War in the Central Pacific, 1943* (New York, 1978).

George P. Hunt, *Coral Comes High* (New York, 1946).

Saburo Ienaga, *The Pacific War: 1931–1945* (New York, 1978).

Allison Ind, *Bataan: The Judgment Seat* (New York, 1944).

Akira Iriye, *Power and Culture: The Japanese–American War, 1941–1945* (Cambridge, Mass., 1981).

_____, *The Origins of the Second World War in Asia and the Pacific* (London, 1987).

Chalmers Johnson, *Blowback: The Costs and Consequences of American Empire* (New York, 2000).

_____, *Peasant Nationalism and Communist Power: The Emergence of Revolutionary China, 1937–1945* (Stanford, 1962).

Sheila Johnson, *The Japanese Through American Eyes* (Stanford, 1988).

F. C. Jones, *Japan's New Order in East Asia: Its Rise and Fall, 1937–1945* (New York, 1954).

E. J. Kahn, *The China Hands: America's Foreign Service Officers and What Befell Them* (New York, 1975).

Stanley Karnow, *In Our Image: America's Empire in the Philippines* (New York, 1989).

_____, *Vietnam: A History* (New York, 1984).

Graeme Kent, *Guadalcanal: Island Ordeal* (New York, 1971).

E. Bartlett Kerr, *Flames over Tokyo: The U.S. Army Air Force's Incendiary Campaign Against Japan, 1944–1945* (New York, 1991).

Lynn Kessler, *Never in Doubt: Remembering Iwo Jima* (Annapolis, Md., 1999).

Harvey Klehr and Ronald Radosh, *The Amerasia Spy Case: Prelude to McCarthyism* (Chapel Hill, N.C., 1996).

Fletcher Knebel and Charles W. Bailey II, *No High Ground* (New York, 1960).

Manny T. Koginos, *The Panay Incident: Prelude to War* (Lafayette, Ind., 1967).

Nakagata Kohachi, *Zozen Gyokai* [*The Shipbuilding Industry*] (Tokyo, 1979).

Dan Kurzman, *Day of the Bomb: Countdown to Hiroshima* (New York, 1986).

Walter LaFeber, *The American Age: U.S. Foreign Policy at Home and Abroad: 1750 to the Present* (New York, 1994).

_____, *The Clash: U.S.–Japanese Relations Throughout History* (New York, 1997).

Robert Leckie, *Strong Men Armed: The United States Marines Against Japan* (New York, 1962).

Melvyn P. Leffler, *A Preponderance of Power: National Security, the Truman Administration, and the Cold War* (Stanford, 1992).

George Liska, *Imperial America: The International Politics of Primacy* (Baltimore, 1967).

Walter Lord, *Incredible Victory* (New York, 1967).

_____, *Lonely Vigil: Coast Watchers of the Solomons* (New York, 1977).

Peter Lowe, *Great Britain and the Origins of the Pacific War: A Study of British Policy in East Asia, 1937–1941* (London, 1977).

David J. Lu, *From the Marco Polo Bridge to Pearl Harbor: Japan's Entry into World War II* (Washington, D.C., 1961).

Donald MacIntyre, *Leyte Gulf: Armada in the Pacific* (New York, 1970).

Harold Macmillan, *The Blast of War: 1939–1945* (New York, 1968).

Tony Mains, *The Retreat from Burma: An Intelligence Officer's Personal Story* (London, 1973).

Mao Zedong, *Selected Military Writings* (Beijing, 1963).

Karal Ann Marling and John Wetenhall, *Iwo Jima: Monuments, Memories, and the American Hero* (Cambridge, Mass., 1991).

Ito Masanori, with Roger Pineau, *The End of the Imperial Japanese Navy* (New York, 1956).

John Masters, *The Road Past Mandalay: A Personal Narrative* (New York, 1961).

Charles L. Mee, Jr., *Meeting at Potsdam* (New York, 1975).

_____, *Playing God: Fateful Moments when Great Men Meet to Change the World* (New York, 1993).

Dillon S. Meyer, *Uprooted Americans: The Japanese Americans and the War Relocation Authority During World War II* (Tucson, 1971).

Franz H. Michael and George E. Taylor, *The Far East in the Modern World* (New York, 1956).

Bernard Miller, *Divine Thunder: The Life and Death of the Kamikazes* (New York, 1970).

E. B. Miller, *Bataan Uncensored* (Long Prairie, Minn., 1949).

John Miller, Jr., *Guadalcanal: The First Offensive* (Washington, D.C., 1949).

Nathan Miller, *Theodore Roosevelt: A Life* (New York, 1992).

Richard H. Minear, *Requiem for Battleship Yamato* (Seattle, 1985).

_____, *Victors' Justice: The Tokyo War Crimes Trial* (Princeton, 1971).

Fuchida Mitsuo and Okumiya Masatake, *The Battle That Doomed Japan: The Japanese Navy's Story* (Annapolis, Md., 1955).

Samuel Eliot Morison, *Breaking the Bismarck Barrier* (Boston, 1957).

_____, *Leyte: June 1944–January 1945* (Boston, 1958).

_____, *The Liberation of the Philippines: Luzon, Mindanao, the Visajas, 1944–1945* (Boston, 1959).

_____, *New Guinea and the Marianas: March, 1944–August, 1944* (Boston, 1953).

_____, *The Struggle for Guadalcanal: August, 1942–February, 1943* (Boston, 1949).

James William Morley, ed., *The Fateful Choice: Japan's Advance into Southeast Asia, 1939–1941* (New York, 1980).

Eric Morris, *Corregidor: The Nightmare in the Philippines* (London, 1982).

Don Moser, *China–Burma–India* (New York, 1978).

Joseph N. Mueller, *Guadalcanal 1942* (Oxford, 1992).

Carl Mydans, *More Than Meets the Eye* (New York, 1974).

Elizabeth M. Norman, *We Band of Angels: The Untold Story of American Nurses Trapped on Bataan by the Japanese* (New York, 1999).

Charlton Ogburn, Jr., *The Marauders* (New York, 1956).

Laurence Oliphant, *Narrative of the Earl of Elgin's Mission to China and Japan* (London, 1861).

F. C. van Oosten, *The Battle of the Java Sea* (London, 1976).

Mark P. Parillo, *The Japanese Merchant Marine in World War II* (Annapolis, Md., 1993).

Graham Peck, *Two Kinds of Time* (Boston, 1950).

Stephen E. Pelz, *Race to Pearl Harbor: The Failure of the Second London Naval Conference and the Onset of World War II* (Cambridge, Mass., 1974).

Hamilton Derby Perry, *The Panay Incident: Prelude to Pearl Harbor* (New York, 1969).

Henri Peyrefitte, *The Immobile Empire: The First Great Collision of East and West; The Astonishing History of Britain's Grand, Ill-Fated Expedition to Open China to Western Trade, 1793–1794* (New York, 1992).

Forrest C. Pogue, *George C. Marshall: Statesman, 1945–1959* (New York, 1987).

John Prados, *The Sky Would Fall: Operation Vulture: The U.S. Bombing Mission in Indo-China, 1954* (New York, 1983).

Gordon W. Prange, *At Dawn We Slept: The Untold Story of Pearl Harbor* (New York, 1981).

_____, *Miracle at Midway* (New York, 1982).

Lewis McCarroll Purifoy, *Harry Truman's China Policy: McCarthyism and the Diplomacy of Hysteria* (New York, 1976).

Robert L. Reynolds, *Commodore Perry in Japan* (New York, 1963).

Richard Rhodes, *The Making of the Atomic Bomb* (New York, 1986).

M. C. Ricklefs, *A History of Modern Indonesia* (Bloomington, Ind., 1981).

Michael Russell, *Iwo Jima* (New York, 1974).

Harrison E. Salisbury, *The Long March: The Untold Story* (New York, 1985).

Ronald Schaffer, *Wings of Judgment: American Bombing in World War II* (New York, 1985).

Michael Schaller, *The U.S. Crusade in China, 1938–1945* (New York, 1979).

Duane Schultz, *The Doolittle Raid* (New York, 1988).

_____, *Wake Island: The Heroes' Gallant Fight* (New York, 1978).

Benjamin I. Schwartz, *In Search of Wealth and Power: Yen Fu and the West* (Cambridge, Mass., 1964).

John S. Service, *The Amerasia Papers: Some Problems in the History of U.S.–China Relations* (Berkeley, 1971).

Aron Shai, *Britain and China, 1941–1947: Imperial Momentum* (New York, 1983).

James E. Sheridan, *China in Disintegration: The Republican Era in Chinese History, 1912–1949* (New York, 1975).

Robert Sherrod, *Tarawa: The Story of a Battle* (New York, 1944).

Michael S. Sherry, *The Rise of American Air Power: The Creation of Armageddon* (New Haven, 1987).

Martin J. Sherwin, *A World Destroyed: The Atomic Bomb and the Grand Alliance* (New York, 1977).

Leon V. Sigal, *Fighting to a Finish: The Politics of War Termination in the United States and Japan, 1945* (Ithaca, 1982).

Philip Chadwick K. Foster Smith, *The Empress of China* (Philadelphia, 1984).

R. Harris Smith, *OSS: The Secret History of America's First Central Intelligence Agency* (Berkeley, 1972).

Edgar Snow, *Red Star over China* (New York, 1938).

Ronald H. Spector, *Eagle Against the Sun: The American War with Japan* (New York, 1985).

R. Conrad Stein, *Fall of Singapore* (Chicago, 1982).

Rafael Steinberg, *Island Fighting* (New York, 1978).

_____, *Return to the Philippines* (New York, 1980).

Alfred Tamarin and Shirley Glubok, *Voyaging to Cathay: Americans in the China Trade* (New York, 1976).

Tang Tsou, *America's Failure in China, 1941–50* (Chicago, 1963).

Ssu-yu Teng and John K. Fairbank, eds., *China's Response to the West: A Documentary Survey, 1839–1923* (Cambridge, Mass., 1954).

Gordon Thomas and Max Morgan Witts, *Enola Gay* (New York, 1977).

John Toland, *But Not in Shame: The Six Months After Pearl Harbor* (New York, 1961).

_____, *The Rising Sun: The Decline and Fall of the Japanese Empire* (New York, 1970).

Eugene Trani, *The Treaty of Portsmouth: An Adventure in American Diplomacy* (Lexington, Ky., 1969).

Thomas F. Troy, *Donovan and the CIA: A History of the Establishment of the Central Intelligence Agency* (Langley, Va., 1981).

Tsuji Masanobu, *Singapore: The Japanese Version* (Sidney, 1960).

Paul A. Varg, *Missionaries, Chinese, and Diplomats* (Princeton, 1958).

John Chalmers Vinson, *The Parchment Peace: The United States and the Washington Conference* (Athens, Ga., 1955).

Milton Viorst, *Hostile Allies: FDR and Charles de Gaulle* (New York, 1965).

Frederic Wakeman, Jr., *The Fall of Imperial China* (New York, 1975).

Denis Warner and Peggy Warner, *The Tide at Sunrise: A History of the Russo-Japanese War, 1904–1905* (New York, 1974).

Bernard Wasserstein, *Secret War in Shanghai* (Boston, 1999).

Michi Weglyn, *Years of Infamy: The Untold Story of America's Concentration Camps* (New York, 1976).

Frank Welsh, *A Borrowed Place: The History of Hong Kong* (New York, 1993).

Kenneth P. Werwell, *Blankets of Fire: U.S. Bombers Over Japan During World War II* (Washington, D.C., 1996).

Keith Wheeler, *The Road to Tokyo* (New York, 1979).

Robert K. Wilcox, *Japan's Secret War: Japan's Rush Against Time to Build Its Own Atomic Bomb* (New York, 1995).

Peter Booth Wiley, *Yankees in the Land of the Gods: Commodore Perry and the Opening of Japan* (New York, 1990).

Peter Williams and David Wallace, *Unit 731: Japan's Secret Biological Warfare in World War II* (New York, 1989).

H. P. Willmott, *Japanese and Allied Pacific Strategies to April, 1942* (Annapolis, Md., 1982).

Dick Wilson, *When Tigers Fight: The Story of the Sino-Japanese War, 1937–1945* (New York, 1982).

Walter Winslow, *The Ghost That Died at Sunda Strait* (Annapolis, Md., 1961).

Lanxin Xiang, *Recasting the Imperial Far East: Britain and America in China, 1945–1950* (Armonk, N.Y., 1995).

Maochun Yu, *OSS in China: Prelude to the Cold War* (New Haven, 1996).

Arthur Zich, *The Rising Sun* (New York, 1977).

INDEX

415